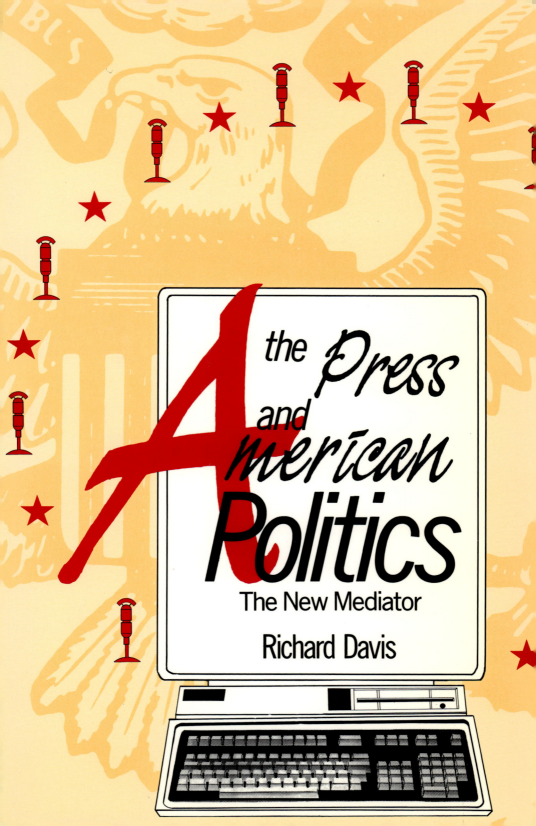

the Press and American Politics

The New Mediator

Richard Davis

the Press and American Politics

The New Mediator

Richard Davis

U.S. Coast Guard Academy

Longman
New York & London

The Press and American Politics:
The New Mediator

Longman, 95 Church Street, White Plains, N.Y. 10601

Associated companies:
Longman Group Ltd., London
Longman Cheshire Pty., Melbourne
Longman Paul Pty., Auckland
Copp Clark Pitman, Toronto

Senior editor: David J. Estrin
Development editor: Virginia L. Blanford
Production editor: Marie-Josée A. Schorp
Cover design: Kevin C. Kall
Photo research: Jack Adams
Production supervisor: Richard C. Bretan

Library of Congress Cataloging-in-Publication Data

Davis, Richard (Richard Dana)
    The press and American politics : the new mediator/Richard
    Davis.
        p.   cm.
    Includes index.
    ISBN 0-8013-0153-X:
    1. Journalism—Political aspects—United States. 2. Journalism—
United States—History—20th century. 3. Press and politics—
United States. 4. Press—United States—Influence. 5. Public
opinion—United States. 6. United States—Intellectual life—20th
century. 7. Journalism—United States—Objectivity. I. Title.
PN4888.P6D38   1991
071'.3—dc20
                                                    90-24754
                                                    CIP

1   2   3   4   5   6   7   8   9   10-MA-9594939291

To Molina

Contents

Preface

The main thesis of this book is that the press has become a new intermediary in the American political system. Although the political role of the press has existed since the dawn of American politics, that role has undergone dramatic change. The press has achieved greater autonomy over time as it has acquired mediating roles in American politics once performed by other institutions.

However, the new role as intermediary does not assume the press possesses enormous power over Americans' attitudes and opinions, that the press is a body intent on imposing a partisan or ideological bias, or, conversely, that the press is merely a tool in the hands of manipulative public officials. These assumptions permeate much of what is written about the press.

They are addressed and discarded in favor of a more complex role for the press as new mediator struggling with other established mediators such as political parties, political elites, and interest groups in the political processes of American politics.

Such an effort requires the assistance of many people—colleagues, students, librarians, reviewers, editors, proofreaders, technicians, etc.—many of whom I do not even know. A few I do know should be acknowledged by name.

Thomas E. Patterson, my friend and mentor, gave much-needed direction and support for his former pupil. He has been a source of guidance for the past eight years and he will recognize much of his contribution on these pages. Tim Cook, Lois Duke, Stephen Flynn, Jarol Manheim, and Robert Savage reviewed the manuscript at various points and provided useful suggestions for improvement.

I wish to acknowledge the support of David Estrin, Ginny Blanford, Marie-Josée Schorp, and Victoria Mifsud at Longman. David offered unfailing encouragement at several crucial points when my vision of this project was clouded. I appreciate his patience throughout this process.

Last but not least, my family endured (or enjoyed, I wasn't always sure which) my absences from them for the past several years since this project's inception. Their love for me even at difficult times like these, and mine reciprocated for them, cannot be expressed in words. Simply, thank you so very much.

Assumptions about Media Power

> *"The press has substantial and specific impacts on policies and policymaking in the federal government."*[1]
>
> *"The images on the nightly news count for everything in a presidential election campaign and beyond . . . [I]n this culture, if something is not on the TV nightly news, it didn't happen, it doesn't exist."*[2]

The political power of the press. Today the subject is on the minds and tongues of politicians, political pundits, presidents, and everyday people. Academics debate it at conferences, roundtables, and in classrooms, and journalists discuss their own power in opinion columns, television documentaries, and even news stories. The press is taken to task for making and then breaking presidential candidates, for glorifying and then condemning individual politicians, for unduly publicizing the activities of terrorists and criminals but failing to address the pressing social issues of the day. How broadly does the press actually influence the electoral process? Do the news media set national policy by ignoring or highlighting certain issues, or pursuing agendas of their own?

The role of the press in American politics has become a major source of discussion and controversy in recent years. Why is the subject such a popular one? Do the news media in fact possess the kinds of power that are attributed to them? When and how were such powers—or the perceptions of such powers—acquired? And, most importantly, how does this perceived power influence the democratic political system in this country—both the electoral process, and the policymaking process?

We need to be clear at the outset about what we mean when we use the words *press* and *news media*. In this book, I use the two terms interchangeably to refer both to those organizations that are in the business of gathering and disseminating news, and to the reporters, editors, and other individuals who are professional newsgatherers and disseminators, primarily at the national level. In other words, the terms *press* and *news media* differentiate the *news* function from the *entertainment* function of the mass media. Although the politics of entertainment and the entertainment of politics are both valid topics for discussion, they are not ours.

Similarly, I use the word *government* to refer to the formal apparatus of United States governance, including its institutions, elected leaders, and agencies. I use the words *political system* to refer to those processes that operate to enable the explicit government of the United States to govern—parties, the electoral system, and so on. Although a number of other players clearly influence how the country functions—lobbyists, special interest groups, corporations and private agencies, among others—they are not our concern here.

HOW THIS BOOK IS ORGANIZED

To understand the implications of the questions raised above, this book is organized around an examination of current perceptions about media power and an attempt to determine their reality and to place them in perspective. Unlike most texts on media and politics, this one is built on the recognition that the American political system and the American press share a long history of interdependency in one form or another. No process operates in a vacuum; we believe that an understanding of history is essential to an understanding of how government and news media work in the 1990s.

Part I of this book identifies the major players in the news business—the newsgatherers and the newsmakers—and explores the operating assumptions of both groups. We look at how journalists gather news, as well as how and why the various "pleaders" for media attention in national government attempt to influence what gets reported.

Part II provides a context for our examination of the news media's role in the political process today, both by tracing the history of the relationship between press and politics from this country's birth to the present day, and by looking at press-government relations in other parts of the world. Chapter 3 examines the period from colonial days through 1830; Chapter 4 focuses on print journalism after 1830; and in Chapter 5 we look at the rise of broadcasting and the twentieth-century shifts in press-politics relations. Chapter 6 traces the history of press regulation in this country, and Chapter 7 provides an overview of the press's role in other countries.

In the next three parts of the book, we explore those areas where the interests of press and government intersect, in order to determine how the changing relationship between the two impacts on the political process. Part III focuses on the relationship between the press and the three major branches of national government—the presidency, Congress, and the Supreme Court. Part IV examines how the press influences policy-making at the national level, with a special emphasis on two policy areas—foreign affairs and national security. Part V provides an analysis of the relationship between the news media and public opinion, particularly in the electoral process.

Finally, in the Conclusion, we reexamine the argument laid out in the next few pages of this chapter, and propose some resolutions to the emerging tensions between an increasingly independent press and the requisites of a democracy.

A PERVASIVE NEWS MEDIA

Indisputably, the media are more pervasive today than they were just thirty years ago. The expanded availability and usage of mass media are facts—perhaps phenomena—of American life. Television, which spread rapidly across the nation during the 1950s, is the primary example, but the print media have also fared well. Over 9,000 newspapers and 12,000 periodicals are published in the United States on a regular basis. Daily newspaper circulation tops 63 million copies—one for every four Americans—and has remained more or less stable since 1970. Weekly newspaper circulation tops 53 million.[3] National newsmagazines like *Time*, *Newsweek*, and *U.S. News and World Report* attract a combined circulation of nearly 10 million, and several nationally circulated newspapers sell in excess of a million copies each weekday—the *Wall Street Journal* (2 million), *USA Today* (1.4 million), the Los Angeles *Times* (1.2 million) and the *New York Times* (1 million). In the past twenty years, circulation for the *New York Times* and the Los Angeles *Times* have grown by 25 percent, and circulation for the *Wall Street Journal* has nearly doubled. Size as well as circulation has increased; between 1950 and 1980, the length of the average newspaper grew from 34 to 60 pages.[4]

Of all the potential media for news, radio is undoubtedly the most pervasive. In 1952, some 3,000 commercial radio stations were licensed in the United States; today, there are more than 10,500. In 1950, about 40 million households had radio receivers. Today, 99 percent of all American households and 95 percent of all cars have radios; and 57 percent of adult American workers have a radio at work. The cumulative weekly audience for radio in the United States is 183 million—about 95 percent of the U.S. population. Over 90 percent of all Americans over 18 say they listen to the radio either daily or every weekday.[5]

Despite radio's massive potential audience, however, it is television that Americans perceive as the most influential medium in their lives. In 1950, 98 television stations operated in the United States, and only about nine percent of American households owned television sets. Today more than 1,000 broadcast television stations hold U.S. licenses. Ninety-eight percent of all American households own at least one set, and over half own two. Once limited to the living room, the TV has now moved into the bedroom, the kitchen, the dining room, and even the occasional bathroom.[6]

Even more remarkable than television's omnipresence is the intensity of our viewing habits. Most Americans say that watching television is their preferred evening activity—outranking reading, or even spending time with the family. Recent additions to television technology—cable and satellite transmissions, VCRs—have affected viewing habits in the 1980s, and network viewership has declined in the last decade. But there is no arguing that television in one form or another occupies a major place in American life.[7]

Americans perceive television primarily as an entertainment medium.[8] Nevertheless, about half of all Americans say they watch television news—more often local than national network news. A variety of new broadcast options arrived on the scene in the 1980s, including Cable News Network (CNN), which broadcasts news 24 hours a day and is available in hotels throughout much of the world; supplementary hard-news shows like "Nightline;" C-SPAN, which broadcasts from the floor of Congress; a proliferation of magazine news shows like "20/20" (modeled more or less on the longtime hit "60 Minutes"); and "docudrama" shows like "A Current Affair" and "Inside Edition." "News junkies" may watch less network news than they once did, but new options assure that they can now watch some form of televised news around the clock.

Public Reliance on the Media

Americans claim that they rely on television more than any other medium for public affairs information. One survey suggests that 66 percent of the American public use television as their main source of news,[9] up from less than 20 percent in 1960.[10] The number who say that they depend on more than one media source for news has dwindled steadily.[11] For political information in particular, Americans tend to turn to television. The 1988 presidential debates were watched by an audience estimated at 160 million, double that of the landmark Kennedy-Nixon debates in 1960.[12]

Americans not only rely on television and other media for information, they give such media high marks for credibility. Between 80 and 90 percent of Americans say they feel the press is generally believable; predictably, particular praise is aimed at the *Wall Street Journal*, the "MacNeil-Lehrer News Hour" on public television, and former veteran news anchor Walter Cronkite.[13] In fact, one recent survey suggests that most Americans rate the press as more believable than the president.[14]

Political Reliance on the News Media

If the governed rely on the news media as a credible and accessible source of information, those who govern also depend on the press, both in electoral politics and in the process of governance. The number of journalists in Washington alone has tripled since the end of World War II to more than 10,000; and the number of reporters accredited by the congressional press galleries grew from 1,300 in 1957 to almost 5,000 in the early 1980s.[15] The White House provides credentials for some

1,500 journalists, three times the number in 1960 (although only about 100 cover the White House full time); and when the president travels, some 100 reporters typically accompany him.

The political press corps is not only larger, it is more visible than it once was. CBS reporter Dan Rather acquired a national reputation—and ultimately the anchorman's chair—through his high-profile adversarial behavior as a White House correspondent, and ABC's Sam Donaldson used the same platform to enhance his own visibility. One 1985 survey demonstrated that more Americans could recognize a picture of ABC journalist Barbara Walters than could identify then Vice-President George Bush or Democratic vice-presidential candidate Geraldine Ferraro.[16]

In part because of its vastly increased size and visibility, as well as because of the extent to which the public relies on it, the press demands more time and attention from politicians and public officials than it once did. Presidential candidates in particular find they must develop new skills and strategies in response to that. A press secretary for one candidate in the 1988 campaign estimated that his candidate spent over one-third of each day in direct contact with the press. "It's not just news conferences, but one-on-one interviews, hotel room briefings, radio and TV shows, editorial board discussions, back-of-the-car interviews and conversations," he explained.[17] More and more, candidates assume that such efforts are necessary to gain the press's attention, to enhance their public recognition and favorable image, and finally to acquire public support.

Once elected, public officials, including presidents, continue to devote large blocks of time to "handling" the press. Former presidential aide John Ehrlichman recounted how President Nixon "used to sit around figuring out how he could get a minute and a half on the evening news,"[18] and Ronald Reagan, who gave fewer formal press conferences than any previous president since Franklin Roosevelt, was a recognized master of the "photo opportunity." Some 3,000 public information specialists work in federal government agencies, and virtually all members of Congress today employ public relations aides. The congressional press galleries are staffed by Congress to facilitate press coverage, and the Senate issues some 30 to 50 gallery passes daily.[19] Elected officials devote this kind of time, money, and energy to press relations only because they believe that such efforts will pay off in terms of reelection or support for their policymaking initiatives.

THE IMPACT OF NEWS MEDIA ON AMERICAN POLITICS

What does this dramatic increase in the size and visibility of the political press in this country—and the concomitant rise in dependency on it by both governed and governors—mean to the way the political process operates? The increase in and of itself is of little concern to political scientists. What we want to know is whether—and how—that increase impacts on the processes, institutions, and individuals of American politics.

In this book, we will examine whether the press possesses the enormous power many politicians, scholars, and political consultants have concluded it has. Here are some samples of these conclusions:

> "The advent of television is the most important change since World War II in just about every aspect of American life and certainly in the environment in which government functions."
> Austin Ranney, *Channels of Power,* New York: Basic Books, 1983, p. 123.

> "[I]n Washington today, correspondents . . . possess a power beyond even their own dreams and fears. They are only beginning to become aware that their work now shapes and colors the beliefs of nearly everyone, not only in the United States but throughout most of the world."
> William L. Rivers, *The Other Government,* New York: Universe Books, 1982, p. 10.

> "A presidential campaign is nothing but dealing with the media. Everything that is done is directly or indirectly related to the media."
> Raymond D. Strother, political consultant, in Dom Bonafede, "Hey, Look Me Over," *National Journal,* November 21, 1987.

> "Modern politics requires television. I don't believe it's possible anymore to run for president without the capacity to build confidence and communications every night."
> Walter Mondale, Democratic presidential candidate, 1984, in Elizabeth Drew, *A Campaign Journal,* New York: Macmillan, 1985, p. 763.

> "The president of the United States ordinarily is brought to you by the news media."
> Michael Grossman and Martha Joynt Kumar, *Portraying the President,* Baltimore, Md.: Johns Hopkins Press, 1981, p. 3.

A fundamental tension exists today between the American news media and American politics, traceable to two developments in recent American political history. The first is the change outlined above—the increased reliance of both citizenry and government on the press as a primary "communications bridge" or linking mechanism. The second, equally important development is the increasingly divergent imperatives of press and politicians, which have moved the press itself into a more and more autonomous position, out from under traditional political controls.

The News Media's Role as a Linking Mechanism

The American political process has grown dependent on the press in recent years in ways that have not traditionally been typical. Political actors and institutions rely on the news media to disseminate information to the public and to garner support; and the public relies on the news media to provide information about how political processes and institutions work, act, and are constituted. What factors have brought about this increased reliance on the press from both producers and consumers?

Changes in Mass Media. Vast technological advances have occurred in the last 40 years in the communications industry. New technology in mass communications has broadened the reach and speed of news transmissions beyond anything imaginable just three or four decades ago. The new technologies include innovations in print, in radio and television broadcasting, and in the widespread use of satellite transmissions. The reach of both broadcast and print media today dwarfs that of communications mechanisms of the past.

In addition to enhanced speed and reach, as we have noted above, the news media can boast an increase in credibility. The press's ability to provide live visual coverage of events half a world away, the role that the press played in uncovering the Watergate scandal, and the increasingly personalized nature of television journalism, among other developments, have contributed to the public's perception that the news is basically "true." This perception in turn increases our tendency to rely on the press for the information on which we base our opinions—and our votes.

Changes in American Politics. The press's role as a linking mechanism between public and government has also been enhanced by various developments in American politics, including the weakening and decentralization of the major political parties, the increasing significance of the national government, and the rise of the "modern presidency."

During the past two decades, political parties have undergone extensive reforms which have affected their ability to influence elections and to operate as centralized political organizations. New party rules about primaries, instituted after the tumultuous presidential nominating conventions of 1964 and 1968, have robbed party leaders of their traditional control over the presidential nominating process and led to the nomination of "outsiders" like Jimmy Carter, Michael Dukakis, and even Ronald Reagan. In addition, new campaign finance laws limit the amount of direct funding that a party can provide to its own nominees, once again removing control from the hands of party leaders. And finally, voters have become less loyal to particular parties than were their parents and grandparents, and more likely to split their tickets and vote for candidates of different parties for different offices.[20] As a result of all these changes, political leaders can no longer count on the infrastructures of their political parties to disseminate information and provide a basis for support.

Changes in the presidential selection process over the last twenty years have produced candidates who rely less on—and therefore owe less to—the centralized structures of their own parties. Instead, candidates who are setting out to win nomination and election find themselves turning to the capabilities of the news media to make their case. In 1976, Jimmy Carter's self-conscious stance as a Washington outsider brought considerable media attention in the wake of the "insider" Watergate scandal; despite the Democratic party's initial lack of interest in his candidacy, national press attention made an otherwise obscure Georgia governor a national figure. Although supported by broad segments of the Democratic party, Michael Dukakis heavily turned to the media rather than to the party to be transformed from a regional candidate into a front runner. The reduced role that political parties now play in the presidential nomination process means that candidates must look elsewhere for mechanisms to reach the public, and the news media, already in place and eager for material, provide the most effective and viable alternative.

During the same period that the influence of political parties has declined, the significance of the national government in American political life has sharply increased. The national government's ability to make policy that affects individual citizens, from the Supreme Court's *Roe v. Wade* decision supporting legalized abortions to the congressional "rescue" of private corporations like Chrysler, has increased the public's need for an information conduit or linking mechanism that is national in scope. The kind of interpersonal and small group communication that was traditionally possible at the local and state levels is simply unachievable for citizens who want to interact with an immense and distant national government. As the locus of power has shifted over the last thirty years to the national level, the mass media, capable of reaching a national audience and doing it quickly, has emerged as a fitting intermediary.

The presidency in particular has changed in recent years. As power has centralized in the Oval Office, and attention has focused there, the office of the president has gradually "decoupled" from the political parties; today's presidency relies very little on political parties to communicate its messages and needs. Presidents typically attempt to set public agendas and produce major changes in a few select policy areas. To accomplish these objectives, they require a mechanism that allows them to influence public opinion and to win legislative support for their policy initiatives. Here again, the media serve their purposes.

All these changes—new technology and enhanced credibility for the media; decreasing power of political parties and enhanced role of national government and particularly of the presidency—have contributed to the rise of the press as the primary linking mechanism between government (or political leaders and political institutions) and the American public. Certainly the imperatives under which the press operates have made the press more aggressive in accepting this role. Indeed, the press has, wittingly or unwittingly, contributed to the changes in political structure by advocating changes in the presidential selection process and nationalizing heretofore local issues by placing them squarely on the doorstep of the White House. The actions of the news media in this area often reflect internal economic or political imperatives, and the increasing independence of the political press.

The Increasing Autonomy of the Press

While the institutions and leaders of the American political system have grown increasingly dependent on the news media, the press itself has emerged as a more and more autonomous force, driven by its own needs and imperatives. Press dependency on political leaders, once a major factor in political communications in this country, has decreased almost to insignificance over the course of the last century.

In the early days of the republic, the American press was typically financially dependent on the resources of political leaders who provided patronage to editors and publishers, start-up loans for newspapers, and continued funds for operation—as well, often, as guaranteed readerships and news material itself. John Fenno relied on Alexander Hamilton's largesse in the form of printing contracts for the funds to publish a newspaper advocating Hamilton's views, and special designations—newspapers published "by authority" of a local government, for example—were common.

Although news organizations today clearly continue to depend on cooperation from government news sources and a "partnership" that we will examine more closely in later chapters, the press no longer depends on the government or individual political leaders for economic stability. Such stability results from a concentration on commercial interests rather than political considerations. News media are funded by subscriptions and/or advertising; they rely primarily on competition in the marketplace, and not political ideology, for their success.

In addition, news media professionals (editors, publishers, reporters, producers) possess far greater control over their "product" than did their counterparts of the nineteenth century. Editors of partisan journals in the late eighteenth and early nineteenth centuries were often accountable to political leaders for the content of their newspapers. Although editor-publishers could and often did resist the pressure applied by such leaders, the likely result of that resistance was the loss of their newspaper's special status with the administration, and the resulting loss of readership and financial support which such status provided. Articles submitted by political leaders who supported the paper were rarely rejected, edited, or balanced with an opposing viewpoint; typically they were printed in full without critical commentary.

Reporters and other professionals now play a much more active role in determining what messages will be transmitted through the media. Decisions about assignments, selection of stories, editing, and time and space allotments are made by the news organizations themselves. Obviously such decisions often reflect the efforts of public relations lobbyists and the availability of material—forms of agenda-setting engaged in by those who "make" news—but only rarely, as in the case of an issue affecting national security, does the press respond to direct intervention from government leaders or institutions. The press of today tends to synthesize and analyze rather than simply repeat what it's told, as it did 200 years ago. The fact that politicians seek influence with the press testifies to the very different role of the press in the political process today.

Because news professionals rather than political leaders control the news product, the press today largely shapes our definition of what is news. Political leaders, for the most part, accept that definition. News is what the journalists say it is. Photo opportunities, ceremonial bill-signings, summits which execute no substantial business, and other *pseudo events*, as political scientist Daniel Boorstin calls them,[21] represent attempts by political leaders to meet needs that are defined for the most part by the news media.

Political leaders in the early years of this country's history actively defined what constituted news. Their definition included texts of speeches and documents, transcripts of legislative proceedings, and articles written by or for politicians. Journalistic definitions of the news occasionally prevailed, but particularly in the political sphere, what got printed more frequently represented a product defined exclusively by political leaders. The influence of government on news certainly continues to exist, as we shall see more clearly in Part III of this book. But that influence is more subtle than it once was, and the press is increasingly independent of it.

Competing Imperatives

The increasing reliance of the political system on the press as a linking mechanism with the public, and the increasing autonomy of the news media, have inevitably created a struggle for control. If the press still depended on political leaders or government authority for funding and readership, the question of control over the news would be irrelevant; the political system's imperative would prevail. Similarly, if the political system did not depend on the press as an intermediary between itself and the citizenry, there would be no tension.

The fact is, however, that the press does shoulder the primary burden of linking public and government at this point in American political history. As a result, political leaders and agencies often pressure the news media to fulfill that function in specific ways—and those pressures often conflict with the press's own imperatives as an independent, autonomous institution.

Political Imperatives. The political institutions and leaders in a democracy need to be able to communicate efficiently with the citizenry. The mechanism that links the government with the public should ideally provide not only a conduit for communication, but also a conduit for the organization of opinion. That such a linking mechanism must exist is not a matter of debate, but the appropriate nature of such a mechanism and the roles that should be played by its various participants is.

A democratic government needs the capability not only to communicate its own policies and decisions to the people, but also to gather and organize the responses and needs of those people in order to make appropriate policy decisions. In the context of elections, the system needs a mechanism capable of presenting candidates and the public debate on the issues. In a non-electoral context, the political system needs a mechanism capable of disseminating information and of gathering and shaping public views for policymakers. In other words, whatever the conduit is that bridges the distance between governed and governors, it must be capable both of expressing the views of the governors and of articulating competently the public response to those views. The imperatives of the political leaders, then, require that the linking mechanism perform certain particular functions that enable the democracy to run more effectively.

Obviously, political leaders also have other imperatives that are often implicit in their criticisms of the press. Both leaders and institutions want the news media to report favorably on their actions and decisions; and both, to maintain their policy-making positions, want an accurate reading of the public response to those actions and decisions.

Press Imperatives. The press has its own set of imperatives, however. The news media are governed, first and foremost, by financial concerns, and their continued operation is contingent upon financial success. This preoccupation with commercial stability is manifested through the drive for audience or circulation and the competition for advertising revenues. The American press operates within a vastly competitive environment.

In addition to the need for commercial or financial stability, the press is governed by its own need for journalistic independence. From before the turn of this century onward, journalists have insisted on the virtue of their independence, and have emphasized the standard of objectivity as their primary credo. The news media have proudly functioned as a "common carrier"—an objective reporter—of information. During the past thirty years, however, and particularly since the press's role in the Watergate scandal in the 1970s, journalists have placed a heightened emphasis on the news media's role as "watchdog" over government, as a trustee of the public good, and as a governmental critic.

The imperatives of press and political system are predictably dissimilar. The relationship is not always adversarial, of course. At many points, the interests of press and government intersect, and cooperation—explicit or implicit—is the order of the day. But as long as the political system seeks to use the press to link the governors and the governed for the continued functioning of democratic government, and as long as the press seeks to meet its own economic needs while remaining independent of government influence, the two institutions will clash. The fundamental tension that exists between government and press is inevitable.

The remainder of this book is devoted to a discussion and analysis of the evolution of that tension and its effects on the various points where press and political system intersect: the newsmaking and newsgathering processes; mass political behavior; electoral campaigns; political institutions; and public policy.

NOTES

1. Martin Linsky, *Impact: How the Press Affects Federal Policymaking*, New York: Norton, 1986, p. 203.
2. Keith Blume, *The Presidential Election Show*, South Hadley, Mass.: Bergin and Garvey, 1985, p. 2.

3. Joseph R. Dominick, *The Dynamics of Mass Communication*, 3d ed., New York: McGraw-Hill, 1990, p. 57.
4. Anthony Smith, "The Newspaper of the Late Twentieth Century: The U.S. Model," *Newspapers and Democracy*, Cambridge, Mass.: MIT Press, 1980, p. 17.
5. See Ray Hiebert, Donald Ungarait, and Thomas Bohn, *Mass Media VI*, White Plains, N.Y.: Longman, 1991, chap. 11.
6. U.S. Bureau of the Census, *Statistical Abstract of the United States, 1987*, 107th ed., Washington: Government Printing Office, 1986, p. 531. Also see Christopher Sterling, *Electronic Media: A Guide to Trends in Broadcasting and News Technologies, 1920–1983*, New York: Praeger, 1984.
7. Gallup Report, May 1986; and *Statistical Abstract*, p. 523.
8. The Roper Organization, *America's Watching: Public Attitudes toward Television*, New York: Television Information Office, 1987.
9. Roper Organization, *America's Watching*.
10. The Roper Organization, *An Extended View of Public Attitudes toward Television and Other Mass Media, 1959–1971*, New York: Television Information Office, 1971.
11. Roper Organization, *America's Watching*.
12. Janet Brown and Ed Fouhy, "The Debates: A View from the Inside Out," *Christian Science Monitor*, November 7, 1988, p. 14; and Elihu Katz and Jacob J. Feldman, *The Great Debates*, Bloomington, Ind.: Indiana University Press, 1962, p. 190.
13. Times-Mirror, *The People and the Press*, January 1986, pp. 20–22.
14. Michael J. Robinson and Andrew Kohut, "Believability and the Press," *Public Opinion Quarterly* 53 (Summer 1988): 174–189.
15. Norman Ornstein, "The Open Congress Meets the President," in Anthony D. King, ed., *Both Ends of the Avenue*, Washington: AEI, 1983; and Dom Bonafede, "The Washington Press—Competing for Power with the Federal Government," *National Journal*, April 17, 1982, p. 664.
16. Times-Mirror, *The People and the Press*, pp. 14–15.
17. From Dom Bonafede, "Hey, Look Me Over," *National Journal*, November 21, 1987, p. 2965.
18. Bonafede, "The Washington Press," p. 668.
19. Per telephone interview with Joseph Keenan, Deputy Superintendent of the Senate Press Gallery, July 24, 1989.
20. Studies about how reforms have affected political parties include Austin Ranney, *Curing the Mischiefs of Faction: Party Reform in America*, Berkeley, Calif.: University of California Press, 1975; Martin P. Wattenberg, *The Decline of American Political Parties, 1952–1980*, Cambridge, Mass.: Harvard University Press, 1984; David Adamany, "Political Parties in the 1980s," in Michael J. Malbin, ed., *Money and Politics in the United States*, Chatham, N.J.: Chatham House, 1980; and Norman H. Nie, Sidney Verba, and John C. Petrocik, *The Changling American Voter*, enlarged ed., Cambridge, Mass.: Harvard University Press, 1979.
21. Daniel Boorstin, *The Image*, New York: Harper & Row, 1961, p. 34.

PART I

Shaping the News

The shaping of the news product can be characterized as a battleground between *newsgatherers* who are pursuing autonomy from politicians while following journalistic and commercial imperatives, and *newsmakers* (politicians and those who seek to influence them) who rely heavily on the news product for political purposes. The news product is an amalgam of the press's mode of newsgathering and the image-making efforts of policymakers acting in accordance with institutional and/or individual objectives.

The purpose of the next two chapters is to describe the interaction of newsmakers and newsgatherers in the formation of news.

CHAPTER 1

The Newsgathering Process

"And that's the way it is."

CBS Evening News anchor Walter Cronkite

Budding journalists are taught that newsgathering includes reporting, editing, and publishing stages. They have also been told by some in the profession that the newsgathering process is intuitive and not really explainable. NBC News commentator John Chancellor and Associated Press writer Walter R. Mears succinctly stated this view: "Former Supreme Court Justice Potter Stewart once said that he could not define pornography, but knew it when he saw it. That's sometimes the way it is with news. The pros know it when they see it."[1] However, the apparently mechanical nature of this cycle (or the mystical nature, according to others) ignores the social forces affecting the process. Journalists are governed by social, political, and cultural forces that significantly shape their work.

Some journalists argue that these forces affecting them are merely those present in the larger society. Journalists, they argue, simply hold up a mirror which reflects the society as it is,[2] and that, explains why the media get blamed for bearing bad news: Society does not want to be reminded of its faults and shortcomings.[3] But, the mirror analogy has been widely rejected because it ignores social forces distinctive to the newsgathering process which have been identified in studies in press work. Even many journalists have admitted the inadequacy of this model in understanding the shaping of news.

A second characterization, perhaps more accurate, is that the news media function as a prism rather than as a mirror—a prism which "picks up rays of information from all directions and refracts them, bends them, before sending them

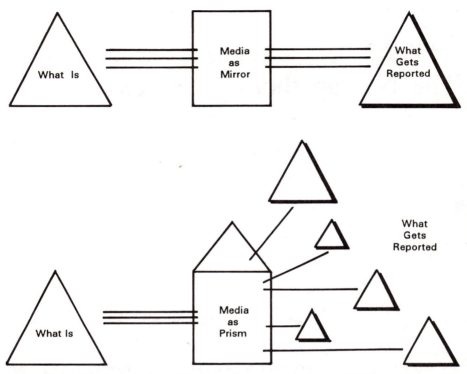

Figure 1.1. Although journalists have often argued in the past that they simply report facts, like a mirror held up to events, scholars agree that the process is more complex than that. One model of news reporting suggests that the media act as a *prism*, gathering rays of information and bending and refracting them as they are transmitted.

out again.''[4] (See Figure 1.1.) The media as prism implies not a mirror accurately reflecting information, but conduits which will ''frame, transform, and invent what they purport to convey.''[5]

If we accept the premise that the newsgathering process itself shapes the news, then what influences the newsgathering process and transforms the nature of news?

Three models have been offered to explain the forces governing the newsgathering process.[6] One pertains to political bias, the second to the influence of the organization, and the third to professional news values and norms.

BIAS

Political Bias

The most popular model explains the news, both broadcast and print, as the product of political bias. This view takes several forms. One holds that those associated with the actual work of journalism—reporters, editors, producers, news anchors—carry ideological biases into their work. News professionals have been primarily accused of injecting a liberal ideological bias into the newsgathering process,[7] an argument supported by the results of various surveys measuring political attitudes of journalists.[8] Also, a large part of the news audience believes the news is politically biased. According to one poll in the mid-1980s, 45 percent of the public believed the press was biased in reporting. Thirty-six percent felt it was not. Of those who saw bias, a majority viewed the bias as ideologically liberal.[9]

Critics of this view argue that the possession of an ideology does not necessarily affect news content, that news professionals may be able to subordinate biases in pursuit of professionalism. These critics also cite the failure of some empirical studies to demonstrate the expected bias.[10]

Others attribute political bias to the corporate boardroom rather than the newsroom. According to this view, the newsgathering process is shaped not by the professionals' ideologies, but by the news corporation's capitalist-oriented perspective. News professionals are dictated to by their corporate bosses.[11] Thus, news content is a reflection of the news corporation's conservative bias.

Still another variation is that, although the news professionals are ideologically liberal, they share the biases of their own society. They do not challenge the underpinnings of society such as capitalism or representative democracy because they share the consensual support for the political, social, and economic institutions. The press then becomes an impediment to social change because of its position as defender of the status quo.[12]

This bias emerges particularly in the area of foreign affairs coverage, some critics argue. The news media present information about foreign countries in a manner consistent with Western ideological interests, and the result is a distorted view of the rest of the world.[13]

There is, however, an abundance of research suggesting media role in social change.[14] For example, Michael J. Robinson has demonstrated the effect of television programming on societal attitudes.[15] Several studies point to media impact on the public agenda.[16] Moreover, those involved in newsgathering even view themselves as social reformers. For example, in the late 1980s, NBC News launched an advertising campaign heralding television's role in societal reform. Such a conservative institution as is described in this literature would resist, not foster such change.

Cultural Bias

Another kind of bias perceived by some critics is that of newsgathering dominated by societal values—not, as in the previous model, American or Western values but rather those of a smaller and more homogeneous specific society. According to this argument, journalists, in particular, share the worldview of their specific cultural milieu—a cosmopolitan, urban upper-class value system.[17]

One example of the existence of such a worldview is the introduction into the newsroom of those who have not been socialized to it. When a Soviet television journalist worked for a Los Angeles television station for a week, the difference in perspective was stark, according to one of the station's news producers:

> You see, a lot of our reporters at KNBC make a lot of money. They're in the upper economic classes. And there's a difference with her. I'm not saying that Svetlana's from the lower economic classes, but she's from a more level society. She identifies with people on a terrific level. So when she goes and interviews people, she's talking *to* them and not *above* them. I rarely see that with American reporters.[18]

The major proponents of this school conclude that "the current intellectual and emotional milieu of the national media is expressed in news coverage of long-term social controversies."[19] In other words, these elite journalists not only hold a shared worldview, but use this view to organize their work. They give greater weight to one side in covering issues—the side that corresponds with their own views of social reality.[20] Moreover, physical proximity and social interaction facilitate continual socialization and reinforcement. Speaking of reporters, political scientists David Paletz and Robert Entman have explained:

> Physically concentrated in the same places, they interact socially, they share the perceptions and gossip that shape stories. The more intimate the physical space, the closer the social relationships, the more similar the news.[21]

The news becomes not only highly similar, but also highly reflective of the group's cultural values.

Overall, however, the political bias model has failed to gain widespread support among scholars. The existence of a liberal slant in the newsroom and a conservative tilt in the boardroom largely have been acknowledged, but the salience of these biases in the formation of the news product (assuming they do not counterbalance one another) has not been conclusively demonstrated.

Succinctly put, do journalists hold political biases? Undoubtedly so. But do these biases shape the news? A single answer to that question has yet to gain widespread support. The problem may be the inadequacy of the model in explaining press behavior. Even if the argument of the salience of these biases is accepted, it is likely they are mitigated by other pressures from the organization and their own standards of professionalism. Unless more persuasive literature appears, we should look beyond bias to other factors with potentially greater power to explain the news product.

Organizational Pressures

One of those other factors is the role of the news media organization in news. A theory of newsgathering holds the process is governed by organizational pressures.[22] According to this model, the economic pressures and organizational strictures shape the process of newsgathering and affect the news product. Some of these strictures include the beat system, deadlines, the audience, advertisers, and owner and/or publisher idiosyncrasies.

The Beat System. Economic pressures of competition impel any news organization to channel its resources in predictable directions. Theoretically, news could happen anywhere at any time, and news organizations must be prepared to report the news wherever and whenever it happens. Practically, news organizations cannot function under such uncertainty. Instead, they predict where news will happen and establish a beat system to assign reporters accordingly. Beats such as the White House, Congress, the Supreme Court, and the presidential campaign are created to anticipate the occurrence of news and inject a measure of predictability. By predicting news, the organization can allocate resources efficiently and compete effectively.

However, the very nature of such beats governs what is considered news. The beat system inherently defines what authority figures and bodies do and say as news. When these bodies and figures take actions and make statements, these actions and statements are duly covered and news is produced.

Also, the beat system has been blamed for the rise of a style of newsgathering called "pack journalism." Pack journalism refers to journalists on a beat converging on a single story, usually in line with the emphases of elite journalists on that beat. The average journalist follows the lead of other journalists due to their close proximity and acceptance that the product of these leading journalists is more likely to be considered news by news executives and the general public. Recently, some departure from the traditional beat system, which consists of coverage of an institution or a department, has been allowed for the elite press. For example, some reporters have been assigned to policy beats, such as science, the economy, and the environment.

Many journalists have opposed such a departure from tradition. Some fear they will be tagged as specialists and never be considered for anchor or editor posts. Another dilemma for the specialist occurs when the "hot" issue suddenly cools. Energy policy, a major beat in the 1970s, faded from public view in the 1980s. Other reporters contend the press should concentrate on events, not issues. Overall, the institutional beat system has not been seriously threatened by the new trend.

Regularized News. Still another economic factor is the establishment of news as a regular daily phenomenon. Presentation of news at regular intervals shapes the newsgathering process. Since the public has come to expect news to be delivered on their doorsteps each morning or in their living rooms each evening, news must be produced day in and day out. For some news outlets, such as the wire services and radio news the intervals are even more frequent.

Hence, the driving factor becomes the process of news delivery whether or not there really is some new thing worth presenting each day as news. A television news anchor cannot appear on the evening news and announce that no news has occurred that day and the broadcast will be dispensed with. The established regularity of the news delivery would be broken. Delivery would be unpredictable. Audience sizes, broadcast schedules, and advertising rates would be affected. The economics of regular presentation of news drives the newsgathering process to produce a fresh commodity daily in order to meet organizational imperatives and public expectations.

Deadlines. The system of deadlines is another economic factor in newsgathering. All forms of media operate under certain deadlines for publication or broadcast of the news. The proverbial reporter who rushes into the newsroom and yells, "Stop the press! I've got a story that's gonna blow this town wide open" simply does not exist. The presses do not stop for news. Newsgathering is organized around the deadline, and stories must be submitted within this rigid time frame. Editing, publishing, and distribution all work on deadline as well. For a newspaper, delays in publication mean delays in dissemination of the paper and loss of revenue. In fact, the later the event occurs, the less likely it is that that event will be included in a timely edition.

Broadcast news programs operate under similar constraints. Reports from correspondents must be submitted early enough for editing prior to the regular news broadcast. News departments are expected to produce news daily or hourly. News programs cannot delay their broadcasts, since viewers or listeners expect the news at a particular time.

Though exceptions are typically made for prestigious beats, such as the White House, late-breaking news, particularly outside the regular beats, is unlikely to air at all. It is too late to include in the upcoming broadcast and it will be old news by the next one.

The Audience. Another organizational pressure is economic consideration of audience response. Newspapers and newsmagazines monitor audience reaction through circulation figures while broadcast news does the same through viewer ratings. Both also use audience surveys. Losses in audience usually mean loss of advertising revenue, prestige, and even the ability to stay in business. Television network news programs rearrange format and style of presentation regularly to attract larger audiences.

Newsgathering can clearly be affected in response to perceived audience interests, including the type and amount of news presented. Although journalists seek to distance themselves from their audience to protect their autonomy in determining the news product, news organizations do alter the style of presentation to meet audience response.[23] For example, network news usually condenses stories into 90-second segments to avoid losing audience interest during lengthy stories. Even the substance of the news presentation has been changed. For example, in the early 1980s, at least one network decided to "de-Washingtonize" its coverage,[24] a decision probably (although not admittedly) based on perceived lack of audience interest.

Advertisers. The effect of advertisers on news depends on the size of the media organizations and the nature of dependence on the advertiser. Although in small news organizations such as local radio and television stations and small circulation dailies advertising and editorial divisions can become enmeshed with the effect of compromising the autonomy of news, larger organizations are typically more immune. Large national news organizations, such as CBS News, *Time*, or the *New York Times*, do not rely on a single advertiser. In fact, they even turn away proffered advertisements, as the three major networks did in the case of Mobil Oil Company ads on current policy issues.

Advertisers no longer possess the power to dictate broadcast news programs as they did in the 1940s and 1950s, when advertisers occasionally bought whole programs like the "Camel News Caravan," a network news program sponsored by Camel cigarettes. Advertisers obviously had greater control over news affecting them. Today, advertisers buy individual 30- or 60-second spots. Rarely does an advertiser sponsor an entire program and never an evening network news broadcast. That is not to say that advertiser pressure does not occur. The relative financial stability of large national news organizations, however, provides some insulation from the pressures of advertisers.

Owners' and Publishers' Idiosyncrasies. As we suggested earlier, political as well as economic considerations can sometimes be injected by the organization on the newsgathering and reporting processes. Owners and publishers of news organizations have been known to impose their will on newsgathering. In the past, William Randolph Hearst of the Hearst Newspaper Syndicate, Robert McCormick of the *Chicago Tribune*, and Henry Luce of *Time* wielded enormous power over the news divisions in their organizations. Hearst and McCormick both used their newspapers to lambast the New Deal, and Henry Luce slanted news in support of Republican candidates and U.S. foreign relations in China.

Editors and reporters were "socialized" into adopting the organization's peculiarities, such as writing stories in a certain style and emphasizing some points while omitting others.

More recently, however, the boardroom has become more removed from the activities of the newsroom. The professionalization of the journalistic corps, discussed in Chapter 5, has diminished the influence of publishers, and large media organizations today are rarely dominated by a single individual who seeks to utilize the organization for political objectives.[25] Many large organizations are either publicly owned or controlled by several individuals.

Moreover, journalists today are trained in the college classroom rather than the newsroom.[26] The result is a journalistic corps imbued with a professional ethic transcending specific news organizations.

Professional Values and Norms

A third model of newsgathering accentuates the role of news professionals and the emerging system of professionalism.[27] Although this model takes several forms, the overriding principle is the salience of professionalism, not the imperatives of the organization nor ideology, in the formation of news.

Professionalism. Professionalism refers to the adoption and inculcation of uniform standards of job performance in newsgathering and reporting. The emphasis on professionalism implies that the dominant role in the newsgathering process is played by reporters, editors, and producers who are directly involved.

Although reporters and editors have been pursuing professional status since the days of Yellow Journalism, professionalism has proved elusive until the last couple of decades. College education, only recently seen as a prerequisite for a journalistic career, has enhanced journalism's search for professional status. Moreover, the rise of college journalism majors has fostered classroom journalistic training over the newsroom training of the past. The career path of office messenger to cub reporter and later to full-fledged reporter has been replaced by a path more similar to that of other professions, and the development of a college journalism curriculum offers a shared experience for news professionals. One study in the early 1980s found that a majority of journalists were products of communications departments versus only 41 percent who had been in 1971.[28] This shared background and training fosters the inculcation of shared values and norms.

Shared Values and Norms. Shared values and norms contribute to heightened group identity, since only those who have been socialized can be assumed to perform a task adequately. Even news organization management personnel, unless drawn from the newsroom, do not share the group identity.

As an example, many journalists contend that only journalists can define what constitutes news. They argue that, due to their training or socialization, only journalists know news when they see it.[29] This argument, of course, prevents the news consumer from being able to judge whether he or she has been well served by the newsgathering process, since only the professional journalist can appropriately make that judgment.

The presence of shared values and norms also eases the transition from classroom to newsroom, and work within the newsroom is facilitated since internal disputes are minimized with adherence to broadly accepted norms.

Since the turn of the century, formations of journalistic societies, publication of trade journals, and adoption of codes of ethics have solidified the professional status and reinforced consensual standards. Trade journals, such as the *Columbia Journalism Review*, the *Washington Journalism Review*, and *Editor and Publisher*, have been useful tools in heightening group identification. According to one survey of journalists, such trade publications are read by a majority of journalists.[30]

The professional model argues first that the news professionals dominate the newsgathering process, and that there is increasing evidence they have become the major determinants in the newsgathering and reporting processes. Secondly, the model argues, journalists are in turn governed in their newswork by shared values

---

What Constitutes *News?*

- Events
- Timeliness
- Drama
- Conflict

- Unusual or unpredictable elements
- Proximity
- Famous names
- Visual appeal

---

and norms. However, identifying those values and norms has been a complicated process, and one only recently attempted. One group of researchers, Lichter, Rothman, and Lichter, has isolated such shared psychological traits in news professionals as fear of power, narcissism, and need for achievement.[31]

Earlier studies of the role of the news media as *gatekeeper* focused on the values of news editors in selecting stories.[32] Scholars wondering what factors drive decision making on what constitutes news have identified the news media as gatekeepers of public information, transforming private information into public knowledge. The question was: Why does some information get past the gate while other information does not? What are the criteria for inclusion or exclusion? Taken as a whole, the gatekeeper studies found that editors—both print and broadcast— did demonstrate a shared value framework in selecting stories for inclusion in the news content. Certain stories, such as those with conflict, proximity, and, for television, those possessing a visual component, were more likely to be selected by editors from among the available stories for broadcast or publication. In one study, the news editors rejected all stories that were timely—that is, that had occurred during the past twenty-four hours—but lacked other news values.[33]

Even before the editor goes to work, however, reporters use shared definitions of news in order to select stories. The role of reporters—their perspectives on news, their usage of sources, their approach to newsgathering—has been the focus of several studies.[34]

Commonly held criteria for newsworthiness of a story include preference for discrete events, timeliness, drama, conflict, the unpredictable or unusual, proximity, and famous names. An additional element unique to television news is the visual element.

Events. News reports events. Events qualify as news for several reasons: An event is easy to identify; it is discrete—with a beginning, middle, and end; and it is tangible for journalists and for the audience occupying a specific time and place. Ideas and concepts, on the other hand, are difficult to define, complex, and often vague.

Many events are actually pseudo events, as Daniel Boorstin describes them.[35] News conferences or ceremonies are designed for press coverage. They are predictable, which enhances their appeal to the press for planning purposes. Covering events also blunts criticism of press bias, since editors and reporters can argue that an event-orientation encompasses all happenings without partisan or ideological bias.[36] Coverage of a presidential press conference and a protest march can both be justified. Not all events are treated equally, however. Official events uniformly receive preference.

Events are "hard" news, and hard news, rather than feature pieces or analysis stories about long-range trends unassociated with a particular event, predominates in news content.[37]

Timeliness. Timeliness refers to news that happened since the last report. For daily media, that means events which have occurred during the past twenty-four hours. In other words, events happening since the last evening news broadcast or issue of the daily newspaper are preferred over events which occurred before that time.

Although timeliness is generally necessary for a story to be considered, we noted earlier that it is hardly sufficient. Thousands of events occur in the course of a day in American national politics alone, and the decisions about which to report hinge on other news values. Without timeliness, however, an event simply disappears. If a peace march down Pennsylvania Avenue or a news conference does not appear in the next issue or broadcast, it is highly unlikely that it will ever appear. Rarely will journalists go back and pick up what they consider "old news."

This preoccupation with timeliness affects coverage of major and minor stories alike. Major stories are not continued to the next day unless another news event occurs which justifies its continuation. For example, a major Supreme Court decision will receive one day's coverage because the Supreme Court itself will not make news again concerning that decision the next day; only if there is some subsequent related event, such as a protest march concerning the decision—a new event—might coverage continue.

Drama. Some stories can acquire a long run in the news due to their dramatic quality. News stories, particularly in the broadcast media, are often dramas. The drama occurs at two levels. One level is the specific report, which is usually treated as a self-contained unit; the beginning, middle, and the end of the drama are encapsulated in the single story. At another level, however, the single story becomes part of an extended dramatic narrative. Examples include a presidential campaign, Supreme Court nomination, or the fate of a presidential policy initiative. One usually uncommon, but highly publicized drama is the scandal. These dramas are covered through a succession of stories over an extended period of time until the dramatic story is somehow resolved, the audience gets bored, or some other drama suddenly intrudes.

Drama is used because it conforms to the journalist's demand for a simple story, and because the readers or viewers attend to the media because they have become interested in the long-running story. Journalists hope the audience will develop concern over the conclusion and stay with the story until its close.

Conflict. Dramas make better news if conflict is present. As in a novel, when two antagonists are clearly identified and a confrontation ensues, the drama is more

What constitutes a "story" is sometimes determined by how many new angles news-gatherers can find to report. During the 1984 presidential election campaign, Geraldine Ferraro's precedent-breaking nomination as the Democratic vice-presidential candidate was virtually overshadowed by press investigation into her husband's finances—an issue which shifted the focus of the campaign from the candidate herself to her spouse, and left her struggling to explain what she did and did not know about her husband's financial dealings. The following headlines appeared over an eight-day period and demonstrate the drama of a continuing story.

G.O.P. SEIZES GENDERLESS ISSUE OF TAX RETURNS TO ATTACK FERRARO

FINANCES OF FERRARO AND HUSBAND ARE INTERWOVEN

ZACCARO: COMPETITIVE, PRIVATE MAN

HUSBAND PLANS TAX DISCLOSURE WITH FERRARO

FERRARO IS TERMED SURPRISED BY LOAN TAKEN BY HUSBAND

FERRARO REVEALS HER TAX FIGURES AND HUSBAND'S

FERRARO DENIES ANY WRONGDOING:
2D LOAN BY ZACCARO FROM ESTATE

Source: Thomas E. Patterson and Richard Davis, "The Media Campaign: Struggle for the Agenda," in Michael Nelson, ed., *The Elections of 1984*, Washington: CQ Press, 1985, p. 119.

compelling, the conclusion less predictable, and the story more newsworthy. Research demonstrates that news professionals prefer stories with conflict.[38] Journalism students are taught that conflict is a central feature of news.[39]

The Unpredictable or Unusual. One classic news definition goes: "If dog bites man, that's not news. But if man bites dog, that's news." In terms of American national politics, the unpredictable action, decision, statement, or behavior is, more likely than not, to be deemed news: the moralistic Gary Hart engaging in extramarital affairs or the staunch anti-Communist Ronald Reagan traveling to China and the Soviet Union.

However, the preference for predictability in gathering news impedes unpredictability as a news value. Only if the unpredictable event occurs in a predictable place and time is it guaranteed the attention of newsgatherers. A presidential stumble or misstatement becomes news because the president is covered as a predictable source of news. Ironically, an even more unpredictable occurrence from an unpredictable source is much less likely to become news.

Proximity. Still another criteria for news is proximity. The closer to home, the higher the likelihood of news coverage. News of national politics and government is proximate to the national network news and national newspapers such as the *New York Times*, the *Christian Science Monitor*, the *Wall Street Journal*, and *USA Today*. However, national political news must compete with—and often is dis-

The uncertain fate of two gray whales trapped in Arctic ice became a long-running dramatic story in the fall of 1988. Attention from the media led to combined U.S.–Soviet rescue efforts that involved ice-cutters, Eskimos, and considerable sums of money. The rescue efforts ran over a period of more than a week, several times as lead stories, despite the fact that a presidential election was only weeks away. Once the whales were rescued, the media turned to other matters—and spent very little time or space analyzing whether or not the story was worth the space it was given. *Source*: © UPI/Bettmann Newsphotos.

placed by—local news in daily metropolitan newspapers because such news is closer at hand and therefore more likely to impact individuals in the locality.

Personalization. News is presented in a personalized manner. This is accomplished by building stories around the human actors who are involved in events.[40] Not only is this true of the style of presentation—television news has become the modern equivalent of a neighborly chat over the backyard fence—but also of substance. News is the story of people. This personalization takes two forms: famous personalities and human interest.

Journalists say "names make news." The presence of a famous name enhances the news value of an event. Stories about people who are familiar to the audience require less explanation for reader or viewer comprehension. These stories are also considered by journalists as more likely to attract and hold audience attention due to the appeal of human interest. Journalists also personalize stories of more complicated issues in order to attract audience attention. Coverage of U.S.-Soviet relations may be reduced to concentration on the personal relationship between the two nations' leaders.

Famous names catch the attention of the audience because of their "familiarity" with them.[41] A continuing drama involving an individual who has become well-known to the audience personalizes a story; the audience may come to identify with such individuals, or at least develop concern for their fate.

Other human interest stories also make up personalized stories. Stories about public policy effects are often personalized by concentrating on a single previously unknown person's experiences. For example, news about released American hostages in 1990 concerned the reaction of their families, their first meal of freedom, and, overall, their initial adjustment to freedom. The causes or effects of that release on U.S. foreign policy are submerged by the personalized angle.

Visuals. Television news seeks to be more than just a talking head accompanied by a still photograph. Understandably, broadcast news professionals want to use television's visual capacity to tell news stories. Such visual capacity also enhances audience interest in the story. Consequently, visuals are crucial for story salience on television.[42]

However, not all stories naturally contain an eye-catching visual component. In fact, many stories of national politics are replete with "talking heads." As we will discuss in the following chapters, political actors attempting to gain or keep press attention have learned to meet this imperative of visual communication.

The search for visuals has led some news departments to create simulations of news events. In 1989, ABC News simulated an alleged spy transaction involving a U.S. diplomat. Although the network was criticized by television critics, other networks said they planned to use the same technique in their future news programs. NBC News producer Sid Feders called the simulations "a natural next step in broadcast news." But others criticize the blending of fact and fiction as confusing for viewers. CNN executive vice-president Ed Turner lamented: "It's all part of this mad search for pictures, pictures, pictures."[43]

SUMMARY

The news media are not merely a mirror reflecting society; their role is more closely akin to that of a prism, which gathers light, bends it slightly, and focuses it. The evidence collected so far indicates that the newsgathering process is not governed by the political biases of the newsgatherers, but organizational perspectives do explain key aspects of newsgathering. The model of newsgathering as the product of rising professionalism best illuminates the approach of newsgatherers to the news. The model also corresponds with the expanded role of reporters and editors in the newsgathering process in recent years.

Employment of shared news values as criteria for news transforms the way journalists approach coverage of American national politics. As will be discussed subsequently, coverage of the performance of governmental institutions, the electoral process, and policymaking is affected by professional news values.

NOTES

1. John Chancellor and Walter R. Mears, *The News Business*, New York: Harper and Row, 1983, p. 5.
2. Sig Mickelson, *The Electric Mirror*, New York: Dodd, Mead, 1972.
3. See William Small, *To Kill a Messenger: Television News and the Real World*, New York: Hastings House, 1970.
4. William Rivers, *The Other Government: Power and the Washington Media*, New York: Universe Books, 1982, p. 212.
5. George Comstock, "Social and Cultural Impact of the Mass Media," in Elie Abel, ed., *What's News: The Media in American Society*, San Francisco: Institute for Contemporary Studies, 1981, p. 243.
6. See Doris Graber, *Mass Media and American Politics*, 3d ed.. Washington: CQ Press, 1989, pp. 76–77.
7. For examples, see Shirley Christian, "Covering the Sandinistas: The Foregone Conclusions of the Fourth Estate," *Washington Journalism Review* (March 1982); and William A. Rusher, *The Coming Battle for the Media*, New York: William Morrow, 1988.
8. For studies of elite journalists' political attitudes, see S. Robert Lichter, Stanley Rothman, and Linda S. Lichter, *The Media Elite*, Bethesda, Md.: Adler and Adler, 1986; and S. Robert Lichter and Stanley Rothman, "Media and Business Elites," *Public Opinion* (October/November 1981). However, a study including non-elite journalists found a more centrist political ideology. See David H. Weaver and G. Cleveland Wilhoit, *The American Journalist*, Bloomington, Ind.: Indiana University Press, 1986, pp. 25–32.
9. Times-Mirror, *The People and the Press*, January 1986, p. 28.
10. See Michael J. Robinson, "Just How Liberal is the News?" *Public Opinion* (February/March 1983): 55–60; and Michael J. Robinson and Margaret A. Sheehan, *Over the Wire and on TV*, New York: Russell Sage Foundation, 1983.
11. For example, see Michael Parenti, *Inventing Reality*, New York: St. Martin's Press, 1986.
12. For samples, see Parenti, *Inventing Reality*; Todd Gitlin, *The Whole World is Watching: Mass Media in the Making and Unmaking of the New Left*, Berkeley, Calif.: University of California Press, 1980; and Gaye Tuchman, *Making News*, New York: Free Press, 1978. For a discussion of this view, see Elihu Katz and Tama Szechsko, eds., *Mass Media and Social Change*, Beverly Hills, Calif.: Sage, 1981. For a critique of the literature, see David L. Altheide, "Media Hegemony: A Failure of Perspective," *Public Opinion Quarterly* 48 (1984): 476–490.
13. For example, see Peter Dahlgren, "The Third World on TV News: Western Ways of Seeing the Other," in William C. Adams, ed., *Television Coverage of International Affairs*, Norwood, N.J.: Ablex, 1982, pp. 45–66; and Edward Said, *Covering Islam*, New York: Pantheon, 1981. For a critique, see Altheide, "Media Hegemony," pp. 476–490.
14. Altheide, "Media Hegemony," pp. 476–490.
15. Michael J. Robinson, "Television and American Politics 1956–1976," *The Public Interest* (Summer 1977): 64–90.
16. For a recent major study, see Shanto Iyengar and Donald R. Kinder, *News That Matters*, Chicago: University of Chicago Press, 1987.

17. Lichter, Rothman, and Lichter, *The Media Elite*.
18. *Los Angeles Times*, November 15, 1989, p. E-4.
19. Lichter, Rothman, and Lichter, *The Media Elite*, p. 301.
20. See Lichter, Rothman, and Lichter, *The Media Elite*.
21. David L. Paletz and Robert M. Entman, *Media Power Politics*, New York: Free Press, 1981, p. 202.
22. See Edward J. Epstein, *News from Nowhere*, New York: Random House, 1973.; Jeremy Tunstall, *Journalists at Work*, Beverly Hills, Calif.: Sage, 1971; and Herbert J. Gans, *Deciding What's News*, New York: Pantheon, 1979.
23. See, for example, Barbara Matusow, *The Evening Stars: The Rise of the Network News Anchors*, Boston: Houghton Mifflin, 1983.
24. See Norman Ornstein and Michael J. Robinson, "The Case of Our Disappearing Congress," *TV Guide*, January 11–17, 1986, pp. 5–6.
25. Two notable exceptions are Australian tycoon Rupert Murdoch, whose newspapers espouse conservative views, and broadcast magnate Ted Turner, who has sought to use his broadcast system to promote better U.S.-Soviet relations. However, actual empirical evidence of their role in the news divisions still is lacking.
26. David H. Weaver and G. Cleveland Wilhoit, *The American Journalist*, Bloomington, Ind.: Indiana University Press, 1986.
27. See, for example, Gaye Tuchman, *Making News*, New York: Free Press, 1978.
28. Weaver and Wilhoit, *The American Journalist*, p. 43.
29. See, for example, John Chancellor and Walter R. Mears, *The News Business*, New York: Harper and Row, 1985.
30. Weaver and Wilhoit, *The American Journalist*, pp. 109–112.
31. Lichter, Rothman, and Lichter, *The Media Elite*, chap. 4.
32. See Dan Berkowitz, "Refining the Gatekeeping Metaphor for Local Television News," *Journal of Broadcasting and Electronic Media* 34 (Winter 1990): 55–88; Eric A. Abbott and Lynn T. Brassfield, "Comparing Decisions on Releases by TV and Newspaper Gatekeepers," *Journalism Quarterly* 66 (Winter 1989): 853–856; and Mark D. Harmon, "Mr. Gates Goes Electronic: The What and Why Questions in Local TV News," *Journalism Quarterly* 66 (Winter 1989): 857–863.
33. James Buckalew, "News Elements and Selection by Television News Editors," *Journal of Broadcasting* 14 (Winter 1969–1970): 47–54.
34. Examples of studies of reporters covering national politics include Dan D. Nimmo, *Newsgathering in Washington*, New York: Atherton Press, 1964; Leon V. Sigal, *Reporters and Officials: The Organization and Politics of Newsmaking*, Lexington, Mass.: D.C. Heath, 1973; Stephen Hess, *The Washington Reporters*, Washington: Brookings Institution, 1981; and Michael B. Grossman and Martha Joynt Kumar, *Portraying the President*, Baltimore, Md.: Johns Hopkins University Press, 1981.
35. Daniel Boorstin, *The Image*, New York: Atheneum, 1972, p. 11.
36. Bernard Roshco, *Newsmaking*, Chicago: University of Chicago Press, 1975, p. 44; and William A. Henry, "News as Entertainment," in Elie Abel, ed., *What's News: The Media in American Society*, San Francisco: Institute for Contemporary Studies, 1981, p. 137.
37. See Grossman and Kumar, *Portraying the President*, p. 266; and Hess, *The Washington Reporters*, p. 15.
38. See Buckalew, "News Elements and Selection by Television News Editors." For samples of emphasis on conflict, see Daniel Riffe and Eugene F. Shaw, "Conflict and

Consonance: Coverage of the Third World in Two U.S. Papers," *Journalism Quarterly* 59 (Winter 1982): 617–626; David L. Paletz and Martha Elson, "Television Coverage of Presidential Nominating Conventions: Now You See It, Now You Don't," *Political Science Quarterly* 91 (Spring 1976): 103–132; and Richard Davis, "News Media Coverage of American National Political Institutions," unpublished doctoral dissertation, Syracuse University, 1986.

39. For a sample of journalistic texts emphasizing conflict as news, see Brian S. Brooks et al., *News Reporting and Writing*, New York: St. Martin's Press, 1980; and Melvin Mencher, *News Reporting and Writing*, 2d ed., Dubuque, Iowa: William C. Brown, 1981.

40. See W. Lance Bennett, *News: The Politics of Illusion*, White Plains, N.Y.: Longman, 1983, pp. 7–13.

41. See Roshco, *Newsmaking*, pp. 15–18; and Herbert Gans, *Deciding What's News*, New York: Pantheon, 1979, pp. 8–10.

42. See, for example, Buckalew, "News Elements and Selection by Television News Editors" and Joseph S. Fowler and Stuart W. Showalter, "Evening Network News Selection: A Confirmation of News Judgment," *Journalism Quarterly* 91 (Winter 1974): 712–715.

43. Bill Carter, "ABC News Divided on Simulated Events," *The New York Times*, July 27, 1989, p. C20.

SUGGESTED READINGS

Bennett, W. Lance. *News: The Politics of Illusion*. New York: Longman, 1983.

Broder, David S. *Behind the Front Page*. New York: Simon and Schuster, 1987.

Epstein, Edward Jay. *News from Nowhere*. New York: Random House, 1973.

Gans, Herbert J. *Deciding What's News*. New York: Pantheon, 1979.

Hess, Stephen. *The Washington Reporters*. Washington: Brookings Institution, 1981.

Lichter, S. Robert, Stanley Rothman, and Linda S. Lichter. *The Media Elite*. Bethesda, Md.: Adler and Adler, 1986.

Roshco, Bernard. *Newsmaking*. Chicago: University of Chicago, 1975.

Tuchman, Gaye. *Making News*. New York: Free Press, 1978.

CHAPTER 2

The Newsmaking Process

"You don't tell us how to stage the news and we don't tell you how to cover it."
Larry Speakes, *Speaking Out*

On June 6, 1989, George Bush called the press together for a news conference at his home in Kennebunkport, Maine, to discuss his accomplishments at the recent summit of Western leaders. The White House envisioned glowing news stories of the president's foreign policy prowess. Instead, news of Bush's press conference got buried in an avalanche of stories about that day's massacre in Tiananmen Square in Beijing, China.

Although this experience and Larry Speakes's statement above apparently contradict one another, they cogently present the reality of newsmaking.[1] Journalists serving primarily as newsgatherers comprise one major participant in the struggle over the shaping of the news. The second major participant, however, is the group of newsmakers—the elected officials, bureaucrats, staff, and interest group representatives—who regularly seek to influence news and who are deemed newsworthy or potentially so by newsgatherers. However, as George Bush learned, even a president doesn't always succeed in the attempt.

Newsmakers as individuals today are dependent on the press as a result of our whole political system's increasing dependence on the press. Most newsmakers try to influence the news coverage about themselves or their organizations.[2] Their relations with the press now constitute a significant aspect of their job. In a survey of public officials conducted in the early 1980s, nearly half of the officials said they spent over five hours a week specifically dealing directly with the press, and even more time is spent considering press coverage of themselves or their departments.[3]

The growing autonomy of the press requires newsmakers to approach the press differently from their counterparts in the past. Unlike nineteenth century public officials, today's newsmakers lack direct control over the news product. Very few own media outlets or support such outlets financially. Nor are very many media outlets governed by owners who, though not politicians, use their newspaper or broadcast station to support a particular political party or political leaders.

Hence, they must seek to influence rather than control the newsgathering process. In most cases, they must appeal to the press to gain its attention through meeting the press on its own grounds. They must be cognizant of news values, journalistic work habits, and media organizational imperatives. They must coordinate political moves with expectations of media performance.

Moreover, they must engage in such activity not in a vacuum, but in competition with many other politicians also seeking access through the media's gates. Newsmakers must attempt to manipulate the press to achieve the coverage they desire; such coverage is not guaranteed.

MANAGING THE NEWS

Who Manages the News?

Collectively, the newsmakers' advantage rests in the fact the press still is dependent on them as sources for news. News primarily is what authoritative sources do and say. But several developments have made the task of managing the news much more complicated. There is greater competition for the attention of the press today than in the past. With the proliferation of federal agencies and departments, the multiplication of congressional staff, and the explosion in Washington-based interest groups and academic think tanks, the range of potential sources is extensive. Like a kid in a candy store, journalists can choose from a wide array of possible sources on almost any subject.

Ironically, press coverage still centers on a few sources such as the White House and the congressional leadership, as will be discussed in later chapters. But the availability of alternative sources complicates the task of managing the news even for these sources. Other potential newsmakers must try harder to capture news attention.

Supply and Demand

Who manages the news depends on the law of informational supply and demand.[4] The question to ask is: Who has what someone else wants? If the newsmaker desperately seeks press notice, then the press acts as gatekeeper, and the newsmaker becomes only one of many pleaders at the media gates. But, if the press yearns for information possessed by the newsmaker, the tables are turned. The newsmaker controls the flow of information to press and public—who receives what and in what form.

Presidents have a distinct advantage due to their possession of both power and information. They often control the supply of information desired by the press. However, depending on the issue or event, other players actually can be in greater demand than the president, causing the president to lose control and become a pleader at the media's gates. These players emerge when a vacuum exists because the expected leader—usually the president—fails to set the agenda. Presidents lacking clear agendas, such as lame ducks, can become secondary figures to agency officials or members of Congress who fill that vacuum with their own issue interests. During his second term as president, Ronald Reagan was upstaged by the Iran-Contra hearings and the 1988 presidential campaign.

Also, if other players are perceived as having more information or expertise than the president about a hot news story, the president can be overshadowed. National Security Council aide Oliver North was just such a player who possessed knowledge highly valued by the press on the Iran-Contra issue. But even those who don't become household names can become newsmakers due to expertise. Senator Richard Lugar, viewed widely as an expert on the Philippines election in 1986, held media attention while observing that election. But it is rare that lesser known and long-shot presidential candidates, agency officials at little-covered agencies and departments, and junior members of Congress become anything but pleaders for press notice.

If supply and demand controls the news, then obviously the more centralized the possession of power and information, the more actual news management becomes feasible. But the system of American national government mitigates against such a monopoly. Constitutional checks and balances combined with political separation through split party control of government effectively decentralizes power and information.

Presidents come closest to possessing a monopoly on certain kinds of information, particularly in areas such as foreign affairs, but even that monopoly has been challenged in recent years by the Congress. On most matters, power and information are scattered across federal agencies, congressional committees, interest groups, and the White House. In such a climate of fragmentation, the press, not politicians, can become the central source from which almost all others draw.

Luck

Even the best of well-laid plans by regular newsmakers for press attention can be thwarted by unexpected events or issues. For example, during the Carter presidency, a presidential press conference designed to explain several policy priorities of the administration was overshadowed by a sudden terrorist kidnapping in Washington, D.C. Such intrusions—events with high dramatic quality, announcements of high political salience nationally or internationally, or the death of a prominent individual—are unpredictable and often frustrate policymakers' attempts to manage the news.

How to Manage the News

Newsmakers employ several techniques in order to attempt management of news. These include providing a flow of news, controlling access by the press, and utilizing to their advantage the journalists' values of news.

Where the demand for information outstrips supply, news management is clearly possible. The White House is almost unique in holding that opportunity on a regular basis. Most of what we will say about news management refers to the White House. Quadrennially, leading presidential candidates are often similarly situated, but possessing the opportunity is not equivalent to using it.

But the White House is unique in holding that opportunity on a regular basis. Hence, its news management is far from typical for newsmakers generally, and can be more accurately portrayed as an "ideal" case. For almost all other politicians, the chance to stand in such a position happens rarely or, more often, never at all. This point is crucial because there is a propensity on the part of critics of the press to make generalizations about press-politician relationships based on the interaction between the presidency and the press. The following discussion represents not the typical, but only the possible for national politicians other than the president.

Providing News. One method of news management is assuring the availability of news for the press. Providing a steady stream of information that the press considers news introduces an element of predictability in newsgathering, and the press can meet the requirement for gathering news with greater certainty. The daily routine of press briefings, prepared texts, official statements, and photo opportunities set up by the White House is specifically designed to keep the press corps happy. Presidential press secretaries have called the exercise "the care and feeding of the press corps."

Moreover, such ready availability of "good news" provides a diversion and can keep journalists from pursuing investigative reporting, which may lead to "bad news" for the public official and require more time and resources.

Controlling Press Access. In addition to the steady supply of information, the press can be catered to by the provision of access. Facilities for reporting provided by newsmakers—office space, phone banks, special entrances—allow the press to report on public officials with greater ease. By providing access to favorable sources of information—the president, key White House officials, and other administration supporters—newsmakers attempt to simplify the newsgathering task of reporters and garner positive coverage. For example, following the U.S. invasion of Grenada in October 1983, the White House sent out favorable sources to sell the Reagan administration's position on the invasion. The Prime Minister of the Caribbean nation of Dominica, who supported the invasion, was flown to Washington by the administration and appeared on all the network evening news programs, "Nightline," and two morning talk shows. She also was interviewed by *U.S. News and World Report* and *USA Today* and spoke at a news conference with President Reagan. Newsgatherers were provided easy access to a supporter of the invasion; access to critics was more problematic.

Simultaneously, however, the tactic of limiting access can be used to manage news. Access to the main news source, usually the president, is parceled out selectively. Availability of news sources is slowed to a trickle or raised to a gush depending on the purposes of the newsmakers.

Since hundreds of events occur in any twenty-four hour period, the determination of what becomes news depends on reporter access and news values. By limiting reporter access to a single event and assuring that the event fits news values, newsmakers hope to narrow the choice of events to one viable alternative—the one provided by them. The event may be a speech, a photo opportunity, or a rally. But the ready availability of only one event generally predicts the nature of press coverage.

Utilizing News Values. By understanding and utilizing news values in staging events, newsmakers can almost predict the subject of stories for the evening news or the next day's newspapers. Newsmakers attempt to stage events that are timely, offer (controlled) drama and emotion, feature a star personality (the president or the candidate), and possess good visuals. Conflict and uniqueness can be useful, if it does not reflect negatively on the newsmaker.

Events. One highly orchestrated White House event during the first year of the Bush presidency was the four-hour trip to Colombia in February 1990. The trip ostensibly was to meet with Latin American presidents, but was actually to demonstrate the administration's fortitude in dealing with drug cartels. The event did not produce substantive policy results; however, it was highly visual and symbolic.

The managers of such events act more like film directors than aides to public officials. When President Reagan visited Grenada in 1986 to meet with citizens there, the White House brought in portable halogen lights to assure good lighting for television and still photographs, presidential staffers checked camera angles at the airport, and paid workers distributed thousands of red, white, and blue posters of the president to encourage Grenadians to attend.[5]

Newsmakers seeking to manage news know journalists cover events, not issues. Events sell newspapers. Few events other than disasters or accidents occur spontaneously; many are staged by newsmakers to attract media attention and convey desired messages.

Even better than a press conference or a ceremony is a staged event with action. Presidential bill-signings used to be private actions without press fanfare, but presidents now use bill-signings as a way to manage news. Bill-signing ceremonies are held with lengthy invitation lists and extensive preparations, and the most important invited guests are the news media, particularly television reporters.

Even the best of staged events can go awry if planners ignore controversial policy issues. Ronald Reagan's visit to the Bitburg military cemetery in West Germany in May 1985 was designed to symbolize U.S. friendship with that country. But when the media discovered that members of the S.S., Hitler's secret police, were also buried there, planners responded to the public outcry not by canceling the trip, but by carefully angling all camera shots so that no Nazi graves were visible. *Source:* © UPI/Bettmann Newsphotos.

Journalists watch as the president makes a speech about the legislation and signs the bill, surrounded by favored members of Congress who have been tapped to share in the limelight. Lyndon Johnson even signed bills on live prime-time television to increase the publicity.

But presidents are not the only ones who sign bills. To gain his own media coverage and upstage the president, House Speaker Tip O'Neill once used the speaker's power to sign bills as they go from Congress to the White House in a staged ceremony one day before the planned White House ceremony.[6]

Although such staged events would seem to have little appeal to the press, reporters continue to cover them because they fit other news values we will discuss shortly and they minimize the uncertainty of the newsgathering process.

Speaker O'Neill's bill-signing ceremony is one example of the competitive staging of events. Attention can shift quickly to other pleaders who may become news managers temporarily and then revert to the role of pleader when supply and demand for information shifts. Even the White House or a front-runner presidential candidate can be upstaged by others.

The proliferation of special pleaders and their various events in American national politics has necessitated attention to other news values to capture the press. A staged event alone certainly cannot assure coverage.

Timeliness. Timeliness is a news value that newsmakers learn quickly if they wish to gain media coverage. For most news outlets, the news cycle is a twenty-four hour period. The reaction to an event must occur in that news cycle, while the event is still a news item. Many members of Congress, for example, are geared to respond quickly to a presidential decision or action in order to catch the wave of press attention before it passes.

Newsmakers also quickly "piggyback" on current stories, to take advantage of positive press attention to good news. In 1988, presidential candidate George Bush arranged to meet with the space shuttle astronauts at the successful completion of their mission, which had attracted considerable public attention because it was the first mission since the 1986 *Challenger* disaster in which seven astronauts were killed.

Timing is especially important with the onset of bad news. Newsmakers hope to limit the political damage of bad news by getting their side out concurrent with initial report of the bad news; failure to respond at the time of the initial announcement tends to drag the story out over several newsdays and may imply acquiescence to the criticism. For example, David Gergen, Director of Communications during the Reagan administration, favored responding to a CBS News documentary that was critical of the administration's social welfare cuts, arguing: "No single show like that will lose you a lot of moderate votes, but if you allow those perceptions to harden over time, it's very difficult to turn them around."[7]

A disaster can present an administration with particularly difficult "bad news." Presidents must act quickly, and their actions must be perceived as effective—not simply a visit to the disaster site. Other kinds of bad news are often defused by the quick appointment of a commission to study causes and options when the issue is first raised in the press.

Conflict. Newsmakers or managers employ conflict with some hesitation, since conflict can prove counterproductive. Many find it very useful, however. Members of Congress, especially those who usually support the administration, can use conflict with the White House to generate press attention.

The Unexpected or Unusual. Since shared news values include a preference for the unexpected and the unusual, newsmakers—particularly desperate ones—often do the unexpected to attract such attention. A member of Congress dons a pig mask to protests congressional porkbarreling; Republican representatives stage a walkout and stand on the Capitol steps to protest heavy-handedness by the Democratic majority.

Visuals. One overriding requisite for television news is the presence of visuals. More visually interesting events will attract more newsgatherers, and thus more press coverage. Candidates will walk through ethnic neighborhoods, don miners' gear, or stand in burned-out slums to dramatize whatever message they wish to send out. In the 1988 presidential campaign, for example, George Bush rode in a powerboat in Boston Harbor, both to demonstrate his own support for the environment and to suggest his opponent's negligence in that area. Michael Dukakis, wearing a business suit, rode in a tank to dramatize his support for a strong national defense, an area in which he was perceived as weak.

White House television news reporters complain the presidential imagemakers have become so adept at creating attractive visuals that they have, in effect, stolen the news cameras. Visuals become more important than the spoken word. In 1984 Lesley Stahl, CBS News White House reporter, delivered a lengthy story highly critical of the Reagan presidency. But the story was a potpourri of visuals of photo opportunities—Reagan hugging Olympic medalist Mary Lou Retton, kissing his wife Nancy, greeting handicapped Special Olympics winners, and speaking at the D-Day anniversary. To her surprise, the White House staff loved it. A Reagan administration official explained that "when you're showing four and a half minutes of Ronald Reagan, no one listens to what you say. . . . The pictures are overriding your message because they conflict with your message. . . . So, in our minds, it was a four and a half minute free ad for the Ronald Reagan campaign for reelection."[8]

The message may be one of image as well as issue. During the 1988 campaign, Michael Dukakis visited several day care centers to highlight his own concern about the issue, but also to defuse charges that he lacked personal warmth.

Visuals are designed precisely to achieve the intended effect. At the D-Day celebration in 1984, White House planners placed television cameras so they could tape both the president's emotional speech and the reaction of a D-Day veteran's daughter who had written to him about the event.

When the supply of news is large, newsmakers resort to news values to capture the attention of the press. But since newsmakers never know what the supply will be on any given day and since they operate in a highly competitive environment with other pleaders, even those frequently in demand utilize news values to acquire positive press coverage.

SUMMARY

Newsmakers, like newsgatherers, are participants in the newsgathering process. They participate in order to affect the news coverage of themselves or their organizations. Whether or not they receive press coverage depends on their skill in making news, controlling press access, and utilizing news values. Their success also is affected by the law of informational supply and demand. Though some newsmakers, such as presidents and front-runner presidential candidates usually are in demand, other newsmakers compete in growing numbers for press notice. The large number of pleaders at the media's gates, aided by governmental fragmentation, creates an atmosphere of uncertainty among those pleaders that even affects the White House. At times, newsmakers can be stunningly successful at achieving their news management goals, while at other times, they fail miserably. Since the news is a product of the efforts of both newsgatherers and newsmakers and both are subject to forces beyond personal objectives, politicians cannot control the news. They can only hope to influence it by pursuing news management strategies and getting very lucky.

NOTES

1. Larry Speakes, *Speaking Out*, New York: Scribner, 1988, p. 218.
2. Martin Linsky, *Impact: How the Press Affects Federal Policymaking*, New York: Norton, 1986, pp. 81–84.
3. Linsky, *Impact*, pp. 81–84.
4. Stephen Hess, *The Government/Press Connection*, Washington: Brookings, 1984, p. 110.
5. Jane Mayer, "It Took Work to Get Reagan into Grenada for Four Hours Today," *Wall Street Journal*, February 21, 1986, p. 1.
6. Richard F. Fenno, Jr., *The Making of a Senator*, Washington: CQ Press, 1989, p. 107.
7. Linsky, *Impact*, p. 164.
8. Quoted in Hedrick Smith, *The Power Game: How Washington Works*, New York: Random House, 1988, p. 412.

SUGGESTED READINGS

Deaver, Michael. *Behind the Scenes*. New York: William Morrow, 1987.
Hertsgaard, Mark. *On Bended Knee: The Press and the Reagan Presidency*. New York: Farrar Straus & Giroux, 1988.
Hess, Stephen. *The Government/Press Connection*. Washington: Brookings Institution, 1984.
Linsky, Martin. *Impact: How the Press Affects Federal Policymaking*. New York: Norton, 1986.
Sigal, Leon V. *Reporters and Officials: The Organization and Politics of Newsmaking*. Lexington, Mass.: D.C. Heath, 1973.

PART II

The Context
of the Media's Role

The role of the press in American politics today must be placed in historical, legal, and comparative context to be understood properly. The relationship between the press and politicians did not originate with Ronald Reagan, Jimmy Carter, or even John Kennedy. The evolution of the role of the press can best be studied by beginning with the colonial era and tracking the historical patterns shaping the relationship today. One purpose of this section is to provide historical context to the present relationship, thereby gaining greater understanding of the forces which have shaped and continue to shape the role of the press in American politics. Another is to present the legal status of the press in American political life and how that status has evolved more recently. Finally, this section compares the media's role in the U.S. system with the role of media in other political systems both similar and dissimilar to the United States.

CHAPTER 3

Colonial America to 1830: Partisan Leaders and the Press

"Professions of impartiality I shall make none. They are always useless, and are besides perfect nonsense."

William Cobbett, editor, *Porcupine's Gazette*[1]

POLITICS AND THE PRESS IN THE COLONIAL AND FOUNDING ERA

On June 10, 1731, an item entitled "An Apology for Printers" appeared in the *Pennsylvania Gazette* under the name of the editor-printer himself. Benjamin Franklin succinctly expressed the role of the press in colonial America:

> [Printers are] educated in the belief that when men differ in opinion, both sides ought equally to have the advantage of being heard by the public; and that when truth and error have fair play, the former is always an overmatch for the latter. Hence they cheerfully serve all contending writers that pay them well, without regarding on which side they are of the question in dispute. . . .[2]

Franklin and other printers of his day sought to maintain their business without offending governmental authorities or the public. They hewed this middle ground in order to survive economically.

Printing was not a lucrative business. Printers managed primarily on small printing contracts, but many also relied on side occupations such as selling books and dry goods (including spices, tea, rum, patent medicine, and stockings). One printer even managed a coffee house. Many also doubled as postmasters. The scarcity of printing business necessitated additional occupations for printers.[3] Newsletters and, later, newspapers became still another means for supplementing income. The newspaper also promoted business by announcing the goods and services available at the printer's shop.

EARLY NEWSPAPERS

The first continuous newspaper in the United States was published in Boston by two brothers, John and Duncan Campbell, who found requests for their popular commercial newsletter outstripping copying speed. The single-sheet Boston *News-Letter* began publication on April 24, 1704.[4] The new paper, which appeared weekly, appeared in content and form much like British newspapers of the time and subsequent colonial newspapers. The paper was filled with news of foreign affairs, natural disasters, ship arrivals, court actions, and political appointments and decisions.[5]

Colonial papers relied heavily on foreign newspapers for news and borrowed liberally from them even though the news was at least two months old. As British citizens, the colonists were highly interested in European events.[6] As newspapers spread throughout the colonies and editors exchanged papers through the mails, news from the other colonies also began to appear.[7]

The emergence of colonial newspapers occurred gradually during the 1700s. In 1725, three newspapers operated in Boston and one each in New York and Philadelphia. By 1750, 13 regular newspapers were printed in the colonies.[8] One major impetus for newspaper publishing was the manufacture of printing presses in the colonies. Before 1750, all colonial presses were imported from England. In 1775, there were only 50 presses operating in the colonies.[9] Newspapers also began to increase in size. By the Revolutionary War, the single sheet newsletters had been replaced by four-page newspapers.[10]

The spread of newspapers throughout the colonies was expedited by the itinerant nature of printers. Printers commonly drifted from colony to colony establishing new papers in regions where they had never appeared. Former apprentices sought their fortunes where no established competition existed. Another boost for newspaper dissemination was the allure of financial gain. Some former apprentices were sent to new communities by their masters with sufficient capital for the enterprise and an agreement to split future profits. Through this entrepreneurial system, Benjamin Franklin established partnerships with fledgling printers in such colonial cities as Newport, Rhode Island, and Charleston, South Carolina.[11]

The spread of the press was undertaken with governmental approval. The press operated with the express permission of colonial authorities. A Boston newspaper appearing in 1690 was suppressed after a single issue because of the failure of the publisher to obtain a government license and because of disapproval of some of the editorial content. Licensing ended by 1695, but government approval for the start-up of a newspaper continued for some time. The Boston *News-Letter* carried a line on its masthead declaring "By Authority." These words alerted readers that the colonial executive routinely read and approved of the contents, and that the newspaper received an official subsidy for publishing the colonial government's official proceedings.[12]

Colonial authorities did not actively use the press to achieve political objectives. Government officials did not attempt to direct newspaper content or shape news articles. The colonial executive exercised tolerance of the press with certain exceptions. Political content offensive to the colonial authorities was subject to prosecution on the grounds of seditious libel. Seditious libel included any editorial content which disparaged the government. Under English common law, the issue in such a case was not the truthfulness of the offending comment, but merely whether or not the accused was responsible for making the disparaging statement. The colonial legislatures possessed, and occasionally exercised, the power to cite editors for breach of legislative privilege or contempt if the lawmakers felt their body had been disparaged by the press. Finally, the colonial government could punish editors by failing to grant much-coveted government printing contracts. The poor remuneration from publishing and necessary reliance on government printing jobs made this threat a very serious one.[13]

On the whole, however, the colonial authorities exhibited a general attitude of benign neglect toward the press. The press conducted business without official intervention unless sensitive political matters involving the colonial government were addressed. Hence, most editors avoided such topics and concentrated on foreign news and nonpolitical content. It would take a revolution, the American Revolution, for the press to fulfill an active political role.

A Revolutionary Press

Political changes wrought immediately prior to and during the Revolutionary War altered the role of the press in political life. The newspaper became useful as an active tool for mobilizing public opinion in the cause of the Revolution. The role of the press in the Revolution has been widely heralded. John Adams believed the "radical change in the principles, opinions, sentiments, and affections of the people was the real American Revolution."[14] Some historians suggest the press played a significant role in affecting that radical change.[15] Historian Arthur Schlesinger, Sr., wrote that the movement for independence "could hardly have succeeded without an ever alert and dedicated press."[16]

Printer-editors of the middle and late 1700s seemed unlikely choices for fomenters of a revolution. Motivated by commercial interests, they stressed their role as impartial mediums for divergent views in the community. Most printers tried to avoid offending any readers or business advertisers for commercial and political reasons by emphasizing their role as objective servants of the public. Colonial printers probably undermined their own influence in the community by suggesting they played a purely mechanical role. But their emphasis was accurate. Printers were craftsmen first; writing and editing were only secondary functions. In fact,

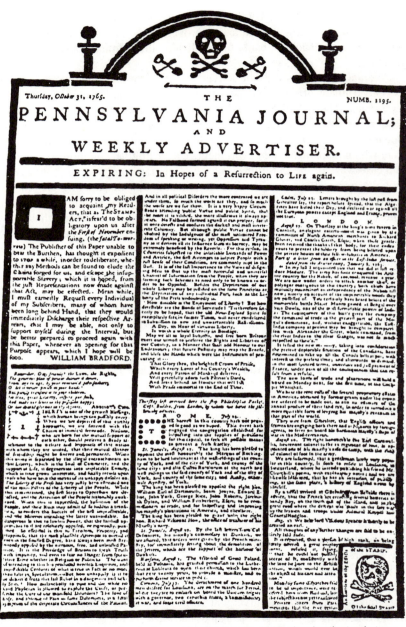

Front page of the Pennsylvania Journal for October 31, 1765, showing the tombstone
makeup used as a protest against the Stamp Act.

most were uneducated and some were even illiterate. The printer-editor was not highly regarded in the social pecking order of the community.

Even worse, the printer-editor was identified in the public mind with the colonial executive. This was due to the printer's role in publishing colonial laws and proclamations and handling government printing jobs, and his unwillingness to criticize the colonial executive in order to avoid governmental coercion.[17] It was the British, ironically, who contributed to pushing the press away from this stance of impartiality by adopting the Stamp Act. The Stamp Act placed a tax on newspapers based on the size of each sheet and the number of advertisements contained in each issue. The act actually played into the hands of those who opposed British authority by uniting newspaper publishers against the government.

The press strongly editorialized against the act and successfully defied it. Schlesinger argued that the Stamp Act changed the role of the press. "No longer mere purveyors of intelligence, they had become engines of opinion."[18] The press had mobilized public opinion, defied government officials, and gained the respect of many colonists, including Revolutionary political leaders.

Political leaders opposing British rule noted the press's role in the demise of the Stamp Act. Although the motive of the printer-editors was largely commercial, the Revolutionary political leaders urged them to adopt a more vocal anti-government stance generally. When many publishers refused to abandon their neutrality, political leaders employed pressure tactics to enlist the press in the Revolutionary cause. The Patriot leaders threatened to start competing papers, which some eventually did. Mobs attacked printers and ravaged their establishments.

Before the Revolution, publishers were caught in the crossfire between the appointed colonial executive and the popularly elected legislature. Many printer-editors still relied on patronage from the colonial governor and were hesitant to oppose the government openly. For example, nearly one-fifth of the advertising space in one Georgia newspaper was bought by the colonial government.[19] Such reliance on the executive's favor was not uncommon.

On the other hand, hostile colonial legislatures punished publishers who sided with the royal governors by withdrawing their own patronage. Printers faced either the wrath of the governor or the fury of the legislature or even mobs of angry Patriots. One North Carolina publisher aptly describer the colonial printer's dilemma:

> What part is now to act? Continue to keep his press open and free and be in danger of Corporal Punishment, or block it up, and run the risque of having his Brains knocked out. Sad alternative . . .[20]

Both the Loyalists and the Patriots sought to win over the colonial press in order to affect public opinion. However, Patriot leaders needed the press as an active weapon on their behalf. Public support for the cause of independence had to be mobilized. Arguments for revolution required some vehicle. News of British acts of tyranny and the Patriots' response in the several colonies had to be disseminated. The revolutionists wanted to establish a network of advocates throughout the colonies. The press could serve as the communication link for that network.

The press served the Patriots by whipping up public enmity toward British rule. The newspapers published lurid accounts of British atrocities in the colonies such as the Boston Massacre and Lexington and Concord. Also reported were the victories of the Patriots such as the Boston Tea Party and defiance of laws of Parliament such as the Stamp Act and the Intolerable Acts. By 1773, newspapers were openly speaking of independence.

Simultaneously, the colonial press denigrated the mother country. Tales of immoral behavior by public figures and corruption in British politics fostered the public belief that the British empire was corrupt and only independence would free the colonies from the stain of British immorality.[21] The Patriots also benefited from more efficient mail service and a liberal exchange of newspapers between colonies. News from other colonies became more readily available than news from London.[22] The spread of information about British moves and Patriot response throughout the colonies fostered a sense of community and identification with other colonies in opposition to England.

By the onset of the war, the Patriot leaders had gained widespread support of the press, either by force of argument or merely by force. The remaining Tory press had been effectively silenced except where British troops offered protection. During the war itself, the Patriot press published positive accounts of the activities of the Revolutionary Army. The capabilities of the Revolutionary forces were exaggerated to promote public support for the war effort.[23]

At the conclusion of the war, the central effort of winning the war was followed by a return to regional or local political concerns similar to the earlier colonial period. Political leaders were no longer intent on using the press in any great national cause. The press briefly returned to chiefly commercial rather than political concerns. The first daily newspapers in the United States were established in this period due to increasing interest in current ship arrivals with their cargoes of goods for local merchants.[24] The decline of newspaper reader interest in politics following the war is suggested by the secondary position devoted to news of politics. However, this period lasted only briefly as political leaders, unhappy with the weaknesses of the Articles of Confederation government instituted after the Revolution, sought the aid of the press in the fight over ratification of the Constitution and the formation of a new, national government.

Newspapers and the Constitution

Newspapers were used to influence the ratification battle by advocates of the Constitution as well as opponents. The exchange of newspapers throughout the states guaranteed a widespread dispersion of arguments pro and con. The vehicle of the press also facilitated the debate by allowing for rapid response to arguments posed by the opposing side. Some of the most widely distributed writings were articles by Alexander Hamilton, James Madison, and John Jay later compiled and titled the *Federalist Papers*. Originally published as separate essays in the New York *Independent Journal*, the articles became the most powerful defense of the Constitution. On the opposing side, the *Letters of a Federal Farmer*, authored by Revolutionary War General Richard Henry Lee, were among the best essays against ratification.[25]

The Anti-Federalists, however, suffered a disadvantage because they organized late and received abuse from the Federalists. Anti-Federalist editors lost circulation through subscription cancellations, had their printing establishments damaged by mobs, and were physically attacked by Federalist mobs.[26] The editor of the *Philadelphia Herald* accused the Federalists of interrupting the mails to prevent the circulation of Anti-Federalist newspapers.[27]

The eventual ratification of the Constitution produced a momentary political consensus in the new nation as national political leaders such as Thomas Jefferson and Alexander Hamilton submerged their deep-seated ideological differences in an effort to foster the new government. However, these differences over such issues as the role of the national government, the function of the presidency, the future of the economy, and the value of democracy did not long remain suppressed. National political leaders began to distinguish themselves into two broad groups later known as Federalists and Republicans.

A Vehicle for Promoting Democracy or the Party

With the objectives of winning elections and influencing national government policy, these national political leaders sought to create a network of political supporters throughout the country. This need was particularly acute for the nascent Republicans who held a minority position in the Congress. The absence of any formal political party structure, as would exist later, necessitated the use of other means, primarily the press, for the propagation of political views and the aggregation of support.

The status of the press in American history to that point had legitimated the press role as such a vehicle. By the 1790s, the press had already become well established as a source of political information and views for the public. This was particularly true for those who could afford subscriptions, but also applied to others who borrowed much-used copies circulated in taverns and other public places.

Moreover, newspapers also were reputed as a significant force in swaying public opinion immediately prior to and during the Revolution. The press also had earned plaudits during the struggle over the ratification of the Constitution.

With its reach and perceived power over public opinion, the press was well suited for the needs of the political leaders. That fitness was even more appropriate with recent technological changes such as new and more efficient presses, an increasing supply of paper due to more efficient paper mills, and decreased costs for printing equipment.[28]

Political leaders even acted to further the capability of the press to act as a vehicle of political ideas. Postal rates for newspapers were set at minimal levels. Exchanges of newspapers between editors through the mails were allowed free of charge.[29]

Political leaders believed the press had a mission to educate the public about the political system to ensure the success of democracy. Thomas Jefferson argued that the way to prevent unwise decisions by the public was to "give them full information of their affairs through the channel of the public papers, and to contrive that those papers should penetrate the whole mass of the people.[30] George Washington, in an address to the Congress, stressed the "importance of facilitating the circulation of political intelligence and information" through the press.[31] The House of Representatives concurred, adding that the dissemination of political information through the press is "among the surest means of preventing the degeneracy of a free government."[32] Later, Washington, urging repeal of a tax on the distribution of newspapers, declared "there is no resource so firm for the Government of the United States as the affections of the people, guided by an enlightened policy; and to this primary good nothing can conduce more than a faithful representation of public proceedings, diffused without restraint through the United States."[33]

Public acceptance and even insistence on this role for the press in a democratic system is also evidenced in the successful campaign to include freedom of the press in the first constitutional amendment, as well as the extension of press freedom in state constitutions.[34] Several state ratifying conventions proposed amendments to the Constitution guaranteeing the freedom of the press. The North Carolina and Rhode Island conventions specifically linked freedom for the press to a role as protector of liberty in a democratic society.[35]

Usage of the press by political leaders to further specific political objectives was augmented by the financial status of the press. Although newspapers appeared well suited to the role as a political system linking mechanism, political leaders would have found the task of appropriating the press for that role far more difficult had the press not been in such a weakened financial position.

The late eighteenth and early nineteenth centuries marked a period of great instability in American journalism. It has been estimated that prior to 1820 more than 500 newspapers folded within one year of establishment. Many others lasted only a few years.[36] But new journals were continually appearing. One survey estimated that sixty newspapers were started in the mid-1780s alone.[37]

One cause of this instability was the Revolutionary War. The war uprooted several newspapers, both Tory and Patriot, as they fled from either angry Patriot mobs or invading British troops.

Still another was the motive for printing a journal. Since newspapers were still sidelines for many printers, they were quickly abandoned when losses accumulated. But the relative ease with which a paper could be printed guaranteed new entries to the business and intense competition. The highly common problem of delinquent subscribers plagued early newspaper publishers. Additionally, many who read the papers did not pay. The cost of the paper was beyond the reach of many people. Nevertheless, many still obtained common copies at public places.

Advertising, which would offer a firm financial base for later generations of publishers, was not then fully realized as a tool for financial stability.[38] The financially weakened state of the press eased the task of political leaders in utilizing the press for political and particularly partisan purposes.

Forging the Link

In a pre-Revolutionary War report to the British government on American newspapers, a Tory newspaper publisher remarked that "Government may find it expedient in the sum of things to employ this popular engine."[39] Political leaders such as Alexander Hamilton and Thomas Jefferson concurred. Hamilton was the first to act, however.

John Fenno was a staunch Federalist from Boston who had come to the attention of Hamilton because of Fenno's well-written defenses of Hamilton's views. Hamilton encouraged Fenno to come to the nation's capital and establish a newspaper to serve as the administration's organ. As Treasury Secretary, Hamilton promised Fenno government printing jobs from his department and financial assistance from well-to-do Federalists.

Thomas Jefferson, James Madison, and other Republicans soon thereafter urged another talented writer and editor, Philip Freneau, to publish a Republican journal in the nation's capital. Freneau also was promised financial inducements for his service to the cause.

Unlike many printers of the day who published journals as a sideline, Fenno and Freneau were men of strong literary talents and intense political views. They represented the first of a new breed of political publishers. Also unlike others, these two men anticipated that their opposing newspapers, the *Gazette of the United States* and the *National Gazette*, would acquire national circulations.

Hamilton, Jefferson, and other political leaders nurtured these young, struggling papers through a variety of support mechanisms. One such mechanism was government printing. Since both Hamilton and Jefferson headed executive branch departments and no central government printing office yet existed, they easily secured government printing jobs for their protégés. Another bond was the allure of a government post. Although the positions were not powerful or lucrative, they provided additional income while requiring little time of the editors. Freneau held a post as translator for the State Department headed by Jefferson.[40] Still another incentive was the authority to publish federal laws and the concomitant stipend. Fenno was the first publisher to hold such authority.

These early political leaders utilized other means to forge binding ties with the press. Hamilton loaned money to Fenno to save his much-valued paper from financial collapse.[41] Jefferson and other Republican leaders solicited subscriptions for Freneau's paper.[42] Jefferson and Hamilton arranged for the editors' proximity to national government officials to give them an advantage in gathering news. The newspaper's identification with the partisan leader also boosted circulation and strengthened its image among readers as the source of the political leader's views.

These supports for the press were essential for continuance. The *Gazette of the United States* and the *National Gazette*, like other succeeding partisan newspapers, were not financial successes. At its peak the circulation of the *Gazette of the United States* was 1,400 and the paper carried a $2,500 debt.[43] It folded in 1798. Freneau's paper suffered similarly and closed down in 1793 after his chief benefactor resigned as Secretary of State. The editor of the *Aurora*, a successor to the *National Gazette*, accumulated a debt of nearly $15,000 in eight years.

The relationship between these editors and their powerful benefactors, however, established a pattern for future similar associations. Political leaders encouraged the start-up of political papers edited by trusted literary partisans. Jefferson advised editor Samuel H. Smith to move to Washington in 1800 to start a Republican paper.[44] Hamilton, John Jay, Rufus King, and other prominent Federalists persuaded Noah Webster to edit a Federalist newspaper in New York.[45] Political leaders offered financial backing for establishment and maintenance of favored journals. At times this took the form of direct loans. Hamilton and other Federalists contributed about $1,000 each for William Coleman to establish the *New York Evening Post*.[46] Jefferson gave money to Republican editors in Pennsylvania and Virginia.[47] A less direct form of financial aid was assistance with subscriptions. As Jefferson had solicited subscriptions for the *National Gazette*, he and other Republican political leaders enlisted subscribers for various Republican papers throughout the country.[48]

Political leaders were instrumental in securing government printing for the favored press. Well-known figures such as John C. Calhoun, John Quincy Adams, and William Crawford who held cabinet posts obtained department printing contracts for publishers who supported them.[49] During Thomas Jefferson's first term in office, Samuel H. Smith averaged several thousand dollars a year in government disbursements for printing contracts from various departments.[50]

As Freneau had been employed by the State Department, a few partisan editors held government positions. An editor allied with John C. Calhoun simultaneously served as federal superintendent of Indian Trade in the War Department headed by Calhoun. Political editors were also tied into the party network through high level posts in the incipient local and state party organizations. Samuel H. Smith held the post of secretary of the Democratic nominating committee in Philadelphia. Peter Freneau, brother of Philip and editor of a Charleston newspaper, served as Jefferson's regional political manager.[51]

Political leaders used the authority to print government laws to favor their party's journals. That authority, vested by Congress in the Department of State, allowed the Secretary of State to choose three newspapers to publish laws and other documents of the federal government. James Madison, Jefferson's Secretary of State, rewarded Republican journals with the designation. Each succeeding Secretary of State used the designation, which was gradually expanded to even more newspapers, to aid partisan papers supportive of the administration.[52]

Editors and political leaders promoted the general view that certain papers were organs espousing the political leader's views. Samuel Smith's *National Intel-*

ligencer was widely known as the Jefferson administration's mouthpiece. The *National Journal* served a similar role during the presidency of John Quincy Adams. Some political leaders contributed pseudonymous writings or urged others to do so. James Madison and Albert Gallatin contributed articles to the *Aurora*, a Republican paper published in Philadelphia.[53]

The relationship was not always harmonious. Politicians and partisan editors often differed in substance and style. For example, the primary Federalist newspaper in Philadelphia during the administration of John Adams was *Porcupine's Gazette*, which served as administration organ. But when the paper began to criticize administration policy toward France, the president withdrew his support. The Republicans had similar problems. Jefferson praised William Duane's *Aurora* for its defense of the Republican cause, but personally did not care for Duane's shrillness and invective.[54]

These differences illustrate the point that political leaders did not exercise absolute control over the press. Newspaper editors could and did act freely without the approval of their benefactors. But, significantly, these actions did jeopardize the relationship with the benefactor, and partisan editors who acted independently did so primarily for political rather than commercial or journalistic reasons.

The relationship between political leaders and editors was maintained through this early period of the nation's history, despite such occasional problems, due to the benefits of the relationship for both politicians and press. For politicians the use of the press offered a largely reliable and effective organ for the dissemination of political views. The dispersion of the population across a wide territory required utilization of a vehicle for propagation of political leaders' views in order to mobilize electoral support. Newspapers, assisted by liberal postage rates and free exchange between editors, facilitated such dissemination. National circulation of partisan papers also connected a growing network of partisan supporters and aided the organization of national political parties.

In a broader, less partisan sense, these politicians were attempting to establish a democratic political system and viewed the press as the vehicle for the effectuation of democracy. A well-informed public became capable of fulfilling a role in a democratic political system. The press served as the means for achieving the goal of a well-informed public.

The arrangement also profited the newspaper editors. In a period of intense competition, the financial support of important political patrons offered a competitive advantage to partisan editors struggling to remain solvent. The known support of powerful backers increased circulation, aided newsgathering, and enhanced overall respectability. The press located in the nation's capital possessed the additional advantage of proximity to national events of interest to a national readership.

The costs which people today would associate with this relationship, such as journalistic independence and objectivity, were not important to the journalists of that day and were even derided by some. Although some newspapers preached neutrality of the press during this period, the vast majority were partisan.[55] From the colonial era through the first decades of the new nation, the press changed from a largely commercial enterprise to a political tool useful to the major political parties and the national political leaders who headed them. Due to the press's role in the Revolution and the ratification struggle, political leaders successfully engaged the press in a role as linking mechanism in American politics. This relationship between early political leaders and the partisan press established during the early years of the nation would intensify under the stress of large-scale changes in the political system and the press.

THE JACKSONIAN PRESS

The relationship between political leaders and the press had been forged in the early days of the United States. But political leaders' democratizing of the political system and the growth of more intense competition within and between parties led political leaders to tighten their links with the press to achieve electoral and policy success. However, their efforts produced the seeds of the eventual destruction of the relationship.

Democracy and Competition

By the 1820s, the two major political parties had experienced a dramatic change in their electoral status. The Federalists, having suffered several national political defeats, were in severe disarray and were virtually extinct as a national political force. The victorious Republicans, however, had their own problems. The party was fragmented into several competing factions, each headed by a national political leader and potential presidential candidate. In the election of 1824, five political leaders—John Quincy Adams, Andrew Jackson, Henry Clay, William Crawford, and John C. Calhoun—led factions of the party and vied for the presidency. The election was the first truly competitive contest since the battle between Thomas Jefferson and John Adams in 1800. By 1828, two clear-cut parties had formed to compete for political power. The presence of real competition at the presidential level, which had been missing since the demise of the Federalist party, spurred interest by the mass of voters in the campaign.

Simultaneously, a trend toward increased democracy, which had been gaining momentum gradually throughout the early 1800s, appeared full-blown by the election of 1828. The political system was beginning to appeal to the ''common man.'' Mass rallies, bonfires, processions, and the formation of political clubs all characterized a political system stirring public enthusiasm for electoral participation. These changes in campaigning had been preceded by more significant structural changes such as popular election of a state's presidential electors, political party nominating conventions, and extension of the suffrage. Voter turnout doubled between 1824 and 1828, and by 1840 nearly four of five eligible voters were participating.[56]

A Nation of Newspapers

The press had undergone significant change as well during the early 1800s. The number of newspapers in the new nation had grown enormously. In the 1830s, more than twelve dailies competed in Philadelphia and six dailies were published in New York.[57] Even Charleston boasted from four to six newspapers during this period.[58] Overall in the United States, the number of newspapers jumped from 200 at the turn of the century to about 1,200 by the mid-1830s. The number of dailies rose from 24 in 1800 to 65 by 1830.[59]

Foreigners remarked that America had become a nation of newspapers and newspaper readers. Alexis de Tocqueville, the Frenchman who toured the United States and described his findings in *Democracy in America*, remarked: "In America, there is scarcely a hamlet which has not its newspaper."[60] Circulation was growing dramatically. For example, in New York, newspapers published one copy for every thirty residents in 1800. By 1830, the figure was one copy for every fifteen persons. But more importantly, circulation of newspapers was beginning to extend beyond the narrow confines of the nation's political elite. In the late 1700s, journals rarely exceeded 1,000 subscribers. By the middle 1830s, circulations in the thousands were common.[61]

Not all observers saw this expanded usage of the press as good for the country. Many viewed journalism as an ignoble profession. One historian of the press has termed this period the "Dark Ages of American Journalism."[62] Alexis de Tocqueville noted that the proliferation of newspapers and the limited financial gain brought from newspaper publishing meant that "persons of much capacity are rarely led to engage in these undertakings. . . . The journalists of the United States are generally in a very humble position, with a scanty education and a vulgar turn of mind."[63] According to another foreign observer, "every booby who can call names, and procure a set of types upon credit, may set up as an editor, with a fair prospect of success."[64]

The press was also viewed as possessing enormous influence over public affairs. Alexis de Tocqueville wrote: "[The press] rallies the interests of the community round certain principles, and draws up the creed of every party . . . . When many organs of the press adopt the same line of conduct, their influence in the long run becomes irresistible."[65] According to Charles Dickens, the American "press has its evil eye in every house and its black hand in every appointment in the state, from a president to a postman . . . ."[66] Edward Everett, one-time Secretary of State and vice-presidential candidate, termed the press "for good or evil, the most powerful influence that acts on the public mind."[67]

Tightening the Link

Increased democracy in politics and more intense competition coupled with an expanding press and a widespread belief in its power to influence public opinion helped create a dynamic and unstable relationship between press and political leaders. Political leaders viewed the press as an essential tool in electoral success. Greater attention to the press as a weapon in the hands of political leaders produced an intensification of their relationship.

The benefits of the relationship were not one-sided. Newspaper editor-publishers profited by association with a national political figure. Not only did the association enhance the prestige of the publication within Washington, but it also provided an opportunity for access to important government news. For the Washington newspaper, designation as the candidate's organ meant national circulation through free exchange of newspapers and a significant role as official administration organ if the candidate won the presidency.

Like their predecessors in the early days of the Republic, the candidates sought a vehicle for expression of their views and the enlistment of public support. The means by which they did so expanded the efforts of their predecessors, however.

For example, since the days of the Patriots during the Revolutionary War, political leaders or their supporters had provided much-needed financial aid to publishers for newspaper start-up. However, the party factions current during this period expanded the practice. In Washington, Jacksonians loaned money for the establishment of the *United States Telegraph* and, later, the *Globe*. But it was also widely rumored that the Jacksonians kept a fund of $50,000 to establish favorable newspapers throughout the country. Other national political leaders did likewise.[68]

Political leaders also were instrumental in securing government printing. The political aspects of awarding printing contracts had become far more significant by the 1820s and 1830s. Three of the major presidential candidates in 1824, for example, headed federal government departments and directed departmental printing to their Washington organs.[69]

Another form of aid was secured through the "by authority" designation. The number of newspapers granted the designation had multiplied since its inception. The designation had become a more wieldy tool for presidential administrations. In 1828, Henry Clay, John Quincy Adams' Secretary of State, withdrew the authority from those papers supporting Andrew Jackson's presidential candidacy. Once in office, the Jacksonians stripped the pro-Adams administration journals of the designation and handed it to their own press supporters. Of 78 newspapers with the designation at the end of the Adams presidency, more than two-thirds were dropped immediately and replaced by the Jacksonian press.[70] Since the authority represented extra income, often much needed by financially encumbered printing businesses, publishers actively solicited the patronage by expressing their fealty to the cause of the political leader.[71]

The most dramatic change came in the expansion of patronage of government offices for friendly newspaper editors. Jackson offered more federal government positions to journalists than had any of his predecessors. It has been estimated that at least ten percent of Jackson's early appointments were journalists. These appointments were rarely major offices (though one editor was offered, but declined, a cabinet position). They included inspector, collector, postmaster, U.S. marshal,

U.S. attorney, and clerk.[72] Although offering government positions to loyal supporters during the campaign was not a new phenomenon, the appointment of journalists
indicated a growing recognition of their role in partisan politics and an attempt to
maintain their political support.

The use of government positions as an inducement and/or reward for the press
was an effective tool at least partially because the line between journalist and
politician was virtually indistinguishable during this period. Many editors of the day
were more interested in politics than journalism. Some, such as Francis P. Blair,
Amos Kendall, and Duff Green, considered themselves politicians as well as
journalists.

Since politicians were appealing to a newly enfranchised electorate, the political appeals of necessity had to match the level of interest and comprehension of
those hearing them. The content of the partisan press reflected both the politicians'
needs to appeal to a broader-based electorate and the shifting readership base for the
press from an elite- to a more mass-oriented audience. The stories were less
sophisticated and more blunt. The press during the days of Hamilton and Jefferson
featured verbose, partisan attacks veiled in a literary style common to social elites.

The political content of the press of the Jacksonian period was much clearer to
the newly franchised and suddenly interested ''common man'' to whom politicians
and editors wished to appeal. Charges hurled at opposing candidates were framed in
plainer language. Jackson's partisan papers portrayed John Quincy Adams as an
unprincipled hypocrite, an anti-democrat, and a Sabbath-breaker. Adams was
accused of prostituting a young American girl to the Russian czar while serving as
U.S. minister to Russia.

The content of the Adams newspapers was equally unvarnished. Jackson was
called a gambler, a blasphemer, an adulterer, and a murderer. His wife was accused
of being a bigamist and circumstances surrounding their marriage were questioned.[73]

Significantly, it was the style of political attacks, not the use of attacks, that
had changed. Earlier political leaders had been charged by opponents with gross
misdeeds, but not with the crudity employed by the mass-oriented partisan press.

However, the changing style of political debate also carried unintended effects.
The blunt attacks had the effect of diminishing the social deference common people
accorded political leaders. Unveiled accusations, such as those made against Jackson and Adams, reduced the distance between political leaders and the mass of
voters. Political scientist Richard Rubin has termed the press of this period ''The
Great Leveler'' due to its role in helping ''desanctify public office and public
leaders, thus opening the possibility of office, leadership, and political activity
generally to the 'unsanctified' ordinary man.''[74]

Through intensive use of various techniques including newspaper start-up,
government printing jobs, federal government positions, and the authority to print
the laws, political leaders were able to tighten the link between themselves and the
press. Newspaper editors, attempting to survive in an increasingly competitive
marketplace and generally committed to the notion of the press as a tool of
partisanship, willingly established closer ties with politicians.

The Seeds of Its Own Destruction

The appointment of journalists to federal government positions may have contributed to the gradual amelioration of their social status, which, in turn, may have contributed to the rise of the Penny Press—by creating a journalistic class enjoying social equality with politicians. Gradually, this journalistic class would not be reticent to dissolve the dependency relationship with political leaders.

The excesses of the Jacksonian subversion of the press, however, may also have hastened the relationship's decline. The proximity of the press to politicians provoked a negative reaction by Jackson's opponents, as well as by some of his supporters. Thomas Ritchie, editor of the *Richmond Enquirer* and a Jacksonian, worried about the freedom of the press under these pressures, wrote to Martin Van Buren: "It really looks as if there were a systematic effort to reward Editorial Partisans, which will have the effect of bringing the vaunted Liberty of the Press into a sort of contempt."[75] Charges that the freedom of the press had been undermined were hurled by Jacksonian opponents and supporters from Georgia to New Hampshire.[76]

Although the accusation, and the appointments which prompted them, evoked little response from the public, they may have disturbed other editors who perceived a growing and discomfiting trend in the relationship between political leaders and the press.

The changing character of both the political system and the press in this period may also have contributed to the demise of the partisan press. As the federal government listened more to the "common man," so the newspapers became more mass-oriented as well. The *United States Telegraph*, for example, claimed a circulation of some 40,000—a figure which suggests a truly national audience. (Many copies of the *Telegraph* were distributed for free, however, and some members of Congress used their franking privileges to distribute copies of favorable newspapers. The Jacksonians were accused, probably accurately, of engaging in this practice to excess.)[77]

SUMMARY

The tide of democracy sweeping the political system and provoking heightened interest in electoral politics may have motivated editors to make financial and editorial decisions leading to a gradual alteration of the press' relationship with political leaders and its role in the political system. The partisan press, at its peak during the Jacksonian era, gradually would be replaced by a press governed by journalistic and economic, rather than political, considerations and engaged in a more egalitarian relationship with politicians and a more autonomous role within the political system.

NOTES

1. Quoted in Frank Luther Mott, *American Journalism, A History: 1690–1960*, 3d ed., New York: Macmillan, 1962, p. 130.
2. Quoted in Carl Van Doren, *Benjamin Franklin*, New York: Garden City Publishing, 1941, p. 100.
3. Arthur M. Schlesinger, *Prelude to Independence: The Newspaper War on Britain 1764–1776*, New York: Knopf, 1966, pp. 53–54; see also Stephen Botein, "Printers and the American Revolution," in *The Press and the American Revolution*, ed. Bernard Bailyn and John B. Hench, Worcester, Mass.: American Antiquarian Society, 1980, pp. 16–17.
4. Alfred McClung Lee, *The Daily Newspaper in America*, New York: Macmillan, 1937, p. 17.
5. Mott, *American Journalism*, pp. 11–12.
6. Schlesinger, *Prelude to Independence*, p. 60.
7. Schlesinger, *Prelude to Independence*, p. 52.
8. Schlesinger, *Prelude to Independence*, p. 52.
9. Lee, *Daily Newspaper in America*, p. 21.
10. Lee, *Daily Newspaper in America*, p. 22.
11. Schlesinger, *Prelude to Independence*, pp. 55–58; see also Lee, *Daily Newspaper in America*, p. 31.
12. Mott, *American Journalism*, pp. 14–15; see also Schlesinger, *Prelude to Independence*, p. 61.
13. Schlesinger, *Prelude to Independence*, pp. 62–64.
14. Schlesinger, *Prelude to Independence*, p. 4.
15. See Philip Davidson, *Propaganda and the American Revolution, 1763–1783*, Chapel Hill, N.C.: University of North Carolina Press, 1941, pp. 225–245.
16. Davidson, *Propaganda and the American Revolution*, p. 285.
17. Botein, "Printers and the American Revolution," p. 22.
18. Botein, "Printers and the American Revolution," p. 82.
19. Robert M. Weir, "The Role of the Newspaper Press in the Southern Colonies on the Eve of the Revolution: An Interpretation," in *The Press and the American Revolution*, ed. Bernard Bailyn and John B. Hench, Worcester, Mass.: American Antiquarian Society, 1980, p. 103.
20. Weir, "Role of the Newspaper Press in the Southern Colonies," p. 103.
21. Merrill Jensen, *The Founding of a Nation*, New York: Oxford University Press, 1968, pp. 316–317.
22. Weir, "Role of the Newspaper Press in the Southern Colonies," pp. 125–129.
23. Carl Berger, *Broadsides & Bayonets*, rev. ed., San Rafael, Calif.: Presidio Press, 1976, p. 2.
24. Mott, *American Journalism*, p. 118.
25. Carl Van Doren, *The Great Rehearsal*, New York: Viking Press, 1948, pp. 188–193.
26. Robert A. Rutland, *The Newsmongers: Journalism in the Life of the Nation 1690–1972*, New York: Dial Press, 1973, pp. 62–63.
27. Robert A. Rutland, *The Ordeal of the Constitution: The Anti-Federalists and the Ratification Struggle of 1787–1788*, Norman, Okla.: University of Oklahoma Press, 1966, p. 62.

28. See Mott, *American Journalism*, pp. 161–162; and Lee, *Daily Newspaper in America*, pp. 98–99.
29. See Lee, *Daily Newspaper in America*, p. 301; and Mott, *American Journalism*, pp. 160–161.
30. Adrienne Koch and William Peden, eds., *The Life and Selected Writings of Thomas Jefferson*, New York: Random House, 1944, p. 411.
31. *Messages and Papers of the Presidents 1789–1908*, vol. 1, Washington: Bureau of National Literature and Art, 1909, p. 128.
32. *Messages and Papers of the Presidents*, vol. 1, p. 132.
33. *Messages and Papers of the Presidents*, vol. 1, p. 142.
34. Culver Smith, *The Press, Politics, and Patronage*, Athens, Ga.: University of Georgia Press, 1977, p. 5.
35. U.S. Department of State, *Documentary History of the Constitution 1787–1870*, vol. 2, Washington: Government Printing Office, 1894.
36. See Lee, *Daily Newspaper in America*, p. 30.
37. See Mott, *American Journalism*, p. 113.
38. Lee, *Daily Newspaper in America*, pp. 32–33.
39. George Henry Payne, *History of Journalism in the United States*, New York: D. Appleton, 1920, p. 120.
40. Donald H. Stewart, *The Opposition Press of the Federalist Period*, Albany, N.Y.: SUNY Press, 1969, pp. 8–9; see also Smith, *Press, Politics, and Patronage*, pp. 14–15.
41. Stewart, *Opposition Press of the Federalist Period*, pp. 8–9.
42. Stewart, *Opposition Press of the Federalist Period*, pp. 8–9.
43. See Mott, *American Journalism*, p. 123.
44. Lee, *Daily Newspaper in America*, p. 480.
45. Stewart, *Opposition Press of the Federalist Period*, pp. 10–11.
46. Mott, *American Journalism*, p. 164.
47. Stewart, *Opposition Press of the Federalist Period*, pp. 10–11.
48. Stewart, *Opposition Press of the Federalist Period*, p. 9. See also Frank Luther Mott, *Jefferson and the Press*, Baton Rouge, La.: Louisiana State University Press, 1943, p. 28.
49. Smith, *Press, Politics, and Patronage*, p. 57.
50. Smith, *Press, Politics, and Patronage*, p. 28.
51. See Smith, *Press, Politics, and Patronage*, p. 57; and Stewart, *Opposition Press of the Federalist Period*, p. 12.
52. See Smith, *Press, Politics, and Patronage*, chap. 4.
53. Stewart, *Opposition Press of the Federalist Period*, pp. 10–11.
54. See Margaret Woodbury, "Public Opinion in Philadelphia 1789–1801," *Smith College Studies in History* 5 (October 1919–1920): 13; and Mott, *Jefferson and the Press*, pp. 47–50.
55. Isaiah Thomas, a Massachusetts printer, categorized American newspapers in 1810 and concluded that only 50 of 350 were not partisan. See Botein, "Printers and the American Revolution," p. 11. For a dissenting view, see Stewart, *The Opposition Press of the Federalist Period*, pp. 624–625.
56. See Richard P. McCormick, *The Second American Party System*, New York: Norton, 1966, pp. 390–391.
57. Mott, *American Journalism*, p. 188.

58. Mott, *American Journalism*, p. 181.
59. See Mott, *American Journalism*, p. 167; and Lee, *The Daily Newspaper in America*, pp. 716–717.
60. Alexis de Tocqueville, *Democracy in America*, ed. Richard D. Heffner, New York: New American Library, 1956, p. 94.
61. See Lee, *Daily Newspaper in America*, p. 78; and Mott, *American Journalism*, pp. 202–203.
62. See Mott, *American Journalism*, chap. 9. For a contrasting view, see Rutland, *Newsmongers*, p. 82–111.
63. De Tocqueville, *Democracy in America*, p. 94.
64. Rutland, *Newsmongers*, p. 85.
65. De Tocqueville, *Democracy in America*, p. 95.
66. Charles Dickens, *American Notes and Pictures from Italy*, ed. Ernest Rhys, New York: E.P. Dutton, 1907, p. 245.
67. Bernard A. Weisberger, *Reporters for the Union*, Boston: Little, Brown, 1953, p. 6.
68. Smith, *Press, Politics, and Patronage*, pp. 60, 68–69, and 122–124.
69. Smith, *Press, Politics, and Patronage*, pp. 56–58.
70. Smith, *Press, Politics, and Patronage*, p. 100.
71. Smith, *Press, Politics, and Patronage*, p. 101–106.
72. Smith, *Press, Politics, and Patronage*, pp. 90, 295–296n; see also James Pollard, *Presidents and the Press*, New York: Macmillan, 1947, p. 161.
73. See Glyndon Van Deusen, *The Jacksonian Era*, New York: Harper & Row, 1959, pp. 26–27; and Robert V. Remini, *Andrew Jackson and the Course of American Freedom, 1822–1832*, vol. 2, New York: Harper & Row, 1981, p. 127.
74. Richard Rubin, *Press, Party, and Presidency*, New York: Norton, 1981, pp. 45–56.
75. Quoted in Smith, *Press, Politics, and Patronage*, pp. 93–94.
76. Smith, *Press, Politics, and Patronage*, p. 94.
77. See Smith, *Press, Politics, and Patronage*, pp. 71–72.

SUGGESTED READINGS

Bailyn, Bernard, and John B. Hench, eds. *The Press and the American Revolution*. Worcester, Mass.: American Antiquarian Society, 1980.
Davidson, Philip. *Propaganda and the American Revolution 1763–1783*. Chapel Hill, N.C.: University of North Carolina Press, 1941.
Mott, Frank Luther. *Jefferson and the Press*. Baton Rouge, La.: Louisiana State University Press, 1943.
Rubin, Richard. *Press, Party, and Presidency*. New York: Norton, 1981.
Schlesinger, Arthur M. *Prelude to Independence: The Newspaper War on Britain 1764–1776*. New York: Knopf, 1966.
Smith, Culver. *The Press, Politics, and Patronage*. Athens, Ga.: University of Georgia Press, 1977.
Stewart, Donald H. *The Opposition Press of the Federalist Period*. Albany, N.Y.: SUNY Press, 1969.

CHAPTER 4

Post-1830: The Penny Press, Yellow Journalism, and Political Independence

"Independent journalism! That is the watchword of the future of the profession."

Whitelaw Reid, Editor, New York Tribune

A NEW KIND OF NEWSPAPER: THE PENNY PRESS

A new daily newspaper appeared on the streets of New York on September 3, 1833. Although budding newspapers were common in the United States at the time, the arrival of the *New York Sun* marked a turning point in American journalism. The *Sun* differed from other newspapers because it sold for a penny and relied solely on street sales. Other newspapers cost about six cents a copy and subsisted on annual subscriptions, many of which were delinquent at any given time. The *Sun* was unique because it appealed to a mass readership—not only with its price, but also with its content. It was directed at the average person, rather than at political or commercial elites.

The *Sun* was also different because it was a financial success. Its success was a harbinger of a new breed of newspapers and journalists, and a significant contributor to a transformed relationship between political leaders and the press.

A Press for the Masses

The traditional partisan press had appealed to a clientele consisting primarily of the relatively well-to-do. Annual subscription rates of $8-$10 per year and single copy prices of up to six cents excluded most others. In the 1830s, with an average daily rate for laborers of one dollar and monthly earnings for farm labor averaging less than nine dollars, a daily newspaper was a luxury well beyond the means of the vast majority.[1] The penny press placed a daily newspaper within the reach of the average person.

In addition to reduced cost, the penny press's content was also designed to attract readers. Although politics remained a major component, the new newspapers featured other topics in news and opinion as well, in accordance with heightened public interest. Nonpolitical stories featured human interest, crime, sex scandals, sports, social events, and other items. News in the penny papers was culled from the police blotter, public trials, events in the street, and any other activities which might conceivably be of interest. Stories were written as much to entertain as to inform; they rarely focused on weighty issues.

The Penny Press and Political Independence

As opposed to their predecessors, which had relied heavily on news submitted by politicians or gleaned from other papers, penny newspapers placed greater emphasis on newsgathering. Aided by increased profits and expanded technologies, and compelled by national crises such as the Mexican War, the slavery issue in the 1850s, and the Civil War, large circulation urban newspapers began to expand their

---

The following items from the New York *Sun* are typical of Penny Press journalism.

Police Office

Margaret Thomas was drunk in the street—said she never would get drunk again "upon her honor." Committed, "upon honor."

William Luvoy got drunk because yesterday was so devilish warm. Drank 9 glasses of brandy and water and said he would be cursed if he wouldn't drink 9 more as quick as he could raise the money to buy it with. He would like to know what right the magistrate had to interfere with his private affairs. Fined $1—forgot his pocketbook, and was sent over to bridewell.

Bridget McMunn got drunk and threw a pitcher at Mr. Ellis, of 53 Ludlow st. Bridget said she was the mother of 3 little orphans—God bless their dear souls—and if she went to prison they would choke to death for the want of something to eat. Committed.

Catharine McBride was brought in for stealing a frock. Catharine said she had just served out 6 months on Blackwell's Island, and she wouldn't be sent back again for the best glass of punch that ever was made. Her husband, when she last left the penitentiary, took her to a boarding house in Essex st., but the rascal got mad at her, pulled her hair, pinched her arm, and kicked her out of bed. She was determined not to bear such treatment as this, and so got drunk and stole the frock out of pure spite. Committed.

Bill Doty got drunk because he had the horrors so bad he couldn't keep sober. Committed.

Source: Frank Luther Mott, *American Journalism,* p. 223.

newsgathering capabilities. In 1840, a chief editor of a New York newspaper hired perhaps two or three editorial assistants. By 1854, the *New York Tribune* boasted a staff of 24 editors and reporters assigned to local and national news.[2] Some of these newspapers doubled their price per copy, but found no deleterious effect on circulation. In return, they doubled the number of sheets from four to eight. The increase in the size of the paper also benefited the news function. Although extra space meant more advertising, the eight-sheet papers eventually allocated approximately equal space to advertising and editorial content. By contrast, the four-sheet press devoted two-thirds to three-fourths of newspaper space of advertising. Additionally, by the 1850s, the larger papers initiated a trend of removing advertising from the front page.[3]

Political News. Standard political news in the partisan press had consisted primarily of correspondence from legislators or others, lengthy transcripts of debate, or texts of speeches. The penny press contained more journalistic accounts of legislators' activities ranging from the sublime to the ridiculous. Newspapers reveled in the dramatic events of the day such as the Mexican War, bloody Kansas, and the Civil War. However, human interest stories involving national politicians also appeared with frequency. The *New York Tribune* published a story about a member from Ohio who brought his lunch to the House chamber and, after eating it, wiped his hands on his bald head and picked his teeth with a jackknife.

National political leaders were finding ways to bypass the press. By the 1850s, members of Congress, fearful of press distortion, used the franking privilege to distribute copies of their speeches. William Seward sent 50,000 copies of one speech in 1850; Daniel Webster distributed 120,000 of another during the same year. In the first five months of 1858, members of Congress mailed 800,000 copies of franked speeches.[4]

Of the three branches of national government, the Congress received more attention from the press than either the presidency or the Supreme Court.[5] Congress was the most accessible of the three institutions. To the reporter, it appeared as a beehive of activity. Also, Congress opened press galleries and allowed reporters to regulate them.

The presidency was closed to the press and made little attempt to woo reporters. Only during presidential election years did the presidency acquire greater press notice than the Congress. However, that notice had more to do with the activities of the parties and candidates during the campaign than to the presidency as a source of governmental activity.[6]

Relations with Politicians. The penny press also contrasted with the partisan press in its relationship with politicians. Some editors eschewed political partisanship. In its first issue, the *New York Transcript* declared that as far as politics goes, "we have none."[7] The *Baltimore Sun* announced the paper would give "no place to religious controversy nor to political discussions of merely partisan character."[8]

Many others, however, served partisan purposes. The inaugural issue of the *New York Tribune,* edited by Horace Greeley, declared: "the political revolution which . . . called William Henry Harrison to the Chief Magistracy of the Nation was a triumph of Right, Reason, and Public Good over Error and Sinister Ambition."[9] The *Washington Post,* a staunch Democratic paper, referred to President Rutherford B.Hayes as "the bogus president" or "his fraudulency."[10] However, such partisanship differed from that of the earlier party press because it was unrelated to patronage or other inducements and also because because these partisans could sometimes be the strongest critics of their own party or candidate. Horace Greeley, editor of the *New York Tribune* criticized Abraham Lincoln during the Civil War, and several Republican newspapers abandoned James G. Blaine when he became the Republican nominee in 1884.[11]

The Penny Press and Financial Independence

Penny Press Finances. The financial basis of the penny press reinforced editorial independence. The penny press succeeded for economic rather than political reasons. Although they were usually highly partisan, their support for political leaders or parties was not related to political patronage, nor was it automatic. At times, they even served as critics, and not just defenders, of their own party.

Penny press publishers were business entrepreneurs like James Gordon Bennett of the *New York Herald,* Charles Dana of the *New York Sun,* and Arunah S. Abell of the *Baltimore Sun* who relied on a strategy of mass circulation and growing advertising revenue. Mass circulation was achieved by lowering the price per copy, stressing street sales over annual subscriptions, and publishing news intended for the mass reader. Mass circulation attracted the attention of advertisers. Advertisers flocked to the penny press because advertising in one mass circulation newspaper was more cost effective than advertising placed simultaneously in several small circulation journals.

Moreover, the penny papers did not screen ads as did the more elite papers. Penny papers ran ads for products such as patent medicines, which were refused by more staid papers.[12]

Penny papers also innovated with advance cash payment for advertising and frequent changes of advertisements. Advance payment solved the problem of cash shortage, which always plagued the partisan press. The large circulation papers bearing production costs such as maintenance of presses, ink, newsprint, and staff salaries, could not afford to carry delinquent accounts.

Frequent changes in advertisements guaranteed new advertising copy which enhanced the fresh quality of the paper. For example, the *New York Herald* initially accepted no advertisement for longer than a two-week period. By 1847, the paper required advertisers to supply new copy daily.[13]

The penny press also forced the development of new presses capable of speedy, efficient printing of newspapers in mass volume. In short, the problem for the penny press was to produce a large volume of newspapers as cheaply as possible.

The stratagem of mass circulation with reliance on advertising and a large readership offered a sharply distinctive financial base for the penny press. In fact, political ties had a dampening effect on mass appeal by restricting the audience to partisan supporters and shaping news content.

Weakening the Relationship between Press and Politicians: Other Factors

The rise of the penny press was only one of several factors contributing to the weakening of the politicians' grasp on the editorial content of the press and the transformation of their relationship. Others included the stronger party organizations, diminished presidential leadership, a fragmentation of American politics, increased reliance on alternative forms of publishing government documents, changed attitudes about the role of the press, the alteration of press financial operations, the rise of technology, and increased professionalism among journalists.

Party Organization. Prior to the Jacksonian era, political parties consisted of loose structures bound together by correspondence between political elites and partisan newspapers. After the demise of the Federalists, the only remaining party, the Republicans, needed little structure to maintain itself. The gradual inclusion of more voters in the electoral process, however, and the eventual fragmentation of the Republican party, led political leaders to look to the political party as a tool for competitive mobilization of voters. Creation of political party organizations on both local and national levels diminished the need for politicians to rely on the press as a network for communication and mobilization of support.

Diminished Presidential Leadership. Similarly, the role of the press changed as the office of the presidency declined in its ability to offer leadership. After Andrew Jackson, virtually none of the presidents elected throughout the remainder of the nineteenth century were major national political leaders with active political agendas. Instead, these presidents were compromise choices, selected by party leaders. Major political leaders like Henry Clay, John C. Calhoun, and Daniel Webster were perceived as unelectable, because they represented sectional interests. Following the Civil War a number of factors—including the impeachment of Andrew Johnson, the scandals in Ulysses Grant's administration, and congressional dominance over Reconstruction and over important policy areas—produced a presidency which lacked forceful direction and leadership. Presidents failed to fully utilize the office, and therefore did not attempt to use the press to bolster public support for policy objectives.[14]

In tandem with the diminished presidency was the demise of the administration organ. Following Andrew Jackson's presidency up until 1860, successive presidents experienced difficulties with the practice of administration organs. Although these incumbents favored the practice, their own organs pursued an increasingly independent course. John Tyler had difficulty establishing an administration organ in Washington. James K. Polk forced the editor of his organ to resign because he believed it was not supportive of his administration. Franklin Pierce was embarrassed by the *Union,* his administration organ, when its editorial stance on a foreign policy issue differed sharply from his own. In 1860, James Buchanan repudiated his own organ when it editorialized in favor of secession.[15] Considering these difficulties, Abraham Lincoln opted not to establish an organ and subsequent presidents followed his example.

Fragmentation of Politics. A movement toward decentralization characterized the politics of the pre- and post-Civil War periods. Prior to the Civil War, power devolved to sectional interests. The post-Civil War period witnessed a preoccupation with local issues rather than national concerns. The fragmentation of politics meant the absence of burning national issues around which major political camps would form and attempt to utilize the press as a tool for articulation and the marshalling of support.

Richard Rubin neatly summarizes the dilemma of American politics in the late nineteenth century:

> On the one hand, the growth in congressional power vis a vis the president combined with the narrow, particularistic nature of congressional activities to undermine concern with and the articulation of national issues. On the other hand, weakened by a combination of post-Reconstruction reaction, ineffective and unimaginative presidents, and narrow . . . electoral contests, the presidency also could not muster popular majorities for particular programs.[16]

Inducements Reconsidered. Politicians had begun to reconsider the value of the relationship, as well. Within a few years, the Congress ended the inducements of printing contracts and the authorization to publish the laws of the United States.

Skyrocketing costs for government printing, hints of scandal in the operation of government printing involving huge profits for newspapers, and the inadequacy of private publishing plants to handle the mushrooming government printing business all contributed to intense criticism of the government's relations with the press.

Moreover, the post of official printer for the houses of Congress, which had originated in 1819, had become a subject of bitter wrangling by partisans seeking to enrich their own partisan organs.[17] In 1860, Congress created the Government Printing Office with responsibility for governmental printing. The creation of this office ended Congressional and executive subsidization of partisan newspapers. A major tool of political leaders and parties in forging relations with a supportive press was gone.

The next victim of reform was the authority to publish the laws, which had been granted to newspapers by the Secretary of State since the time of George Washington. The radical Republican Congress following the Civil War stripped the State Department of the power of designating newspapers in the South. Soon thereafter, the Congress removed the power for all other newspapers as well and vested it in the clerk of the House of Representatives.[18] Shifting this power to the Congress had no significant partisan impact since Republicans controlled both the presidency and the Congress. However, this power was useful to the Congress in drumming up press and public support for the impeachment and conviction of President Andrew Johnson.[19] The fragmented Congress lacked the ability to utilize this power, as the executive branch had done in the past. This may help account for the short period during which Congress held the power. By 1872, the Congress had ended this form of patronage after a congressional committee selected to study the problem pointed to excessive costs and the damage to the independence of the press. The committee report noted that it was "questionable whether the dominant political party should thus aid those newspapers which only reflect its partisan views instead of being mirrors of public opinion."[20]

Attitudes about the Role of the Press. The committee's report was reflective of a general reversal of attitudes about the role of the press in American politics. Increasing acceptance by the public, the press, and even politicians was given to a view of the press as an independent force unshackled by connections with parties and candidates. Under this argument, the partisan press had failed to fulfill adequately the information function due to its obsequiousness to politicians. *New York Tribune* editor Whitelaw Reid expressed dramatically a common sentiment:

> Independent journalism! that is the watchword of the future of the profession. An end of concealments because it would hurt the party; an end of one-sided expositions . . .; an end of assaults that are not believed fully but must be made because the exigency of party warfare demands them; an end of slanders that are known to be slanders . . . of hesitation to print the news because it may hurt the party . . . of doctoring the reports of public opinion . . . of half truths . . . that is the end which to every conscientious journalist a new and beneficent Declaration of Independence affords.[21]

This view was promoted by many journalists. However, widespread acceptance by political leaders and the public as well produced the demise of governmental supports for the long-standing, though frayed, relationship.

Changing Press Finances. Other changes in the press also contributed. From the perspective of the press, government patronage became increasingly irrelevant for large dailies reliant on circulation and advertising. Weeklies located in less sparsely populated areas still subsisted on government patronage. However, the urbanization of the population made their role less significant. Moreover, in light of technological developments, the original intent of government aid seemed antiquated. The multiplicity of newspapers throughout the country assured that the vast majority of the population would receive news of national politics without the aid of government support.

Technological Developments and Partisanship in the News. Improved communication and transportation facilities, particularly with the invention of the telegraph, allowed for more rapid exchange of news across the country. The role of the telegraph in enhancing transmission of news cannot be underestimated. Prior to the invention of the telegraph and extension of wire across the country, editors sought various means to speed the transmission of news. These included chartering loco-motives, sending semaphore signals, launching balloons, and sending carrier pi-geons.[22] The telegraph far surpassed any of these means for speed and reliability.

Additionally, the telegraph resulted in the creation of the wire service. Origi-nated by several upstate New York newspapers, the concept of the wire service was to improve nonlocal newsgathering capabilities of small metropolitan newspapers. The idea soon spread, leading to the creation of several wire services by the turn of the century, including the Associated Press, the United Press, and Scripps. Use of the wire service expanded quickly.[23] By 1872, more than 350 newspapers, about half of the dailies in the country, were served by a national wire service.[24]

An unanticipated effect of the wire service was the suppression of partisanship in news content. The wire service decreased reliance on the mail exchange of newspapers, which had been a bulwark of the partisan press network. The Washing-ton partisan organs played increasingly minor roles as conveyors of national politi-cal news. Wire service news also affected the partisan content of news by offering a more neutral content acceptable to a wide array of newspapers. Since the wire services profited by expanding membership and lowering costs to its members, the strategy of neutering the news met economic exigencies.

Simultaneously, newspapers began to separate news and opinion. The com-mon practice of editorializing leads of news stories diminished gradually. Horace Greeley developed the concept of an editorial page, which further separated news and opinion.[25] Still another factor limiting the role of partisanship was the sheer volume of the press. Between 1853 and 1903, the number of dailies in the United States mushroomed from less than 400 to 2,400.[26] The plethora of newspapers competing for the same market assured that partisanship, which would be shared by several newspapers, could not be the major competitive difference. Publishers were forced to rely on other types of appeals to convert and hold readers.

Changing Status of Journalism. Also important was the changing status of jour-nalists and journalism. First editors and then reporters acquired social acceptance and professional prestige through the 1800s. The professional standing of editor was boosted by the model of an independent crusader courageous enough to tackle parties and presidents. Nineteenth century editors such as Horace Greeley *(New York Tribune)*, James Gordon Bennett *(New York Herald)*, William Cullen Bryant *(New York Evening Post)*, and E. L. Godkin *(The Nation)* became nationally known figures equal in notoriety and prestige to national politicians. Greeley, with the support of some other editors, even became a presidential candidate in 1872.

The Civil War served as an impetus to the acceptance of the journalist as a professional. Large metropolitan newspapers devoted significant financial resources to news coverage of the war since they viewed the conflict as an opportunity to prove the value of the press. The *New York Herald,* one of the most aggressive in war reporting, spent half a million dollars on war coverage and employed more than 40 correspondents in the field at any one time.[27] Correspondents' stories included harrowing accounts of penetrating enemy lines and escaping to safety in order to transmit the news. Editors enhanced their correspondents' status by printing by-lines giving the reporter's name. The practice increased the prestige of individual journalists particularly at a time when readers were most interested in national news.

Following the war, some reporters became known personalities. Names such as Richard Harding Davis, Henry M. Stanley, and Henry Raymond became familiar to newspaper readers. Some of these reporters, such as Raymond, later moved to editorial positions.

Most reporters still received little public attention, worked long hours, and earned low salaries, usually between $15 and $30 per week.[28] However, the reporter had gained a respectable niche in American life.

One sign of the increased prestige of journalists was their status in political life. Editors and even some reporters actively rotated from journalistic to political positions. Journalists were frequent and often successful candidates for public office. Thirty-four journalists served in the Forty-first Congress and twenty-four in the Forty-second. Presidential candidates Horace Greeley and James G. Blaine had been editors. Journalists were appointed to federal government posts from clerk to cabinet official.[29]

These developments in both the political system and the press reduced system dependence on the press since political leaders could rely on other vehicles and national politics had become fragmented lacking clear direction from the presidency. The tangible political inducements for the press to accept partisan leadership were reduced significantly.

The press began to place economic considerations above the political. The press no longer played mouthpiece for political leaders. The penny press with its independent financial base sparked a gradual revolution in the relationship of the press to political leaders.

YELLOW JOURNALISM
AND PRESIDENTIAL NEWSMAKING

With political independence established for the press, particularly elite dailies, and with political parties and political leaders no longer reliant on the press in either the electoral process or governance, the dependency relationship of an earlier era seemed gone forever. However, major developments at the turn of the century would initiate changes in the press and political leaders leading to reestablishment of the relationship under new ground rules and involving players whose relative strength had been transformed significantly in the ensuing years.

Origins of Yellow Journalism

Increasingly established as an independent force, the press at the turn of the century was driven by commercial versus political concerns. These commercial interests sparked a tumultuous phase in journalistic history commonly titled "yellow journalism.'' The term ''yellow journalism'' originated with the use of yellow ink in comic illustrations. In the 1890s, larger dailies installed color presses initially for use in comic sections, but later appearing on the outside pages, as well. (The most popular cartoon of the period was the ''Yellow Kid of Hogan's Alley'' starring a boy dressed in a yellow gown, first published in the *New York World* and later in the *New York Journal.*)

Some of the other New York dailies panned the new technique. The *New York Times* advertised itself as a paper that ''does not soil the breakfast cloth.''[30] In fact, the term was used to encompass a genre of press attitudes and behavior highlighting sensationalism and emotion-laden copy in pursuit of more and more readers.

This type of journalism was hardly new; it can be traced to the early penny dailies such as the *New York Sun* and the *New York Herald* where the human interest story was a staple of news content. The Civil War and post-war period, however, had established the news business as one of a search for facts and information. Since the war reporters and editors had been acquiring more respectability and journalism had veered from its penny press roots. Yellow journalism took news reporting back to those roots.

Michael Schudson has described two models of journalism.[31] One is the ideal of information. The reporter's function is to provide pure, unframed information to the reader. The second model is the ideal of the story. Journalism is storytelling. Hence, facts must be framed to tell the story. According to Schudson, under this model, news ''serves primarily to create, for readers, satisfying aesthetic experiences which help them to interpret their own lives and to relate them to the nation, town, or class to which they belong.''[32]

While the former model characterized the reporting during and following the Civil War and was epitomized in the content of dailies such as the *New York Times,* the latter model was the foundation for yellow journalism.

Characteristics of Yellow Journalism

Circulation and Advertising.   The best known characteristic of yellow journalism is the preoccupation with circulation at the turn of the century in New York City. These circulation wars can be linked to the changing role of advertising in the economic base of newspapers. Although advertising had long affected newspaper economics, the growth of large department stores and the increased consumer demand for goods led advertisers to seek mass circulation for their newspaper advertisements and prompted publishers to boost circulation to capture key advertising accounts. Circulation became a gauge for advertisers of the suitability of a newspaper as a mass medium. Whereas in previous years newspapers had minimized the importance of wide circulation and even concealed their circulation figures, newspapers and advertisers developed a more businesslike attitude toward publication of circulation figures and newspapers even used such figures for self-promotion and solicitation of additional advertisers.[33]

Growing circulation figures required the presence of additional readers. Where were these readers coming from and why did they suddenly begin to buy news-papers? Skyrocketing purchases of newspapers have been attributed to the rapid influx of immigrants during the 1880s and 1890s, particularly in large urban centers. These immigrants offered newspapers a previously untapped audience if editorial content could be made appealing to them.[34]

Additionally, changing life-styles and the new status of women as newspaper readers contributed. The growth of population and the rise of manufacturing created a social environment increasingly turbulent and complex. The newspaper was one constant that aided people in coping with this large and ever more complicated environment. Women were solicited as newspaper readers because department store advertisers and publishers believed they held primary responsibility for purchases of family goods.[35]

Although the components of yellow journalism success were present, an entrepreneurial spirit provided the igniting spark. In New York of the middle 1890s, two newspaper publishers—Joseph Pulitzer of the *New York World* and William Randolph Hearst of the *New York Journal*—were pitted against each other in a circulation war intended to crush one or the other. Instead, both prospered while some other papers unwilling or unable to match their journalistic style eventually folded.

Sensationalism. The search for competitive advantage led both publishers to utilize new approaches to journalism to attract new readers in large numbers. This would be a journalism not like the staid, unsensational style of other New York news-papers such as the *New York Times,* the *New York Tribune,* and the *New York Evening Post.* As Hearst explained his success after one year of publication, he admitted: "It is the Journal's policy to engage brains as well as to get the news, for the public is even more fond of entertainment than it is of information."[36]

Yellow newspapers dwelled upon human interest, particularly stories of crime and sex. Pseudo-scientific articles such as supposed ancient discoveries, miracle

---

The worst of yellow journalism has been termed "the new journalism without a soul." The movement can be characterized by excessiveness—scare headlines in bold black type, full-page line drawings and illustrations, heavy black or red borders, and highly dramatized text. Shocking headlines were designed to grab reader attention, like the following examples:

STARTLING CONFESSION OF A WHOLESALE MURDERER WHO BEGS TO BE HANGED

STRANGE THINGS WOMEN DO FOR LOVE

SCHOOL GIRL'S SAD FATE. DECOYED INTO HOUSE OF ILL-FAME AT CONEY ISLAND

TOTS BURNED TO DEATH

Source: From Edwin Emery and Michael Emery, *The Press in America,* Englewood Cliffs, NJ: Prentice-Hall, 1984, p. 282.

cures, and major medical discoveries were highlights of yellow journalism. Another characteristic was the recurrence of campaigns against social injustice. The *New York World* proclaimed itself a paper that would "expose all fraud and sham, fight all public evils and abuses. . . ."

One aspect of that excessiveness was the use of various gimmicks to attract readers. These included sponsoring around-the-world trips and contests for newspaper slogans and offering large rewards for solving noted crimes.

Some yellow press innovations even survived the period to become staples of American newspaper format—full-color Sunday supplements, lengthy feature articles, popular comic sections, use of pictures, and occasional banner headlines.

Critics of Yellow Journalism

Opposition to the practices of yellow journalism arose quickly from a variety of sources—civic groups, religious leaders, and especially non-yellow newspapers. Several prominent newspapers held out against the onslaught of yellow journalism. Some of these strongly criticized the yellow press. An *Evening Post* editorial charged: "Everyone who knows anything about 'yellow journalism' knows that everything they do and say is intended to promote sales . . . these papers are public evils, and a national disgrace to be got rid of if possible. . . ."[37]

Economics also affected criticism of yellow journalism. Hearst and Pulitzer discovered that huge circulations did not mean high profits. New readers either lacked purchasing power or were simply resistant to advertising. Meanwhile, the older and more prosperous readers defected to the non-yellow papers. The circulation of the *New York Times,* a prominent non-yellow paper, rose from 25,000 in 1898 to 121,000 by 1905 and agate lines of advertising climbed from 2.4 million in 1897 to six million by 1905.[38] The success of the *Times* in the heyday of yellow journalism signaled to other publishers that an emphasis on accurate, fast, comprehensive reporting also could sell newspapers.

Also, a significant political event intensified criticism of the yellow press. President William McKinley's assassination was linked to the bitter criticism of McKinley in the editorial columns of the Hearst newspapers.[39] Non-yellow papers placed blame for the deed on the practices of the yellow press:

> The journalism of anarchy shares responsibility for the attack on President McKinley. . . . Let us hope it is really sorry. Then let us hope its sorrow will last long enough to persuade it that the selling of more papers . . . is not the chief end of journalism . . . when it leads one to defamation as a delight, to vilification as an industry, and to printed, pictorial, or platform blackguardism as a trade.[40]

Yellow Journalism's Impact on the Press

Despite opposition by several prominent dailies, yellow journalism did have a temporary widespread effect on the newspaper business. Many newspapers around the country copied yellow press practices. These include the *Philadelphia Inquirer,*

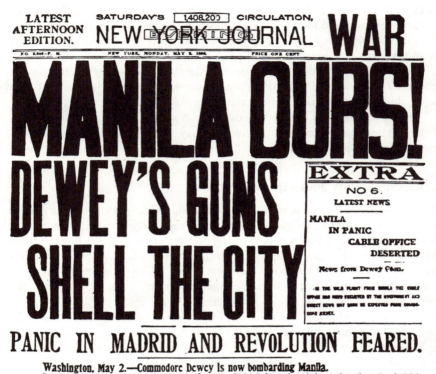

The most significant impact on national politics commonly attributed to yellow journalism is the outbreak of the Spanish-American War in 1898. According to one study of newspapers' role in the war, lurid accounts of atrocities in Cuba prompted mass meetings throughout the country in support of American retaliation and influenced members of Congress to initiate war. Screaming headlines called for action:

AMERICAN MOTHER OF *MAINE* VICTIM APPEALS TO THE NATION FOR REVENGE

SUICIDE LAMENTED THE *MAINE*. AGED MARY WAYT INHALED GAS THROUGH A TUBE.

> **GRIEVED OVER OUR DELAY. "THE GOVERNMENT MAY LIVE IN DISHONOR," SAID SHE. "I CANNOT."**
>
> The *New York Journal* went even further; it initiated a contest with a $50,000 reward for information leading to the conviction of those responsible for the explosion aboard the *Maine,* and solicited funds for a memorial for the *Maine*'s victims.
>
> Source: Compiled from Marcus M. Wilkerson, *Public Opinion and the Spanish-American War*, Baton Rouge, La.: Louisiana State University Press, 1932; Joseph Wisan, *The Cuban Crisis as Reflected in the New York Press*, New York: Columbia University Press, 1934; Frank L. Mott, *American Journalism*, New York: MacMillan, 1962, pp. 527–33; and W. A. Swanberg, *Citizen Hearst*, New York: Scribner, 1961, p. 144.

the *New York Herald,* the *Denver Post,* and the *St. Louis Globe-Democrat.* Duplication of the *World* and the *Journal*'s techniques produced temporary circulation increases for yellow newspapers. The *New York Herald* circulation jumped from 235,000 to 500,000 by 1898. Circulation of the *Philadelphia Inquirer* shot up from a minuscule 5,000 in 1889 to 300,000 by the turn of the century.[41]

One study of 21 large metropolitan areas throughout the country found one-third of the newspapers practicing yellow journalism.[42] Some of those papers were owned by Hearst or Pulitzer.

Even non-yellow papers were forced to alter their policies to meet the new trend. Some papers like the *Times* lowered prices to a penny per copy to remain competitive and appeal to a larger readership.

OTHER MAJOR PRESS DEVELOPMENTS

The turn of the century marked a salient turning point in American journalism. yellow journalism was just one of several major developments changing the press and affecting its role in American politics.

Newspapers as Big Business

One of those developments was the emergence of a corporate-operated press. Unlike a century before, urban dailies were becoming corporate entities employing hundreds of workers and incurring massive expenses for items such as salaries, paper, ink, and the most modern printing presses.

Start-up costs for new dailies in established markets had been steadily climbing. In the 1790s, the Federalist paper, the *Evening Post* in New York, had been started with $10,000. The *New York Times* in 1851 was opened with a capital amounting to $69,000. By the turn of the century, from several hundred thousand up to a million dollars was required to start up a competitive metropolitan newspaper.

The most common way to enter a major market competitively was to buy out an existing newspaper. Existing newspapers possessed the value of existing large circulations, advertising contracts, and franchises for wire services, in addition to physical assets such as printing facilities and staffs.[43]

However, buy-outs had become extremely expensive by the turn of the century. The *New York World,* the largest newspaper in the country at that time, expended $2 million annually and was said to be worth $10 million. The owner of the *Chicago Tribune* refused an offer of $4 million in 1892. Although dailies in smaller cities did not carry that kind of price tag, many experienced growth similar to the *Washington Post,* which sold for $210,000 in 1889 and sixteen years later majority control was resold for over half a million dollars.[44]

Annual incomes for these dailies equalled those of large corporations of the time. In the 1890s, the *New York Herald and Telegram* netted for its owner a million dollars a year. Not only did single newspapers such as the *New York Times* and the *New York Tribune* become large financial operations, but chains of newspapers under a single owner began to appear. E. W. Scripps and his brothers, James and George, started dailies in Detroit, Cleveland, St. Louis, and Cincinnati in the 1880s. William Randolph Hearst, Joseph Pulitzer, and Frank Munsey also headed newly forged chains throughout the country. Chains enhanced the business quality of the press and buried the image of the free-thinking editor of an independent newspaper. However, the influence of chains or groups, as they would later be called, would not peak until a later period.

Undoubtedly, newspapers were big businesses with rich potential as money-making ventures. Joseph Pulitzer reportedly amassed a fortune of over $18 million. E. W. Scripps's earnings were estimated at $50 million.[45] Obviously, most newspaper owners made less. However, newspapers as business ventures were increasingly attractive. The value of U.S. newspapers and magazines rose from $89 million in 1879 to more than $250 million by 1904.[46]

Also, competition was diminishing. Although the number of dailies was increasing, the growth was occurring in areas without existing dailies. Large financial investments required for start-ups or buy-outs and continued operating costs limited new competitors in large urban areas with established newspapers. Smaller existing dailies unable to compete with the established dailies were frequent targets for mergers. In New York City, between 1912 and 1925 the number of dailies declined from 14 to 9.[47] Diminished competition meant greater stability for existing newspapers.

The Role of Advertising

In line with a trend prevalent throughout the late 1800s, advertising constituted an ever-increasing source of income for newspapers. In 1879, advertising made up 44 percent of total income for newspapers and periodicals. By 1904, that figure had climbed to 56 percent. Between 1892 and 1914, newspaper and periodical advertising sales multiplied three and a half times.[48]

A heightened role for advertising in the revenue for newspapers made them more dependent on advertisers. Business relations with advertisers were regularized with formation of advertising companies and the Audit Bureau of Circulations which provided periodic, accurate information on circulation figures.[49]

Newspapers and periodicals no longer fit the nineteenth-century model of the scandal sheet. Journalism was big business and those who ran it were business tycoons.

Professionalization

The changes occurring in the newspaper's boardrooms also spilled over into the newsrooms. Reporters had long held the image of antinomians. However, journalism was moving gradually toward professionalization. Professionalizing the newsgathering process also can be linked to the unfavorable reaction by the public and even many journalists to the excesses of yellow journalism.

One manifestation of the professionalization of the news business was the formation of trade associations such as the National Editorial Association and the American Newspaper Publishers Association. Reporters also formed their own press clubs, the most famous of which is the National Press Club formed in 1908 by Washington reporters.[50] Also, the publication of new trade journals such as *Editor and Publisher, The Journalist,* and *The Fourth Estate* marked this trend.

Journalism organizations also began to establish codes of ethics for journalism. A reaction to yellow journalism, the codes were an attempt to delineate the role of the press in society and the rights and responsibilities of the press.[51]

Another sign of professionalization was the movement for structured journalistic education. Prior to the turn of the century, journalists were largely self-trained. Although newspaper magnate E. W. Scripps viewed a college education as a detriment to a reporter, concern for journalism training and inculcation of professional standards increased. Commencing with Joseph Pulitzer's endowment of a journalism school at Columbia University, journalism majors were established in schools across the country.[52]

Professionalization affected attitudes concerning the function of the press. Journalism educators compared journalism to law and medicine—professions acting as a public trust. A public trust possessed responsibilities to the society. For the journalistic profession, they included accurate portrayal of events sans sensationalism. Professionalization impacted on the newsgathering process itself. The definition of news, procedures and practices for gathering news, and relations with sources, were revised by professionalization.

Relations with Political Parties

This period also marked growing distance between newspapers and political parties. In 1899, more than two of three newspapers were clearly partisan. Thirty years later, less than half were.[53] A new type of independent publisher, professionalization leading to changing conceptions of the role of journalism, and the rise of the wire services all contributed to weakening press ties with political parties.

The first generation of penny press publishers, men such as James Gordon Bennett and Horace Greeley, separated themselves from the political parties financially, but still retained their intensely held partisan affiliations. The second generation, including Whitelaw Reid *(New York Tribune)*, Henry Watterson *(Louisville Courier-Journal)*, and Charles Dana *(New York Sun)*, were considerably less partisan and more likely to place journalistic concerns before partisan loyalty. They were more willing to break with the party, as many Republican editors did in 1884 to support Democratic presidential candidate Grover Cleveland. However, the traumatic nature of their temporary opposition was powerful evidence of their loyalty. Primarily, they saw their role as critics from within the party.

The succeeding generation, however, consisted of publishers who lacked the party ties held by their elders. The rhetoric of the second generation about the virtues of independent journalism was taken seriously by the third generation. Younger publishers like William R. Nelson of the *Kansas City Star* and Melville Stone of the *Chicago Daily News* rejected the role of internal party critics and largely faithful party adherents. This new generation exhibited a higher degree of detachment from the partisan fervor of an election campaign by staking out a role as independent observer. Their stance was not merely nonpartisan, but, at times, even anti-partisan. In 1924, an editorial in the *New York Times* declared "while it is too soon to despair of government by party, many of us have become heartily ashamed of it."[54] They possessed a strong drive for commercial success. The justification for their newspapers rested on business and journalistic, rather than political, principles. For example, the *Kansas City Star* launched its first issue with the explanation that the city needed "a cheap afternoon newspaper, of the highest class."[55] It would be independent of all parties. Nelson wrote:

> The most sensible appeal that can be made to young voters . . . would urge them not to surrender their consciences and their judgments to the keeping of party bosses, but to maintain their independence and exercise the suffrage according to their own convictions.[56]

Conceptions of the role of journalism were evolving; for example, the newspaper's function in shaping public opinion on political issues. While the party organs implicitly assumed voters needed guidance on political matters, newspapers began to abdicate that role. Many newspapers abandoned editorials. Moreover, some journalists stressed their role as fact finders shorn of any requirement to guide public opinion.

Even their mottoes reflected newspapers' changing conception of their role as purveyors of news vs. opinion:

"All the News That's Fit to Print."	The *New York Times*
"If It's News and True, It's Here."	*New Haven Journal Courier*
"First to Last—The Truth."	*New York Herald Tribune*

The claims of non-interference in voters' decision making rang hollow. Independent newspapers were hardly reticent to launch campaigns to alter public opinion, as discussed earlier. But, these campaigns rarely had a partisan component and, in fact, often attacked both major political parties such as reform of political machines.

The new generation of publishers contributed to the changing conception of the newspaper. Also, the call for liberal reforms during the Progressive Era at the turn of the century tainted the partisan-leaning press and redounded to the benefit of the independents. Moreover, the commercial success of the independent papers pointed to the appeal of their nonpartisan, and even anti-partisan, content.

Another blow to the partisan papers was the rise of the wire services as the primary source of nonlocal news. The wire services had grown from small cooperative regional ventures during the 1840s and 1850s to national associations by the 1890s. These services included the Associated Press, the American Press Association, and the Scripps Press Association.

For national political news, the wires had to compete with the newspapers' own reporters. In 1871, at least 130 newspapers had their own Washington correspondents. However, wire service membership grew. By 1908, the Associated Press had nearly 800 members. The output of wire service news also had increased. In the 1850s, the AP had sent upwards of 1000 words daily to subscribers. By 1910, that figure had soared to 35,000 words.[57]

PRESIDENTIAL NEWSMAKING

These developments had contributed to increased press autonomy from political leaders, decreased reliance by politicians on the press for party service, and lowered expectations about the press as a political tool. Newspapers could no longer be relied upon to perform as loyal organs for political parties or individual politicians. Yet, necessity soon led to the reestablishment of a symbiotic relationship between political leaders, particularly presidents, and the press.

Changing Conception of the Presidency

That sense of necessity appeared to touch both sides simultaneously. The office of the president had not been viewed as a vigorous position since the impeachment of Andrew Johnson in 1868. However, when Theodore Roosevelt succeeded to the presidency in 1901 after the assassination of William McKinley, the conception of presidential role began to change. Roosevelt saw the office in broad terms:

> My belief was that it was not only [the president's] right but his duty to do anything that the needs of the Nation demanded unless such action was forbidden by the Constitution or by the Laws. Under this interpretation of executive power I did and caused to be done many things not previously done by the President. . . . I did not usurp power, but I did greatly broaden the use of executive power."[58]

Moreover, the office itself was expanding for reasons other than the personality of the president. One cause was increasing United Statesrole in foreign affairs. Events such as the Spanish-American War, the establishment of a small American colonial empire, U.S. military involvement in Latin America, and World War I all enhanced the president's role as one of several world leaders. The United States entered world affairs as a major participant and the office of the presidency acquired a new and weighty responsibility as one of several major world leaders.

In domestic affairs, Roosevelt's own efforts and those of Woodrow Wilson elected in 1912, eventually propelled Congress to place more responsibility for governance in the hands of the president. However, the resources for the presidential office would increase more gradually and much later.[59] Also, a significant dissenting view advocating a circumscribed presidency similar to those of the nineteenth century persisted.[60]

Roosevelt faced a dilemma. He entered office with the poorest relationship with his own political party of any president since the Civil War. Roosevelt's expansive view of the presidential office could not be fulfilled through the traditional party machinery. The solution would be to turn to some other vehicle for transforming the presidency into a "bully pulpit" for conveying his ideas about social and political reform and mobilizing congressional and public support. That vehicle would be the press.

Political scientist Jeffrey K. Tulis argues Roosevelt was the father of a "rhetorical presidency," where the president acts as leader of public opinion. Such a conception was largely unknown to nineteenth-century presidents. Obviously, the news media become a vital tool for such a role.[61]

Fulfilling Journalistic Imperatives

Identification of the needs of the presidency for a vehicle for exercising power does not explain why the press would be willing to serve such a function.

Newspapers, particularly the elite dailies, were by this time highly autonomous of political leaders and possessed certain journalistic-driven imperatives. These included a steady generation of news with color and drama, predictable sources of news, and ready access to those available sources.

Presidents, beginning with William McKinley, were willing to meet such imperatives in pursuit of their own political objectives of strengthening the office and affecting public policy formulation. McKinley was the first to encourage White House coverage. His secretary met with reporters daily to brief them on the day's events. Also, he provided reporters with a place to pass the time between news briefings.[62] Not all succeeding presidents were eager to do so. Some such as William Howard Taft and Herbert Hoover were disdainful of the expectations placed on them by the press. But the model of presidency-press relations established by Theodore Roosevelt has been followed by most presidents in this century.

Theodore Roosevelt formalized and expanded McKinley's press efforts. He had been doing this long before entering the White House. From the ride up San Juan Hill during the Spanish-American War as a Rough Rider to his actions as New York City's Police Commissioner, Roosevelt's unorthodox behavior and colorful life-style provoked controversy. Although Roosevelt attempted to shield his family from reporters' prying eyes, the antics of his children, particularly his daughter Alice, contributed to the drama of White House news coverage.

However, Roosevelt's personal or family life-style alone was not the main ingredient of most White House news nor would that kind of news have served Roosevelt's purpose. Roosevelt provided a steady stream of news about his administration's policy statements and actions. The White House issued a continual supply of news statements. The intent was to keep reporters too busy to pursue critical stories.

He also met regularly with reporters in news conferences, usually during his daily shave. These sessions were designed to expose reporters to his thinking and shape the stories written about his administration.[63]

Roosevelt offered reporters a predictable source of authoritative and colorful news. Unlike nineteenth-century presidents, Roosevelt made news regularly. This saved reporters covering the White House from the dreaded job of telling their editors there was no news today as their predecessors had done. This policy also pleased publishers and editors seeking to justify paying a reporter or correspondent to wait outside the White House for news. More and more editors began to assign reporters to cover the White House since it now became a predictable source of news. The expectation of a daily news happening lingers today, even though no major news story actually occurs.

Steady news generation was one way Roosevelt met journalistic imperatives. Another was his attempt to cultivate a sense of camaraderie with journalists. Journalists viewed Roosevelt as more of a journalist than a politician. Like them, he sought to rectify social problems and battle established interests. He emphasized his distance from traditional politicians. The image was one Roosevelt did not attempt to alter. In fact, Roosevelt fostered such notions through his easy rapport with the press corps and keen interest in their work.

Roosevelt clearly appreciated the needs of journalists. He understood the need for timing in issuing news. Statements issued on slow news days were likely to be magnified in emphasis while bad news could be buried in a flood of releases. He also knew the journalistic ethic of objectivity, which was acquiring greater weight among journalists, would work to his benefit as reporters would attempt to be accurate in their descriptions of the president's statements.[64]

Journalists also required access to decisionmakers in order to observe events and report them in true journalistic style. Roosevelt accommodated them by inviting them into the White House for press conferences and interviews with the president. He set aside a room in the White House for use by the press corps. He designated a member of his staff to aid the press. The regular press conferences and the barrage of official statements also suggested to the press corps that they had access to White House decision making.

Institutionalizing Presidency-Press Relations

Roosevelt institutionalized presidency-press relations. He established a model for presidency relations with the press, but he also undertook reforms that most presidents have continued—a White House press room, regular news conferences and interviews, and White House staff assistance for the press.

A later president, Woodrow Wilson, added to Roosevelt's reforms. He personally delivered State of the Union speeches to Congress, a practice discarded for over a century, which had the intended effect of ensuring greater press attention to the president's message. He also kept these speeches short to facilitate publication of the full text in the newspapers. Also, he kept to a single theme to avoid diluting its impact.[65] Whereas, presidents such as Jefferson, Adams, and Jackson had their speeches published in full on request or as a matter of course, by Wilson's time, the president had to structure the speech to meet journalistic needs.

However, it was Franklin Roosevelt's presidency that permanently altered both the role of the presidency and the president's relations with the press. Roosevelt

Franklin Delano Roosevelt appointed the first full-time White House press secretary, Stephen Early, a former newspaper reporter who made himself available to the press corps at all times. Roosevelt also initiated twice-weekly press conferences, which became legends among journalists because of the friendliness of the meetings and the deluge of information that the president provided. Roosevelt was an acknowledged master at communication with both press and public. *Source:* © Wide World Inc., FDR Library.

copied cousin Theodore's views of the presidency and relationship with the press. He also added his own reforms.

Although he had never been a journalist, Roosevelt appeared to understand journalism. Sometimes he gave journalists hints for their work. On one occasion he commented: ''If I were going to write a story, I would write it along the lines of the decision that was actually taken last Saturday. . . .'' On another, he advised, ''. . . that is the trouble, you haven't got a spot news story. You have an interpretive long-range story.''[66]

He cultivated good relations with the reporters covering the White House. He praised them for their articles, which demonstrated he was an avid reader. He helped them understand the difficult technical issues of the Depression so they could explain them to their readers.

Roosevelt also attempted to curry the favor of both reporters and the general public by creating a class war between reporters and editors and the newspaper publishers. He issued continual attacks on newspaper publishers claiming 85 percent of them opposed the New Deal. Although overdrawn, his charges fit neatly into his more general attacks on the wealthy and big business and solidified his implicit alliance with the common man.

Roosevelt's adroitness in working with the press even prompted charges that the White House press corps had become propagandists for the administration. However, the model of a president actively seeking to utilize the White House press corps for the administration's purposes, particularly by meeting press imperatives, was reinforced by FDR and has become the yardstick for measuring successive president's relations with the press.[67]

THE NEW RELATIONSHIP VS. THE OLD

The reestablishment of a close relationship between the presidency and the press indicated both needed the other. However, the new relationship was not the same as the old. Significant differences existed between the two.

The press had acquired a high level of autonomy from political leaders and political parties during the intervening period. Presidents no longer could rely on the financial weakness of the press to gain support through financial supports. The elite newspapers with influence nationally were large corporations governed by economic rather than political concerns.

Presidents also could not turn to partisan loyalty since journalism now valued independence more than loyalty and objectivity in reporting more than partisan editorializing in the news. The rise of the wire services had contributed to that trend. Although some smaller dailies continued the tradition of partisan mouthpieces or editorializing in news content, the larger and more influential newspapers set the trend of an independent press.

The press had achieved such a status that whereas in the past, presidents had interacted with publishers and editors, now their primary contact was with reporters. This change was a product of the diminished stature of presidents and the enhanced status of the press. The news component affected the type of reporting. Initially, the close involvement with reporters resulted in a more reverential attitude toward the presidency. While editors and publishers felt equal to most presidents, particularly those of the late nineteenth century, reporters still did not.

Presidents realized they needed the cooperation of the press in order to expand the role of the office and meet the increasing expectations placed on the incumbent. The declining role of the party and the distance of some presidents from their own party necessitated other resources.

Significantly, the press would have to be met by presidents on the grounds set by the press. The president had to meet press imperatives in order to acquire press coverage and a forum for influencing public opinion and national policy. The president had to appreciate news values, journalistic norms and ethics, and the operation of the news business in order to gain this forum. Presidents who were willing to do these things were successful in utilizing the press to their advantage in fulfillment of administration objectives.

The shift of the ground rules from political imperatives to press imperatives indicated the highly developed autonomy of the press in relation to American political leaders, including presidents.

NOTES

1. U.S. Bureau of the Census, *The Statistical History of the United States,* introduction by Ben J. Wattenberg, New York: Basic Books, 1976, p. 163.
2. Alfred M. Lee, *The Daily Newspaper in America,* New York: Macmillan, 1937, pp. 611–613.
3. Frank Luther Mott, *American Journalism, A History: 1690–1960,* 3d ed., New York: Macmillan, 1962, p. 295.
4. Thomas C. Leonard, *The Power of the Press,* New York: Oxford University Press, 1986, p. 93.
5. See Samuel Kernell and Gary C. Jacobson, "Congress and the Presidency as News in the Nineteenth Century," *Journal of Politics* 49 (1987): 1016–1035.
6. Kernell and Jacobson, "Congress and the Presidency as News," pp. 1016–1035.
7. Quoted in Michael Schudson, *Discovering the News,* New York: Basic Books, 1978, p. 21.
8. Schudson, *Discovering the News,* p. 22.
9. Bernard Weisberger, *Reporters for the Union,* Boston: Little, Brown, 1953, p. 10.
10. Chalmers M. Roberts, *The Washington Post: The First 100 Years,* Boston: Houghton Mifflin, 1977, p. 5.
11. See James Pollard, *Presidents and the Press,* New York: Macmillan, 1947, pp. 351–359. See also Allan Nevins, *The Evening Post,* New York: Boni and Liveright, 1922, pp. 458–468.
12. Edwin Emery and Michael Emery, *The Press in America,* Englewood Cliffs, N.J.: Prentice-Hall, 1984, p. 142; and Lee, *Daily Newspaper in America,* pp. 317–318.
13. See Lee, *Daily Newspaper in America,* pp. 317–318.
14. Jeffrey K. Tulis, *The Rhetorical Presidency,* Princeton, N.J.: Princeton University Press, 1987.

15. See Robert Seager, II, *And Tyler Too*, New York: McGraw-Hill, 1963, pp. 221–222; Philip Shriver Klein, *President James Buchanan*, University Park, Pa.: Pennsylvania State University, 1962, p. 374; and Pollard, *Presidents and the Press*, pp. 233–240, 289–290.
16. Richard Rubin, *Press, Party, and Presidency*, New York: Norton, 1981, p. 74.
17. See Culver Smith, *Press, Politics, and Patronage*, Athens, GA.: University of Georgia Press, 1977, pp. 210–211.
18. Smith, *Press, Politics, and Patronage*, pp. 237–238.
19. Smith, *Press, Politics, and Patronage*, p. 240.
20. Quoted in Smith, *Press, Politics, and Patronage*, p. 241.
21. Quoted in Mott, *American Journalism*, p. 412.
22. Frederic Hudson, *Journalism in the United States from 1690 to 1872*, New York: Harper & Brothers, 1873, pp. 596–598.
23. For a discussion of the early growth of the wire services, see Richard Schwarzlose, *The Nation's Newsbrokers*, vol. 1, Evanston, Ill.: Northwestern University Press, 1989.
24. Lee, *Daily Newspaper in America*, p. 512.
25. See Lee, *Daily Newspaper in America*, chap. 16; and Mott, *American Journalism*, pp. 295–296.
26. Lee, *Daily Newspaper in America*, p. 64.
27. Emery and Emery, *Press and America*, p. 200.
28. See Mott, *American Journalism*, p. 406; and Emery and Emery, *Press and America*, p. 264.
29. See Hudson, *Journalism in the United States from 1690 to 1872*, pp. 699–700; and Pollard, *Presidents and the Press*, pp. 241, 292, 376, and 544.
30. Schudson, *Discovering the News*, p. 112.
31. Schudson, *Discovering the News*, pp. 89–120.
32. Schudson, *Discovering the News*, p. 89.
33. Schudson, *Discovering the News*, pp. 93–94.
34. Schudson, *Discovering the News*, pp. 97–98.
35. Schudson, *Discovering the News*, pp. 100–101. See also Mott, *American Journalism*, p. 599.
36. Quoted in W.A. Swanberg, *Citizen Hearst*, New York: Scribner, 1961, p. 90.
37. Quoted in Marcus W. Wilkerson, *Public Opinion and the Spanish-American War*, Baton Rouge, La.: Louisiana State University Press, 1932, p. 126.
38. Schudson, *Discovering the News*, p. 114.
39. Mott, *American Journalism*, pp. 540–541.
40. *Brooklyn Eagle*, September 11, 1901. Quoted in Allan Nevins, *American Press Opinion: Washington to Coolidge*, Boston: D.C. Heath, 1928, p. 467. Reprinted by University Microfilms, Ann Arbor, Mich., 1970.
41. Sidney Kobre, *The Yellow Press*, n.p., 1964, pp. 86, 135.
42. Mott, *American Journalism*, p. 539; Lee, *Daily Newspaper in America*, pp. 271–272.
43. Lee, *Daily Newspaper in America*, p. 170.
44. Chalmers M. Roberts, *The Washington Post: The First 100 Years*, Boston: Houghton Mifflin, 1977, pp. 43, 83; also see Mott, *American Journalism*, pp. 546, 560.
45. See Willard Bleyer, *Currents in the History of American Journalism*, Boston: Houghton Mifflin, 1927, p. 351; also Mott, *American Journalism*, p. 551.
46. Lee, *Daily Newspaper in America*, pp. 170–171.
47. Frank O'Brien, *The Story of the Sun*, New York: Appleton, 1928, pp. 206–207.
48. See Lee, *Daily Newspaper in America*, p. 172; and Mott, *American Journalism*, p. 593.

49. Bleyer, *Currents in the History of American Journalism,* p. 420. For a more detailed discussion of the changes in advertising and their effects on newspapers, see Michael Schudson, *Advertising, The Uneasy Persuasion,* New York: Basic Books, 1984, pp. 147–177.
50. Lee, *Daily Newspaper in America,* pp. 228–240, 666–677.
51. See Nelson A. Crawford, *The Ethics of Journalism,* New York: Knopf, 1924.
52. See Lee, *Daily Newspaper in America,* pp. 658–666; and Mott, *American Journalism,* pp. 604–605.
53. Lee, *Daily Newspaper in America,* p. 182.
54. See Nevins, *American Press Opinion,* p. 582.
55. Bleyer, *Currents in the History of American Journalism,* p. 310.
56. Quoted in Michael E. McGerr, *The Decline of Popular Politics,* New York: Oxford University Press, 1986, p. 118.
57. Lee, *Daily Newspaper in America,* pp. 510, 526–528.
58. Theodore Roosevelt, *An Autobiography,* New York: Macmillan, 1921, pp. 388–389.
59. Examples include the Budget and Accounting Act of 1921 and the growth of the federal bureaucracy during World War I. For a brief discussion of the expansion of the presidency during this period, see James MacGregor Burns, *Presidential Government,* Boston: Houghton Mifflin, 1966, pp. 67–71.
60. See William Howard Taft, *The President and His Powers,* New York: Columbia University Press, 1916, pp. 139–157.
61. Tulis, *Rhetorical Presidency.*
62. George Juergens, *News from the White House,* Chicago: University of Chicago Press, 1981, p. 15.
63. Juergens, *News from the White House,* pp. 17–18.
64. For further discussion of Theodore Roosevelt's relationship with the press, see Juergens, *News from the White House,* pp. 7–90; and Pollard, *Presidents and the Press,* pp. 569–600.
65. Juergens, *News from the White House,* pp. 126–166
66. Quoted in Pollard, *Presidents and the Press,* pp. 776–777.
67. For a discussion of FDR's relations with the press, see Graham J. White, *FDR and the Press,* Chicago: University of Chicago Press, 1979; and Pollard, *Presidents and the Press,* pp. 773–845.

SUGGESTED READINGS

Juergens, George. *News from the White House.* Chicago: University of Chicago Press, 1981.
Kobre, Sidney. *The Yellow Press.* n.p.: 1964.
Leonard, Thomas C. *The Power of the Press.* New York: Oxford University Press, 1986.
Mott, Frank Luther. *American Journalism: A History 1690–1960.* New York: Macmillan, 1962.
Nevins, Allan. *American Press Opinion: Washington to Coolidge.* Boston: D.C. Heath, 1928. Reprinted by University Microfilms. Ann Arbor, Mich., 1970.
Schudson, Michael. *Discovering the News.* New York: Basic Books, 1978.
Tebbel, John, and Sarah Miles Watts. *The Press and the Presidency.* New York: Oxford University Press, 1985.
Wilkerson, Marcus, W. *Public Opinion and the Spanish-American War.* Baton Rouge, La.: Louisiana State University Press, 1932.

CHAPTER 5

1900 to the Present: The Rise of Broadcasting, Media Conglomerates, and the New Journalism

> *"[Radio] will make the long speech impossible or inadvisable . . . the short speech will be the vogue."*
>
> John W. Davis, 1924, Democratic presidential candidate[1]

On Christmas eve 1906, ship operators along the eastern coast of the United States heard over their wireless telegraph receivers "a human voice coming from their instruments—someone speaking! Then a woman's voice rose in song. It was uncanny! Many of them called their officers to come and listen; soon the wireless rooms were crowded. Next someone was heard reading a poem. Then there was a violin solo; then a man made a speech, and they could hear most of his words."[2] The broadcast is believed to be the first radio broadcast to the public. Sent by Reginald Fessenden, a professor of electrical engineering at the University of Pittsburgh and former research assistant to Thomas Edison, the broadcast was one of many technological developments leading to commercial use of, and a political role for broadcasting.

In the decade following Fessenden's experiment, several other inventors built transmitters and attempted continuous radio transmission. In 1909, weekly programs of news and music originated from a bank building in San Jose, California. In 1915–1916, similar operations were started in New York and Pittsburgh and at Tufts University and the University of Wisconsin. Even these few experimental stations were closed with the onset of World War I.

These breakthroughs in radio broadcasting still had little value for mass usage due to the dearth of radio receiving sets. The early audience consisted of amateur wireless enthusiasts who constructed homemade sets. In 1920, sets became available in a few large department stories with prices ranging from $25-$60—a price out of reach for many consumers. Moreover, there were few radio stations transmitting and even those broadcast only a few hours per week.

EARLY BROADCASTING

Following the war, radio stations began to flourish as a variety of groups and individuals began to perceive value in radio transmissions. Department stores, hotels, and restaurants began to construct stations as sidelines to attract business. Other groups such as churches and social clubs joined the growing station ownership. Many stations were owned by newspapers. Radio transmitting equipment was not a severe financial drain—costs ranged from less than $3000 to more than $50,000 for the few powerful stations.[3]

However, continued operating costs were another matter. One station started for less than $4,000 in 1920 was spending more than $80,000 by its third year of operation. Smaller stations could not shoulder such costs. Costly increases in power and equipment improvements were required to compete with other stations. Smaller stations unable to afford these expenses soon closed down. Only with the widespread use of advertising by the late 1920s did radio acquire a solid financial base.

The set-up of radio stations throughout the country (566 by March 1923) spurred public interest in the medium and created a rush for receivers in the 1920s. By 1924, two and a half million were in use. Two years later, it was estimated that one in six families had sets.[4] Mass radio had come of age.

Government's Role

The role of the federal government also shaped the development of radio. Since its inception as a public medium, debate had ensued over the government's role in regulating the medium. The industry's growth preceded government's interest in radio and affected the shape of the policy toward the new medium.

The plethora of stations had created a chaotic situation with continuous signal interference. After discussions involving broadcasters, amateur radio operators, and government officials during several radio conferences during the 1920s, the Commerce Department sought statutory authority to regulate the burgeoning industry.

The government's initial reaction to radio was a laissez-faire attitude. Not until several years after the phenomenal growth of radio as a mass medium did the Congress pass legislation regulating radio broadcasting. A federal court decision prohibited the Department of Commerce from issuing regulations for broadcasting. The department had performed regulatory tasks such as issuing station licenses, assigning wavelengths, and setting limitations of times of operation and station power—all technical aspects of broadcasting.

Congress enacted the Radio Act of 1927 which eliminated small low-power stations producing interference with the signals of the more powerful stations, allocated more frequencies, and reassigned station frequencies. The act also established the Federal Radio Commission to regulate radio broadcasting. In the spirit of the 1920s, however, the commission was regarded as more servant than regulator of the industry.[5]

Even after the Federal Radio Commission was initiated under the Radio Act, the regulatory emphasis was on the technical, rather than the editorial aspect of broadcasting. Government censorship was strongly opposed.

Given the existing problem of a multitude of signals, it is significant that there was widespread fear of a monopoly of radio broadcasting and support for government intervention to prevent it.

Some saw broadcasting as a publicly owned utility. Herbert Hoover, then Secretary of Commerce, argued that the people owned the broadcast waves and broadcasting should be treated as a utility existing to serve the public. Hoover contended that radio should be the subject of even greater governmental scrutiny than print media because radio was more pervasive.

But Hoover's views conflicted with the laissez-faire attitude toward business, including the broadcast industry, which was common in the 1920s. Within a year, Hoover, broadcasters, and the Congress would take a middle path preserving private ownership with a modicum of government regulation, primarily over technical facets. Hoover's concern, shared by broadcasters, by this point was not radio's perniciousness but the potential of government limitation of free speech.

> This decision has avoided the pitfalls of political, religious, and social conflicts in the use of speech over the radio which no Government could solve—it has preserved free speech to this medium.[6]

This middle path—private ownership with government regulation primarily over technical aspects—became the basis of U.S. telecommunictions policy. The approach met broadcasters' demands for government regulation over the chaotic free enterprise system, as well as a hands-off policy toward programming and the industry's profits.

Though government ownership was avoided, broadcasters feared the potential of government intervention in programming and the newly formed National Association of Broadcasters adopted a formal code of ethics to forestall moves for further government action.

Complaints about the FRC and a growing mood to unite all forms of communication—radio, telephone, and telegraph—under one regulatory body led Congress to pass the Communications Act of 1934. This new act created a Federal Communications Commission which supplanted the FRC and possessed broader powers than the old commission. The FCC could determine whether new licenses and renewals would be granted. It could not censor programs, but past performance in programming could be used as a criterion in determining the station's service to the public at the time of license renewal. However, license revocation was rare and license renewal generally a perfunctory task for the FCC.

The existence of federal legislation and a commission regulating broadcasting placed radio in a class distinct from the print media, which lacked these regulatory controls. Significantly, however, the Communications Act prohibited government control of program content. License renewal was highly routine. Government intervention in programming was rare, and even then primarily motivated by issues of obscenity rather than politics. Governmental regulation did not impinge on the autonomy of the press. Regulation of the industry, for the most part, was internal. Radio's rise in an era of journalistic codes of ethics adopted by the print media (and soon thereafter also by broadcasters) affected the broadcast industry, as well. Such self-regulation was designed to avoid governmental interference.

Early Political Usage

Most politicians, including presidents, either did not understand the political possibilities of radio or were reluctant to employ them during its early days. Some politicians viewed radio as potentially harmful and sought to mitigate its effects through editorial control. Radio broadcasts of the Democratic National Convention in 1924 were allowed by the Democratic party officials only if disorder was not aired.[7] In 1926, one member of Congress proclaimed in debate that radio "is going to be the most powerful political instrument of the future."[8] But other politicians did not share that view or, if shared, did not attempt to realize it. Presidents Coolidge and Hoover made radio broadcasts, but did not actively utilize the medium for fulfillment of policy objectives.

Radio also had a news function beginning with its early days. Environmental stations broadcast news programs as early as 1910. During the 1920s and 1930s, news became a more significant radio feature. Stations began to hire news staffs. In 1930, one Beverly Hills station carried a news staff of ten reporters. Broadcasters approached political happenings as newsworthy events and such broadcasts became dramatic firsts: the first broadcast of a national political convention (1924), a presidential inauguration (1925), a congressional session (1923), and a nationwide speech by a president of the United States broadcast coast to coast (1923).[9]

The creation of broadcast networks across the continent furthered news capability. Radio news was capable of covering national and international news without exclusive reliance on the print-oriented wire services. In fact, radio could provide audio coverage which enhanced the dramatic quality of the news. During the 1920s and 1930s, radio covered events such as national political conventions, presidential campaigns, the Bonus March on Washington in 1931, and the crash of the airship *Hindenburg* in 1937.

Radio news initially was hampered by ownership connections with newspapers which used radio only as a gimmick to attract newspaper buyers. Also, newspapers, which carried exclusive wire service contracts, waged a war against wire service use by radio news. However, the networks developed their own newsgathering capabilities causing the newspapers eventually to abandon their efforts.

EFFECTS OF BROADCASTING

The Print Media

The emergence of radio news broadcasting as a viable news medium would soon have a significant impact on newspapers. Some of the qualities possessed by broadcasting would affect newspapers' newsgathering and news dissemination functions.

The expanding reach of radio was a remarkable phenomenon. By 1930, daily newspaper circulation reached a figure of 40 million.[10] The same year there were an estimated 14 million radio receivers in use constituting 45 percent of all households. A decade later, newspaper circulation, though it had experienced a roller-coaster sales record during the Depression, was similar to 1930. But radio receivers more than tripled in number to an estimated 44 million sets representing 81 percent of all households.[11] By the advent of commercial television in the late 1940s, radios were found in 95 percent of all households.

Thanks to a proliferation of stations, the emergence of networks, and the increasing affordability of mass-produced radio receiving sets, radio had quickly entered the vast majority of American households. This occurred despite a severe economic depression.

Not only did radio possess tremendous reach, but the medium achieved a pervasiveness previously unknown among news media. According to a 1940s survey of radio use, the average radio listening time was nearly five hours per day.[12] Radio news did not account for the majority, or even a significant minority, of that time. According to a 1938 Federal Communications Commission (FCC) survey, one-sixth of radio's programming was devoted to news and public affairs programming. However, during a period of great interest in news, radio news was pervasive. The amount of news programming during the war years constituted up to 20 percent of network programming.[13]

The speed of transmission by radio also was a characteristic of great significance. Although this feature of radio was utilized only rarely in the 1930s, the wartime years of the 1940s demonstrated radio's capacity for rapid dissemination of news and information. During the 1938 Munich conference, NBC made 460 broadcasts in 18 days.

These characteristics of radio impinged on the long-held function of newspapers as carriers of late-breaking news. Newspaper publishers could not halt radio's growth, but they could alter their own approach to news in response. Newspapers began to concentrate less on late-breaking news and more on exhaustive descriptions and analysis of the news. Newspaper journalism was given still another reason, in addition to the complexity of the issues, for greater emphasis on interpretation.

Newspapers began to redesign layout to allow scanning of news more quickly. News was departmentalized and brief summaries were placed on the front page. Although the appearance of newsmagazines such as *Time* and *Newsweek* in the

1920s and 1930s also contributed, radio's rapid style of delivery forced newspapers to alter their own format.

The effects on newspapers were bolstered by the close relationship of radio and newspapers. By 1940, one-third of all radio stations were owned by or affiliated with a newspaper.[14]

Radio also quickly became a centralizing force as a news medium. The rapid formation of national networks and the predominance of network programs in programming schedules pitted the more decentralized newspapers against a rising national medium. Although both newspapers and radio began as local units, many local newspapers had become part of newspaper groups during the early 1900s. By the 1930s, about one-third of daily newspapers were owned by newspaper chains.[15]

Radio made that transition much more rapidly and completely. NBC network debuted in 1926; CBS formed one year later. By 1934, about one-third of all commercial radio stations were network affiliates. By the World War II years, more than 60 percent of stations were affiliated with the networks.[16] Moreover, radio effectually robbed local affiliates of the editorial function over news that local dailies possessed over wire service stories. Affiliates might refuse to carry network news, but the likely consequence would be loss of network affiliation and abandonment by listeners.

This centralizing tendency was a phenomenon affecting newspapers as well. Some chains formed at the turn of the century, such as Hearst, Scripps, Gannett, and Ridder, had mushroomed in size. In the 1930s, the Hearst chain included 26 dailies in 19 cities constituting alone more than 13 percent of daily circulation.[17] By 1933, the six largest chains controlled 81 dailies representing 26 percent of daily newspaper circulation.[18]

The rise of chains was linked to the consolidation of newspapers. Their number dropped precipitously between 1900 and 1930 with a net loss of nearly 300 newspapers. Also, the number of cities with only one daily newspaper doubled.[19]

The reasons for consolidation and chain acquisition included: economic pressures placed on smaller newspapers by technological advances in publishing, advertising preference for one large circulation newspaper rather than several dailies dividing local readership, and the economy of combining morning and evening papers. In addition, the lack of continued need for dailies representing various parties and factions, the increased standardization of the news product through shared journalistic and editorial attitudes and practices, and the attempt to appeal to general readership all fed consolidation.[20] Some of these causes had been affecting the newspaper industry gradually since the era of the penny press.

Effects on the Electoral Process

There is little evidence of the influence of radio broadcasting on the electoral process, particularly vote decisions. Voting studies in the 1940s indicated little media influence.[21]

Radio broadcasting did alter campaigns somewhat. The actual effects were far less than widely assumed. There was an effect on how politicians *viewed* the new medium. They originally envisioned radio dramatically recasting campaigns. Some observers predicted that radio would improve the quality of campaign speeches and even the quality of candidates. But the actual effects were far more limited. Parties and presidential candidates did use radio to convey their messages. In the 1924 presidential campaign, the Republican party even established its own radio station in New York and transmitted until election day.[22] That same year, Calvin Coolidge delivered an election-eve speech carried by 26 stations across the country. Partisan use of radio grew from election to election. In 1932, the two parties together bought more than 120 hours of network time. By 1936, it was up to 160 hours.

The costs of radio time began to worry politicians. In 1928, the combined cost for time for the two major political parties exceeded one million dollars. However, radio advertising still accounted for less than 20 percent of the Democratic party expenses and only ten percent of the Republicans. In 1932, NBC and CBS donated three time slots for political addresses. However, costs still rose. By 1944, the two parties spent $700,000 each for radio time.

Radio coverage of the national political conventions did provoke some changes in their operation. For example, in 1924, Democratic party leaders sought to avoid use of the name of the Ku Klux Klan during debate over an anti-Klan resolution.[23]

But neither the candidates nor the campaigns were dramatically changed by radio. Candidates continued to stump the country rather than rely on radio broadcasts. Improved transportation facilitated such cross-country campaigning. Political leaders did not appear to take the candidates's radio voice and personality into account when selecting presidential nominees.

Candidates did find radio a highly effective medium for reaching voters, if not influencing them. But the closed nature of the nomination process—selection of national convention delegates by party leaders and activists—shunted radio from that process. Radio was a more useful medium in the general election campaign.

The effects of radio broadcasting of political messages on voting were predicted to be quite powerful. The nature of the medium prompted fears of mass suasion by politicians, particularly demagogues. The success of Adolf Hitler in Germany was linked to his radio oratorical skills. In the United States, political speakers such as Father Charles Coughlin, who castigated the New Deal and supported the Union Party in 1936, and Huey Long, who proposed a populist "share-the-wealth" plan during the Depression, achieved widespread popularity. Coughlin's listeners were estimated to number up to 30 million.[24] But these fears were unrealized. The Union party garnered less than one million votes and Roosevelt and the New Deal continued to enjoy widespread public approval. Consistently in the 1930s and 1940s, the political party buying the most radio time lost the presidential election.

Effects on Political Institutions

The rise of broadcasting did not alter the internal functioning of the presidency, Congress, or the Supreme Court. However, the medium did impact on the external relations of the presidency and the Congress.

The Presidency. When radio became a national medium, presidents did not immediately perceive this new invention as a political tool. Calvin Coolidge spoke often on radio and in a 1920's poll was even voted the fourth most popular radio figure, even ahead of Will Rogers.[25] Herbert Hoover also delivered frequent radio addresses. Hoover spoke 95 times on radio during his four-year term, only nine times less than Franklin Roosevelt during his first term.[26] However, few of these early presidential radio broadcasts involved public policy. Most were general remarks to various groups such as the YMCA and the 4-H Club, and included the radio listeners more as eavesdroppers rather than part of the intended audience. Daniel Boorstin called them speeches along the lines of commencement addresses rather than direct attempts to influence public opinion.[27]

Remarkably, Hoover did not lack vision of the potential of radio, as indicated earlier. However, his own aloof and even frigid radio persona prevented more effective usage of the medium. Moreover, Hoover's views of more limited government involvement in American life did not propel the former engineer to employ the medium to fulfill major domestic policy objectives.

Conversely, Franklin Roosevelt exuded personal warmth and possessed a broad political agenda. Not surprisingly, Roosevelt was the first president to use radio effectively as a presidential tool.

At first glance, FDR did not appear to need radio to help affect public opinion. His election coattails in 1932 swept into Congress a large majority of his fellow party adherents. But voters were reacting more to the unpopular Republicans than providing a specific mandate for Democrats. Roosevelt needed to sell his New Deal both to Congress and the American public and seek their cooperation during its implementation. Since he perceived the newspapers as enemies, radio served as the most appropriate medium. Additionally, FDR was not unfamiliar with radio. While governor of New York, he had utilized radio to gain public support and bypass the Republican-dominated press.[28]

Roosevelt not only held the motive, but also the capability to wield radio as a medium for communication and persuasion. His exuberant personality conveyed personal warmth and sincerity through a voice well suited to the vehicle of radio.

An extra advantage was his knack at reducing complex social and economic problems to simple terms understandable by average citizens. One commentator of the time explained:

> His ability to create a feeling of intimacy between himself and his listeners, his skill placing emphasis on key words, his adroitness in presenting complicated matters in such simple terms that the man in the street believes he has a full mastery of them, have won him admiration from even his political enemies.[29]

FDR also understood radio speeches could not be written or delivered like speeches at rallies or other large assemblies. The radio speech must be geared to a listening, not a reading audience. Also, FDR viewed radio as an interpersonal medium and he employed it as such. He talked to the millions listening on radio as if he spoke to a small group of people. According to one administration official who watched Roosevelt deliver his radio addresses, "His face would smile and light up as though he were actually sitting on the front porch or in the parlor with them."[30]

Moreover, fireside chats, as they were termed, were scheduled infrequently to maintain their fresh appeal. In his dozen years as president, Roosevelt delivered only 28 such chats or an average of less than three per year.[31] Timing also was crucial. The fireside chats usually occurred between 9 and 11 p.m.—prime radio listening time—and lasted, on average, about one half hour.

Roosevelt's use of radio probably not only fostered public support for his domestic policy moves, but also changed the relationship of the average citizen to the office of president. The presidency no longer seemed a distant office. New ties with the White House and even national government were forged. One evidence of these new ties was presidential mail. While Hoover received several hundred letters a day, FDR received 5,000 to 8,000 letters daily with the deluge increasing after each fireside chat. Many of these letters sought help for personal problems, assuming both the president's sympathy and power.

Skillful use of radio provided the president with a forum for explaining administration policies, cultivating public support, and pressuring Congress to enact presidential priorities. This forum became more attractive due to the president's ability to frame the message as he wished. FDR's use of radio as a presidential tool not only impacted his own presidency, but also served as model for presidential use of broadcast media, radio and television, for his successors.

Congress. While Franklin Roosevelt was making use of the medium for altering public policy and the presidency, the Congress was conducting business as usual. Institutionally, the Congress functioned the same way after radio as it had before. The legislative process remained unchanged. Some members of Congress used radio as a forum for communication and persuasion locally. According to one study, approximately 40 percent of members used radio to broadcast messages to constituents. (That same usage would be true after the commercial development of mass television. During the 1950s, just under one-half of members regularly used television programs to reach constituents.)[32] Members also spoke on national network radio on policy issues. For example, between 1928 and 1940, members of Congress spoke more than 1,000 times on CBS network alone.[33]

But, individual members spoke for themselves, not Congress as a whole. In fact, the very number of members of Congress speaking diversified congressional response and illuminated the problem of congressional usage of radio. A wide variety of members speaking fragmented the congressional reply to presidential use. The Congress suffered a handicap vis-à-vis the president in effective usage of radio as a medium for the institution's external relations. This weakness aided the president in utilizing radio for linkages with the public.

Summary

The rise of broadcasting accelerated the press's struggle towards autonomy. Radio aided the financial stability of the media. Following the initial shake-out of low power radio stations, broadcast media became highly profitable. Additionally, the initial fear that radio would endanger newspapers by robbing them of audience and advertisers was not borne out. Although the newspaper industry did suffer losses of both to radio, the intrusion of radio primarily stimulated the media market as a whole. Advertisers utilized both radio and print, as did audiences. Radio supplemented rather than displaced newspapers. Developing unique functions for both— radio use as a source of spot news and newspaper reading for more detailed information—enhanced dual usage.

Declining intra-industry competition also strengthened both broadcast and print media. Less competition within each industry bolstered financial stability.

Mergers into newspaper groups and formation of national radio networks centralized the news function as it related to American national politics. Given the highly localized nature of the newspaper industry, the rise of broadcasting and the conglomeration of newspapers strengthened the press's capability to serve as a linking mechanism for national politics while concurrently retaining and even expanding press autonomy in decision making about editorial content.

Press autonomy was not threatened, but reinforced by the rise of broadcasting and conglomerates. Political system dependency, on the other hand, increased, at least in relation to the electoral system and the external relations of the Congress and the presidency. New technology, which had played a major role in the hastening of these historical patterns, was primitive, however, compared to the inventions of the next period.

TELEVISION, NEW JOURNALISM, AND POLITICAL CHANGE

Television and News

> When television has fulfilled its ultimate destiny, man's sense of physical limitation will be swept away and his boundaries of sight and hearing will be the limits of the earth itself. With this may come a new horizon, a new philosophy, a new sense of freedom, and greatest of all, perhaps, a finer and broader understanding between all the peoples of the world.[34]

That is how one early commentator saw the future effects of television on society. High hopes for television long preceded its actual commercial marketing. The technology for television had been in existence since the 1930s, but World War II and a post-war television station freeze to resolve technical problems temporarily halted television's commercial development.

However, continued technological advances enabled the new medium, when finally introduced to the national public in the 1950s, suddenly to acquire a large niche in American life. After the freeze, the number of VHF stations nearly tripled in four years. By 1960, nearly 500 stations operated throughout the country.[35] The number of television sets mushroomed. In 1950, less than four million households owned television sets. Four years later, 26 million did. By 1958, sets were in over 41 million homes or 83 percent of all households.[36]

Because the national networks were already established and possessed the technology and financial resources, television became a national medium even more rapidly than had radio. Local television stations were much more likely to affiliate with one of the major networks given the high costs of programming compared with radio. Until the mid-1960s, no more than ten percent of television stations remained unaffiliated.[37]

The News Function

Network television possessed a news component from the very beginning. However, television, unlike newspapers, was primarily an entertainment medium. News was a distinctly secondary function in terms of time allocation, financial resources, and profitability. During the 1950s, news and public affairs programming constituted less than ten percent of network programming. Prior to 1963, regular network news consisted of a 15-minute evening broadcast, and news departments received smaller budgets than entertainment divisions. Moreover, the news departments were not profitable. Advertisers were attracted to the programs by promises of visible reminders of their sponsorship, such as the Camel News Caravan sponsored by Camel cigarettes. The networks used news to satisfy Federal Communications Commission standards for public service and as a showcase of the network's social responsibility.

Early television news was not very sophisticated compared with today's programs. The news consisted of no more than a reporter reading from a script on camera with still slides in the background and, if all went well, a few stories on film.

By the early 1960s, national news gained greater attention in American life. Events such as the Civil Rights movement and the Cuban Missile Crisis dominated the news. The youthful president, John F. Kennedy, and his family also attracted the attention of the nation. Also, televised events such as the 1960 presidential candidate debates and Kennedy's live news conferences drew large audiences to television.

CBS and NBC decided to expand the network evening broadcasts to one half hour and allocate more resources to news. During the 1960s, the news departments also began to show a profit.

Network television news received its greatest boost during a national crisis— the assassination of John F. Kennedy. For several days, Americans gathered around their television sets to participate in the national mourning. Television news profes-

The Westinghouse Corporation not only sponsored broadcasts but financed a network of its own in the early days of television. This historic photo of CBS-Westinghouse coverage of the 1952 presidential election includes broadcast journalism superstars (l. to r.) Eric Sevareid, Edward R. Murrow, Walter Cronkite, and Lowell Thomas. The light-colored suits worn by Murrow and Cronkite suggest an early lack of "camera smarts"—or perhaps less emphasis on physical appearance. *Source:* © CBS.

sionals faced the greatest test to date of their ability to transmit news quickly, accurately, and professionally in a severe national crisis.[38]

Television News and Newspapers

The way television handled news was distinctive from print media. The emergence of television news, like radio news a generation earlier, was bound to have an impact on the print media. Television news brevity, rapidity, and transience all impacted on newspapers eventually. However, initially, television as the child of print journalism was more affected by print media than vice versa. Early television reporters such as David Brinkley, Walter Cronkite, Harry Reasoner, and John Cameron Swayze were drawn from print journalism.[39] Guidance on determination of news was sought from the print media. Until television news could determine its own identity separate from print journalism, it continued to maintain an inferior status vis-à-vis the daily newspapers.

Economics of the News Media

In the years following World War II, the news media business—both print and broadcast—solidified its strong financial position. Newspaper profits remained healthy, profits routinely exceeded those of Fortune 500 companies.[40] Network profits were highly attractive. In 1977, the news divisions of the three major networks earned over $400 million.[41] By the late 1980s, the annual budget of CBS News alone was over $300 million.[42]

One major cause of financial vitality as an industry was declining competition. The three major networks enjoyed a monopoly on national television due to the demise of the Dumont network in 1955 and the absence of any new competitors. Cable, which would later threaten network profits, was largely in the planning stages.

The survivors of newspaper attrition were those dailies associated with newspaper groups. Such groups were becoming larger and more pervasive. In 1960, the 25 biggest chains—such as Gannett, Thomson, Knight-Ridder, and Newhouse—controlled 38 percent of daily newspaper circulation. By 1976, they controlled 52 percent of circulation. In 1960, all group-owned newspapers constituted nearly half of U.S. daily circulation. By 1976, the figure was 71 percent; and in 1985, it was 77 percent.[43]

Another media industry financial development was cross-ownership of media. Ownership of various media—newspapers, broadcast stations, magazines, and book publishing—by conglomerates became common. According to its 1988 annual report, Gannett Corporation owned not only 89 daily newspapers and 35 non-daily newspapers (usually weeklies), but also 10 television stations (reaching a combined total of over 10 million households), 16 radio stations (with a listening population of approximately 44 million), a radio service delivered to 2,000 radio stations, and an outdoor advertising division with subsidiaries in 18 major markets. Although large, Gannett is not unusual in the diversity of its holdings. Another conglomerate is the Knight-Ridder Company, which owns 30 daily newspapers, a cable television company, and the *Journal of Commerce*. It is probably best known for its news syndicate, which serves more than 250 daily newspapers in the United States.

Conversely, broadcasting companies moved into the print media. For example, according to its 1989 annual report, Capital Cities/ABC owned not only ABC TV and Radio and 29 affiliated radio and television stations, but additionally 10 daily newspapers, 77 weeklies, and 80 specialized periodicals.

These developments were highly beneficial to the autonomy of the press. A solid financial position diminished the possibility that the industry would become dependent on others, particularly politicians. The trends of centralization discussed in the previous chapter had become more pronounced by this period and aided newsgathering capabilities, as well as the capability to encounter national politicians and political institutions as equals.

Changing Status of Journalism

Journalism as a profession was acquiring a new, more respectable status. Long perceived as a lower middle-class profession staffed largely by technicians, journalism by the 1960s began to be viewed quite differently.

Journalism began to be seen by many younger people as a tool for affecting policymakers and influencing events. The image of television news anchors personifying journalism likely contributed to enhanced journalistic status. A new generation of students was exposed to television journalism—watching reporters and anchors mingle with important political leaders and present at crucial events.

Enrollment at journalism schools increased. By the 1970s, over 200 journalism programs existed with over 36,000 majors.[44] Many students perceived journalism as an interesting career with high utility for society.[45]

As the perception of journalism changed, a new type of individual became attracted to the profession. Students from prestigious liberal arts schools began to gravitate to journalism as a worthy career option. Increasingly, college graduates generally populated newspaper and broadcast news reporter staffs. Journalism had acquired a professional status through the changing character of journalists.

However, one major consequence was the growing chasm between the socioeconomic and educational backgrounds of journalists versus average Americans. Journalists were significantly more likely than the general population, even among younger Americans, to be college graduates.[46] Journalists themselves became aware of the increasing gap between themselves and middle Americans. Many Washington reporters began to feel that they were out of touch with the rest of the nation, and most believed that was a serious problem.[47]

New Journalism

The consensus among journalists on the role of journalism forged in reaction to the excesses of yellow journalism began to unravel in the 1960s with the emergence of competing schools of thought. Terms such as "new journalism," "advocacy journalism," and "adversarial journalism" were used to identify approaches advocated by various groups of journalists. These terms engendered strong debate within the journalistic profession over the role of journalists in society particularly and American politics specifically.

The first new school of thought was the "new journalism," approach which appeared in the 1960s. New journalism rejected traditional journalism as stultifying and even dishonest. Advocates of new journalism argued that journalists could not exercise freedom of expression because they were locked into roles as conduits of official information. Traditional journalism also was dishonest because its neutral approach actually aided the authoritative source on which journalists relied for news. Traditional journalism did not provide the reader with the journalist's own observations and analysis which would serve to balance the official statement. Hence, traditional journalism did not print all the truth.

Jack Newfield, an advocate of new journalism, explained:

> The truth, and even the hard news, usually rests beneath the surface of any event or social conflict. Yet, reporters rarely question what they are told by any politician with a title.[48]

Critics of traditional journalism pointed to press treatment of accusations by Senator Joseph McCarthy in the 1950s, acceptance of politicians' statements about the Cold War, and pro-military editorial content as examples of press complaisance as a conduit for authoritative sources' political objectives.[49]

New journalists argued that members of the press could not remain objective in the face of moral evils in society:

> The goal of all journalists should be to come as close to the truth as possible. But the truth does not always reside exactly in the middle. Truth is not the square root of two balanced quotes. I don't believe I should be 'objective' about racism . . . or lead poisoning. . . . Certain facts are not morally neutral.[50]

According to new journalism, journalists must become more a part of the story they were telling. Journalists could participate through offering personal insight, critique, and analysis.[51]

Advocacy Journalism

Also related to this participatory approach was advocacy journalism—the practice of using news stories to support issue positions advocated by the journalist. Advocacy journalism was distinct from press opinion and commentary, which had always been present, because of its concentration on news rather than editorials.

Proponents of advocacy journalism concluded objectivity was impossible to achieve. Therefore, journalists should not even attempt to achieve it. They could not stand by as neutral observers and recorders of social and political events, but should use their journalistic tools in morally just causes.

Advocacy journalists approached their job from a world view varying from that shared by traditional journalists. Advocacy journalists perceived conflicting interests in society struggling to achieve their goals. However, the struggle was not being fought on level ground. Some interests—such as the poor, minorities, non-profit groups—lacked powerful spokesmen to express their viewpoints. The journalist must intervene on the side of those who lack such power and equalize the struggle. Traditional journalists saw the players on the field as already equal.

Critics of advocacy journalism charged this approach was contradictory even to the objectives of new journalism. Rather than achieving greater reporter autonomy, the effect would be greater association with and dependence on interest groups who would use journalists as conduits.

Also, critics argued, advocacy journalism failed in its task of providing the basic description of events—who, what, when, where, and why—in the rush to serve various interests. This approach also endangered the mass audience the press had won since the demise of the party press and had been steadily expanding throughout the years. Advocacy would refactionalize the press and diminish its credibility.

Advocacy journalism enjoyed wide appeal among journalists and did alter their approach to news.[52] However, it did not replace traditional journalism, probably due to the waning of fervor for social causes by the 1970s and the persuasive argument that the advocacy role diminishes the autonomy of the press from groups and individuals promoting various political causes.[53]

Adversarial Journalism

Another byproduct of the new journalism was a trend termed adversarial journalism. Adversarial journalism referred to the press's critical stance in relation to political leaders and institutions, particularly the presidency. The primary role of the adversarial press was to challenge the administration. The press was to act as the political opposition—not with responsibility for offering policy alternatives, but to question administration policies and actions.

Adversarial journalism was born of the anti-establishment attitude among many intellectuals during the 1960s and the credibility gap created by the use of lying by the government during peacetime. Events such as the U-2 incident, the Bay of Pigs invasion, the Vietnam War, and Watergate convinced many in the press that government officials were prone to lie to save themselves or the administration politically and that they would attempt to use the press to do so. Hence, press cooperation with administration officials was viewed as partnership with devious politicians and a deception of the general public.

Adversarial journalism earned a large following among journalists due to its consistency with the autonomy of the press.[54] Theoretically, an adversarial relationship reinforced that autonomy by placing the press in a hostile position vis-à-vis politicians and diminishing the likelihood of manipulation by politicians.[55]

However, the adversarial approach came under attack even within the journalistic profession. In 1982, Michael O'Neill, then president of the American Society of Newspaper Editors, criticized the trend:

> We should make peace with the government. We should not be its enemy. . . .
> We are supposed to be the observers, not the participants—not the permanent
> political opposition. . . . The adversarial culture is a disease attacking the nation's
> vital organs.[56]

Still another development related to adversarial journalism was the emphasis placed on investigative reporting. Investigative reporting as it related to politics rested on the assumption that politicians were hiding corrupt practices and the job of the press was to ferret out such behavior. The goal of reporters, as Tom Wicker once expressed it, was to "catch the scoundrel with his hand in the till."[57] The success of *Washington Post* reporters Bob Woodward and Carl Bernstein in uncovering the Watergate story sent shock waves through journalism.

Finding the exclusive story on political corruption or malfeasance became the objective of many journalists. Newspapers and television news departments created investigative reporting staffs and allocated significant resources for them. Public affairs programming such as "60 Minutes" on CBS and "20/20" on ABC became popular.

However, the news industry soon found investigative reporting was expensive, controversial, time-consuming, and often not very productive. The spate of legal suits following investigative reporting pieces made many publishers leery of future efforts. Reporters assigned to beats found investigative reporting impractical given the demands of deadlines and editors' preoccupation with daily events.

New Journalism and Press Autonomy

New journalism was not a sudden creation of underground journalists in the 1960s, but the product of increasing press autonomy with ancestors reaching back to the penny press of the 1830s and including the yellow press at the turn of the century and the interpretive reporting of the 1930s. New journalists were the most recent generation descended from a long line of journalists pressing for media autonomy.

Although advocacy journalism could be viewed as a return to the partisan press, the other aspects of new journalism corresponded with enhanced autonomy of the press.

The changing socio-economic and educational background of journalists had altered journalism and attitudes about politicians. The increasing complexity of events in the 1960s and 1970s lent weight to the argument that the audience must be informed about more than just facts and that the journalist must be interposed between the facts and the audience to offer necessary explanation and interpretation. Although this reasoning had also been used in the 1930s, journalists had relied heavily on non-journalists as columnists and commentators. By the 1960s and 1970s, journalists began to rely more on themselves for such roles. Higher socio-economic status and educational level may have contributed to the attitude among journalists that they could fulfill that role. Journalists saw themselves as social equals to their authoritative sources.

By the early 1980s, journalism and journalists had undergone major transformations most of which enhanced press autonomy. With the rise of television, a strong financial position, and the new journalism, the press possessed firmer control than ever before as gatekeepers of the media and greater desire and capability to scrutinize political activities independent of politicians.

POLITICAL DEVELOPMENTS

The Presidency in the Nuclear Age

World War II and the events following recast attention on the office of the president. From one of several world leaders, the president suddenly became premier world leader. The United States had become a superpower with the dawning of the nuclear age, and the president, as the nation's foreign policy representative and commander-in-chief, acquired a new, more complicated role in world affairs.

Due to the U.S. position as a superpower and the onset of the Cold War with the Soviet Union, the president held responsibility to make decisions impacting on most of the world.

With the break-up of the colonial powers and the emergence of the Third World, the ability of the United States to affect events diminished. Many of the new states declared neutrality in the bipolar conflict between superpowers. The United States' inability to attain military or political victory in the Vietnam War was symptomatic of this new development.

The expectations of the president in world affairs had risen to enormous levels, but the capabilities of the president had not. In fact, one could argue they had been reduced.

Complicating the president's dilemma was the resurgence of Congress in foreign-policy making, as well as national security policy. Until the Vietnam War, the president and Congress had usually forged a bipartisan foreign policy with the president in the leadership role. In the aftermath of Vietnam, that consensus unraveled and Congress sought a greater role in decision making concerning the United States' role abroad. A struggle over the direction of foreign policy has ensued.[58]

Given the complexity of the president's situation, incumbent presidents turned to the media as a tool for informing and persuading the American public and, indirectly, the Congress of the president's foreign policy objectives. Presidents Kennedy, Johnson, Nixon, Ford, and Carter attempted to employ the media, particularly television, to garner public support and forestall congressional opposition regarding the president's foreign policy decisions.

The President as Domestic Policy Leader

By the 1950s and 1960s, the president also was expected to offer domestic policy proposals and, generally, set the agenda for domestic policy. The familiar phrase—"the president proposes and the Congress disposes"—succinctly describes this relationship. The Kennedy, Johnson, Nixon, and Carter administrations opened their terms with major domestic policy proposals to Congress for consideration. The president's task was to convince the Congress that his initiatives should be enacted.

This description is too simplistic, however, and congressional scholar Randall Ripley has suggested there are at least three models of presidential-congressional relations in addition to the executive dominance model discussed above. Joint program initiation, congressional dominance, and stalemate are the other three models.[59]

However, the most dangerous for the president is stalemate, which fails to produce policies due to unwillingness to compromise. This situation was common during the 1950s to 1970s due to split partisan control of Congress and the presidency. From 1945 to 1981, differing parties controlled the Congress and the White House for 16 years.

Expectations of presidential performance rose, but the president's capabilities did not keep pace. Stalemate reflected more negatively on the president who was perceived as domestic policy leader than on the Congress.

In order to acquire more leverage with the Congress in achieving domestic policy objectives, presidents turned to the media to mobilize support.

Presidential Selection

The mode of selecting presidents underwent a major transformation during the 1960s and 1970s which impacted on American national politics and the role of the press.

The nomination process experienced the most radical change. The two major parties adopted major reforms designed to democratize the selection process after the 1968 Democratic National Convention which selected a nominee, Hubert Humphrey, who had not competed in the primaries. Charges of political boss control led to national party commissions recommending broader participation in the nomination process.

The main vehicle of change was the presidential primary. Though primaries existed prior to the party reforms, most delegates to the national conventions were selected in party caucuses or by party leaders. Winning the primaries was used as a gauge of popularity, but was not the means for acquiring delegates to the nominating convention. Following the reforms, in 1972 two-thirds of the delegates to the Democratic national convention were selected by primaries. By 1980, 71 percent were chosen in primaries.[60] Although Democrats have tinkered with their system continually since that time, the candidate's dependence on primary victories to gain the nomination has remained constant.[61]

In addition to the changes in delegate selection, the parties were affected by reforms in campaign finance. In the wake of Watergate, Congress enacted new campaign financing laws designed to limit the amount of money candidates could raise and spend, including financial support from the party. Matching funds during the primary season and total public financing during the general election further reduced the role of the party in campaign finance.[62]

The role of party leaders was clearly diminished by these changes. Scholars also argued they weakened the presidency's ability to govern by delinking presidential candidates from the party support needed once in office.[63]

Changes in the presidential selection process caused by the weakening of political party role provided a more salient role for the news media in the process, particularly at the nomination stage. This role will be discussed in Chapter 15.

The Electorate

Not only were the institutions and processes experiencing change, but the electorate was not remaining static. A significant difference between voters of the 1940s and those of the 1970s was in their adherence to a political party. By the end of the 1970s, the number of independents had risen to one-third of the electorate. Voters were shaking off political party affiliation in favor of a more detached stance from either of the major political parties. This development meant candidates had to appeal to voters less on the basis of political party. Even those voters who still identified with parties were less devoted to their affiliation.

The voters also were more likely to split their tickets between parties. This tendency helped create the split party control of national government.[64]

Without the guide of party identification as a cue for assessing the candidates and the campaign, voters sought the assistance of other vehicles. The extent of usage of the media and media effect on the vote decision will be discussed more extensively in Chapter 14.

The voters also became more cynical and discontent with governmental leaders. Public distrust of politicians and feelings of political inefficacy rose during the 1970s.[65] Although scholars have differed over the nature and causes of discontent, a series of policy crises—Vietnam, Watergate, energy, inflation—at least did not ameliorate this sense of failure on the part of politicians, if not the political system as a whole.

Some scholars have suggested the news media portrayal of national politics has contributed to public discontent. The role of the media in cultivating public attitudes of cynicism will be discussed further in Chapter 14.

COMMUNICATIONS REVOLUTION

The past two decades have witnessed a communications revolution in the United States and in the world. This communications revolution has had consequences for the role of the mass media in American politics.

New Technologies

The cause of this communications revolution is the introduction of new technologies which have significantly altered the mass media, particularly the broadcast media. Several new technologies or variations of existing technology have emerged and/or been implemented in the past 20 years. We will discuss the emergence of cable, satellite, and low power television, as well as their effect on the role of the news media in American politics.

Cable. The most dramatic of these new technologies has been the introduction of cable. Cable operates through a network of underground wires. Individual households can be linked to a central point transmitting program signals from satellite services or locally originated broadcasts. Because each wire can hold several signals simultaneously, cable theoretically can offer an infinite number of signals since the cable size can be expanded to accommodate as many wires as needed. The spectrum for over-the-air broadcast frequencies on the other hand is limited, resulting in only a handful of television stations possible in any geographical area.

Although initiated in the late 1940s as a response to a limitation by the Federal Communications Commission on licensing of new stations, cable mushroomed in the 1970s and 1980s with the deregulation of the industry. Originally, cable systems relied on microwave transmissions from over-the-air broadcast stations. But the growth of satellite communications and the start-up of various satellite services signalled even greater diversity of programming through specialized offerings.

Cable offers consumers a wider range of program options than ever possible before. Initially providing up to 12 channels, cable systems usually now offer 30 to 50 channels and are potentially capable of carrying up to 100 program alternatives.

Mass audience usage of cable has been inhibited by the fact that households must actually be connected to a cable strung from a central clearinghouse. Only since 1987 have more than 50 percent of U.S. homes had access to cable. But cable has become a popular option. Nearly 50 million households or two-thirds of those accessible subscribe to a cable service, and the number is growing annually. It is estimated that by 1995 cable will have nearly 60 million subscribers.[66] By contrast, in 1960, 650,000 homes or 1.4 percent of U.S. households had cable.[67]

Cable viewing also has been increasing. Between 1987 and 1988 alone, audience viewing of cable programming increased 33 percent. Cable programs, superstations such as WTBS (Atlanta) and WGN (Chicago), and pay services such as HBO and Disney Channel combined accounted for more than one-third of prime-time audience viewing. In 1980, such programs constituted only 12 percent of prime-time audience viewing.[68]

Although some media observers have speculated that the spread of cable signals the demise of the print media, newspapers and newsmagazines have reacted to cable the same way that they did towards early radio and television; they have bought into the new medium. News media organizations with substantial cable investments include, for example, Time-Life Company, the New York Times Company (publisher of the *New York Times*). Times-Mirror (publisher of the *Los Angeles Times*), and Newhouse Corporation.

One characteristic of cable not shared by other mass media is its interactive capability. The mass media traditionally have been unidirectional. The mass media transmit and the audience receives, but no inherent feedback mechanism existed.

Although perfectly sane people may talk to their television sets on occasion, that talk is not fed back to the source of transmission.

Cable, however, does have an interactive capability. Several experiments in interactive cable have been conducted in cable-connected cities; the best known and the prototype has been the QUBE system developed by Warner-Amex Corporation in Columbus, Ohio. The system can be used for such actions as selecting entertainment services, transacting personal financial affairs, and shopping at home.[69]

Satellite. An ideal companion for the growth of cable has been the use of commercial satellites for transmitting television programming. Communication satellites orbiting in space operate by receiving signals from transmitters called uplinks, amplifying the transmission, and beaming it back to receivers known as downlinks, "earth stations," or "dishes," within the range of transmission.

Through satellite, news and entertainment programming originating from one location can be received simultaneously by earth stations all over the country.

Satellites are equipped with transponders or channels which allow up to 54 programming options from as many different locations to be received and then beamed back to earth stations. Also, earth stations can receive transmissions from more than one satellite simultaneously.

Satellites have been used by cable systems for programming options since HBO became the first satellite programming service in 1975. Superstation WTBS in Atlanta joined HBO by offering its signal via satellite one year later. WTBS was the first of several superstations to use satellite. A large number of satellite programming services now compete, which has greatly expanded the offering of local cable systems beyond local over-the-air stations and superstations.

Low Power Television (LPTV). Another facet of the communication explosion has been the development of low power television stations—stations to which a reduced amount of broadcast power is allowed. Low power television with wattage power only for about a 20-mile radius is designed to serve small cities, suburban areas, and even inner city neighborhoods. With low construction costs, estimated at less than $250,000 versus several million for full-power stations, the LPTV station was seen as an ideal medium for serving highly specialized audiences which are ignored by the large market full-power stations. It is not a new technology, rather it is a novel variation of existing television broadcasting since it reduces rather than enlarges broadcast power. However, it is a fast growing one.

In the late 1970s, cable was growing at a slower rate than expected while satellite services were expanding rapidly. In order to tap the potential of satellite, the FCC authorized the development of low power television stations, which were likely to use these services for programming, and encouraged applications for licensing.

However, several barriers temporarily halted the development of LPTV. The FCC had not resolved what directions LPTV should take. Initially, the FCC hoped the new stations would offer a local-access channel in areas without cable. However, the scope of the stations was soon altered to encourage interconnection of markets with no limitations on programming sources. Without limits on programming, it was feared LPTV stations could become subscription pay TV outlets. This innovation also incurred the wrath of existing broadcasters, who feared competition from LPTV stations. They brought pressure to bear on the FCC to restrict severely LPTV development.

During the mid-1980s, however, the FCC restarted LPTV development. The FCC now issues licenses at the rate of 250 per month. Currently over 600 low power television stations have been licensed and construction permits have been granted for 1700 more.[70]

Effects on Broadcast Industry

The existing media conglomerates have attempted to stop the growth of competition by investing in the new technologies. Conglomerates such as Newhouse, Time, Inc., Times-Mirror, and Storer Broadcasting have become major owners of cable systems. The second largest cable company in the United States with 4 million basic customers in 32 states is owned by Time, Inc. Time also owns HBO which, according to Time, Inc.'s 1988 annual report, has 17 million subscribers nationwide. According to Times-Mirror's 1987 annual report, it owns cable subsidiaries with a combined total of almost a million basic subscribers. Storer Broadcasting owns nearly 1,500 cable systems nationwide. Newhouse has over a thousand.

The expansion of cable has merely extended the monopolization of media. Four cable firms hold 30 percent of the market and gain 77 percent of the advertising and programming revenue.[71] Many of the applications for LPTV stations have been submitted by existing media conglomerates.

However, even these efforts have not stopped the fragmentation of the broadcast industry with new networks such as the Fox Network and the satellite networks emerging. As mentioned earlier, the audience share for independent and superstations and cable programs has grown at the expense of the three major networks. The networks, faced with declining advertising revenues, have instituted cutbacks. These cutbacks have affected the news divisions since their audiences have dropped dramatically. Network news divisions, financially well-to-do during the 1970s and early 1980s, are no longer prosperous. NBC News, lost as much as 90 million annually during the late 1980s and dismissed over 100 news division employees.[72]

The fragmentation is not limited to greater competition, but also to the specialization of programming content. One distinguishing feature of these new satellite networks is their specialization. In the highly competitive environment that broadcast television has become since the introduction of satellite and cable transmission, the audience share for the new specialized networks separately is small and distinguishable from others.

The fragmentation of audience has occurred along various cleavages. Networks such as Black Entertainment Television (BET), which provides African-American entertainment and Galavision, Univision, and Telemundo, Hispanic networks, serve specific racial or ethnic audiences. The Christian religious audience is served by networks such as the Christian Broadcasting Network (CBN), the Inspirational Network, and Eternal Word TV. The latter two can be seen in 10 million homes, while CBN is available in 41 million households.[73] Music buffs can choose from among the Nashville Network, Music Television Videos (MTV), or VH-1 and VH-2. Business related offerings include Dow Jones Cable News and the Financial News Network. All-news and public affairs programming is available on other networks such as Cable News Network (CNN) and C-SPAN, which offers complete coverage of congressional floor proceedings, as well as interviews, news conferences, speeches, and seminars.

In news in particular, these new technologies have enhanced the surveillance capability of the press. Satellites allow for almost immediate transmission of news from bureaus, as well as live transmissions from remote areas.

However, satellite transmission also has reduced the dominance of the major networks over broadcasting national news. Entire news networks such as CNN, and

One of the most dramatic success stories of the 1980s in broadcast journalism was the Cable News Network (CNN) founded by Ted Turner in 1980. Despite slow growth in the early years, CNN now plays with the "big boys." It filed suit to be included in pool coverage of major political and government events—a status formerly awarded only to the three major networks—and its CNN International now broadcasts by satellite to 54 countries, including more than 25,000 European hotel rooms. The CNN World Report also broadcasts unedited, uncensored segments from news broadcasts in other countries, and CNN provided the only live coverage of the explosion of the shuttle *Challenger*. *Source:* Joseph R. Dominick, *The Dynamics of Mass Communication*, 3d ed., New York: McGraw-Hill, 1990, p. 57. Reproduced by permission.

separate news programs such as Independent Network News, USA Today, and Monitor have emerged on cable with the capability of reaching local television stations throughout the country. CNN, for example, is carried by 8,000 cable systems and can be viewed in 46 million households.[74]

Satellite particularly has strengthened local network affiliates since now they can bypass the networks in favor of alternative programming through satellite transmission. Local stations also can rent transponder time in order to broadcast from anywhere in the country; rather than depending on network reporters they can actually send their own to cover national events from a local perspective. Larger local broadcast stations use satellite to cover national news, such as a presidential campaign or a national party convention.

Political Consequences

These new technologies have real or potential consequences not only for the broadcasting industry but also for the political system. One highly significant consequence results from the increasing fragmentation of the broadcasting system. Arguments for government regulation of the broadcast industry have traditionally been based on the limited number of available broadcast frequencies. With the proliferation of cable, satellite, and low power television, almost unlimited broadcasting ''space'' has opened up, and the argument for regulation has been weakened. Deregulation has even spurred the fragmentation, which in turn has sparked calls for further deregulation. The eventual result is diminished governmental control over broadcasting.

Another political consequence is the potential fragmentation of the body politic. One study found two-thirds of Hispanic Americans said they watched Spanish-language television daily. On average, they watched for two-and-a-half hours per day. These networks also have their own news programs. Telemundo and Univision both have evening news programs. It has been estimated Univision's evening news program reaches four million U.S. Hispanics. Univision also has an early morning and a late night news program.[75]

With the increasing availability of broadcast channels which appeal primarily to specialized audiences, will subcultures be encouraged to flourish and to foster separate political cultures? What is the political impact of greater fragmentation of the American electorate—a fragmentation which is enhanced by the fragmentation of the broadcast audience, including the news audience?

There is also debate over whether the new technologies will produce the evolution of direct democracy. It is conceivable that future voting could occur in the privacy of the home with the touch of a button. Just as members of Congress vote with electronic cards (although they must be present in the chamber to do so), voters at home could use similar cards to participate in elections at all levels.

Short of actual voting, the interactive capabilities of new technologies can potentially facilitate communication of public views on policy proposals, pending legislation, and executive decisions. The general public could register an immediate response to governmental action or even any proposed action. This response also could be made without a single interactive technology if two existing technologies—television and touchtone telephone—were combined.[76]

The use of interactive cable has been encouraged by some scholars as a means to make democracy work better—a kind of electronic complaint box.[77] Assessing public reaction would be easier and less expensive through interactive cable.

But fears also have been expressed that the availability and use of such technology would pose serious problems for American politics.[78] The immediate interactive capability might make possible a direct democracy, where citizens would make decisions and strongly influence policy-making. The filter of representatives acting in a slower, more deliberate manner might be lost.

One scholar dismisses such concerns as unrealistic:

> One science-fiction fantasy has the public engaged in a national town meeting on cable TV with various issues being debated and then decided by a push-button vote. War could be declared on Monday, cancelled on Tuesday, and declared again on Wednesday. . . .[79]

The lack of realism lies in the suspicion that new technology inevitably will replace established institutions and processes. Rather, experience suggests that, instead, new technologies will simply augment those processes already in place. The new technology may well facilitate greater understanding of issues, but mediating institutions would still be necessary to avoid an overload of issue concentration and to offer a ''cooling off'' period between public response to issues and events and public policy.[80]

POLITICAL SYSTEM DEPENDENCY AND PRESS AUTONOMY

This historical sketch has detailed the growing autonomy of the press and the concomitant political system dependency on the press. As the press became more capable of functioning as an independent force in American politics, components of the political system—the presidency, Congress, and the electoral process—have become increasingly dependent on the press to perform functions previously carried out by political actors such as political parties. Other linking mechanisms of the past such as the political party were failing as channel for public opinion and political leaders, shaper of the public agenda, and gatekeeper of the nomination process. New roles for the presidency in relation to Congress and the public deepened that institution's reliance on the press.

As the nation begins its third century, the political system is highly dependent on a more and more autonomous press for its basic functioning. The succeeding chapters discuss the effects of this trend on press role in American politics currently.

NOTES

1. Edward W. Chester, *Radio, Television and American Politics,* New York: Sheed and Ward, 1969, pp. 18–19.
2. Helen Fessenden, *Fessenden,* New York: Coward-McCann, 1940, p. 153. Quoted in Eric Barnouw, *A Tower in Babel,* New York: Oxford University Press, 1966, p. 20.
3. Barnouw, *A Tower in Babel,* p. 105.
4. See Edwin Emery and Michael Emery, *The Press and America.* Englewood Cliffs, N.J.: Prentice-Hall, 1984, pp. 372–378; and Christopher Sterling and John M. Kittross, *Stay Tuned,* Belmont, Calif.: Wadsworth, 1978, pp. 79–81.
5. Eric Barnouw, *The Golden Web,* New York: Oxford University Press, 1968, p. 28.
6. "Proceedings of the Fourth National Radio Conference November 9–11, 1925," in John Kittross, ed., *Documents in American Telecommunication Policy,* New York: Arno Press, 1977.
7. Barnouw, *A Tower in Babel,* p. 150.
8. Carl Friedrich and Evelyn Sternberg, "Congress and the Control of Radiobroadcasting," *American Political Science Review* 37 (October 1943):747–818.
9. Chester, *Radio, Television, and American Politics,* pp. 16, 23; and Barnouw, *A Tower in Babel,* pp. 146–148.
10. Alfred M. Lee, *The Daily Newspaper in America,* New York: Macmillan, 1937, p. 727.
11. Frank Luther Mott, *American Journalism, A History: 1690–1960,* New York: Macmillan, 1962, pp. 679, 784; Sterling and Kittross, *Stay Tuned,* p. 533.
12. Columbia University Bureau of Applied Social Research, *The People Look at Radio,* Chapel Hill, N.C.: University of North Carolina Press, 1946, p. 96.
13. Sterling and Kittross, *Stay Tuned,* pp. 175–176.
14. Mott, *American Journalism,* p. 680; Sterling and Kittross, *Stay Tuned,* p. 191.
15. Mott, *American Journalism,* p. 648.
16. Sterling and Kittross, *Stay Tuned,* p. 512.
17. Emery and Emery, *Press and America,* pp. 427–430.
18. Lee, *Daily Newspaper in America,* pp. 215–216.
19. Emery and Emery, *Press and America,* pp. 398–404.
20. Mott, *American Journalism,* pp. 635–636; Emery and Emery, *Press and America,* p. 399.
21. See Paul Lazarsfeld, Bernard Berelson, and Hazel Gaudet, *The People's Choice,* New York: Columbia University Press, 1968; and Bernard Berelson, Paul Lazarsfeld, and William McPhee, *Voting,* Chicago: University of Chicago Press, 1954.
22. Chester, *Radio, Television, and American Politics,* pp. 18–19.
23. Robert K. Murray, *The Longest Ballot: Democrats and the Disaster in Madison Square Garden,* New York: Harper & Row, 1976, pp. 160–161.
24. Emery and Emery, *Press and America,* p. 449.
25. Chester, *Radio, Television, and American Politics,* p. 16.
26. Chester, *Radio, Television, and American Politics,* p. 97.
27. Daniel Boorstin, *Hidden History: Exploring Our Secret Past,* New York: Harper & Row, 1987, p. 141.
28. James MacGregor Burns, *Roosevelt: The Lion and the Fox,* New York: Harcourt Brace Jovanovich, 1956, p. 118.

29. Quoted in Chester, *Radio, Television, and American Politics*, p. 31.

30. Quoted in Burns, *Lion and the Fox*, p. 205. See also Barnouw, *Golden Web*, pp. 7–8.

31. Chester, *Radio, Television, and American Politics* pp. 32–33.

32. Dorothy Hartt Cronheim, "Congressmen and Their Communication Practices," doctoral dissertation, Ohio State University, 1957, p. 112. Cited in Timothy E. Cook, *Making Laws and Making News*, Washington: Brookings, 1989, p. 25.

33. Chester, *Radio, Television, and American Politics*, p. 62.

34. Quoted in Joseph H. Udelson, *The Great Television Race*, Tuscaloosa, Ala.: University of Alabama Press, 1982, p. 47.

35. Sterling and Kittross, *Stay Tuned*, p. 515.

36. Sterling and Kittross, *Stay Tuned*, p. 535.

37. Sterling and Kittross, *Stay Tuned*, p. 515.

38. See Bradley S. Greenberg and Edwin B. Parker, *The Kennedy Assassination and the American Public: Social Communication in Crisis*, Palo Alto, Calif.: Stanford University Press, 1965.

39. Barbara Matusow, *The Evening Stars: The Making of the Network News Anchor*, Boston: Houghton Mifflin, 1983.

40. Ernest C. Hynds, *American Newspapers in the 1980s*, New York: Hastings House, 1980, pp. 136–137.

41. A. Frank Reel, *The Networks*, New York: Scribners, 1979, pp. 61–62.

42. "CBS News to Debut A.M. Makeover and Prime Contender," *Broadcasting*, October 26, 1987, p. 102.

43. Ben Bagdikian "Newspaper Mergers—The Final Phase," *Columbia Journalism Review* (March/April 1977):17–22; and *Columbia Journalism Review* (November/December 1986): 47.

44. David H. Weaver and G. Cleveland Wilhoit, *The American Journalist*, Bloomington, Ind.: Indiana University Press, 1986, pp. 43–44.

45. Thomas A. Bowers, "Student Attitudes toward Journalism as a Major and a Career," *Journalism Quarterly* 51 (Summer 1974), p. 267.

46. Weaver and Wilhoit, *American Journalist*, pp. 46–48; Herbert Gans, *Deciding What's News*, New York: Pantheon, 1979.

47. Stephen Hess, *The Washington Reporters*, Washington: Brookings, 1981, p. 12.

48. Jack Newfield, "Journalism, Old, New, and Corporate," in Ronald Weber, ed., *The Reporter as Artist: A Look at the New Journalism Controversy*, New York: Hastings House, 1974, p. 59.

49. See James Aronson, *The Press and the Cold War*, Indianapolis, Ind.: Bobbs-Merrill, 1970; J. Fred MacDonald, *Television and the Red Menace: The Video Road to Vietnam*, New York: Praeger, 1985; and Michael J. Parenti, *Inventing Reality*, New York: St. Martin's Press, 1986.

50. Newfield, "Is There a New Journalism?" in Weber, ed., *The Reporter as Artist*, p. 304.

51. For a compilation of views on new journalism, see Weber, *The Reporter as Artist;* Michael L. Johnson, *The New Journalism*, Lawrence, Kans.: University of Kansas Press, 1971; and Paul H. Weaver, "The New Journalism and the Old—Thoughts after Watergate," *The Public Interest* (Spring 1974): 67–88.

52. A comprehensive survey of journalists in 1971 found 30 percent supported advocacy journalism. Another 35 percent favored journalistic neutrality. The remainder sought some middle ground between the two approaches. See John Johnstone, Edward J.

Slawski, and William Bowman, *The Newspeople,* Urbana, Ill.: University of Illinois Press, 1976.

53. A cogent analysis of advocacy journalism can be found in Morris Janowitz, "Professional Models in Journalism: The Gatekeeper and the Advocate," *Journalism Quarterly* 52 (Winter 1975): 618–625. For a sample of sympathetic views, see Edie Goldenberg, *Making the Papers,* Lexington, Mass: D.C. Heath, 1975; and Gaye Tuchman, "Objectivity as a Strategic Ritual: An Examination of Newsmen's Notions of Objectivity," *American Journal of Sociology* 77 (January 1972): 660–679. A more critical perspective is offered in Weaver, "The New Journalism and the Old," pp. 67–88.

54. For a defense of adversarial journalism, see Peter Stoler, *The War against the Press: Politics, Pressure, and Intimidation in the 80s,* New York: Dodd, Mead, 1986. For a scholarly discussion of the theory, see William Rivers, *The Adversaries,* Boston: Beacon Press, 1970. A critique is found in Michael B. Grossman and Francis E. Rourke, "The Media and the Presidency: An Exchange Analysis," *Political Science Quarterly* 91 (1976): 455–470.

55. See Jay G. Blumler and Michael Gurevitch, "Politicians and the Press: An Essay of Role Relationships" in Dan Nimmo and Keith R. Sanders, eds., *Handbook of Political Communication,* Beverly Hills, Calif.: Sage, 1981, pp. 467–493.

56. Quoted in James Boylan, "Declarations of Independence," *Columbia Journalism Review* (November/December 1986): 44.

57. Tom Wicker, *On Press,* New York: Viking Press, 1978, p. 185.

58. For more discussion of this topic, see Arthur M. Schlesinger, Jr., "Congress and the Making of Foreign Policy," in Thomas E. Cronin and Rexford G. Tugwell, *The Presidency Reappraised,* 2d ed., New York: Praeger, 1977, pp. 201–227; and Louis Fisher, *The Politics of Shared Power,* 2d ed., Washington: CQ Press, 1987, pp. 105–111.

59. Randall Ripley, *Congress: Process and Policy,* 3d ed., New York: Norton, 1983, pp. 28–31.

60. Stephen Hess, *The Presidential Campaign,* Washington: Brookings, 1988.

61. For a discussion of the national party reforms during the 1960s and 1970s, see Austin Ranney, *Curing the Mischiefs of Faction: Party Reform in America,* Berkeley, Calif.: University of California Press, 1975; Byron E. Shafer, *Quiet Revolution,* New York: Russell Sage Foundation, 1983; and James W. Ceaser, *Presidential Selection,* Princeton, N.J.: Princeton University Press, 1979.

62. For more on campaign reform, see Michael Malbin, ed., *Parties, Interest Groups, and Campaign Finance Laws,* Washington: American Enterprise Institute, 1980; Michael Malbin, ed., *Money and Politics in the U.S.,* Washington: American Enterprise Institute, 1984; and Frank J. Sorauf, *Money in American Elections,* Glenview, Ill.: Scott, Foresman, 1988.

63. For a critique of the effects of reforms, see Nelson W. Polsby, *Consequences of Party Reform,* New York: Oxford University Press, 1983; and David E. Price, *Bringing Back the Parties,* Washington: CQ Press, 1984.

64. For a sample of work on these trends in the 1960s and 1970s, see Everett Carll Ladd, *Where Have All the Voters Gone?,* 2d ed., New York: Norton, 1982; Norman H. Nie, Sidney Verba, and John R. Petrocik, *The Changing American Voter,* Cambridge, Mass.: Harvard University Press, 1979; and Walter DeVries and V. Lance Tarrance, *The Ticket-Splitter,* Grand Rapids, Mich.: Eerdmans Publishing, 1972.

65. For a sample of this literature, see Joel D. Aberbach and Jack L. Walker, "Political

Trust and Racial Ideology,'' *American Political Science Review* 64 (December 1970): 1199–1219; Arthur H. Miller, ''Political Issues and Trust in Government: 1964–1970,'' *American Political Science Review* 68 (September 1974): 951–972; and Seymour Martin Lipset and William Schneider, ''The Decline of Confidence in American Institutions,'' *Political Science Quarterly* 98 (Fall 1983): 379–402.

66. U.S. Bureau of the Census, *Statistical Abstract of the United States 1989*, Washington: Government Printing Office, 1988, p. 548.

67. Christopher H. Sterling and Timothy R. Haight, *The Mass Media: Aspen Guide to Communication Industry Trends*, New York: Praeger, 1978, p. 56.

68. Jeremy Gerard, ''Even with 'Remembrance,' a Ratings Month to Forget,'' *New York Times*, December 5, 1988; and Watson James, *Transition in Television*, Chicago: Crain Books, 1983, p. 1–3.

69. For an extensive discussion of the future of cable in the United States and elsewhere, see Ralph M. Negrine, ed., *Cable Television and the Future of Broadcasting*, New York: St. Martin's Press, 1985.

70. For a discussion of LPTV, see Don Le Duc, *Beyond Broadcasting*, White Plains, N.Y.: Longman, 1987, pp. 100–102; and Patricia Watkins, ''Refranchising and Low Power Television,'' in Jean Rice, ed., *Cable TV Renewals and Refranchising*, Washington, D.C.: Communications Press, 1983. For current figures on LPTV, see the latest issue of *Broadcasting* magazine.

71. ''Concentrating on Concentration,'' *Broadcasting*, June 5, 1989, pp. 46–52.

72. See Peter J. Boyer, ''NBC News Still Has Money Worries,'' *New York Times*, April 12, 1988, p. C19; and Peter J. Boyer, ''NBC News Dismisses 110 Employees,'' *New York Times*, September 12, 1988, p. C19.

73. *Broadcasting*, August 22, 1988.

74. *Broadcasting*, August 22, 1988.

75. See Ana Veciana-Suarez, *Hispanic Media USA: A Narrative Guide to Print and Electronic Media in the United States*, Washington: The Media Institute, 1987.

76. Frederick Williams, *The Communications Revolution*, Beverly Hills, Calif.: Sage, 1982, p. 193.

77. Ithiel de Sola Pool, ed., *Talking Back*, Cambridge, Mass.: MIT Press, 1973, pp. 237–246.

78. Edward V. Dolan, *TV or CATV? A Struggle for Power*, Port Washington, N.Y.: National University Publications Associated Faculty Press, Inc., 1984, pp. 69–70; Vernone Sparkes, ''Cable Television in the United States,'' in Ralph M. Negrine, *Cable Television and the Future of Broadcasting*, New York: St. Martin's Press, 1985, pp. 41–42.

79. Pool, *Talking Back*, p. 237.

80. Pool, *Talking Back*, p. 244.

SUGGESTED READINGS

Dolan, Edward V. *TV or CATV? A Struggle for Power*. National University Publications. Port Washington, N.Y.: Associated Faculty Press, Inc., 1984.

James, Watson. *Transition in Television*. Chicago: Crain Books, 1983.

Johnson, Michael L. *The New Journalism*. Lawrence, Kans.: University of Kansas Press, 1971.

MacDonald, J. Fred. *Television and the Red Menace: The Video Road to Vietnam*. New York: Praeger, 1985.

Nie, Norman H., Sidney Verba, and John R. Petrocik. *The Changing American Voter*. Cambridge, Mass.: Harvard University Press, 1979.

Polsby, Nelson W. *Consequences of Party Reform*. New York: Oxford University Press, 1983.

Shafer, Byron E. *The Quiet Revolution*. New York: Russell Sage, 1983.

Sterling, Christopher H., and John M. Kittross. *Stay Tuned*. Belmont, Calif.: Wadsworth, 1978.

Stoler, Peter. *The War Against the Press: Politics, Pressure, and Intimidation in the 80s*. New York: Dodd, Mead, 1986.

Udelson, Joseph H. *The Great Television Race*. Tuscaloosa, Ala.: University of Alabama Press, 1982.

Weaver, David H., and G. Cleveland Wilhoit. *The American Journalist*. Bloomington, Ind.: Indiana University Press, 1986.

CHAPTER 6

Regulating the Press

"Congress shall make no law . . . abridging the freedom of the press."
The First Amendment

PRESS FREEDOM AND DEMOCRACY

Despite the wording of the First Amendment, government has regulated the mass media since the invention of the printing press. Regulations on the press are the formal means whereby governments circumscribe the role of the press in society. No country allows complete freedom of the press. As will be discussed in the next chapter, in fact, many politicians view the press as an ideological tool. Accordingly, as policymakers they strictly mandate press activity.

In the United States, since the framing of the Constitution, freedom for the press to function has traditionally been perceived as facilitating the effective functioning of a democratic society. As John Adams wrote in the Massachusetts Constitution: "The liberty of the press is essential to the security of the state."

As a result, regulation of the press has been shaped by the belief that a free press is essential to a democracy. Restrictions on the press which hamper the press's functioning are believed also to hamper the functioning of the democratic system itself.

The Framers of the Constitution did not include a provision securing freedom of the press in the document as adopted by the Constitutional Convention, not because of opposition to such a freedom, but because the Framers saw it as unnecessary. In their view, the enumerated powers of the central government did not include power to violate such rights as freedom of the press or to override guarantees of a free press already stated in many of the state constitutions.

But others successfully argued that freedom of the press, along with other specific rights, needed to be protected in the federal Constitution since some states did not guarantee them. The proscription on Congress's power over freedom of the press was included in the first amendment to the Constitution.

Regulation of the press was approached cautiously. The Framers did not seek to reimpose licensing of the press, for example, which had been a common practice in early colonial government.

But, freedom of the press to publish was not firmly grounded in American political culture, as evidenced by the Alien and Sedition Acts of 1798. A widely held view by early American political leaders was that prior restraint of publication was prohibited by the First Amendment, congressional power over seditious libel—editorial content which disparaged the government—had never been altered by the Constitution.[1]

When Republican newspapers criticized the Federalist administration's moves to go to war with France and the Federalist Congress responded with the Sedition Act, the political leaders were maintaining, not abandoning, their views about government control of the press. Editorials, news reports, even printed letters from readers viewed by the government as false, scandalous, or malicious against the president, Congress, or the government could become the basis for a criminal charge.

The Sedition Act of 1798, which had the most impact on the press, turned published criticism of the government into a criminal activity. The Sedition Act, resulted in 25 arrests and eventually 10 convictions.[2] Several of the leading opposition party newspapers were targeted for prosecution. One Republican was imprisoned for six months and fined $100 for calling the president an incompetent.[3] The Acts were later repealed in 1800 when the Republicans gained a majority in Congress.

However, the Republicans were not advocates of a free press. During Jefferson's presidency, a few Federalist editors were indicted for seditious libel.[4] The press was not united against the Sedition Act. Federalist newspapers favored the act while Republican papers opposed it. One Federalist editor wrote that it "is patriotism to write in favor of our government—it is sedition to write against it."[5] The Supreme Court as a body never received a case derived from the Sedition Act, but individual justices on the Federalist-controlled body upheld the cases on a lower level.[6]

Even in World War I, the press was restricted by another Sedition Act passed in 1917, which prohibited publishing any criticism of the government, the flag, the Constitution, or the war effort.[7] However, since that time, the power of the government to declare a published statement against the government as the basis for criminal activity has been severely curtailed by the Supreme Court.[8]

Prior restraint was prohibited by Congress, but it was not until 1925 that First Amendment guarantees for freedom of the press were applied, through the Fourteenth Amendment, to the states.[9] The First Amendment only prohibited congressional action. Limitation on actions by the states over freedom of the press was omitted by Congress.[10]

In 1931, prior restraint of publication by a Minnesota state law was declared unconstitutional by the Supreme Court. The Court did leave open the possibility of the constitutionality of prior restraint of publication in extreme situations such as wartime, obscenity, and incitement to violence, but in a subsequent opinion the justices warned that "any system of prior restraints of expression comes to this Court bearing a heavy presumption against its constitutional validity."[11]

Since the turn of the century, the press has undertaken some measures of self-regulation to forestall governmental regulation. As discussed in Chapter 4, journalists, in the wake of widespread criticism of the excesses of yellow journalism, sought to impose a code of ethics.

Another tactic has been the concept of the press council. At the national level, the National News Council was a body armed with power to handle journalistic excesses. Founded in 1973 by a consortium of ten foundations, the council's task was to handle complaints concerning the performance of the major national suppliers of news—wire services, newsmagazines, national dailies, national syndicates, and television networks. The council was disbanded in 1984 because of lack of support by some major news organizations and lack of enforcement power.[12] Press councils have succeeded in other Western democracies such as Britain, New Zealand, Switzerland, and Italy. In the United States, successful local press councils were formed in a few cities and one state (Minnesota). However, at the national level, the National News Council was largely ineffective and short-lived. Many journalists have opposed press councils. They fear such bodies will rob them of First Amendment guarantees and they reject the role of non-journalists who also sit on the councils in determining how well they do their job.[13] Ironically, these fears were not realized through the National News Council. For instance, during its first two years, the Council received 59 complaints concerning the press, only five of which were upheld by the Council as valid.[14]

Concern for self-regulation also figured in the appointment of an ombudsman by several major dailies such as the *Washington Post* and the *Los Angeles Times*. The ombudsman reviewed the newspaper's own internal operations in covering news and published those findings in the newspapers. The role of ombudsman was demonstrated in the critique by the *Washington Post*'s ombudsman of the paper's handling of the story of a reporter who faked a Pulitzer Prize-winning story about child drug addicts. For those relative handful of newspapers who used them, the ombudsman helped keep public criticism at a minimum by demonstrating the news organization's sensitivity to its own faults.[15]

Trends in Increased Press Autonomy from Government Regulation

Since the founding of the republic, but more particularly during this century, the news media generally have become increasingly free of governmental regulation.

These actions have enhanced the opportunity on the part of the press to act as an independent force in American politics.

Prior Restraint

One clear trend is the decreasing governmental power to censor news media content directly. Government censorship had been employed in the past. Abraham Lincoln shut down two newspapers with Confederate sympathies during the Civil War. The Post Office at times refused to handle abolitionist literature before the Civil War because it was viewed as politically extreme.

Prior restraint, or pre-publication censorship, by the government has been severely limited by the U.S. Supreme Court. The court has viewed pre-publication censorship as inimical to First Amendment guarantees, except in the most extreme circumstances. Several Supreme Court cases in this century have asserted that freedom. The court has prohibited restraints on the distribution of circulars, the publication of election-day editorials, and even taxes on the press when used as a vehicle for government control.[16]

The most significant test of prior restraint occurred in the "Pentagon Papers" case.[17] The case involved a conflict between liberty of the press and perceived national security interests of the U.S. government. In June 1971, both the *New York Times* and the *Washington Post* began publication of a series of secret government documents which outlined the history of U.S. policy in Vietnam. The Justice Department successfully obtained a temporary court injunction against the publication of some of the material, which was deemed harmful to national security. The newspapers appealed, and both cases moved quickly to the Supreme Court.

The Court struck down the injunction against publication. But the decision produced no new legal doctrine on the issue because of the deep divisions among the justices. A majority affirmed that the government possesses a heavy burden in justifying prior restraint but admitted the justification of prior restraint by government under certain extreme circumstances.[18]

Succeeding court injunctions of publication have been extremely rare and probably would not be supported by the Supreme Court. In 1979, a district court judge issued an injunction against *The Progressive*, a monthly magazine, to stop publication of secret plans to make a hydrogen bomb. The plans were published in another newspaper and ultimately the government dropped its case.[19]

Deregulation

A second trend has been the deregulation of the broadcast industry. Deregulation has moved the government away from regulation of broadcast programming, and it has allowed broadcasters greater flexibility in decisions about programming and other aspects of the industry. Though the Reagan administration was identified with deregulation, the initial impetus for deregulation actually came from the Carter administration.

Two major factors—one technical, the other normative—explain the success of the move toward deregulation. As we pointed out in an earlier section, technological developments such as satellite network transmission for both radio and television, cable transmission, and low power stations have provided solutions to the problem of scarcity of broadcast frequencies. That scarcity of airwave frequencies was a major reason for treating broadcasting differently from the print media.

Hand in hand with these technical developments has emerged a reinforced argument for more limited government role in the regulation of business, including broadcasting. Since 1980, this argument has won the support of a majority of the commissioners of the FCC. Proponents contended the government should allow market forces to dominate the industry. Moreover, they argued, broadcast media should be equated with print media and accorded the same rights under the First Amendment.

Deregulation has come in the form of relaxation or elimination of several rules set by the FCC to govern broadcast stations. Advertising rules limiting commercial time to 18 minutes per hour were eliminated, for instance. These rules had been technically voluntary, but license renewal had been contingent on compliance.

Rules governing programming content also were set aside. The FCC rules had specified a certain percentage of non-entertainment, local, and informational programming, but the new proliferation of all-news, all-talk broadcast stations was used as justification for abolishing the requirement.[20] (The FCC has stated the importance of public service programming content in evaluating license renewal.)

License renewal itself has undergone significant deregulation. In 1981, licenses were extended by the FCC from three years to five and seven years for television and radio respectively. Moreover, license renewal controversies during the 1980s have been weighted towards the incumbent license-holders.[21]

Other non-content-related rule changes included relaxation of the limitation on ownership of broadcast stations. Under the old formula, a single owner could not possess more than seven AM, seven FM, and seven television stations. In August 1984, that formula was changed to 12-12-12, as long as the combined markets of those television stations do not include more than 25 percent of television households nationwide.[22]

Deregulation has increased press autonomy by relaxing the governmental control of broadcasting. The potential for a governmental role in programming, particularly in news and public affairs, has been significantly minimized by the deregulation of the broadcast industry. Although theoretically the public owns the airwaves, in fact private industry controls all the means for utilizing those airwaves. The public service expectations codified in law have been reduced. Thus, broadcast media have become far more like the print media in freedom from governmental regulation during the last decade.

Libel

Another trend noticeable in the past 30 years has been in the area of libel. Although pre-publication censorship has occurred rarely and lacks legal footing except in extreme circumstances, the press nevertheless is subject to *post*-publication legal action for content. Libel laws allow redress for press content damaging an individual's reputation.

Libel laws, an outgrowth of seditious libel laws, have been consistently upheld by the Supreme Court. Seditious libel involved criminal penalties, but libel cases today are purely civil cases prosecuted not by the government but by the party who seeks legal redress.

However, the U.S. Supreme Court has broadened news media immunity from libel, especially in cases involving public officials. In the case of *New York v. Sullivan*, the U.S. Supreme Court in 1964 held that a public official suing for libel must prove "actual malice" on the part of the press. If there is no malice, then no libel has been committed by the press. In other words, an error in reporting is not sufficient for libel; the public official must prove the statement was made "with knowledge that it was false or with reckless disregard of whether it was false or not. . . . "[23]

The heavy burden in proving libel is apparent in two recent cases involving well-known public figures and national media organizations. General William Westmoreland, former commander of U.S. troops in Vietnam, sued CBS in 1982 for accusing him in a documentary of deceiving political officials about the strength of the North Vietnamese and Viet Cong during the Vietnam War. Simultaneously, Israeli Defense Minister Ariel Sharon sued *Time* magazine for charging Sharon with complicity in the 1982 massacre of Palestinian refugees.

In both cases, the plaintiffs claimed they had been libeled by the press. Lengthy court trials ensued. Neither plaintiff actually won: In the Sharon case, actual malice was not proved; and Westmoreland dropped his case before its conclusion because his lawyers could not prove actual malice. Hence, the press's libel protection was not endangered by the resolution of these well-known cases.[24]

The very bringing of the suits by two internationally known figures against major press organizations—in conjunction with a popular movie about libel in the early 1980s called "Absence of Malice"—was a measure of widespread public interest in, if not dissatisfaction with current libel law. According to a poll conducted in the mid-1980s, 49 percent of the public believed the growing number of libel suits was a good thing. Only 10 percent felt it was bad. There also is a lack of sympathy among the public for the need to prove malice. Two-thirds believed news organizations should pay damages if a story is false even if they believed at the time the story was true. Also, there was little support for the *New York v. Sullivan* decision. Seventy-five percent of the public believed it should not be more difficult for a public official than a common citizen to sue for libel.[25] Apparently, widespread sentiment exists for less press immunity from libel and probably indicates the public perceives there is too little press restraint.

The Fairness Doctrine

Yet another trend involving regulation of the press is represented by the repeal of the Fairness Doctrine. The Fairness Doctrine was adopted by the Federal Communications Commission in 1959, following the passage of an amendment to the Communications Act which stated that broadcasters had an obligation to facilitate the discussion of controversial public issues by offering reasonable opportunity for contrasting views to be expressed. The broadcaster retained the right to decide how this obligation would be fulfilled. The Fairness Doctrine itself was a source of controversy; broadcasters felt they were being unfairly discriminated against. Since print media had no such obligation, broadcasters had long sought repeal of the rule.

The Reagan administration's appointees to the FCC concurred and abolished the rule in 1987. An attempt by Congress to codify the doctrine into law was killed by President Reagan's veto and the inability of the doctrine's proponents to muster a two-thirds majority in both houses to override the veto.

The debate over the doctrine is not over, however. Attempts to resurrect the doctrine will likely continue because the controversy over its necessity lingers.[26]

Broadcasters argue that the Fairness Doctrine unfairly singled them out—that they should enjoy First Amendment rights equal to those of the print media. They contend that the Fairness Doctrine allowed the government to control the press in violation of the First Amendment. Bill Monroe, a television news correspondent charged that the "Fairness Doctrine idea—that government can improve the American media—is in brutal confrontation with the First Amendment. It is unworkable in practice, and philosophically subversive of the amendment."[27]

Opponents of the doctrine also argue that the scarcity of frequencies problem has been resolved by the proliferation of broadcast channels through cable, and that public debate of issues is now conducted through a diversity of broadcast alternatives, so that diversity is no longer needed on each broadcast station.

Finally, they argue that the doctrine actually inhibited debate of controversial public issues, because broadcasters shied away from allowing any statements which might lead to license renewal challenges or litigation from various interest groups.

Proponents of the doctrine counter the broadcast airwaves are and always have been public property and are not for the private use of broadcasters. Since broadcasters do not own the airwaves, government regulation of programming content to facilitate public discussion of issues is both proper and necessary. Proponents point out that the Communications Act of 1934 and subsequent court decisions do not grant ownership of the airwaves to broadcasters, but allow them to hold a public trust with a responsibility to serve the public.[28]

Proponents argue that, although the number of frequencies has expanded, the available number is still finite. Moreover, the cost of owning a broadcast station is prohibitive for all but a few. Should only those with money to own a broadcast station be allowed to air their views?

Support for the Fairness Doctrine also stems from the belief that without legal requirement, broadcasters will not offer access to others who do not share their views. Nicholas Johnson, a former member of the FCC, contended:

> There is no regulation that limits a broadcaster's right to say whatever he or she wants over the air—including personal attacks on others. The Fairness Doctrine doesn't censor them, it prevents them from censoring the rest of us.[29]

The debate over the Fairness Doctrine continues. Efforts have been made in Congress to restore the doctrine to law. Although future presidents may not share former President Reagan's links to the broadcast industry, it is guaranteed broadcasters will continue to be vigorous in opposition to any reduction of their newly acquired freedom.

The Right of Access

Due to the concentration of ownership in the news media and the centralization of information sources, the issue of right of access by those who do not own or run news media organizations has arisen. The right of access is the right of individuals or groups to use the media to express their views. The broadcast media before deregulation were bound to provide some limited right to access, but print media have never been so bound.

Those with broadcast licenses have right of access to the airwaves. Additionally, any who wish to publish printed material have similar rights. Not everyone, however, can buy radio or television time. Nor is access guaranteed to established print media, such as newspapers and news magazines, which are the preeminent sources of news and opinion. Is there a right to be able to participate in the exchange of ideas through guaranteed access to the existing mass media?

Some scholars have argued for such a right. Jerome Barron has urged the U.S. Supreme Court to assert such a right. He contends the absence of such a right inhibits freedom of speech since media gatekeepers can censor who has access to the press, which is the primary mechanism for the public debate of issues. According to Barron, the long-held belief that government can be the only censor is antiquated, and "private censorship serves to suppress ideas as thoroughly and as rigidly as the worst government censor."[30] Benno Schmidt has supported narrow access guarantees in print media in the areas of reply to personal attack of acceptance of commercial advertisements (if a newspaper accepted advertisements from a company it must accept them from others in the same business.)[31]

No such right has been furthered by the courts or the FCC; this despite attempts by those seeking access to establish such a right. However, narrow related rights have existed for broadcast media alone. Before its abolition by the FCC, the Fairness Doctrine asserted the right to broadcast a point of view if an opposing view had already been aired.[32] But no single group could declare a right to use broadcast time to state that view; the broadcaster could determine the manner of presentation.

In fact, the U.S. Supreme Court has denied any right of access. In a case over whether the First Amendment provides right of access to air political advertisements at regular commercial rates, the Court rules the First Amendment guarantees no such right.[33] The court has upheld the right of reply in certain situations involving broadcasting such as personal attack and editorializing on political candidates.[34] But such right of reply specifically has not been applied to the print media.[35]

Despite the calls for the establishment of a right of access to mass media, the trend has actually been in the opposite direction. The deregulatory process has bolstered broadcasters in their right to deny access by reducing government regulation.

SUMMARY

Formal legal constraints on the press have diminished over time, enhancing the autonomy of the press. The print media historically have been subject to less restraint than broadcasting. However, with the demise of the Fairness Doctrine and the deregulatory moves of the 1980s, broadcast media are subject to fewer legal restraints than at any time in the history of governmental regulation of broadcasting.

Although the federal government possesses the power to restore those legal controls through statute and regulation, such action is unlikely given the current political climate of pro-business Republicanism.

The result of the diminuition of such legal constraints is the loss of a lever by politicians to affect news media actions. Moreover, media organizations are increasingly relieved from legal requirements to serve the public's interests at the very time when their ability to affect those interests has increased. Although the absence of such legal power prevents politicians from using it for nefarious purposes, it also prevents them from using it for good ones either.

NOTES

1. John Lofton, *The Press as Guardian of the First Amendment*, Columbia, S.C.: University of South Carolina Press, 1980, p. 27.
2. Frank Luther Mott, *American Journalism, A History: 1690–1960*, New York: Macmillan, 1962, p. 149.
3. Mott, *American Journalism*, pp. 151–152.
4. Lofton, *Press as Guardian*, pp. 45–47.
5. Lofton, *Press as Guardian*, p. 34.
6. Leonard W. Levy, *Emergence of a Free Press*, New York: Oxford University Press, 1985, p. 280.
7. Lofton, *Press as Guardian*, pp. 179–187.
8. Schenck v. U.S., 249 U.S. 47 (1919); and Dennis v. U.S., 341 U.S. 494 (1951).
9. Gitlow v. N.Y., 268 U.S. 652 (1925).
10. Levy, *Emergence of a Free Press*, pp. 258–268.
11. Near v. Minnesota, 283 U.S. 697 (1931); New York Times Co. v. U.S., 403 U.S. 713 (1971).
12. See Norman C. Isaacs, *Untended Gates: The Mismanaged Press*, New York: Columbia University Press, 1986, chap. 7.
13. See David Cassady, "Press Councils—Why Journalists Won't Cooperate," *Newspaper Research Journal* 5 (Summer 1984): 19–25.
14. Isaacs, *Untended Gates*, chap. 7.
15. See James Boylan, "Declarations of Independence," *Columbia Journalism Review* (November/December 1986): 30–45.
16. Near v. Minnesota, 283 U.S. 697 (1931); Lovell v. Griffin, 303 U.S. 444 (1938); Mills

v. Alabama, 384 U.S. 214 (1966); Grosjean v. American Press, 297 U.S. 233 (1936); and Bantam Books, Inc. v. Sullivan, 372 U.S. 58,70 (1963).

17. New York Times v. United States, 403 U.S. 713 (1971).

18. For a discussion of the case, see Sanford J. Unger, *The Papers and* the Papers; New York: Columbia University Press, 1989; and Don R. Pember, "The 'Pentagon Papers' Decision: More Questions Than Answers," *Journalism Quarterly* 48 (1971): 403–411.

19. Lofton, *Untended Gates*, p. 278.

20. For a discussion of deregulation, see Erwin G. Krasnow, Lawrence D. Longley, and Herbert A. Terry, *The Politics of Broadcasting*, 3d ed., New York: St. Martin's Press, 1982, pp. 22–23, 197–200; and Jeremy Tunstall, *Communications Deregulation*. London: Basil Blackwell, 1986.

21. Tunstall, *Communications Deregulation*, p. 234.

22. Tunstall, *Communications Deregulation*, pp. 146–147, 151.

23. New York Times v. Sullivan, 376 U.S. 254 (1964).

24. For a discussion of the cases, see Renata Adler, *Reckless Disregard*, New York: Vintage, 1986; and Don Kowet, *A Matter of Honor: General William Westmoreland versus CBS*, New York: Macmillan, 1984. For a description of the CBS News inquiry into the ethics of the broadcast's reporting and editing, see Burton Benjamin, *Fair Play*, New York: Harper & Row, 1988.

25. Times-Mirror, *The People and the Press*, January 1986, p. 35.

26. For a discussion of the arguments over the Fairness Doctrine, see Fred W. Friendly, *The Good Guys, the Bad Guys, and the First Amendment*, New York: Random House, 1976; Ford Rowan, *Broadcast Fairness*, White Plains, N.Y.: Longman, 1984.

27. David Bollier, "The Strange Politics of 'Fairness'," *Channels*, January/February 1986, p. 49.

28. See National Broadcasting Co. v. U.S., 319 U.S. 219 (1943); and Red Lion Broadcasting v. FCC, 395 U.S. 367 (1969).

29. Bollier, "The Strange Politics of 'Fairness'," p. 48.

30. See Jerome Barron, *Freedom of the Press for Whom: The Right of Access to Mass Media*, Bloomington, Ind.: Indiana University Press, 1973.

31. See Benno Schmidt, *Freedom of the Press vs. Public Access*, New York: Praeger, 1976.

32. Red Lion Broadcasting v. FCC, 395 U.S. 367 (1969).

33. See CBS v. Democratic National Committee, 412 U.S. 94 (1973).

34. Red Lion Broadcasting v. FCC.

35. Miami Herald Publishing Co. v. Tornillo, 418 U.S. 298 (1974).

SUGGESTED READINGS

Adler, Renata. *Reckless Disregard*. New York: Vintage, 1986.

Barron, Jerome. *Freedom of the Press for Whom: The Right of Access to Mass Media*. Bloomington, Ind.: Indiana University Press, 1973.

Friendly, Fred. *The Good Guys, the Bad Guys, and the First Amendment*. New York: Random House, 1976.

Krasnow, Erwin G., Lawrence D. Longley, and Herbert A. Terry, *The Politics of Broadcasting*, 3d ed. New York: St. Martin's Press, 1982.

Levy, Leonard W. *Emergence of a Free Press*. New York: Oxford University Press, 1985.

Rowan, Ford. *Broadcast Fairness*. New York: Longman, 1984.

Schmidt. Benno. *Freedom of the Press vs. Public Access*. New York: Praeger, 1976.

CHAPTER 7

The News Media
in Other Systems

The relationship between the press and politics in the United States is not universal. The role of the press in our political system is defined quite differently than it is in other systems, even in industrial democracies such as Japan, Canada, New Zealand, and the Western European nations. In no other nation, however, is the press so independent and the political system so dependent as in this country.

One distinction inheres in the theoretical base for the press's role. In the United States, the press remains largely free of government regulatory control, and that freedom is justified both on the basis of economic freedom, and because it is perceived as advantageous to the democracy because it allows the exchange of ideas necessary for mass decision making.

Due to the high level of freedom granted the press in the United States in its own operation, it possesses latitude in defining its role in society and, more particularly, in politics. Journalistic and commercial imperatives are allowed to govern. The press can choose to fulfill a variety of roles—simultaneously or exclusively—such as common carrier of information, watchdog over government, critic, or public trustee. It can even choose not to perform any of the above and ignore politics altogether.

Such freedom to operate has been the product of a process of evolution previously described. Other very different models of political-press relationship exist in other societies, however.

Four models of press relationship with government, first identified in 1956 by Fred S. Siebert, Theodore Peterson, and Wilbur Schramm and somewhat restructured by John Merrill and Ralph Lowenstein, include: social-centralist, authoritarian, libertarian, and social-libertarian.[1]

In the *social-centralist* model, the press functions as an arm of the governing party or the state. It possesses no independence since it is one element of the governmental structure, and it assists in governance through propaganda. The model was derived from the role of the press in Communist nations. However, recent changes in the Soviet Union and Eastern Europe have led to modifications of the model in those nations. The continued flux in those nations' political systems makes determination of the role of the press extremely difficult at this time. The social-centralist model does continue to prevail in some hardline Communist nations such as China and Cuba.

In the *authoritarian* model, the press is expected to support the state, though it may not be a part of the government. A privately owned press is allowed to operate, but it must not oppose the state. Many Third World nations fit this model.

The *libertarian* model describes a press with nearly total freedom from government control. The press serves its own interests, and the independence of the press serves the political system's needs by providing a vehicle for information surveillance of government and a debate over public issues. The only controls on the press are post-publication punishment for areas such as obscenity, defamation, and wartime sedition.

Under the libertarian model, the press may or may not fulfill its implicit democratic functions in pursuit of economic and journalistic interests. Therefore, the press must be forced to accept a minimum of government controls to assure access to all views and the maintenance of the free exchange of ideas.

This modification of the libertarian model is the *social-libertarian* model, in which the press has a responsibility to society which is more explicit than in the libertarian model. The social-libertarian model anticipates that the press may use its freedom to choose not to perform tasks for the democratic system. Since such roles are required, the press will be subject to some governmental requirements to fulfill them. In the United States, press control for the broadcast industry has included regulations on the handling of public issues designed to facilitate rather than limit public discussion, but even these regulations have been significantly reduced in the last decade, as discussed in the previous chapter.

Therefore, to assume that the press/political system relationship in the United States is social-libertarian would be inaccurate. United States government regulations apply only to the broadcast media, not print.

The United States can be more accurately described as a libertarian system with some social-libertarian components, particularly in relationship to the broadcast industry, such as public ownership of the airwaves leading to government regulation of technical aspects of broadcasting and an extremely vague obligation on the part of private broadcasters to perform public service in order to obtain license renewal.

THE LIBERAL DEMOCRACIES

Few other political systems share this position with the United States. Although several industrial democracies such as the United Kingdom, France, Germany, Italy, and Japan have undergone similar deregulation movements in the 1980s, compared to the United States they still occupy a position closer to the social-libertarian model. At least since the Second World War, these nations possess a heritage of press independence combined with government controls to assure press compliance. Press responsibility is more explicit, and the government plays a significant role in defining that responsibility. The government typically does not have the power of prior censorship, but it does have significant power to define the responsibility of the press through controls.

In Japan, for example, according to national law, broadcasting must contribute to the "development of a healthy democracy." Program content cannot be interfered with except by law, and candidates receive air time free of charge.

Formal controls on broadcasting in other liberal democracies include requirements for balance in presenting controversial issues, prohibitions on editorializing about issues, and mandates to provide coverage of sessions of Parliament.

The differences between the United States and other industrialized liberal democracies are more stark in the operation of broadcasting than in the print media. The print media in these nations are typically libertarian, as is that of the United States. However, press relations with parties and with interest groups does stand in contrast to those in the United States. In several Western countries, newspapers are either owned by or strongly affiliated with political parties or interest groups.

In the Scandinavian countries, newspapers have traditionally been closely tied to political parties, and party thinking is often reflected in editorial content. Recent economic changes have toned down the obvious partisan tone to some degree, but the labor press still dominates much coverage. Even in liberal democracies, governments aid newspapers through subsidies, preferential tax treatment, postal privileges, and government advertising. Some government subsidization in Western countries is tied to financial need and has not been used as a partisan tool. Tax and postal privileges are common for all newspapers, for example, in the United States and many European democracies; in Sweden, an elaborate system of subsidies, mainly supported through advertising taxes, supports newspapers facing economic difficulties.[2] The Japanese government exempts the press from a number of taxes, as well as from the requirement that the public be allowed to buy shares in a corporation.[3]

Unlike the United States, political parties in many other Western democracies possess close relationships with the news media. In some countries, interest groups also share such a relationship. For example, political parties are guaranteed a share in the governance of the broadcast corporation in Italy. Interest groups and parties play a unique role in the broadcasting system in the Netherlands. Parties and groups do not own or operate broadcast stations, but they are allotted time for their own programming—information and entertainment.[4]

The United States also differs from other nations, even liberal democracies, in the control of wire services. In the United States, all wire services, including the two major services—the Associated Press and United Press International, are privately owned and operated. Elsewhere, government typically runs the wire service. Nations fitting the social-centralist model, such as the USSR, China, and Cuba, control their own news services and prohibit all others. Many Third World nations do so as well. But even some liberal democracies own their own wire services. In France, Agence France Press (AFP) is owned by the French government. AFP receives 60 percent of its funding from the French government, a relationship which occasionally leads to government intervention in newsreporting.[5] EFE, the Spanish news agency which is popular throughout Latin America, is government-owned.

The greatest distinction between the United States and other similar nations in control of broadcast media is the issue of ownership. While the United States has encouraged private ownership, other liberal democratic nations have adopted some form of government ownership ranging from near government monopoly to a mixed public/private system. The British Broadcasting Corporation (BBC) became the model for the public corporation, usually funded by government through license fees and, to some degree, advertising, but not dependent on government for daily operation. The BBC has acquired a distinguished reputation for independence from government control. However, as noted earlier, even in Britain the government legally possesses the power to affect program content. Most other public corporations are less independent of their respective governments than the BBC. In several liberal democracies, government can affect appointments in broadcast organizations. In Germany and Italy, for example, journalists are hired on the basis of their partisan affiliation.[6]

NON-DEMOCRACIES

No other broadcast system has placed so much reliance on private ownership as has the United States. However, most nations have followed neither the private ownership model nor the public corporation model. Government ownership has been adopted in order to maintain control of the media and has been applied to both print and broadcast.

Most nations follow the authoritarian model, in which the press is placed in the service of the state. William Rugh has identified three types of authoritarian systems: a *mobilization* press, where the press is used as a tool in the development of the nation; a *loyalist* press, which exists to provide fealty to the state rather than as a change agent; and a *diverse* press, where some degree of pluralism is tolerated and government control is more limited.[7] Significantly, the role of the press in an authoritarian model is highly explicit. Political leaders, not the press itself, define the press's functioning within the political system. In the 1960s, for example, one Asian head of state asserted that "the press is an instrument to mobilize the masses to realize the achievements of the revolution."[8] African-owned newspapers in the 1960s performed much the same function; prior to the independence of their countries, many African leaders were journalists or newspaper owners. Now, in the 39 independent African nations that support daily newspapers, the majority have only one and it is government-owned.[9]

Partisan or government-ownership of the press obviously bars the kind of independence that characterizes the press in the United States. Criticism of the government, expression of opposing views, and pursuit of goals other than those espoused by the government (goals dictated by journalistic imperatives or commercial profit, for example) are impossible, since they do not further the development of the nation. But many journalists in developing countries accept the trade-off. As one African journalist articulated this acceptance:

> When governments need to explain policy, transmit their decisions, instructions, wishes, suggestions, or laws, or discuss new projects and ideas with their electorate, they must have a forum which is not antagonistic to the overall goals of national policy.[10]

The predominance of the authoritarian and social-centrist models and the government ownership of mass media worldwide indicate that a low level of autonomy for the press is the rule, and not the exception. Even within liberal, industrialized democracies, the press typically enjoys less autonomy from government control than exists for the press in the United States.

The press in other systems is governed to a greater extent than is the United States press by the imperatives of the political system—such as nation building or maintenance of the status quo—or of individual political leaders, parties, or interest groups.

That is not to say, however, that the relationship between the state and the press in these other nations has been static. In some nations, the government's role has recently diminished. In France and Italy, for instance, deregulation has resulted in a dramatic increase in privately owned radio stations. In Great Britain, more privately owned television stations have been permitted during the past decade.

DEPENDENCE ON THE NEWS MEDIA

The United States is unique not only in the high level of press autonomy, but also in the extent of political system dependence. It is true that many political leaders in Third World nations rely on the mass media, particularly radio, for modernization and national development. In authoritarian and social-centralist systems, the press serves as a tool of politicians and acts primarily as the means by which political institutions or individual leaders perform political functions. The press does not act in such functions as autonomous actors, but as arms of the state.

Among liberal democracies, the United States political system is the most dependent of any nation on the press for performance of its functions. This is particularly true for the electoral process. In other similar political systems, such as Britain, France, and Germany, the selection process for the party's candidate is largely an internal party process and the mass electorate is not directly involved in decision making. The press are therefore less engaged in the selection process.

Moreover, party affiliation is more intense and more widespread in many other liberal democracies. The political party designation of the candidate serves as a strong cue to the voters. Election outcomes are more predictable in Western European nations, due to strong partisan attitudes and the rarity of defection.

In this atmosphere, the political parties play a much stronger role in the organization of the electoral process than do parties here. In these countries, political parties still perform the functions the press has acquired in the United States. Hence, these political systems are not as dependent on the press.

The system of governance in other liberal democracies also mitigates against an extended press role because the political party is a salient factor in governance as well. The political party's control of the selection of candidates and the significant role in elections contributes to candidate/elected official allegiance to party positions and strengthens the party in governance. The very structure of government common in these systems, a parliamentary system, enhances party strength.

The strength of the party in the electorate, as an organization, and in government does not open a vacuum which invites the press to play a major role in areas such as setting the policy agenda, framing debate, and providing reaction to policy decisions.[11]

The structure of government in other nations also mitigates against the same level of dependence on the press. Most liberal democracies are parliamentary systems with single party control of both executive and legislative branches. In such systems, the executive and legislative branches are more united in governance, which minimizes use of the press by either institution for influencing the other. For example, the British prime minister rarely uses national television to urge citizens to lobby their member of parliament in the prime minister's behalf.

SUMMARY

The role of the press in the United States has developed differently from that of mass media in other political systems. No other nation has granted the press as much freedom from political control as has the United States. No other nation has relied so extensively on private ownership of the press as has the United States.

In no other country do political leaders have as minor a part in determining the press role. This fact alone distinguishes the United States political-media system from almost every other system.

The absence of political system strictures on the media guarantees that the press will determine its own role. Moreover, where the political system lacks effective organizing mechanisms for the electoral process, agenda-setting, and the shaping of public opinion, and where the system of government is fragmented to invite external influences, the vacuum left by the weakened state of other political actors can be filled by the press.

This highly favorable environment for press role is uncommon throughout the world, but exists in the United States and has contributed significantly to the influence of the press and the salience of press-politician relationships in American politics.

NOTES

1. See Fred S. Siebert, Theodore Peterson, and Wilbur Schramm, *Four Theories of the Press*, Urbana, Ill.: University of Illinois Press, 1956; and John Merrill and Ralph Lowenstein, *Media Messages and Men*, White Plains, Longman, 1979, p. 160ff.
2. Emmanuel Paraschos, "Europe," in John C. Merrill, ed., *Global Journalism*, 2d ed., White Plains, N.Y.: Longman, 1991.
3. Hisao Komatsubara, "Japan," in John A. Lent, ed., *Newspapers in Asia*, Hong Kong: Heinemann Asia, 1982, p. 125; and William Horsley, "Press As Loyal Opposition in Japan," in Anthony Smith, ed., *Newspapers and Democracy*, Cambridge, Mass.: MIT Press, 1980, pp. 200–227.
4. Roland S. Homet, Jr., *Politics, Culture, and Communication*, New York: Praeger, 1979, pp. 62–63; and Anthony Smith, *The Shadow in the Cave*, Urbana, Ill.: University of Illinois Press, 1973, pp. 264–278.
5. Joseph Fenby, *The International Wire Services*, New York: Schocken Books, 1986, pp. 159–170.
6. Homet, *Politics, Culture, and Communication*, pp. 17–18.
7. William Rugh, *The Arab Press*, 2d ed., Syracuse, N.Y.: Syracuse University Press, 1987.
8. Lloyd Sumerland, *The Press in Developing Countries*, Sydney, Austral.: University Press, 1961, p. 141.
9. L. John Martin, "Africa," in John C. Merrill, ed., *Global Journalism*, 2d ed., White Plains, N.Y.: Longman, 1991.
10. Dennis L. Wilcox, *Mass Media in Black Africa*, New York: Praeger, 1975, p. 21.
11. For a discussion of the role of political parties in liberal democracies, see Leon D. Epstein, *Political Parties in Western Democracies*, New York: Transaction, 1980; and Stanley Henig, ed., *Political Parties in the European Community*, London: Allen and Unwin, 1979.

SUGGESTED READINGS

Altschull, Herbert. *Agents of Power: The Role of the News Media in Human Affairs*. White Plains, N.Y.: Longman, 1984.
Atwood, Rita, and Emile G. McAnany, eds. *Communication and Latin American Society*. Madison, Wis.: University of Wisconsin Press, 1986.
Dunnett, Peter J. S. *The World Newspaper Industry*. London: Croom Helm, 1988.
Homet, Roland S., Jr. *Politics, Culture, and Communication*. New York: Praeger, 1979.
Merrill, John C., ed. *Global Journalism*. White Plains, N.Y.: Longman, 1990.
Ochs, Martin. *The African Press*. Cairo, 1987.
Rugh, William. *The Arab Press*, 2d ed. Syracuse, N.Y.: Syracuse University Press, 1987.
Smith, Anthony. *The Shadow in the Cave*. Urbana, Ill.: University of Illinois Press, 1973.
Smith, Anthony, ed. *Newspapers and Democracy*. Cambridge, Mass.: MIT Press, 1980.

PART III

Covering Political Institutions

Although early attention to the role of the media in American politics centered on the electoral process, events such as the election of a telegenic president, John F. Kennedy, in the 1960s and the downfall of Richard Nixon in the Watergate scandal contributed to the growing perception of media power in affecting institutional performance, particularly the presidency. In fact, a decade and a half of presidencies which are perceived to have failed—Lyndon Johnson, Richard Nixon, Gerald Ford, and Jimmy Carter—has been associated with press influence. Ironically, Ronald Reagan's perceived success also has been partially attributed to the press's treatment of him.

The purpose of this section is to explain the nature of the press's relationship with national political institutions—the presidency, the Congress, and the Supreme Court—and to analyze the effects of those relationships on the institutions and their relationships to each other and to the citizenry.

CHAPTER 8

The Presidency

"If there is a balance of powers within the government, it rarely shows on television."

Political scientist Thomas Cronin[1]

STARRING THE PRESIDENT

The president is the star. This is true not just when an actor resides in the White House. In news coverage of American national political institutions, the president is the star.

No other individual in American government receives as much time and space in the news media as the president.[2] Rarely does an issue of a major daily newspaper or a network evening news broadcast not include a story from the White House. And, according to Michael Grossman and Martha Kumar, the White House story "is the president: who he is, what he does, and what his programs, actions, and goals are."[3]

The presidency as an institution benefits from extensive news coverage of the president. The presidency dominates news from Washington to the point that other institutions—the Congress and the Supreme Court—pale by comparison.

There are indications that this preoccupation with the president has grown over time.[4] When we include coverage of extensions of the person of the president—policy proposals, decisions, and related activities—the president's dominance is even greater. Much national news coverage of the federal bureaucracy, Congress, and even state and local government is attention to the president's initiatives and decisions—still part of the continuing saga of the president.

The argument could legitimately be made that virtually all coverage of national government is primarily the drama surrounding the president—from the story of the initial policy proposal through the Congress's handling of the issue to the president's subsequent reaction to Congress. It may even extend to the role of interest groups, the states and localities, the federal bureaucracy, and the Supreme Court. Energy programs, budget cuts, anti-inflation plans all receive elongated coverage if they emanate from the White House and are considered top priorities of the president.

Not only does the president get a lot of press coverage, but most of it is favorable, or at worst neutral. Although the number of unfavorable stories has increased since the late 1960s and early 1970s (Vietnam and Watergate) the president still receives more favorable than unfavorable press.[5]

MANAGING THE NEWS

The president's media coverage is generally positive primarily because of White House efforts to manage the news. The White House usually does not need to solicit the press's attention (although it cannot take such attention for granted), but the president's staff does try to affect the content that is transmitted. A vital and time-consuming job of the president and his senior advisors is the shaping of news coverage to the president's advantage.[6]

Former White House Communications Director David Gergen aptly describes this preoccupation:

> We had a rule in the Nixon [presidency] that before any public event was put on his schedule, you had to know what the headline out of that event was going to be, what the picture was going to be, and what the lead paragraph would be.[7]

Image-Making

The White House works to create an image of the president which supports the president's policy objectives and creates a reservoir of political capital (that is, popular support), for the president in his battles with Congress and others. This imagemaking is especially crucial in the first year of a new administration when the new president seeks to translate an electoral mandate into congressional and public support for the administration's proposals. The president not only can be more successful in accomplishing policy objectives, but he also can draw an image of himself which will form the first strong impression in the public mind. Fortuitously, the press also concentrates on the personality of the new president in this first year. (See Table 8.1.) Since such information is new, it is considered newsworthy. The White House, aware of this emphasis, seeks to take advantage of it through imagemaking. According to Grossman and Kumar, the image created generally encompasses the president's personal characteristics, leadership ability, and policy.

TABLE 8.1. PRESIDENCY STORIES PRIMARILY ABOUT PERSONS BY YEAR IN CBS EVENING NEWS, LOS ANGELES TIMES, AND SYRACUSE NEW YORK POST-STANDARD (%)

	1969*	1971	1973*	1975	1977*	1979	1981*	1983
Number of stories	40	37	44	37	42	46	52	52
Stories about persons (%)	63	43	48	65	55	48	60	46
Stories not about persons (%)	37	57	52	35	45	52	40	54

*presidential inauguration years (*Source:* Davis, "News Media Coverage of American National Political Institutions.")

The President Is Human. The White House attempts to "humanize" the president, particularly in the first year of a new administration. Reporters are quick to pick up on such stories, since they appeal to a natural human interest in an important personality and his family.

Typically, the White House portrays the president as one who is close to the concerns of the citizenry, whether that be through an emphasis on Jimmy Carter's small-town roots, his experiences as a farmer and small businessman, and his preference for staying in voters' homes during campaign trips, or on George Bush's predilection for pork rinds, backyard barbecues, and playing horseshoes. The public flap over Nancy Reagan's designer dresses was the other side of this coin. The press is vital in communicating this image to the public: the president as common man.

The First Family. The president's family is used to demonstrate his compassion as well as a model home life. The First Lady's involvement in noncontroversial causes such as Barbara Bush's work on adult illiteracy aid the president's image as a concerned individual. In the case of Barbara Bush, her matronly figure and grey hair has reinforced an image as a typical woman, particularly by comparison with Nancy Reagan, who was petite and dressed in fashionable designer clothes. Children, particularly younger children, can soften the public image of the president. Even animals, when presidential offspring are adults, can serve a similar role, as evidenced by the attention to Millie, the Bush's pregnant spaniel who was featured on the cover of *Life* magazine.

Emphasis on family can backfire, however, given inappropriate context or behavior. Jimmy Carter's mention during the 1980 presidential debate that he had discussed nuclear arms policy with his 13-year-old daughter Amy was met with derision, since it implied he received policy advice from his teenage daughter,[8] and Carter's brother Billy became involved in an embarrassing scandal over his role as a lobbyist for Libya. Ronald Reagan's children undercut both his "family man" image and his positions on moral issues; son Ron appeared on *Saturday Night Live* in his underwear, and daughter Patti wrote a derogatory novel based on her relationship with her father.[9]

> The following excerpts from an article by Maureen Dowd, *New York Times* White
> House correspondent, in the July 27, 1989, *Times* reflect the kind of information the
> White House likes to see disseminated about a new president. Written in the first year
> of the Bush presidency, it focused on Bush's penchant for letter-writing.
>
> > Not since Thomas Jefferson wrote some 5,000 letters in his time in office has
> > there been such a Presidential pen pal . . .
> > Mr. Bush [averages] about 200 notes and postscripts a week . . .
> > Of the 12,000 to 15,000 letters that come in every day to be answered on the
> > azure Presidential stationery by 130 staff members and 400 volunteers, Mrs. Green
> > [Director of the White House Correspondence Office] sends Mr. Bush a weekly sample
> > of 20 to 40 pro and con letters on major issues. He also gets a larger pack of touching or
> > amusing letters, plus any that appear to be from his vast circle of acquaintances.
> > The analysts note that the Bushes' mail has a more intensely personal quality to it
> > than that of recent predecessors. "The kinder, gentler thing, the points of light thing
> > have struck a chord," Mrs. Green said.
> > One recent letter was from a woman who had opened a youth outreach center in a
> > black neighborhood in Houston. She reminded Mr. Bush that as a teenager in the
> > 1960s, she had played on an all-girl softball team called the George Bush All-Stars that
> > he had sponsored there. 'In those days it was very seldom that whites would come into
> > that all-black community,' she wrote, 'but you were an exception.'
> > A short story written by a little boy was passed along to Mr. Bush. It was about
> > two boys, lost in the White House one night, who bump into the President 'wearing his
> > Mickey Mouse slippers and carrying his Teddy Bear and his blanky' and a can of
> > Sprite. Mr. Bush replied in kind: 'After I saw you and the other kid that night, I finished
> > my Sprite, put my Teddy Bear to sleep with Millie our dog. I gave my Blanky to
> > Marshall, my granddaughter. Then I went back to sleep. Just kidding.' "

Leadership. Our expectations for the presidency today demand presidential leadership, or at least the appearance of such. In fact, the president is severely hampered
by the Constitution, by statute, and by the resistance of the Congress in his decision-
making role. Hence, the White House concentrates on projecting an image of
leadership in order to gain public and congressional support. Grossman and Kumar
identify several components of the image as a leader.[10]

Military Decisiveness. The president must appear militarily decisive. Early in his
presidency, George Bush's use of the military in Panama and the Middle East
successfully reinforced this image. However, Jimmy Carter's failed attempt to
rescue the Iran hostages and the Reagan administration's inability to oust Panama-
nian leader Noriega in 1988 contributed to a perception of military impotence.

Control of Subordinates. The president also is expected to demonstrate leadership
by firing disruptive subordinates. The continued presence of a subordinate who
challenges the president or politically damages him is viewed as a sign of weakness.
President Reagan's firing of the air traffic controllers in 1981 projected a strong,

decisive image, but his later refusal to remove his embattled chief of staff Donald Regan in 1986–1987 conveyed the opposite impression.

Intellectual Ability. The president is expected to show leadership through his command of the issues and his overall intellectual ability. Presidents Kennedy, Nixon, and Carter projected images of highly knowledgeable experts on complex matters, although their expertise usually was demonstrated in controlled settings. Ronald Reagan lacked this intellectual or technical ability, but successfully lowered expectations of presidential expertise by drawing the analogy of a corporate chairman of the board rather than a hands-on manager. George Bush, however, has restored the practice of showing leadership through intellectual command of the issues.

World Leader. Finally, Grossman and Kumar argue that the president must show leadership through his role as a world figure. Presidents have often turned to foreign policy—and particularly to foreign travels—to boost sagging popularity at home. Richard Nixon's visit to the Soviet Union and later to the Middle East in the midst of Watergate and the Camp David Summit arranged by Jimmy Carter to bring together the leaders of Israel and Egypt in 1978 are two examples.

Foreign travel can also backfire. Gerald Ford's tumble down an airplane stairway on a trip to Austria reinforced an already-established image of incompetence, and Ronald Reagan's failure to achieve an arms agreement with the Soviet Union at the Iceland Summit in 1986 initially attracted critical stories from the press, which the White House sought to manage by sending a phalanx of top officials to the major news organizations. Even that trip finally confirmed the image-building value of foreign travel as Reagan's public approval rating jumped eleven points.[11]

Foreign travel generally reaps benefits for presidential image. A study of fifteen presidential trips abroad between 1953 and 1978 found overwhelmingly favorable news coverage.[12]

Activity. Another component of image-making is the illusion of activity. As the president moves about with speeches, ceremonies, travel, he leaves in his wake a plethora of news stories. Such reporting sustains the image of an active president, even when such activity may be more symbolic than real.

Moreover, all of these stories serve to direct the attention of the press toward favorable presidential news and away from investigative reporting.

Policy. The tactics to improve the president's image with the press and the public are designed primarily to lay the groundwork for congressional and public support of the president's policy objectives.

The president himself specifically presses his policy agenda through the news media. Presidents use speeches to various audiences to push policy initiatives. These include the State of the Union addresses, televised "fireside chats," and speeches to the numerous groups offering him invitations to speak. The selection of the audience is done with the press coverage in mind. The setting for the speeches is fitted with the particular policy objective in order to provide the backdrop and visual reinforcement of the verbal message. For example, in 1988, Ronald Reagan used a visit to the U.S. Coast Guard Academy to press for formation of a bipartisan executive-legislative commission on drug interdiction.

Press Access

As Reagan's presidency emphasized, one recurring point of contention between the press and the White House has been access to the president. While nearly all members of Congress, including the leadership, are readily available for questioning, the president has sometimes maintained an aloofness from the press.

Historically, the White House has gone to great lengths to encourage reporters and offer access. Presidents have provided office space within the walls of the White House for the press's operations, and those facilities have gradually improved. Ironically, Richard Nixon moved the press even closer to the Oval Office by covering over the swimming pool and moving the press into the West Wing. In addition to office space, the White House arranges for press access to the president as he travels.

But press access nevertheless is controlled by the administration. The press is kept in a confined environment at the White House, and reporters are prohibited from wandering at will. Formal access to senior officials is granted at the administration's discretion, and presidents have discouraged, although usually unsuccessfully, unauthorized contacts between staff and the press.

Access is extended when it serves the administration's purposes and denied when it does not. Favored reporters and columnists are granted private interviews with the president and exclusive stories, for example, while others who are viewed as unfriendly are denied such access.

According to Reagan press secretary Larry Speakes, favorites during the Reagan years, for example, included columnists James J. Kilpatrick and George Will, Hugh Sidey of *Time*, Bill Plante and Gary Schuster of CBS. But other reporters were accorded different treatment. For example, during the Reagan presidency, reporters for the *Washington Times* were shunned by the White House Press Office for printing stories about Nancy Reagan's dislike for Larry Speakes.[13]

Speaking for the President

Managing the news about the presidency means controlling the statements emanating from the White House. Such control eludes presidents since not all who speak about the president, or even those who speak for him, are saying what he would want said. Presidential spokespersons include the president himself, and also a wide array of persons ranging from the press secretary to a lowly White House staff member.

According to Colin Seymour-Ure, there are six types of spokespersons who are differentiated on the basis of their regularity in meeting with the press, their authorization to speak to the press, and their specialization as public relations professionals.[14]

Presidential press secretaries, authorized specialists, meet with the press routinely. The press secretary speaks formally for the president in daily (and sometimes more often) briefings with the press. Some of the most effective press secretaries have been individuals who have had close personal relationships with the president, such as Jody Powell to Jimmy Carter and Bill Moyers to Lyndon Johnson. However, other secretaries have included government public relations professionals such as Larry Speakes (Reagan presidency) and Marlin Fitzwater (Reagan and Bush), and former White House reporters such as Jerry Terhorst and Ron Nessen in the Ford presidency.

Although the press secretary is the spokesperson usually most visible to the press and the public, presidential assistants such as the White House Chief of Staff, the National Security Advisor, assistants, deputy assistants, and special assistants to the president also meet with the press routinely, though usually for background purposes. Policymakers have devised ground rules for these interviews, which generally have been accepted by the press. (See page 144.) The practice allows aides of the president to say things the president cannot. For example, these sources can float trial balloons on policy options or potential appointments without directly linking the president to the suggestion. Moreover, the aide's relative anonymity is preserved, while the limelight is retained for the president.

White House staff members, including top aides, also can serve as unauthorized spokespersons. Attempts to serve personal or policy objectives in contrast to those of the president can lead to unauthorized contacts. These "leaks" are made to affect the outcome of policy or personnel decisions. Some leaks are made to enhance the leaker's reputation or diminish that of another administration official. A classic example of the former is David Stockman's unflattering portrayal of Reaganomics given an *Atlantic Monthly* reporter who published them in 1981. An example of the latter is the press leak by some Bush officials of negative portrayals of Vice President Dan Quayle's performance during the 1988 campaign.

Other leaks, however, are inadvertently made. For instance, former press secretary Jody Powell, in social conversation, told a wire service reporter that President Carter had been attacked by a large rabbit. The journalist reported the story, which sparked strong derision of the president for more than a week.[15]

The goal for a president is to manage the news by minimizing the transmission of unauthorized information from those who "speak for" him. However, such a task has been an impossible one for modern presidents.

PRESIDENTIAL PRESS CONFERENCES

The press continues to demand greater access. One key barometer of access to the president in the eyes of the press corps is the frequency of presidential press conferences.

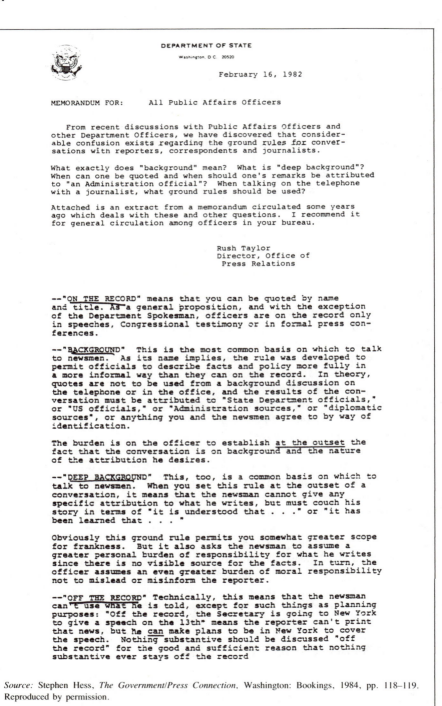

DEPARTMENT OF STATE

Washington, D.C. 20520

February 16, 1982

MEMORANDUM FOR: All Public Affairs Officers

From recent discussions with Public Affairs Officers and
other Department Officers, we have discovered that considerable confusion exists regarding the ground rules for conversations with reporters, correspondents and journalists.

What exactly does "background" mean? What is "deep background"?
When can one be quoted and when should one's remarks be attributed
to "an Administration official"? When talking on the telephone
with a journalist, what ground rules should be used?

Attached is an extract from a memorandum circulated some years
ago which deals with these and other questions. I recommend it
for general circulation among officers in your bureau.

Rush Taylor
Director, Office of
Press Relations

--"ON THE RECORD" means that you can be quoted by name
and title. As a general proposition, and with the exception
of the Department Spokesman, officers are on the record only
in speeches, Congressional testimony or in formal press conferences.

--"BACKGROUND" This is the most common basis on which to talk
to newsmen. As its name implies, the rule was developed to
permit officials to describe facts and policy more fully in
a more informal way than they can on the record. In theory,
quotes are not to be used from a background discussion on
the telephone or in the office, and the results of the conversation must be attributed to "State Department officials,"
or "US officials," or "Administration sources," or "diplomatic
sources", or anything you and the newsmen agree to by way of
identification.

The burden is on the officer to establish at the outset the
fact that the conversation is on background and the nature
of the attribution he desires.

--"DEEP BACKGROUND" This, too, is a common basis on which to
talk to newsmen. When you set this rule at the outset of a
conversation, it means that the newsman cannot give any
specific attribution to what he writes, but must couch his
story in terms of "it is understood that . . ." or "it has
been learned that . . . "

Obviously this ground rule permits you somewhat greater scope
for frankness. But it also asks the newsman to assume a
greater personal burden of responsibility for what he writes
since there is no visible source for the facts. In turn, the
officer assumes an even greater burden of moral responsibility
not to mislead or misinform the reporter.

--"OFF THE RECORD" Technically, this means that the newsman
can't use what he is told, except for such things as planning
purposes: "Off the record, the Secretary is going to New York
to give a speech on the 13th" means the reporter can't print
that news, but he can make plans to be in New York to cover
the speech. Nothing substantive should be discussed "off
the record" for the good and sufficient reason that nothing
substantive ever stays off the record

Source: Stephen Hess, *The Government/Press Connection*, Washington: Bookings, 1984, pp. 118–119.
Reproduced by permission.

These encounters have been compared with the question period in the British Parliament where the Prime Minister and other cabinet officials stand to answer questions from other members, especially those of the opposition.[16] Journalists argue that since no such opportunity for official questioning exists in the United States, press conferences serve a similar purpose of exposing the president to questions from the people's representatives—the press.

According to political columnist David Broder, press conferences are useful because "they bring presidents into the political dialogue, by requiring them to answer the arguments and evidence introduced by critics of their policies. They guarantee that the American people hear from the man they elected—and not merely from some hired spokesman."[17] Broder argues that press conferences are good for presidents, too, since facing frequent news conferences "forces a president to be sure he knows what is happening around him."[18]

Former presidential press secretary Jody Powell contends that Americans "have a right to see how their Chief Executive and Commander in Chief handles himself under tough cross-examination,"[19] and scholar Lewis Wolfson suggests that such encounters are valuable because they allow "reporters momentarily to sweep aside the layers of counsellors and toadies that surround the president."[20]

Presidents and their advisors in the White House have typically viewed press conferences somewhat differently. They see press conferences as a tool available to the president to communicate his policy objectives and gain political support to achieve them. They are less inclined to view the sessions as an institution they must preserve. Not surprisingly, presidents are inclined to use this tool when it serves their own purpose. John Kennedy enjoyed press conferences because of his skill in bantering with reporters; his press conferences reinforced the image of a president in command of the issues.

Succeeding presidents have been measured against Kennedy's performance, and presidents such as Nixon and Ford, who sometimes compared poorly with Kennedy, scheduled news conferences less frequently and found the conferences less helpful as a tool in presidential communication and persuasion. Jimmy Carter, like Kennedy, initially enjoyed the give-and-take of the sessions and committed himself to meet with reporters twice a month, although later in his presidency he found less and less to enjoy in the encounters and met more sporadically with reporters.[21] George Bush also began his presidency at ease with the press in these gatherings. Like Kennedy, he enjoyed bantering with reporters. One example is the following frank exchange between a reporter and Bush as president-elect:

Q: Mr. Vice-President, you seem to be dancing around just how much your administration would—will spend on housing.

A: Yes.

Q: Would you talk about that?

A: I wouldn't have phrased it that way but that's exactly what I was doing.[22]

For Ronald Reagan, press conferences were fraught with danger. Although he usually maintained a congenial manner, Reagan often misspoke on key issues and demonstrated ignorance on others. A representative from the Press Office frequently met with reporters afterward to correct the president's misstatements, an effort which only fueled speculation Reagan was too detached from his own administration.[23]

Reagan sought to avoid press conferences. In the first seven years of his presidency, he averaged only one news conference every other month while previous presidents such as Gerald Ford and Jimmy Carter averaged over their presidencies twice that.[24]

Press conferences can be a useful forum for conveying messages to the press and the public about the president personally as well as about policy. Since the White House press corps places such a strong emphasis on the press conference as an indicator of presidential capability, a press conference can be seen by the White House as a means to retrieve confidence and respect. For example, President Reagan used a press conference in March 1987 to demonstrate that he was on top of the Iran-Contra affair.[25] President Ford once briefed reporters on the budget and faced their questioning for nearly three hours in order to demonstrate his intellectual prowess on policy issues.[26] Harshly phrased press conference questions during the Nixon presidency actually won public sympathy for the president.[27]

Presidents attempt to manage the news emanating from press conferences just as they do other White House news. One effective tactic is scheduling, which is at the president's discretion. Timing is significant. Presidents are often more willing to hold press conferences when there is good news to announce or bask in; while news conferences are apt to be less frequent during bad times for presidents.[28] Jimmy Carter decided to abandon his schedule of regular news conferences following widespread criticism in the press,[29] and Ronald Reagan generally avoided press conferences during investigation of the Iran-Contra affair.

John Kennedy enjoyed press conferences and held them frequently. Succeeding presidents have often been measured against Kennedy's performances and have scheduled conferences less often. Ronald Reagan, although projecting an almost unflappable congeniality, often misspoke or misunderstood questions; press aides spent considerable time and effort "mopping up" after Reagan's press conference errors. *Source:* JFK Library; the White House.

Choosing a time for a press conference also means choosing the topic. By scheduling a news conference at a time when certain issues are current, the president can anticipate the line of questioning from the press.

He can also direct press attention by opening with a statement on a topic he wishes to address in the press conference, but the attempt will be unsuccessful if press attention is focused on other topics.

Presidents also try to direct the line of questioning through the selection of reporters to ask questions. Presidents are bound by tradition to choose regularly the representatives of the three major networks, the wire services, national news-magazines, and major national newspapers such as the *New York Times* and the *Washington Post*. However, the president can intersperse that selection with "backbenchers"—reporters from other news organizations such as regional news-papers or news syndicates. Their questions usually are more friendly to the president because of a desire to be asked again in the future, or may serve to change the subject if the president is unhappy with the line of questioning.

Former Reagan press spokesman Larry Speakes explained the efforts of the Press Office in directing the president's question-taking:

> We also tried to identify people who might ask softball questions, and I would put three or four people on the right-hand side of the front row. I would tell the President, 'If you get battered from the left or the center, go to your right.'[30]

Given the extensive news coverage guaranteed to press conferences and their primetime live coverage, presidents usually devote large blocks of time to preparation. The president meets with key advisors to review likely questions and rehearse appropriate answers. A briefing book also may be used to refresh the president's memory on pending issues.[31] Such extensive preparation is time-consuming, as Jimmy Carter's press secretary Jody Powell admits:

> Our commitment to hold two a month was foolish. A president simply has more important things to do with his time than prepare for two full-blown press conferences each month.[32]

Powell suggests a press conference be held every four to six weeks.

Early on, before live television coverage, both presidents and reporters benefited from presidential press conferences. Presidents used press conferences to present the administration's viewpoint and explain policies in an informal manner; the White House press corps derived both news and an insider's understanding of the president's thinking. Reporters were bound by certain rules: no direct quotations could be used without approval; most information was for background; information that was off-the-record could not be shared with other reporters not in attendance.

At the same time, the reporters were given the opportunity of a frank exchange in a setting where the president was usually relaxed and willing to take reporters into his confidence.[33]

As Edward Follard, a former *Washington Post* correspondent explained:

> The value of the press conference, as we saw it was that by asking questions and getting answers from the president, we found how the president felt about, oh, the issues of the day; found what his hopes were; what his worries were; had a chance to, oh, size him up, so to speak.[34]

However, the mutual benefits have diminished. Presidents today usually feel that they can communicate their policies more effectively in other formats. Journalists find that the conferences offer little in the way of news and often generate hostility with the president or the public.

The most dramatic change has been the introduction of television. Televising the news conference placed both the president and the reporters in the public's view. The president could no longer share information with the press during a news conference on an off-the-record basis. The senior aides to the president now perform that function in non-televised interviews. The president's answers became more formal and less insightful as they were formulated for a mass audience rather than for reporters. As presidents went "over reporters' heads"—directed more of the content of their answers to the television audience—the reporters present grew resentful of their being used as props and intensified the critical questioning.

Broadcast reporters, particularly, well-known figures in their own right, designed questions to elicit the most newsworthy answers—questions to catch the president off-guard and burst the bubble of the administration's forum for presenting administration views to the public.

All of these developments of the past quarter century and repeated with each president have resulted in fewer regularly scheduled news conferences. Although newly inaugurated presidents initially have guaranteed the press frequent access through regularly scheduled news conferences, the pattern typically recurs and the encounters become less frequent.[35]

Certainly the modern news conference has been widely criticized as ineffective. Criticism has come from the press corps, who deride it as a "theatrical event,"[36] or criticize it because they perceive it as the absolute tool of the president.[37] Hugh Sidey of *Time* calls it "a dinosaur that deserves burial."[38] Administration officials, on the other hand, pan the sessions because of their inability to use it effectively.

The growing dissatisfaction towards a vehicle with declining utility has prompted both the White House and the press to seek alternatives to the sessions. Presidents have experimented with other types of encounters, including the mini-news conference where a few reporters are invited to ask questions of the president in a less formal session. The Carter and Reagan administrations tried mini-conferences but reporters not included in the pool complained. To reduce growing tension over news conferences, President Bush also has relied on impromptu daytime televised press conferences rather than the formal, prime-time gatherings with much larger television audiences. Bush has also turned to the mini-news

---

Are press conferences useful?

According to Jimmy Carter's press secretary Jody Powell,

> As transmitters of information, [press conferences] are vastly overrated. I often felt the nation would have been better informed about what President Carter was up to had his town hall meetings been televised instead of his press conferences. Not because the citizenry asks more intelligent questions than the press, but because they ask questions about things they want to know about. (Powell, p. 305)

And Larry Speakes, press secretary for Ronald Reagan, argues:

> In the wake of Watergate and Vietnam, press conferences have deteriorated into a game of "How can I trip him up?" and "I gotcha." Instead of asking legitimate questions on matters of importance, most of the reporters who attend press conferences are there only to trap the President. They are trying to make news, not report it. (Speakes, p. 235)

---

conferences with a small number of reporters. One White House aide explained: "We're looking at various alternative ways of letting the press ask questions of the president."[39] The search continues for a mutually acceptable format for both president and press.

BYPASSING THE PRESS

Presidents have often sought a direct, credible link with the public which allows them to bypass the press altogether. With a direct link, the president could transmit his message without the prism of reporting which transforms an event according to news values.

Presidents frequently blame the press for distorting their messages and not providing the opportunities to communicate with the public. In exasperation, Dwight Eisenhower once told his senior aides: "Just let me get up and talk to the people. I can get through to them that way."[40] Jody Powell argues that the press "fails to provide the President with an adequate channel for communicating with, for moving, shaping, and directing the popular will."[41]

As a result, presidents have devised methods to bypass the press. The White House press office bypasses the national press by reaching out to the non-Washington press. This office disseminates news directly to daily and weekly newspapers and local radio and television stations around the country.

The Reagan administration revived a technique used by Franklin Roosevelt— radio speeches. Reagan delivered a weekly radio address, which was a comfortable vehicle for Reagan, the former radio sportscaster, to lobby the Congress and the public for policy support. George Bush, however, chose not to continue the practice.

The State of the Union speech, which is televised live to the nation and is given in a historic location with members of Congress as props, is a prime vehicle for the president to get the attention of Congress and the public. Presidents have used it to press a bevy of proposals. Some, such as budget and tax cuts pushed in Reagan's 1981 speech, come to fruition. Others such as Nixon's government reorganization plan in 1971 and Reagan's New Federalism failed to achieve the necessary support. Presidents can make the speech more dramatic by focusing on a single high-priority issue, which creates the impression that is their primary, if not sole, interest.

Televised "fireside chats," following the model of Franklin Roosevelt's radio chats, are still valuable in cultivating public support for the president's policy agenda, since they allow the president to speak directly to the American public to announce and defend policies. When they seek public support, presidents request time from the networks for a televised address to the nation.

Although the networks usually comply, they have at times refused. Two networks failed to provide Lyndon Johnson with requested time because network executives felt his speech would not address a major policy issue; and two speeches by Jimmy Carter—one on the Panama Canal treaties and the other on civil service reform—were not carried by all the networks.[42] Ronald Reagan was refused live network coverage for several speeches.

Denial of television time to the president by network executives clearly raises a question of power: Who should decide whether the president's speech is important enough to give him time to address the nation live? No resolution currently exists. Both sides have sought to accommodate the other. Network news executives have been cautious in refusing time to avoid charges of suppressing the president's messages. In turn, presidents have spaced out their requests to prevent audience boredom and network refusal. George Bush waited nine months before delivering his first prime-time televised address to the nation. Moreover, the availability of alternative news sources such as CNN and C-SPAN, which will become more widespread with the increasing penetration of cable, could make the question moot within the next few years.

The president's use of televised addresses is rendered less effective by the networks' granting response time to the opposition party, usually immediately following the presidential address. But the president maintains an advantage simply because he offers a single program and possesses the status of the presidency. Opposition party members of Congress lack that status and often differ among themselves on alternatives to presidential programs, which limits their ability to blunt the president's message.

Visual messages often are as effective as—or more effective than—the content of prepared speeches. To demonstrate his administration's anti-Washington message, for example, President Reagan used the backdrop of his California ranch to sign the historic tax cut bill in 1981. Reagan's visit to Normandy to commemorate the 40th anniversary of D-Day showed the president nearly embodying American patriotism.

Ingratiation and Intimidation

Presidents also have used other methods to attempt to manage the news. Some of these methods have been more personal and blatant than others. Lyndon Johnson tried to ingratiate himself with reporters through gifts.[43] Presidents have used dinner and other social invitations to gain journalists' favor.

Presidents also have used intimidation to gain journalistic quiescence. Methods directed at journalists include denying access or special privileges such as accompanying the president on foreign trips. The White House has used contacts with news executives to affect the tone of journalists' stories. One CBS correspondent at the White House remembered meeting Lyndon Johnson for the first time and being told by the president in his Texas drawl: "Ah'm a good friend of yo' boss, Frank Stanton. Anything Ah can do for you, just let me know. Ah know we're going to get along just fine."[44]

Pressure has been directed less at the journalists and more at their organizations. Kennedy tried to get reporters reassigned, while Johnson tried to get them fired. The Nixon administration threatened to deny license renewal to network-owned stations and sought to use the IRS to investigate news organizations.[45] Spiro Agnew, Nixon's vice president, used speeches to win public sympathy for Nixon in his battles with the press and to pressure the news media into moderating critical coverage of Nixon.[46]

THE PRESS CORPS

The Body Watch

The reporters who cover the president observe him every moment he is in the public eye. Although most regular White House reporters engage in the "body watch," as they call it, it is a particularly vital function for the wire service reporters whose stories are the staple of national news coverage for hundreds of small daily newspapers. Helen Thomas, chief White House reporter for UPI, estimates that over 80 percent of her job consists of following the president or getting information about him.[47]

Sometimes this physical shadowing is referred to as a "death watch," because of the imperative for reporters to be there if anything happens to the president. Reporters who were present in Dallas on November 22, 1963, have the experience seared in their memories, and some such as Dan Rather of CBS and Tom Wicker of the *New York Times* saw their careers catapulted because of their reporting of that event. Careers can be made or broken by such crisis reporting. As one editor put it: "The worst thing in the world that could happen to you is for the President of the United States to choke on a piece of meat, and for you not to be there."[48]

The press corps also defends the body watch as a public service, through which the public is kept informed of the president's activities. But the body watch is pursued primarily because what the president does, says, and decides is defined, quite simply, as news.

Competition perpetuates the body watch. As long as other reporters are there, no reporter can afford to be elsewhere. The chance is too great of missing a big story or even a little story covered by the wire services. But, as far as presidential news coverage is concerned, it makes no sense from an economic standpoint since a few reporters could easily perform the same function. In some cases, the networks have pooled their efforts to reduce the number of camera crews, but editors often demand that the story they use originate from their own staff reporter, even though a similar story can be obtained from the wire services.

The body watch is perpetuated by journalists and their editors and producers. The presidential body watch is favored as an efficient, even economical, way to report on national government activity, since it allows the press to cover a single individual and report that as the activity of the national government during that day. Former ABC White House Correspondent Sam Donaldson has termed the body watch a "convenient way of filling up time and being able to defend it by saying it is the presidency after all."[49]

The president can use the press's saturation coverage as a forum for pushing his own agenda of issues. Since the press defines what presidents say and do as news, presidents can say and do what fits their own political purposes. But the body watch also can be confining both administratively and personally. Administratively, the element of secrecy is damaged in such matters as personnel appointments. Personally, the effect can be damaging. Gerald Ford suffered from news coverage of his accidents—falling down as he skied or tripping on an airplane ramp. Jimmy Carter tried to elude the press corps once to go fishing in Pennsylvania, and presidential retreats to Camp David or other homes have been attempts to escape the body watch, if only temporarily. Even in those settings reporters stay as close as they can. The press corps routinely observed the Reagans at their California ranch through telephoto camera lenses perched on nearby mountaintops.

Getting News

Reporters complain that the body watch deters them from more investigative reporting of the White House, but most national circulation newspapers and news-magazines go beyond the body watch in their reporting of the presidency.

News is what the president has done, is doing, or plans to do. Reporters get news by personal observation, but such observation is sporadic and highly controlled by the White House. The photo opportunities and speeches allow the White House to show off the president, but almost always in the way the White House desires.

As a result, reporters also turn for news to the press secretary's briefings, which occur at least daily, statements from the president or other officials, and to transcripts of presidential speeches.

Background meetings with White House aides can offer more accurate and detailed information than the public news conferences or briefings. Members of any administration are more likely to speak candidly in sessions where the information will not be attributed directly to them, and such briefings can be used to educate reporters about the background of a policy issue or decision.

Obviously, the instruction is intended to benefit either the administration or the individual official. These briefings are opportunities for administration officials to launch trial balloons of policy decisions or personnel appointments without direct administrative responsibility. Officials may be sending messages to others—other administrative figures, members of Congress, or foreign leaders—in an unofficial manner. In 1986, for example, administration officials used background briefings to persuade Libyan leader Muhammar Qaddafi that the United States was attempting to overthrow him.

Some sources in backgrounders carry their own motives for working with reporters. They may be on the losing side of a policy debate and want outside support, or they may wish to derail a policy decision by premature leaking.

Congress also serves as a valuable source of administration news. Members of Congress gain information about administration actions and often pass such information on to reporters. When the U.S. planes bombed Libya in April, 1986, for example, Senator Robert Byrd, after meeting with the president about the attack, leaked to reporters that the president would make a major announcement on television.

Barriers to News

Journalists who cover the White House are sometimes overfed but feel undernourished. The White House Press Office blankets them with statements, briefings, and other material, but nevertheless limits their access to the president. They cannot question White House sources at will; they are restricted to the press area of the White House, unless otherwise authorized; and even their best sources usually talk only when they want to and not otherwise.

The access may be stopped altogether if the reporter is "frozen out" by the White House because of coverage perceived as unfavorable. A succession of critical stories or negative references to the president, White House aides, or the administration generally can result in a denial of access. Interviews are not arranged, phone calls remain unreturned, and foreign travel reservations are not made. However, such tactics are primarily used against media outlets the White House believes it can temporarily do without, such as regional newspapers or news syndicates. Rarely are they applied to news organizations such as the *New York Times* or the major networks with strong influence among elites or broad circulation. Representatives of the two major wire services—Associated Press and United Press International—are never excluded because their information feeds almost all other news outlets in the nation.

Sometimes the barriers to newsgathering are raised not by the administration, but by the press. Editorial demands for the body watch can take reporters away from more in-depth stories, and reporters sometimes complain their serious articles on public policy issues are shunted aside for personality pieces. Andrew Glass, a news syndicate reporter complained during the Carter years that "it's a lot easier for me to get into several newspapers in the chain with a story about Amy [Carter] than with a story about an important policy decision."[50]

The habits of reporters also contribute to a reporting style that misses some major stories. The huge flow of materials from the White House leads many reporters to concentrate on that information and ignore or overlook other possible stories not being discussed by the White House. Reporters at the White House also enjoy a cozy relationship with sources that can inhibit attempts at investigation. One White House reporter anonymously commented: "The White House Press Corps is the last place the Watergate story would have broken."[51] As a result, White House reporters do miss major stories about the presidency. The Watergate story was uncovered by two reporters who were not part of the White House press corps, and the Iran-Contra affair during the Reagan administration similarly escaped the White House reporters.

The Journalists

Although terms such as White House press corps connote a monolithic quality, the reporters who cover the White House actually fall into at least two broad categories.

Elites. The most visible and influential are the reporters who represent national newspapers such as the *New York Times* and the *Wall Street Journal*, major metropolitan newspapers such as the *Washington Post* and the *Los Angeles Times*, the wire services, the newsweeklies such as *Time* and *Newsweek*, and network television news.

The elites are influential for a number of reasons. First, they are read or watched by other reporters for cues on stories. Because these journalists represent national or major regional news outlets, White House officials accord them special privileges such as scoops, entrée to private briefings, a speedier return of phone calls, greater assistance in developing stories, the best seating at daily White House press briefings, and almost guaranteed recognition at presidential press conferences.

The elites are influential not only because of their national scope, but also because they are read by power holders in government, including the president. Reporters from these elite news sources set the tone for coverage by others, and they engage in analysis which is read or heard by policymakers in Washington and issue activists around the country. The wire service reporters, on the other hand, are influential not because they are well read in Washington, but due to the wide circulation of their stories throughout the country.

Non-elites. The rest of the press corps comprises a wide array of representatives from other media outlets including smaller metropolitan dailies, news syndicates, radio stations, special interest publications such as *Fortune* and *Business Week*, and the foreign press. This group can be subdivided into two groups—those who cover the White House full-time and others who, representing small media organizations, cover national politics and divide their time between the White House and other locations.

The dichotomy between elites and non-elites, which is recognized by both the press corps and the White House, can be useful to the White House press office. Since the non-elites often resent the privileges accorded the elites, the press secretary can use this animosity against the elites by occasionally taking sides with the non-elites.

The View from the Press Section

Just as the administration possesses certain goals in its relationship with the press, so too do the reporters who cover the White House. Reporters seek news that satisfies their editors and readers and, if possible, enhances their own status among colleagues. They seek exclusives—or at least they seek to avoid being scooped. Current sources need to be maintained and new, reliable sources acquired.

Reporting on the White House is the pinnacle of a journalistic career for many reporters. The proximity to power, the centrality of the source in American politics, the visibility among colleagues and, for broadcast news reporters, across the nation are alluring.

For other reporters, the White House beat is a critical stepping-stone to other positions such as news anchor, senior editor, or columnist. Occasionally, the beat may even take a reporter on the other side of the podium. Ron Nessen of NBC News and Jerry Terhorst of the *Detroit News* both moved from the White House press corps to the post of White House press secretary.

Reporters face a professional dilemma in cooperating with the White House. Many middle-aged journalists are products of new journalism, and younger journalists grew up during the Vietnam/Watergate period. An adversarial stance gains much rhetorical support. However, cooperation is essential to job performance. Getting stories, obtaining interviews, gaining access to background briefings all hinge on a willingness to cooperate with White House officials. Hence, cooperation is really the rule, not the exception.

The press corps regularly complain about manipulation by the administration, but resisting such manipulation is a complicated matter. Not to cover what the White House presents is defying news values because the White House has orchestrated events to conform to those values.

For example, television reporters who seek their own stories likely will show pieces with "talking heads"—pictures of people being interviewed—since visual drama is rare in unofficial White House news. Given a rough equality on the other news values, faced with the choice between those stories and White House-produced news, the news media opt for the choice that is more visually entertaining. Moreover, editors and producers who also receive the wire service stories will wonder why the main event provided by the White House was not covered.

Reporters often react to proffered news stories with thinly veiled cynicism. In the network news story, for example, the reporter's voice-over may pan administration actions or decisions, and the reporter's closing remarks may impugn administration motives. But since audiences tend to remember the visual image more than the audio message, the effect of the cynicism may well be lost. As Sam Donaldson commented, "Presidents have learned that they don't need [reporters]. They just have to capture our cameras."[52]

Reporters' hostility toward White House manipulation attempts is often directed at the press secretary in press briefings. David Halberstam compared the hostility at the White House briefings to that at the military reports received during the Vietnam War:

> The guys who went to the [briefings] . . . were ferocious there. They would tear flesh off the briefer, and they would never get anything. There was a lot of combat and scratching of flesh and flaring of whatever. For all of it, they really got nothing. . . . Some of it, some of the anger they were taking out on the briefing officer was their own frustrations.[53]

Overt public complaints about manipulation are unlikely. Such complaints would shift attention from the story to the press. The press has come to accept the manipulation, but reporters continue to assert their independence by private criticism and complaint, cynicism, and occasional outbursts of hostility.

SUMMARY

The White House press corps has undergone dramatic change since the days of FDR, not only in terms of the number of reporters, but also in the journalists' conception of their role and their capabilities in surveillance of the presidency. Grossman and Kumar note:

> The President and the White House staff today are faced with a press corps vastly more sophisticated than the one that existed before World War II, news media that actually produce stories about some of the ways in which the White House tries to manipulate them. . . .[54]

The trends in journalism of the 1960s and 1970s have altered the perspective of White House journalists. Reporters feel a responsibility to do more than describe events; they must also interpret them. The experiences of Vietnam and Watergate have deepened press mistrust of politicians, and the press now also feels an obligation to warn the public about activities of government officials—to play the watchdog.

Presidents have become more sophisticated in their usage of the press and have devised a variety of methods to manage the news. However, they still must compete with other players in national politics. They cannot take for granted that the press will always offer them all the coverage they feel they need.

Due to the increased autonomy of the press, the public spotlight for the president often means bad news descends on the White House first. The blame for national problems is routinely laid at the president's doorstep by the press. Managing the news is an attempt to lessen the damage of that bad news.

Despite press accusations that the White House creates news content and White House claims that the press completely controls the president's image, the battle continues. Neither player can dominate the other. The very persistence of the struggle indicates that the press has become increasingly autonomous in its relations with the White House, while the president has become ever more dependent on the press for help in governing, and both sides are fully aware of it.

NOTES

1. Thomas Cronin, *The State of the Presidency*, 2d ed., Boston: Little, Brown, 1980, p. 96.
2. Richard Davis, "News Media Coverage of American National Political Institutions," unpublished doctoral dissertation, Syracuse University, 1986, p. 50.
3. Michael B. Grossman and Martha Joynt Kumar, *Portraying the President*, Baltimore, Md.: Johns Hopkins University Press, 1981, p. 263.
4. See Elmer E. Cornwell, Jr., "Presidential News: The Expanding Public Image," *Journalism Quarterly* 36 (Summer 1959): 275–283; Alan Balutis, "Congress, the Presidency, and the Press: The Expanding Presidential Image," *Presidential Studies Quarterly* 7 (Fall 1977): 244–251; Grossman and Kumar, *Portraying the President*, chap. 10; and Davis, "News Media Coverage," p. 46.
5. See Grossman and Kumar, *Portraying the President*, pp. 255–263.; and Fred Smoller, "The Six O'Clock Presidency: Patterns of Network News Coverage of the President," *Presidential Studies Quarterly* 16 (Winter 1986): 31–49. For a discussion of unfavorable coverage, see Michael J. Robinson et al., "With Friends Like These . . . ," *Public Opinion* (June/July 1983): 2–3.
6. For a discussion of the White House efforts during the Reagan presidency, see Mark Hertsgaard, *On Bended Knee: The Press and the Reagan Presidency*, New York: Farrar Straus & Giroux, 1988.
7. Quoted in Hedrick Smith, *The Power Game: How Washington Works*, New York: Random House, 1988, p. 406.
8. See, for example, Jeff Greenfield, *The Real Campaign*, New York: Summit Books, 1982, pp. 239–240.
9. Georgia Dullea, "First Family's Foibles: A Drama in Two Acts," *New York Times*, February 28, 1986, p. B6.
10. Grossman and Kumar, *Portraying the President*, pp. 232–238.

11. "Duel of the Spinmeisters," *Newsweek*, October 27, 1986, p. 23.
12. Grossman and Kumar, *Portraying the President*, p. 236.
13. Larry Speakes, *Speaking Out*, Scribners, 1988, pp. 219, 240
14. Colin Seymour-Ure, *The American President: Power and Communication*, New York: St. Martin's Press, 1982, pp. 79–89.
15. Jody Powell, *The Other Side of the Story*, New York: William Morrow, 1984, pp. 104–108.
16. Lewis Wolfson, *The Untapped Power of the Press*, New York: Praeger, 1985, p. 24.
17. David Broder, "Remember Presidential News Conferences," *Washington Post*, July 26, 1987, p. B7.
18. Broder, "Remember Presidential News Conferences," p. B7.
19. Powell, *The Other Side of the Story*, p. 306.
20. Wolfson, *The Untapped Power of the Press*, p. 21.
21. Grossman and Kumar, *Portraying the President*, pp. 244–245.
22. "Remarks by Bush and Kemp at News Conference in the Capital," *New York Times*, December 20, 1988, p. B8.
23. Hertsgaard, *On Bended Knee*, pp. 138–140.
24. Hedrick Smith, *The Power Game: How Washington Works*, New York: Random House, 1988, p. 432.
25. Steven V. Roberts, "Reagan Sets Thursday News Session," *New York Times*, March 18, 1987, p. A17.
26. Grossman and Kumar, *Portraying the President*, p. 234.
27. Grossman and Kumar, *Portraying the President*, pp. 247–248.
28. See Jarol B. Mannheim and William W. Lammers, "The News Conference and Presidential Leadership: Does the Tail Wag the Dog?" *Presidential Studies Quarterly* 11 (Spring 1981): 177–186.
29. Grossman and Kumar, *Portraying the President*, p. 245. See also Wolfson, *The Untapped Power of the Press*, p. 22.
30. Speakes, *Speaking Out*, p. 238.
31. Speakes, *Speaking Out*, pp. 236–239.
32. Powell, *The Other Side of the Story*, p. 305.
33. See B. H. Winfield, "Franklin D. Roosevelt's Efforts to Influence the News During His First Term Press Conference," *Presidential Studies Quarterly* 9 (Spring 1981): 189–199.
34. Grossman and Kumar, *Portraying the President*, p. 241.
35. For a discussion of the introduction of television at presidential news conferences, see Laurence Lorenz, "Truman and the Broadcaster," *Journal of Broadcasting* 13 (Winter 1968–1969): 17–22; and Harry Sharp, Jr., "Live from Washington: The Telecasting of President Kennedy's News Conferences," *Journal of Broadcasting* 13 (Winter 1968–1969): 23–32.
36. Charles Krauthammer, "Opposition Party: The Press," *Washington Post*, March 27, 1987, p. A27.
37. Wolfson, *The Untapped Power of the Press*, p. 22.
38. Hugh Sidey, "A Waste of Everybody's Time," *Time*, September 30, 1985, p. 27.
39. Bernard Weinraub, "Bush, on the Mound, Puts His Spin on Pitch to Press Corps," *New York Times*, January 26, 1989, p. B6.
40. Robert H. Ferrell, ed., *The Diary of James C. Hagerty*, Bloomington, Ind.: Indiana University Press, 1983, p. 41.

41. Powell, *The Other Side of the Story*, p. 35.
42. See Robert Locander, "Carter and the Press: The First Two Years," *Presidential Studies Quarterly* 10 (Winter 1980): 106–120.
43. Tom Wicker, *On Press*, New York: Viking Press, 1978, p. 131. Robert Pierpoint, *At the White House*, New York: Putnam, 1981, pp. 105–106.
44. Pierpoint, *At the White House*, p. 102.
45. See William Porter, *Assault on the Media: The Nixon Years,* Ann Arbor, Mich.: University of Michigan Press, 1976, pp. 53, 169.
46. See Dennis T. Lowrey, "Agnew and the Network TV News: A before/after Content Analysis," *Journalism Quarterly* 48 (Summer 1971): 31–41.
47. Grossman and Kumar, *Portraying the President*, p. 43.
48. Grossman and Kumar, *Portraying the President*, p. 43.
49. Quoted in Dick Kirschten, "The White House Press: Public Watchdog or Megaphone for President's Messages?" *National Journal* (November 16, 1985): 2585.
50. Quoted in Grossman and Kumar, *Portraying the President*, p. 231.
51. Quoted in Grossman and Kumar, *Portraying the President*, p. 187.
52. Kirschten, "The White House Press," p. 2585.
53. Grossman and Kumar, *Portraying the President*, p. 185.
54. Grossman and Kumar, *Portraying the President*, p. 226.

SUGGESTED READINGS

Denton, Robert E., Jr. *Presidential Communication: Description and Analysis*. New York: Praeger, 1986.
Grossman, Michael B., and Martha Joynt Kumar. *Portraying the President*. Baltimore, Md.: Johns Hopkins University Press, 1981.
Hertsgaard, Mark. *On Bended Knee: The Press and the Reagan Presidency*. New York: Farrar Straus & Giroux, 1988.
Pollard, James. *The Presidents and the Press*. New York: Macmillan, 1947.
Powell, Jody. *The Other Side of the Story*. New York: William Morrow, 1984.
Speakes, Larry. *Speaking Out*. New York: Scribners, 1988.
Tebbel, John, and Sarah Miles Watts. *The Press and the Presidency: From George Washington to Ronald Reagan*. New York: Oxford University Press, 1985.

CHAPTER 9

Congress

*"Each side holds important power—members of the House [of Representatives]
by controlling whether, where, and how to grant access, journalists by deciding
whether, when, where, and how to pay attention."*

Timothy E. Cook[1]

When the Senate began live televised coverage of its floor proceedings in 1986,
Ronald Reagan, no stranger to television, reportedly advised a group of senators on
how to act in front of the cameras. The president told them to wear blue shirts, stand
on the white chalk marks on the floor, and keep their mouths closed when they kiss.

The Senate's premiere on live television is one example of the growing role of
the press in the legislative process. The Congress institutionally and members
individually have been exerting themselves to try to attract more news media
attention. An explosion in press relations has occurred and Congress has become
more accessible to print and broadcast media than ever before in its history.
According to one estimate, the congressional press galleries distribute 15,000 press
releases a year.[2] Another anomaly is that Congress has more journalists covering it
than any other governmental institution. In the mid-1980s, more than 1,500 reporters were accredited to the daily press gallery.[3]

COVERING CONGRESS

A Disappearing Congress?

Ironically, despite these exertions and news stories of Congress, particularly those
involving ethics violations, recently grabbing national press attention, the Congress
has not earned more coverage or more favorable coverage in the news. In fact, on

both counts, there has been a decline. Political scientists Norman Ornstein and Michael J. Robinson found network television news coverage of Congress during one month in 1985 was half what it had been the same month ten years earlier,[4] and another study confirmed this conclusion and also found a similar although less marked decline in newspaper coverage of Congress.[5] Also, many stories mentioning Congress are not stories primarily about Congress, however, but lead-ins to other stories. One reporter who covers Congress lamented:

> Congress will get on where there's a vacuum of power elsewhere. It might be an element of someone else's story. Just look at my assignment sheets if you want to see how much the networks care about Congress.[6]

This shift is not attributable to reporters. In fact, reporters attempt to overcome the diminution of congressional news by tying the subject of their stories to other stories emanating from the White House, State Department, or the Pentagon.[7] It is the editors and producers who have minimized congressional news. Apparently, what Congress does has become less and less newsworthy to them.

Remarkably, this decline has occurred at a time when the Congress has become more assertive in its relationship with the presidency. In foreign and defense affairs in particular, Congress has become a powerful player in policy-making, as evidenced by the congressional role in the Gulf War, the Panama Canal Treaty, U.S. aid to Nicaraguan Contras, and arms control negotiations.[8]

Moreover, when Congress is the subject of news coverage, the view is more often than not uncomplimentary. Studies have consistently suggested that congressional coverage both on network news and in newspaper editorials is generally negative.[9]

Why has coverage apparently declined, and why is Congress often portrayed negatively when it is covered? One scholar, Susan Heilmann Miller, proposed that Congress's problem is its lack of an ultimate spokesperson.[10] Its bicameral structure and the partisan divisions in both houses ensure that at least four leaders will compete for the role of congressional spokesperson, and the profusion of congressional committees and subcommittees, of which there are over 250, adds to the confusion. Congress offers the press a shifting array of leaders and experts. No one person speaks for the whole body, as a single individual does for the presidency.

This fragmentation is both a blessing and a curse for Congress. On the one hand, many reporters prefer covering Congress to covering the president precisely because of its more open atmosphere and the abundance of sources. As one CBS correspondent has put it:

> It's like night and day. There [at the White House] you are at the mercy of a handful of people. They can make or break you. . . . You can't roam around the White House and the Executive Office Building. Up here, in contrast, there are 535 sources, most of them eager and available to the press, and their aides, thousands of them.[11]

On the other hand, editors and producers, and some reporters, may be confused by the cacophony inherent in the Congress, especially given the greater time and space constraints discussed earlier. The White House, by contrast, offers a highly structured presentation with a single personality. Reporters may prefer the confused environment, but if the amount of news coverage actually devoted to Congress is an accurate yardstick, editors and news executives apparently tilt toward the more structured and more familiar personalities at the White House.

Even some reporters who cover Congress have noted the problem. Although they enjoy the freedom and the availability of sources, they realize the problems with lack of structure in covering the institution. James McCartney of Knight-Ridder complained that "Congress does a lousy job in telling a reporter what goes on. The problem with Congress is that it has no organization and is just babble. It needs to present its information better, like the White House."[12]

Explaining national political activity in the time and space constraints provided is more easily accomplished by focusing on a single individual—the president—than the multifaceted activity of the Congress.

The trend to less congressional coverage also marks a new autonomy in the press's relationship to Congress. With so many simultaneous events to choose from, reporters, especially broadcast reporters, often become the object of inter-committee competition for hearing coverage. The press, however, now are capable of relying on a widely disparate amalgam of sources. They may broadcast only a snippet of the hearing itself, and then use the setting as a lead-in to a media-arranged collage of sources and backdrops. According to Roger Mudd, "Today, if [the networks] cover a [congressional] hearing, they'll stay in the hearing itself for maybe 15 seconds—then switch to a coal mine in West Virginia or somewhere else out of Washington to finish the story."[13] For example, a 1983 CBS Evening News story on sex discrimination in insurance industry rates began with a reference to a bill in Congress, but cut to interviews with a small business owner, a life insurance spokesperson, a member of Congress, and a representative of a women's group.[14]

Conversely, while the press has acquired increased autonomy from Congress, the Congress as an institution has become more dependent on the press. Congress as an institution relies on the media to communicate its activities and gain leverage in policy-making vis-à-vis the president. As the president increasingly has become the star of national government news, Congress has become more dependent on the media to remain a significant visible force in the public eye.

C-SPAN Coverage

One of the steps Congress as an institution has taken to compete with presidential news is the introduction of television coverage of floor proceedings. The House first allowed television cameras to broadcast legislative proceedings in 1979.[15] The move was taken in response to a widespread belief the House was losing the contest for media attention to the Senate and the president.[16] Although opposed by members who feared their colleagues would play to the cameras, the presence of cameras is now widely accepted.

Consistent access to television, however, did not immediately enhance the status of the House in news coverage of Congress. Stories about the House were likely to be longer and include more filmed reports following the initiation of C-SPAN, but the number of stories did not change significantly.[17] One barrier was that the House insisted on control of the camera system, which the networks vehemently protested. Although the broadcasts are aired by the Cable Satellite Public Affairs Network (C-SPAN), a small, non-profit company funded by the cable industry, the actual broadcasting system is controlled by the House leadership. C-SPAN picks up only the broadcast pictures provided by the six cameras in the House chamber, which are controlled by the House. The other networks use only snippets of the live coverage for their news programs. House leadership feared that press control of the cameras would diminish respect for the House, particularly if cameras were able to focus on an empty chamber, snoozing members, or protesters in the visitors' gallery. But now the House itself allows camera shots of the usually empty chambers during special orders—time periods when members give speeches usually designed for consumption by the district constituency back home.

The House's position as the sole source of opposition party control during most of the 1980s did turn press attention towards that chamber and its members. The C-SPAN coverage already in place just made the task easier.[18]

The Senate installed eight cameras and started their own broadcasts in 1986 in response to a widespread belief that the House had gained the upper hand due to C-SPAN coverage. Live coverage of their floor action is aired on another network called C-SPAN II, run by the same company. Many members of the Senate feared that the introduction of live television coverage would radically alter the behavior of members—that senators would spend more time and effort trying to curry public favor through live television coverage than in conducting legislative business. Business would be delayed because of grandstanding. Senator Russell Long of Louisiana warned: "Statesmanship is all too scarce a commodity as it is now. It will be even more scarce with television."[19]

But even senators initially in opposition have come to accept the cameras, and have minimized their effect on legislative behavior. Senator Robert Byrd, an early opponent of live television coverage, now calls the coverage a major development in the history of the Senate by opening the deliberations of that body to the view of millions of Americans.[20]

The effects of C-SPAN floor proceeding broadcasts are still little known. An estimated 20 million Americans watch C-SPAN monthly.[21] That figure is nearly ten times the audience size in 1982.[22] C-SPAN is now carried on more than 3,000 cable systems and is available in more than 43 million households. C-SPAN II—the Senate channel—is offered to more than 17 million households.[23] Average household viewing time is more than seven hours a month for C-SPAN II and nearly 10

Who Watches C-SPAN?

From a national telephone poll of 2,379 randomly selected households conducted in late 1988 describing the C-SPAN audience.

- Average household viewing time (C-SPAN)   9.9 hours per month
- Average household viewing time (C-SPAN
  II)   7.7 hours per month
- College educated   49%
- Advanced degrees   11%
- Registered voter   84%
- Voted in 1988   78%
- Discuss politics at least 3 times a week   23%

Source: "National Survey Shows C-SPAN Audience Nearly Doubled in 1988 As It Grew Broader, Younger, More Diverse," C-SPAN press release, January 9, 1989.

---

hours a month for C-SPAN. Viewers are more politically active than the general public. For example, 78 percent voted in the 1988 election compared with only 50 percent of the general public. (See box.) There is little evidence C-SPAN coverage has had much effect on Congress's legislative performance.[24] It is unclear what effect the coverage has had on public opinion.

WHO GETS COVERED

Institutional Coverage

Most press coverage of Congress is not about individual members, but about the institution—or more accurately about the two institutions.[25] Journalists treat the two houses of Congress much as members of Congress do: as two separate bodies with little interaction. Most stories originate from one house or the other.[26]

The Senate, which has fewer members than the House, receives more attention from the press than does the House. Senators tend to be generalists who serve on a wider range of committees and represent a broader constituency. Senators become more easily identified with particular issues, since the competition for "squatters' rights" on the issues is not as intense as in the House. Moreover, the Senate possesses powers such as confirmations of appointments and ratification of treaties which are highly newsworthy. And, at any one time the Senate contains more current or prospective candidates for the presidency than the House.[27]

However, these advantages may be overshadowed by the exigencies of news coverage. As we mentioned above, the House received more attention from the press between 1981 and 1987 than it had in the past, and perhaps more than the Senate, because it was the only part of the national government controlled by the opposition.

News Media and the Party Leadership

The names of Thomas Foley, George Mitchell, Robert Michel, and Robert Dole may not be household words, but they are familiar to more Americans than those of almost any other member of Congress. As the leaders of the House and the Senate, they receive more attention from the press than other members of the Congress. One reason for this attention is that these leaders, unlike the president, also are available to the press on an almost daily basis. They meet with the press in daily news conferences while Congress is in session. But as we discussed earlier, availability does not guarantee press coverage.

Rather, along with the law of informational supply and demand, the leaders possess something journalists are demanding. The congressional leadership provides a center point to the multi-faceted activity of the Congress. They are the only members of Congress who provide a wholistic perspective on congressional activity. Moreover, the leaders respond to the political aspects of policy rather than the technical, much like the journalists who cover Congress.

The press also is following the path to power. Overall, the leadership of the Congress possess more power over legislation than any single group of members. In recent years, congressional leaders have been more assertive in offering leadership on policy and party matters. More coverage of the House vis-à-vis the Senate during the 1980s coincided with a more vigorous House leadership more willing to use the media in the legislative process.

Consequently, in electing their leadership, members have become more cognizant of press relations and televised images. In the party leadership races in the late 1980s, the telegenic nature of the candidates for leadership positions was considered an important factor in the selection process.[28] Congressional leaders today are more visible and accessible to the press than leaders of 15 to 20 years ago. Aware that White House stories receive higher priority than those from Congress, Tip O'Neill, while Speaker of the House, once even phoned reporters at the White House to make a Congress story into a White House story.[29]

Members versus Congress

One dominant theory of the news media's role in Congress suggests that television has created a new breed of member, a ''show horse,'' who seeks publicity, rather than concentrating on legislation.[30] As the theory goes, the news media, particularly television, gravitate toward members of Congress who are telegenic and tailor their work for media consumption. This thesis is summed up by Lewis W. Wolfson:

> Television has created a new breed of senator and congressman—the carefully coiffed show horse who pushes a few favorite causes but scorns legislative chores and serious homework.[31]

The emergence of this new breed of member impinges on the performance of the future of the institution. Michael J. Robinson argues:

> The implications are straightforward enough—a Congress that is less likely to get along with itself, more likely to focus on higher office, less likely to behave as a group than as a disjointed collection of individuals.[32]

As the conventional wisdom goes, both houses have experienced greater fragmentation of power, undermined central authority, and the influx of members who choose media relations over serious legislative duties.

Scholars supporting this theory point to past studies of news coverage which suggest activist, but junior, senators receive more than their expected share of news attention.[33]

Another group of scholars has disputed the empirical evidence for deleterious media effects. One study found the preponderance of attention in news coverage of the Senate was devoted to legislative leaders, including committee chairs and ranking minority members. The press concentrated on institutional leaders, not junior legislators.[34] A similar study of the House confirmed that leadership and seniority are the main determinants for coverage of members and that the media actually contribute toward the concentration of power.[35]

This concentration of power may have an impact on the role of the non-leaders:

> As news media organizations seemed to have reduced coverage, more attention has been devoted to the institution as a whole and to the leaders. . . . As news coverage is constricted and increasingly centralized, the furtherance of individual goals through the national news media may be a more difficult task [for junior members]. . . .[36]

However, still a third possibility exists; neither the journalists nor the members of Congress singly determine the shape of coverage. Rather, both do. Timothy E. Cook suggests the press and members of Congress negotiate power. Both follow unwritten ground rules for interaction designed to promote the goals of both. According to Cook: "Politicians need publicity and journalists need copy, and the two sides can and do perform valuable services for each other."[37]

Media and Non-Leaders

What members of Congress get covered and why? As we have noted, leaders are favored over non-leaders because the press follows the path of power—it focuses primarily on those members who are in positions to achieve their own legislative goals and block the goals of others.

Members of the party in power receive more coverage than opposition party members.[38] (See Table 9.1.) Its members are the committee and subcommittee chairs and those party leaders who control floor debate and the movement of legislation.

TABLE 9.1. MEDIA COVERAGE OF SENATORS BY PARTY, 1978 AND 1983 (%)

Item	Senate Composition	Media Coverage	Bonus
1978—Democrat control			
Democrats	59	69	+10
Republicans	41	31	
1983—Republican control			
Republicans	54	59	+5
Democrats	46	41	

Source: Stephen Hess, *The Ultimate Insiders: U.S. Senators in the National Media,* Washington: The Brookings Institution, 1986, p. 57. Reprinted with permission.

Prospective or former presidential nominees also receive greater press attention. The Senate has been termed a presidential incubator, but it should be more accurately termed a presidential candidate incubator since it produces many candidates (five in 1988), but in fact few presidents are directly drawn from its ranks. For example, Senator Edward Kennedy, a perennial prospective presidential candidate since 1968, receives more press coverage than almost any other member of Congress.[39] Senators Edmund Muskie, George McGovern, John Glenn, and Gary Hart received heavy press notice immediately before or after their presidential races.

Even in the House, or perhaps especially there, those members who run for president or vice president receive additional attention. Former presidential candidates Morris Udall and Paul McCloskey appeared frequently on the network evening news following their unsuccessful campaigns.

Beyond leaders and prospective or former presidential candidates, other members can gain press attention. However, the initiative in such encounters is largely that of the press. Members of Congress may engage in publicity-seeking opportunities such as flurries of press releases, news conferences, and staged events, but these are not strong determinants of coverage. Members who are perceived as seeking publicity for publicity's sake run the risk of being portrayed negatively as media hounds by the very journalists they seek to impress.

When members do solicit relations with the press, the primary objectives of such operations tend to be local, not national, media representatives. Members have learned that the national press is more difficult and unpredictable, and that national news coverage may backfire, since they cannot control the final news product.[40]

But that doesn't mean members of Congress don't seek national exposure. Members do so in order to aid their role as legislators.

USING THE NATIONAL MEDIA

Strategies for National Media Use

In the past, members of Congress eschewed the "outsider" strategy, that is, turning to the press to place issues on the legislative agenda. But, the outsider strategy is more and more a common part of many members' legislative tools.

According to David Mayhew, members of Congress engage in three types of activities for electoral purposes—advertising, position-taking, and credit-claiming.[41] The press is an aide in each of these activities.

The press plays an obvious role in advertising, since voters utilize news for informational purposes. Members of Congress like constituents to see them on the news working on the constituents' behalf.

Position-taking also is accomplished through the press, since the press is the main vehicle through which constituents learn where representatives stand on many issues. Members actively disseminate press releases explaining their support for or opposition to various legislative proposals.

Credit-claiming is a widespread congressional activity. Members still pass legislation the old-fashioned way; they introduce legislation and gather political support. However, public notice for such accomplishments is gained through the press. Most credit-claiming is pursued for local consumption, but benefits may accrue from claiming credit in the national media, if possible. Constituents back home are impressed when they see their representative on national network news. The message also is sent to others in Washington, particularly to colleagues in Congress, that the member is informed and effective, and such a message increases the member's credibility.

According to Timothy E. Cook, members of Congress attempt to utilize the media to establish credibility on favored issues, to move issues onto both public and congressional agendas, and to pressure colleagues to act or react.[42] Credit-claiming is an art requiring skill in timing and positioning. Mayhew argues that members are always seeking opportunities to claim credit for governmental action.[43] However, quick action is needed to lay claim to an action before some other enterprising member does so.

Vice President Dan Quayle's press secretary explained how, as a new senator from Indiana, Quayle failed to put these skills to work to claim credit in the national press:

> He didn't get the credit he deserved. . . . Instead of staying here [in Washington] he went to Indianapolis to hold a press conference to announce and explain his position. When he got back to Washington, the wave had rolled over him. . . . When he got back, he found that . . . another senator had taken credit for being "THE guy," and that he wasn't disposed to share it."[44]

Credibility means establishing the member as the expert on a selected issue and the media's primary source in the House or the Senate on that particular issue. Stephen Hess has termed this acquiring "squatters' rights" on an issue:

> A legislator can acquire such squatters' rights to an issue because of a vacuum (the natural leader declines to come forward); expertise (enough knowledge to impress the press corps); timing (early recognition of the issue's news values); publicity skills (scaring off equally legitimate competitors by calling attention to one's claim); and good luck (picking an issue that circumstances elevate to the front page).[45]

Though many members of Congress attempt to stake out areas of expertise, few see those areas become "hot" in the media's eyes as issues of great importance. Two junior members in their respective houses, Senator Bill Bradley of New Jersey and Representative Richard Gephardt of Missouri laid claim to the field of tax reform and became well known when the issue later acquired priority status. Their own careers were furthered as Bradley was touted widely as a presidential candidate and Gephardt later became House majority leader. Representative Jack Kemp of New York staked out an early reputation as an expert on economic policy, particularly supply-side economics and became a frequent news media source in the 1980s, but when Senator Paula Hawkins of Florida tried a similar tactic with the issues of child abuse and missing children, her priorities never won her sustained expert status in the press, she was criticized as pushing a "mini-agenda," and she ultimately suffered defeat in her reelection bid.

The news media can serve to raise the visibility of an issue. By publicizing the issue in prominent media outlets, such as the *Washington Post*, the *New York Times*, or one of the national news magazines, members hope that "their" issue will catch on with other media and colleagues in Congress who will hear from constituents and place the issue on the priority list before Congress. Press coverage then may move colleagues to action. A member may utilize the press to force a committee chair to hasten work on a bill, or legislation may be killed. For example, New Mexico Senator Pete Domenici found high interest among other senators in a bill on waterway user fees he introduced after the *Washington Post* gave the bill extensive coverage. Domenici attributed the heightened interest to the news coverage: "You know, there's probably 500 good-policy ideas floating around the hill at any one time, but most of them just aren't getting on the front page of the *Post* every week."[46]

Why Members Don't Use the National Press More Often

Using the press to achieve legislative objectives may seem a quick and easy way to achieve legislation. It is not. It is a long, complicated path contrasted with other paths available to members of Congress.

Stephen Hess explains the difference:

> Trying to use the media to get legislation through Congress is a Rube Goldberg design based on (A) legislator influencing (B) reporter to get information into (C) news outlet so as to convince (D) voters who will then put pressure on (E) other legislators. Given all the problems inherent in successfully maneuvering through the maze, no wonder that legislative strategies are usually variations of (A) legislator asking (E) other legislators for their support through personal conversation, "Dear Colleague" letters, caucuses, or other means. . . . [47]

Some evidence also indicates that national news attention does not help individual members' reelection chances.[48] In fact, such attention may weaken electoral chances by attracting stronger challengers or generating negative responses from voters.[49] In 1980, for example, Representative Richard Nolan of Minnesota gained national news attention by suggesting during the Iran hostage crisis that the United States should give the Shah back to Iran. Nolan's nationally reported remark generated hostility among voters in his district and prompted him to forego a reelection bid.

Positions do not even have to be extreme to lose support back home. Members who have been too closely identified with national policy-making can be vulnerable to charges that they are callous toward local concerns. For example, both then House Majority Leader Thomas Foley of Washington and House Minority Leader Robert Michel of Illinois faced close races in the 1980s at least in part due to their party leadership positions.

MEMBERS AND THE LOCAL MEDIA

Although the scope of this book is limited primarily to the national press, we will take a few pages here to discuss members of Congress and the local media. We have suggested that the local press constitutes the primary object of attention for members of Congress. Obviously, the courting of the local media is an indirect courting of the district or state constituency which members view as relevant to their reelection chances.

However, the local media also are highly dependent on the members of Congress from their area. This symbiotic relationship produces a more favorable approach to coverage of individual members of Congress by local media. Unlike reporters for national media outlets who have a wide array of senators and representatives as potential sources, local journalists stationed in Washington can be severely hurt by denial of access to local members. As Cook notes, the reporter's reliance on the member for news easily outweighs the value of a scoop on something potentially embarrassing to the member. Also, local journalists, he argues, are merely following the traditional standards of news—depend on authority figures for sources.[50] Similarly, members' reliance on the local press as a conduit for publicity prevents a parasitic relationship and encourages a symbiotic one.

The symbiotic relationship has been criticized as a partnership in propaganda.[51] Local media do provide a positive image of members of Congress. Much of the news, especially for weekly newspapers, consists of press releases from the member's office printed almost verbatim.[52] Even daily news outlets are sympathetic. In sum, local media, for the above reasons, tend to be reactive not assertive in handling news about their region's members of Congress.[53]

Incumbents also benefit during election periods, when they almost invariably get more coverage than their challengers. Remarkably, this is even more true in tight races where the incumbent is vulnerable enough to draw a strong challenger. Moreover, the incumbent's coverage, as Peter Clarke and Susan H. Evans found, is typically directed at positive attributes such as experience in office and constituent service.[54]

Members of Congress have taken advantage of modern techniques for local media relations. Members have at their disposal, for a small fee charged to their office budgets, the use of broadcast recording studios (six in the House and three in the Senate) where tapes can be produced and sent to local stations in the district or states. Some members use these facilities to broadcast monthly television programs aired on cable public affairs channels. About one-third of House members hold regular broadcast programs.[55] Members also tape public service announcements to be shown locally. Costs for these facilities are subsidized by the Congress.

The introduction of 800-number telephone lines, computers, and telecopiers has made it easier to send news releases and "actualities" (a recorded statement by the member to radio and television stations and newspapers in the home state or district).[56] More than one-half of members write weekly newspaper columns.[57] Today it is the rare member who does not utilize these techniques for working with the local media. According to congressional observer Norman Ornstein: "With Federal Express, fax machines, and satellites, [the member] can be on TV and in the newspapers continually in a way that simply wasn't possible before."[58]

THE CONGRESSIONAL COMMITTEE

Woodrow Wilson once wrote: "Congress in session is Congress on public exhibition, whilst Congress in its committee-rooms is Congress at work."[59] The press apparently concurs. Coverage of Congress is Congress-in-committee more than Congress in floor proceedings.[60]

However, this bias in favor of committees in the past, particularly for television, can be linked to the availability of visuals. Since the early 1970s, almost all committee sessions have been accessible to television cameras. Prior to the C-SPAN coverage of the House and the Senate, only committees allowed broadcast of proceedings. As floor proceedings have become available to television, the emphasis may be changing, though no empirical evidence yet exists.

In covering committees, the press shows equanimity towards the two houses by covering both about equally. But Stephen Hess explains the larger number of House committees and hearings means the House must work twice as hard as the Senate to get the same amount of coverage.[61]

Of all Senate committees, press coverage focuses most often on those over foreign relations, judiciary, budget, and governmental affairs.[62] (See Table 9.2.) More generally, the press focuses in on committees responsible for broad policy areas as opposed to constituency committees which serve particular narrow constituencies, such as Veterans Affairs, Agriculture, and Small Business.

These committees dominate news coverage of committees because of their areas of jurisdiction, the level of conflict involved, and the people who serve on them. For example, Foreign Relations is responsible for international relations, which usually is the subject of presidential emphasis. At least since Vietnam, members of the committee have become experts in opposition to the president's

TABLE 9.2. RANKING OF SENATE COMMITTEES BY AMOUNT OF MEDIA ATTENTION, AVERAGE, 1953–1983

Committee	1953–1983 Ranking[a]	Type
Foreign Relations	1.8	Policy
Judiciary	2.6	Policy
Budget	3.0 (1983 only)	Policy
Governmental Affairs	5.0	Policy
Armed Services	6.0	Policy/Constituency
Labor	6.8	Policy
Banking	7.2	Policy/Constituency
Appropriations	8.2	Constituency
Finance	9.0	Policy/Constituency
Commerce	10.6	Constituency
Agriculture	11.2	Constituency
Energy	12.0 (1983 only)	Constituency
Environment	13.8	Constituency
Small Business	15.0 (1983 only)	Constituency
Veterans' Affairs	15.0 (1973–74, 83)	Constiuency

[a]These figures reflect an average of the collective rankings of the members of each committee for the years 1953–54, 1965–66, 1969–70; 1973–74, and 1983. For example, the members of the Foreign Relations Committee ranked 1 (1953–54), 3 (1965–66), 2 (1973–74), and 1 (1983) for an average of 1.8. (*Source:* Stephen Hess, *The Ultimate Insiders: U.S. Senators in the National Media,* Washington: The Brookings Institution, 1986, p. 35. Reprinted with permission.)

foreign policy. Even when the Senate majority has shared party affiliation with the White House, this has been true. Witness the cases of Senator William Fulbright during the Johnson administration, who became a vocal critic of the administration's Vietnam policy and used his position to oppose the war; and more recently of Senator Jesse Helms during the Reagan presidency, who, from the Foreign Affairs Committee, sought to move foreign policy by opposing negotiations with the Soviet Union, holding up Senate confirmation of key diplomats, and publicly supporting right-wing foreign governments.

The issues committees address may provoke heated conflict at one time, but not at others. For example, due to the oil shortage in the 1970s, the Congressional Energy committees received more attention in the 1970s than in the 1980s when there was an oil glut and calls for government action diminished.

Also, news coverage flows from personalities. Foreign Relations usually boasts several prospective presidential candidates. In the 1980s, in the Senate these have included Howard Baker, Joseph Biden, Alan Cranston, John Glenn, and Paul Simon.

In turn, members who seek national news exposure gravitate to those committees already in the press spotlight, while others who seem to want to avoid such notice likely choose less visible slots. For example, Senator Paul Simon, though still a freshman senator, had acquired seats on the three most publicized committees in the Senate. On the other hand, Senator Quentin Burdick of North Dakota left the highly visible Judiciary Committee to serve as chairman of the much less noticed Environment and Public Works Committee.

However, serving on a committee with a high level of press visibility can be a two-edged sword. Voters may see the member, particularly true for senators, as too involved in national issues and not sufficiently concerned with those of the state or district. For example, Senators Frank Church of Idaho and Charles Percy of Illinois were both defeated in their reelection bids after serving as chairmen of the Foreign Relations Committee.

When committees are covered, what attracts the press? In addition to the general area of committee jurisdiction and the personalities involved, other factors like the particular issues addressed, the witnesses called, and the tenor of the hearing all contribute to newsworthiness.

Committees are covered when the issues they handle suddenly become news. The economic committees become newsworthy during times of economic difficulty, for instance; and during scandals involving members of Congress, the ethics committees suddenly gain media attention. Select committees much as the Senate Watergate Committee in 1973–1974 and the joint committee which investigated the Iran-Contra affair in 1987 are typically the objects of heavy media coverage.

Members seeking national attention compete to be appointed to such committees, and careers can be made or broken through such participation. Senator George Mitchell earned the plaudits of Democrats for his performance in the Iran-Contra hearings in 1987, which contributed to his subsequent selection as Senate majority leader. Conversely, Senator Daniel Inouye, who had been highly regarded by fellow senators, was criticized for his leadership of the Iran-Contra hearings and was defeated by Mitchell in the race for Senate majority leader.

Witnesses who testify at committee hearings also can attract the cameras. Well-known entertainers, sports figures, or business executives can command media notice. For example, when the lead singer of the rock group Twisted Sister testified at hearings on pornography in rock lyrics and videos, the networks devoted more time to the hearings on one day than they had to coverage of the budget-deficit crisis for an entire month.[63] Unusual witnesses such as mob figures masking their faces are popular for television coverage.

For television particularly, heated exchanges between witnesses and members of Congress become newsworthy. Members of Congress must approach such exchanges cautiously because they may not always emerge as the victor. Members must be careful not to generate a public backlash in support of a perceived congressional hearing victim, as occurred with Oliver North during the Iran-Contra hearings and with Supreme Court nominee Robert Bork during questioning related to his first wife's illness and subsequent death.

Congressional committees establish a symbiotic relationship with the press. A congressional committee and the press work together to publicize issues. By focusing attention on a certain issue, the press can provide the justification for a committee investigation, which in turn stimulates more press coverage. The impetus may be committee members or staff leaking information to a reporter, which initiates the process. Susan Heilmann Miller suggests the symbiotic relationship is a more accurate description than the adversary relationship commonly portrayed.[64]

SUMMARY

Although the presidency's changing relations with the news media have received greater notice from scholars, the Congress also has been affected by the media. In the late 1970s, a political consultant summed up the widespread consensus on the media effects on Congress in describing the current typical congressional candidate and members of Congress:

> Guys with the blow-dried hair who read the script well. That's not the kind of guy who'd been elected to the Congress or Senate ten years ago. You've got a guy who is not concerned with issues; who isn't concerned about the mechanics of government; who doesn't attend committee meetings; who avoids taking positions at any opportunity and who yet is a master at getting his face in the newspapers and on television. . . . You get the modern media candidate . . . [65]

However, as this chapter has demonstrated, the presence of the media has not accomplished the radical overhaul implied in the consultant's assessment. Although members of Congress are accused of using the national media to accomplish legislative and electoral objectives, such usage, even if attempted, is fraught with problems and dangers.

Actually, press coverage of Congress is a process of members of Congress offering a wide variety of potential stories to choose from, while reporters select which fit news values. As in any similar buyer's market, members of Congress must tailor their offerings to national news media along the lines of news values. Viewing realistically the chances of success, many members, particularly those in the House, do not even bother to actively court national media attention. Their press operations are geared to the local level.

Hence, the real competition exists among a much smaller group of members who attempt to establish reputations through the national press for future leadership bids, presidential races, or legislative prowess.

Given this wide array of possible stories, it is not surprising that the press turns to the leadership who have proven expertise, power, and, in most cases, widespread visibility. They constitute the stable lead players in a congressional cast of hundreds.

NOTES

1. Timothy E. Cook, *Making Laws and Making News: Media Strategies in the U.S. House of Representatives*, Washington: Brookings, 1989, p. 31.

2. Lewis W. Wolfson, *The Untapped Power of the Press*, New York: Praeger, 1985, p. 37.
3. See Martha Joynt Kumar and Michael Baruch Grossman, "Congress: The Best Beat in Town," paper presented at the annual meeting of the American Political Science Association, Washington, D.C., August 28–31, 1986.
4. Norman Ornstein and Michael J. Robinson, "The Case of Our Disappearing Congress," *TV Guide*, January 11–17, 1986, pp. 4–10.
5. See Richard Davis, "Whither the Congress and the Supreme Court? The Television News Portrayal of American National Government," *Television Quarterly* 22 (1987): 55–63.
6. Cook, *Making Laws and Making News*, p. 46.
7. Cook, *Making Laws and Making News*, pp. 46–58.
8. For arguments on congressional reassertiveness, see James L. Sundquist, *Decline and Resurgence of Congress*, Washington: Brookings, 1981; Thomas M. Franck and Edward Weisband, *Foreign Policy by Congress*, New York: Oxford University Press, 1979; and I. M. Destler, "Executive-Congressional Conflict in Foreign Policy: Explaining It, Coping with It," in Lawrence C. Dodd and Bruce Oppenheimer, *Congress Reconsidered*, 3d ed., Washington: CQ Press, 1985, chap. 15.
9. See, for example, Michael J. Robinson and Kevin R. Appel, "Network News Coverage of Congress," *Political Science Quarterly* 94 (Fall 1979): 407–418; Charles Tidmarch and John C. Pitney, Jr., "Covering Congress," *Polity* 17 (Spring 1985): 463–483; and Arthur H. Miller, Edie N. Goldenberg, and Lutz Erbring, "Type-Set Politics: The Impact of Newspapers on Public Confidence," *American Political Science Review* 73 (March 1979): 67–84.
10. Susan Heilmann Miller, "News Coverage of Congress: The Search for the Ultimate Spokesman," *Journalism Quarterly* 54 (Autumn 1977), pp. 459–465.
11. Quoted in Dom Bonafede, "The Washington Press—It Magnifies the President's Flaws and Blemishes," *National Journal*, May 1, 1982, p. 769.
12. Quoted in James McCartney, *National Journal*, November 21, 1983; p. 2376.
13. Norman Ornstein and Michael J. Robinson, "Television's Coverage of Congress," *TV Guide*, January 11, 1986, p. 6.
14. CBS Evening News, February 22, 1983.
15. For a discussion of legislative history of the decision, see Ronald Garay, *Congressional Television: A Legislative History*, Westport, Conn.: Greenwood Press, 1984; and Cook, *Making Laws*, pp. 25–30.
16. For a discussion of the disparity in coverage between the two houses, see Robinson and Appel, "Network News Coverage," 407–418; Susan H. Miller, "News Coverage of Congress," pp. 459–465; Stephen Hess, *The Washington Reporters*, Washington: Brookings, 1981, pp. 101–102; and Richard Davis, "News Media Coverage of American National Political Institutions," unpublished doctoral dissertation, Syracuse University, 1986, pp. 84–87.
17. See Lynda Lee Kaid and Joe Foote, "How Network Television Coverage of the President and the Congress Compare," *Journalism Quarterly* 62 (Spring 1985): 59–65.
18. For data on increased coverage of House members post-1981, see Timothy Cook, "House Members as Newsmakers: The Effects of Televising Congress," *Legislative Studies Quarterly* 11 (May 1986): 203–226.
19. Quoted in Jacqueline Calmers, "Senate Agrees to Test of Radio, TV Coverage," *Congressional Quarterly Weekly Report*, March 1, 1986, pp. 520–521.

20. Robert Byrd, Remarks at C-SPAN Seminar for Professors, National Press Club, Washington, D.C., July 31, 1987.
21. Norman J. Ornstein, "Political Scientists and Journalists Watch Congress," *News for Teachers of Political Science* (Summer 1987), p. 1.
22. Garay, *Congressional Television*, pp. 136–142.
23. For audience figures, see latest issue of *C-SPAN Update*.
24. See Garay, *Congressional Television*, pp. 136–142; and Roger H. Davidson, "Congress and the American People," in Christpher J. Deering, *Congressional Politics*, Chicago: Dorsey Press, 1989, pp. 318–319.
25. See Robinson and Appel, "Network News Coverage," 407–418; and Davis, "News Media Coverage," pp. 106–109.
26. See Kumar and Grossman, "Congress: The Best Beat in Town"; and Davis, "News Media Coverage," pp. 84–87.
27. For a discussion of the Senate's media advantages, see Richard F. Fenno, Jr., *The United States Senate: A Bicameral Perspective*, Washington: AEI, 1982.
28. See, for example, Janet Hook, "Gingrich's Selection as Whip Reflects GOP Discontent," *CQ Weekly Report*, March 25, 1989, pp. 625–627; and Ronald Elving, "Politics in the Age of TV," *CQ Weekly Report*, April 1, 1989, p. 722.
29. Kumar and Grossman, "Congress: The Best Beat in Town," p. 9.
30. See Michael J. Robinson, "Three Faces of Congressional Media," in Thomas E. Mann and Norman Ornstein, eds. *The News Congress*, Washington: AEI, 1981, pp. 55–96.
31. Wolfson, *Untapped Power of the Press*, p. 40.
32. Robinson, "Three Faces of Congressional Media," p. 95.
33. See, for example, David H. Weaver and G. Cleveland Wilhoit, *News Media Coverage of U.S. Senators in Four Congresses*, Lexington, Ky: Association for Education in Journalism, 1980.
34. Hess, *Washington Reporters*.
35. See Cook, *Making Laws and Making News*. Also, for a partial confirmation of Cook's study, see Ferill Squire, "Who Gets National News Coverage in the U.S. Senate," *American Politics Quarterly* 16 (April 1988): 139–155. For a conflicting result, however, see Charles M. Pearson, "Explaining National News Coverage of Members of the U.S. Congress, 1977–1980," paper delivered at the annual meeting of the American Political Science Association, Washington, D.C., August 28–31, 1986.
36. Davis, "News Media Coverage," p. 114.
37. Cook, *Making Laws and Making News*, p. 9.
38. See Eric P. Veblen, "Liberalism and National News Coverage of Members of Congress," *Polity* 14 (1981): 153–159; and Hess, *Washington Reporters*, pp. 55–57.
39. Hess, *Washington Reporters*, pp. 116–142.
40. See Timothy Cook, "Marketing the Members: Evolving Media Strategies in the House of Representatives," paper delivered at the annual meeting of the Midwest Political Science Association, Chicago, Ill., April 18–20, 1985.
41. David Mayhew, *Congress and the Electoral Connection*, New Haven, Conn.: Yale University Press, 1974, pp. 49–79.
42. See Cook, "Marketing the Members."
43. Mayhew, *Congress and the Electoral Connection*, p. 53.
44. Quoted in Richard F. Fenno, Jr., *The Making of a Senator*, Washington: CQ Press, 1989, p. 28.
45. Stephen Hess, *The Ultimate Insiders: U.S. Senators in the National Media*, Washigton: Brookings Institution, 1986, p. 39.

46. T. R. Reid, *Congressional Odyssey*, New York: W.H. Freeman, 1980, p. 130.
47. Hess, *Ultimate Insiders*, p. 103.
48. See Timothy E. Cook, "Show Horses in House Elections: The Advantages and Disadvantages of National Media Visibility," in Jan Pons Veermeer, ed., *Campaigns in the News: Mass Media and Congressional Elections*, Westport, Conn.: Greenwood Press, 1987, pp. 161–181.
49. See Lyn Ragsdale and Timothy E. Cook, "Representatives' Actions and Challengers' Reactions: Limits to Candidate Connections in the House," *American Journal of Political Science* (1987): 45–81.
50. Cook, *Making Laws and Making News*, p. 116.
51. See Ben Bagdikian, "Congress and the Media: Partners in Propaganda," *Columbia Journalism Review* (January/February 1974).
52. For a discussion of positive coverage by local media, see Michael J. Robinson, "Three Faces of Congressional Media," pp. 75–82.
53. Cook, *Making Laws and Making News*, pp. 116–117.
54. Peter Clarke and Susan H. Evans, *Covering Campaigns*, Palo Alto, Calif.: Stanford University Press, 1983, pp. 57–72. See also Douglas Kelley, "Press Coverage of Two Michigan Congressional Elections," *Journalism Quarterly* 35 (1958): 447–449.
55. Cook, *Making Laws and Making News*, pp. 93–94.
56. See Robinson, "Three Faces," pp. 63–64.
57. Cook, *Making Laws and Making News*, p. 94.
58. Norman Ornstein, "The Hardest House to Break Into," *Washington Post* National Weekly Edition, September 5–11, 1988, p. 16.
59. Woodrow Wilson, *Congressional Government*, Cleveland, Ohio: World Publishing, Meridian Books, 1965, p. 69.
60. See Robinson and Appel, "Network News Coverage," pp. 414–415; Tidmarch and Pitney, "Covering Congress," *Polity* 17 (Spring 1983): 463–483; and Davis, "News Media Coverage," pp. 114–119.
61. See Hess, *Washington Reporters*, p. 106; and Davis, "News Media Coverage," pp. 115–116.
62. See Hess, *Ultimate Insiders*, p. 30. See also Steven S. Smith and Christopher J. Deering, *Committees in Congress*, Washington: CQ Press, 1984, p. 67.
63. Ornstein and Robinson, "Television's Coverage of Congress," p. 6.
64. Susan Heilmann Miller, *Reporters and Congressmen: Living in Symbiosis*, Lexington, Ky.: Association for Education in Journalism, 1978.
65. Quoted in Robinson, "Three Faces," p. 94.

SUGGESTED READINGS

Blanchard, Robert, ed. *Congress and the News Media*. New York: Hastings House, 1974.
Clarke, Peter, and Susan H. Evans. *Covering Campaigns*. Palo Alto, Calif.: Stanford University Press, 1983.
Cook, Timothy E. *Making Laws and Making News: Media Strategies in the U.S. House of Representatives*. Washington: Brookings, 1989.
Garay, Ronald. *Congressional Television: A Legislative History*. Westport, Conn.: Greenwood Press, 1984.

Hess, Stephen. *The Ultimate Insiders: U.S. Senators in the National Media*. Washington: Brookings Institution, 1986.

Miller, Susan H. *Reporters and Congressmen: Living in Symbiosis*. Lexington, Ky: Association for Education in Journalism, 1978.

Veermeer, Jan Pons, ed. *Campaigns in the News: Mass Media and Congressional Elections*. Westport, Conn.: Greenwood Press, 1987.

CHAPTER 10

The Supreme Court

The courts are a political institution, and we don't cover them as such.
Washington Post editor Bob Woodward[1]

THE COURT AND THE PUBLIC

"Your Honors: Before You Vote on *Roe Vs. Wade*, Listen to one final opinion: America's." So read full-page advertisements in major newspapers in the spring of 1989—advertisements unusual because the object of their lobbying was not elected officials, but the justices of the U.S. Supreme Court.

The U.S. Supreme Court is the most reclusive American political institution. In the past, the press has contributed to that reclusive nature, but the future may be a different matter.

The Court is aloof from the day-to-day policy formulation interaction involving the presidency and Congress. When policy struggles do involve the Court, years have often passed since the original formulation of the issue.

The Court has carefully avoided such involvement in part because the appointment process and the Congress's ability to affect the court's jurisdiction and size hold the potential of involving the Court and subordinating it to other political actors, and this impels the justices to adopt means to maintain judicial independence. The judicial aloofness is not elitism, but an effort to perpetuate the image of a legal institution resolving cases on the basis of legal rights rather than a political institution in which political considerations influence decisions.

The Court's continued success in gaining compliance with its decisions is contingent on the public perception that the Court is largely apolitical. Alexander

What extremists couldn't do with 100 firebombs, the Supreme Court might do with one decision.

Frustrated because they haven't been able to outlaw abortion for everyone, extremists are using desperate maneuvers to stop specific groups of women from being able to obtain safe, legal abortions.

On July 3, in the *Webster* case, the Supreme Court gave states more power to restrict access to abortion, touching off a legislative and political firestorm.

And anti-choice zealots are pushing for states to use their power against the young and the poor.

Right now, in two cases before the Supreme Court (see box above), anti-choice forces are attempting to strip young women who seek a safe, legal abortion of their privacy and protection against harassment and physical abuse.

Another measure headed for Supreme Court review might have shut *three out of four* clinics offering family planning and abortion services.

Confronted with public outrage at such threats to women's health, the state attorney general in that case backed away, but medically unnecessary "clinic standards" (see box) are a favorite extremist weapon and will doubtless appear on the Supreme Court's docket again.

A bad Supreme Court decision in any of these cases would do more to deny women

WHAT'S WRONG WITH "PARENTAL CONSENT"?
The Hodgson case before the court challenges a Minnesota requirement that a woman under 18 notify both parents before an abortion. Most teens already consult a parent, without such laws. Almost half don't live with both parents. One in four teens seeking a judicial "bypass" of the law is accompanied by the parent who has custody, pleading not to have to involve the other parent. Most Americans agree a teen who can't talk with her parents should be able to consult another responsible adult. Indeed, after hearing evidence of family conflict and brutal violence, an appeals judge wrote "compelling parental notice... is almost always disastrous." We're also contesting an Ohio law with a similar destructive impact.

access to safe, legal abortion than a decade of firebombings and clinic blockades.

President Bush has continued the attack started by President Reagan. Allied with anti-choice extremists, his administration has again asked the court to reverse *Roe v. Wade*, the historic decision that legalized abortion nationwide and ended the back-alley carnage sixteen years ago.

He has overruled Congress three times and vetoed the right of poverty-stricken rape and incest victims to terminate their pregnancies.

The White House must take responsibility for the chaos in abortion laws and the growing danger to women.

When voters get the chance to reject extremism, they do so, as the races in Virginia, New York and New Jersey made clear.

America stands for choice.

And it's time for our elected officials to respect the views of the majority, undo the damage done by the Reagan-packed court, and act to preserve the safety and privacy of *all* women — including the millions who happen to be young or poor. Please mail the coupons immediately.

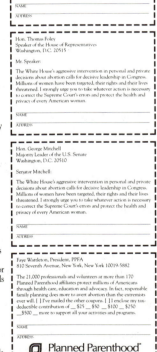

CLINIC MARAUDERS RAISE "SAFETY" CONCERNS? Abortion is practically risk-free... one hundred times safer than an appendectomy. Yet extremists now call for every clinic to be equipped and staffed like a major hospital. Net effect? To padlock 75% of women's health centers. Outrage against such extremist tactics forced Illinois' Attorney General to settle the Ragsdale case just days before the Supreme Court was to hear it. But similar assaults are proposed in other states. Catastrophe is still only five Supreme Court votes away.

Don't wait until women are dying again.

President George Bush
The White House
Washington, D.C. 20500

Mr. President:

Your vetoes of federal legislation protecting the right of the disadvantaged to make responsible, safe decisions about abortion were cruel and unjust. Don't you realize you are accountable to the majority of Americans who want the health and privacy of women protected? Reject narrow extremism and take a responsible position on abortion and family planning.

NAME
ADDRESS

Hon. Thomas Foley
Speaker of the House of Representatives
Washington, D.C. 20515

Mr. Speaker:

The White House's aggressive intervention in personal and private decisions about abortion calls for decisive leadership in Congress. Millions of women have been targeted, their rights and their lives threatened. I strongly urge you to take whatever action is necessary to correct the Supreme Court's errors and protect the health and privacy of every American woman.

NAME
ADDRESS

Hon. George Mitchell
Majority Leader of the U.S. Senate
Washington, D.C. 20510

Senator Mitchell:

The White House's aggressive intervention in personal and private decisions about abortion calls for decisive leadership in Congress. Millions of women have been targeted, their rights and their lives threatened. I strongly urge you to take whatever action is necessary to correct the Supreme Court's errors and protect the health and privacy of every American woman.

NAME
ADDRESS

Faye Wattleton, President, PPFA
810 Seventh Avenue, New York, New York 10019-5882

The 21,000 professionals and volunteers at more than 170 Planned Parenthood affiliates protect millions of Americans through health care, education and advocacy. In fact, responsible family planning does more to avert abortion than the extremists ever will. [ ] I've mailed the other coupons. [ ] I enclose my tax-deductible contribution of __ $25 __ $50 __ $100 __ $250 __$500 __ more to support all your activities and programs.

NAME
ADDRESS

⊡ Planned Parenthood®
Federation of America

A 1989 advertisement which appeared in major newspapers. Reprinted with permission of Planned Parenthood© Federation of America, Inc.

Hamilton argued that the Supreme Court would be the weakest branch of the federal government and that its power would rest in "neither force nor will but merely judgment."[2] The Court has not proved weak, largely because it has maintained the perception of good judgment that is imperative to public acceptance of its role in public policy.

The Court does not follow public opinion as closely as do presidents and members of Congress, but its members are cognizant, however, of the public's view of how they are performing.[3]

This watchfulness is heightened by the fact that public opinion of the Court does not remain static. In the 1960s and early 1970s the Supreme Court was viewed as doing only a fair or even a poor job,[4] and a plurality of the population viewed the Court's decisions as too liberal. That image has improved during the 1980s; in recent years, a plurality or a majority view the court as doing a good to excellent job.[5]

Although we often think of the Court as disconnected from and uninfluenced by public opinion since it is perceived as a legal body interpreting the Constitution rather than as a political branch, the relationship between public opinion and the Court's activities is stronger than expected. Gregory Caldiera has demonstrated the public responds to the activities of the Court, and this responsiveness impacts on public confidence in the judiciary.[6]

First, the public keeps track of Court decisions more closely than is generally recognized, and public attitudes toward the Court correspond to perceptions of which way the Court is heading. As we noted above, in the 1960s and early 1970s a plurality of the American public believed the Court was too liberal and wanted it to move in a more conservative direction;[7] by the 1980s, the public perceived the Court's ideological direction as just about right.[8] The public's confidence in the Supreme Court rose. According to one survey, in 1973 only a plurality expressed confidence in the Court. By 1987, a majority said they felt that way.[9]

Secondly, like other institutions, the Court depends on public opinion for its continued vitality. Lack of public confidence can damage the Court's ability to participate in public policy-making. In the extreme, the Court will no longer be taken seriously. Compliance would be problematic.

The power of the institution could be gutted by a Congress imposing limits on the Court's jurisdiction or by a president seeking to make the Court a political servant of the administration. All this could be done in retribution for actions taken by the Court which are radically divergent from the views of the majority.

The Court has suffered such severe setbacks in public approval such as after the *Dred Scott* case in 1857 when it upheld slavery, and during the 1930s when the Court opposed popular New Deal programs. The Congress and the presidency may, with public approval, combine against the Court in a variety of ways.[10]

In the Court, the broader objective of its relations with the press is to perpetuate public confidence through maintaining its public image of aloofness from politics. No other governmental institution is as persistent nor as successful in accomplishing its objective. Individual presidents have achieved policy or personal objectives in press relations, and many members of Congress have been similarly successful, but for neither were the goals and accomplishments institutional in nature.

The Court possesses several distinct advantages over the other two branches of government in such a process. First, the small body of justices at any one time and the absence of innate and permanent factions such as divisions by political party aids in maintaining the public solidarity of the justices. And second, the continuity of the Court also supports institutional objectives. Where representatives, senators, and even the president must constantly look toward reelection challenges, the turnover of justices is usually extremely gradual and generally precipitated by choice on the part of the resigning justice.

On the other hand, the very small size of the Court and the independence of its members can lead to fragmentation. Fragmentation would mean each justice pursuing his or her own agenda in a manner potentially harmful to the court's ability to maintain public deference.

Moreover, the danger of fragmentation is always real due to the nature of the justices' relations with each other. Each possesses an equal vote, they rarely owe their appointment to any other justice, nor is their continuance on the Court affected by the other justices. The justices primarily work separately. The Court has even been characterized as nine separate law firms.[11] The justices must be wary of pursuing individual objectives which may diminish the institution's strength.

The Court has even been generally successful in obtaining press cooperation in advancing Court objectives. The court attempts to gain press coverage that reflects aloofness from politics and enhances public respect for the institution.

The press typically accepts the Court's objectives in regards to public perceptions, and this is reinforced by the language the press uses: the justices of the High Court, donned in their solemn black robes, "hand down" decisions. Two political scientists have argued that "journalistic language makes it less apparent to the public that nine unelected justices make policies as significant as those of the elected president and Congress."[12]

Also, the justices are successful in drawing attention away from themselves or the decision-making process and toward the decision itself. Almost none of the news coverage of the Court concerns the way the justices make decisions.[13] Reporters rely on the authoritative Court sources, which fail to provide this information.

We learn of the structure of decision making—oral arguments, conferences, opinion writing, and final announcement—but the press does not examine that process in conjunction with specific decisions. The press does not because the Court has not made such reporting easy.

Hence, the Court's image as a body that proclaims the law with finality on the basis of legal factors is not undermined by an examination of the variables—legal or political—present in the process leading up to that decision.

Justices' Relations with Reporters

The justices of the U.S. Supreme Court individually have maintained their distance from journalists, traditionally, rarely giving interviews to reporters and then usually only on a background basis. The justices do not hold press conferences except when retiring from the Court, and other employees of the Court are prohibited from talking with reporters.

As a result, news stories about the Court, rarely focus on the individual justices, personally or professionally.[14] There is a great deal of coverage of the nominees to the Court. (See Table 10.1) However, once justices come on the bench, stories specifically about them are uncommon. Those that do occur tend to be reports on justices' health or occasional speeches.

Since the Court consists of only nine individuals, each of whom possesses an equal vote capable of shifting majorities and radically altering the direction of Court decisions—since each justice is, in fact, one-ninth of a national political institution—this paucity of news coverage of the individual justices can only be a testament to the success of the justices' strategy of press relations.

The justices conduct press relations in order to preserve respect for the Supreme Court through which they can exercise political power. The potential weakness of the Court in the American political system necessitates active efforts to preserve the court's revered position in national government.

Individual justices no doubt recognize that their places in public policy-making are largely determined by the continued strength of the Court as a national political institution. Hence, the justices have been wary of pursuing individual objectives which may diminish the institution's strength.

The justices, then, possess strong incentives to cooperate with one another in order to forge majorities.[15] In particularly significant cases, such as *Brown v. Board of Education* (1954) and *U.S. v. Nixon* (1974), the justices have even achieved unanimity in order to accentuate the force of the opinion. Unanimity diminishes the

TABLE 10.1. NUMBER OF CBS EVENING NEWS STORIES ABOUT THE U.S. SUPREME COURT BY TERM (1984–1989)

	1984	1985	1986	1987	1988
Case-related	17	13	14	11	35
Confirmation/Retirement	2	11	23	38	0
Personal	5	0	4	1	2
Total	**24**	**24**	**41**	**50**	**37**

Note: Source is a content analysis by the author of CBS Evening News transcripts obtained from the CBS Research Library for the period between October 1, 1984, and July 7, 1989. Only news stories covering the Court or about the Court were used. Case-related stories include those about cases before the Court at some stage of the Court's decision-making process. Confirmation/retirement includes stories about a justice retiring. It also includes stories of nominees to the Court, even those not finally confirmed. Personal includes stories about the justices' personal activities, which encompassed personal health, speeches, and other statements. Some overlap did ƨxist, although very rarely. Categorization in those cases was based on the primary theme of the story.

opportunity for critics to point to cracks in the majority reasoning outlined by the minority. A unanimous decision conveys the message that, on this issue, the interpretation of the law is unmistakable.

Pursuing Media Strategies

Recent years have provided indications that some of the justices intend, at least temporarily, to abandon that shared strategy of institutional aloofness for individual style. Several justices, including Thurgood Marshall, Harry Blackmun, and former member William Brennan before he resigned, have made themselves more available to reporters for on-record interviews. Some interviews, such as those conducted in conjunction with a public television series in 1987, have been limited to a discussion of the operations of the Court.

Others, however, have included topics the justices have usually avoided in the past such as involvement in public debates on issues or criticism of colleagues personally and the direction of Court decisions generally.[16] Some of the justices such as John Paul Stevens and Harry Blackmun have used speeches for such purposes. In 1985–1986, Justice William Brennan engaged in an extended colloquy with then-Attorney General Edwin Meese, III, over the right of the president to interpret the Constitution.

Although the justices still are far from media stars, this recent increased availability to the press suggests a possible change in the justices' relations with reporters and their attitudes toward the relationship between the Court and the press.

If a change has occurred, why? The justices may have opened up to the press in order to participate in the celebration of the bicentennial of the Constitution in the mid- to late 1980s. They would be ideally suited to explain the role of the court in the expanded public discussion of the Constitution and the American system of government. The political environment is salient. The issues pushed to the Court in the 1970s and 1980s have been highly emotional ones unresolved by other political institutions. These have included, for example, abortion, school busing, affirmative action, and the death penalty.

Another explanation is related to the larger social environment within which the justices live. Not unlike others, the justices have experienced the communications revolution and the attending openness. They may be reacting by adopting the norms of greater forthrightness.

Within a year of taking office as chief justice, William Rehnquist wrote a book explaining the procedures of the Court.[17] Other justices have offered insights on the Court's operations and the justices' relations with one another.[18] Justice Antonin Scalia has participated in symposia with scholars and journalists. The justices have sought to achieve an openness about the Court and its operations which fits an age of candor and lessened formality.

The justices also probably have been affected by the press's greater access to the other institutions of government. Since the 1970s, the press, including televi-

Cartoon of February 12, 1990. © 1990, *Washington Post* Writers Group. Reprinted with permission.

sion, has enjoyed largely unlimited access to congressional committee hearings. Floor proceedings are opened to live television coverage. While other institutions facilitated greater access for the press, the Court apparently has remained largely static.

Perhaps closer to home for the justices, lower courts have begun opening courtrooms to cameras. The Court has upheld the right of states to grant access to cameras.[19]

But the Court has been reluctant to follow suit itself. Former Chief Justice Warren Burger has suggested the justices might be distracted by the cameras and that highly selective coverage of all arguments, as the networks would provide, would give the public a distorted conception of the case.[20] Under Chief Justice William Rehnquist, the justices in November 1988 experimented with the televising of oral arguments. In late 1989, after polling his colleagues on the Court and finding a majority opposed to the presence of cameras, Rehnquist announced the Court would not change its policy.

One overriding issue in the debate over televising the Court, as with the televising of Congress, has been control of the television system. The justices desire power over the image and would demand control of the cameras. But the press responds, as one newspaper editorial, that "giving the Court such editorial control would be too high a price for public access."[21]

Less intrusive radio coverage also has been rejected, although three of the justices expressed support. Before retiring, Justice Brennan remarked that "There is no reason in my judgment why only those who can gain entrance to the courtroom should be able to witness these proceedings."[22] ABC Radio requested such coverage for the oral arguments in the 1989 case of *Webster v. Reproductive Health Services* involving abortion, but Rehnquist denied it.[23]

The justices' wariness is probably reinforced by the way in which the justices have seen the Court used as a political football in recent presidential elections. In 1984, Democratic presidential candidate Walter Mondale declared: "This election is . . . about Jerry Falwell picking justices for the Supreme Court." That same year, then-Vice-President George Bush contended "the American people want a Supreme Court that will interpret the Constitution and not legislate.[24] The 1988 Democratic presidential candidate, Michael Dukakis, raised the issue of presidential appointments to the Court in a debate with George Bush. Even one of the justices, Harry Blackmun, contributed to that rhetoric when he commented that if George Bush were elected, the Court could become "very conservative well into the twenty-first century."[25]

We don't know what effect making the Court a campaign issue has on public perceptions, but the Court's image as an independent legal body can hardly be enhanced. Although the Court has been the object of presidential campaign rhetoric in the past, the justices may have sought to defuse the issue this time through candor about the Court's functioning.

Some of the justice's new emphasis on individual visibility may be an attempt to pursue personal or policy objectives, however. Those who have made themselves most visible have been the justices viewed as liberals or centrists on the bench, such as Harry Blackmun, John Paul Stevens, and Thurgood Marshall. They have watched a more conservative majority form among the four Reagan-appointed justices and Justice Byron White, and they have seen their influence within the Court wane. They have watched the conservatives become more assertive on the Court and have observed changes external to the Court which favor the conservatives. The "liberal-centrists" may be pursuing an "outsider" strategy designed to bring public pressure on their colleagues or, at the least, to explicate their own roles.

If, however, these justices are using the press to achieve outside the confines of the Court what they have failed to achieve inside, it is not unreasonable to assume that debates within the Court's conference room will eventually begin to spill out into public view. If justices on both sides of an issue begin running to the cameras to air their sides of the issue, such activity would constitute a radical change in the justices' use of and dependency on the press.

The justices also may be turning to the press to affect specific decisions by other institutions. For example, on March 15, 1989, Chief Justice Rehnquist held a press conference to urge Congress to raise salaries for federal judges. Although press conferences are held continually in Washington to push for legislation, this one was truly unique because never before had a justice held a news conference to announce anything but his own resignation from the Court.[26] Also, during the confirmation hearings for Supreme Court nominee Robert Bork, two of the justices took the highly unusual step of speaking out in favor of the appointment.

Reporting the Decisions

On the days when decisions are announced, the twenty-five reporters assigned to the Court full-time are at their busiest. This is so because when the press covers the Court, it reports its decisions. Only rarely are news stories not about the decisions. But the press is highly selective even in reporting decisions. But the press is highly selective even in reporting decisions. One study of newspaper coverage of Court decisions in the late 1970s found that most decisions were never reported by local media, and that even a national newspaper never reported one-third of the decisions. According to another study, newsmagazine coverage of the Court decisions missed 80 percent of the decisions.[27] On the other hand, a few other decisions are accorded near saturation coverage for a short period. On the day of the announcement of the Webster case in July 1989, the television and radio networks went live for a half hour after the decision and then continued with periodic reports throughout the day. The decision received several pages of editorial space in the next day's major daily newspapers.

Another study suggested that press coverage concentrates on social policy such as abortion, school prayer, capital punishment, and civil rights and ignores other, more complex issues such as search and seizure and legal standing to sue.[28]

The explanation for press reporting of decisions rests with the way the Court releases its decisions as well as the way journalists approach reporting them. The Court offers extensive written explanations of their decisions. However, justices do not make themselves available to reporters following the announcement of decisions, which leaves reporters largely on their own to describe, explain, and analyze the decisions. As a result the journalists who cover the Court come to rely on non-Court sources, such as summaries of cases provided by legal groups and interviews with prominent legal scholars or representatives of affected interest groups.

Those decisions that are covered by the press tend to be reported briefly and sketchily, particularly by network news and non-elite daily newspapers.[29] The effect of the decision on the parties involved may be reported, but for all except a handful of decisions little or no attention is paid to the decision's impact, to explanation of the decision-making process, to the context of the decision, or to the reaction of affected parties.

The press has frequently been criticized for serious errors in its reporting of Court decisions. Critics have argued that some reporters and many headline writers miss the subtleties of Court decisions.[30] For example, David L. Grey documented misreporting of the 1962 school prayer case, and Frank J. Sorauf found news coverage of the Court's campaign finance rulings inaccurate and misleading.[31]

Who is to blame for sketchy and sometimes inaccurate reporting of decisions? Reporters complain that the fault lies with the Court. First, it speaks not to the

Legal fireworks keep network news teams busy

With Supreme Court's 'Webster' decision on Monday and North sentencing on Wednesday, journalists scrambled to be first

As the hands of the clock in the Supreme Court press room approached one minute past 10 last Monday morning (July 3), a press aide sang out to a mob of hundreds of reporters, "Webster!" Almost immediately, Tim O'Brien, ABC News's law reporter who had made sure he was in a position to grab one of the first copies released of the court's opinion in *Webster v. Reproductive Health Services*, was seen slicing through the horde like a halfback racing through an opposing line. His goal was the cubbyhole assigned to ABC and a telephone connected to Barry Serafin at ABC News headquarters in New York. By 10:02 a.m., he had absorbed enough from the seven-page syllabus and the following 77 pages of opinion and separate statements to report on the air that *Roe v. Wade*, the court's 1973 decision affirming a woman's constitutional right to an abortion, had not been overturned—that is what he considered "the bottom line" in the case—but that provisions of the Missouri state law narrowing the right to an abortion had not been declared unconstitutional.

It was that kind of a morning for the law reporters of all the networks. Grab a copy—or have someone grab one for you and relay the results to you—and report "the bottom line" and a bit more to a waiting country, and world, of the most eagerly and nervously awaited opinion of the court's 1988-89 session. O'Brien appeared to be first on the air with word of the decision, but not by much. Everyone was racing. CNN's David French, for instance, was on the air, talking into a camera on the plaza in front of the court at 10:02. But he was dependent for his information on a producer who was skimming the opinion in the press room and relaying word by cellular telephone, as an intern was racing from the press room to deliver a copy of the opinion to French. But as in all such competitions among broadcast journalists, being first by a couple of minutes provided not much more than bragging rights.

The tension in the press room and on the plaza had been palpable. And the release of the tension, with word from the court, provided a fitting climax to weeks, months of anticipation. The plaza was crowded with demonstrators on both sides of the issue and with correspondents interviewing leading members of the warring factions as well as legal scholars. In the principal stakeout position, C-SPAN's camera was cheek by jowl with one from an Australian company. The networks had their own camera locations. And O'Brien, who had emerged from the press room—reading the opinions as he went—was seen interviewing, live, Bruce Fein, known to the communications industry as a former FCC general counsel but generally described as a legal scholar and close monitor of the Supreme Court. By 10:29, the first wave of reports was concluding, as CBS News's Bruce Morton was wrapping up a special, anchored by Connie Chung in New York, that had begun 27 minutes earlier and had included a report by law correspondent Rita Braver.

The story provided additional evidence of the flexibility available to today's broadcast journalist. After O'Brien's telephoned report, Serafin, in the New York studio, interviewed Kate Michelman, leader of a pro-choice group, and Nellie Gray, a pro-life activist, in the ABC News bureau in Washington, and Sarah Weddington, the Dallas attorney who represented the "Roe" in *Roe v. Wade*, in the network's Dallas bureau. CNN's Mary Tillotson, who covers the President, was reporting from Kenne-

bunkport, Me., at 10:04 and again at 10:25. John Cochrane, NBC's White House correspondent, was also reporting from Kennebunkport. And CBS's Linda Taira and NBC's Andrea Mitchell were doing live interviews on Capitol Hill with members of Congress on opposing sides of the issue. It was a major story, and the networks were playing it for all it was worth.

And not only the networks. Some of the 10 satellite trucks that lined the street outside the Supreme Court served stations and groups that wanted their own piece of the story. A Conus spokesman, for instance, said that Conus and its member stations produced 39 live and taped reports on The Day. (Among those providing reports were KMBC|TV| Kansas City, which moved a truck to the state capital in Jefferson City for interviews with principals in the case, and WCVB|TV| Boston, whose correspondent obtained reaction from White House chief of staff John Sununu with the President in Kennebunkport.) And all of the trucks at the court were operated by staffers grateful the long wait was over. Said a tech.ician in the CBS truck, waiting for the correspondents and producer to finish their work, "We've been coming up here two or three times a week for the past month."

For the network news operations and, particularly, their law correspondents, it was well that Independence Day provided a holiday on Tuesday. Because there was another major court story on Wednesday morning, one that imposed renewed pressure on the networks to get a story fast and get it right. It was the sentencing of former White House aide Oliver North by U.S. District Judge Gerhard Gesell. The courtroom was crowded. And outside, the cameras and correspondents were stationed, ready to go live with the news as to whether North, convicted of three felonies, would get jail time.

Again, there were some ingenious techniques involved. ABC News's Bill Greenwood was in the courtroom and, as soon as the sentencing was concluded, at about 11:06 a.m., dashed out and informed a producer, Alan Speck, who was in the corridor and equipped with a walkie-talkie. He relayed the word to O'Brien, who was at a camera position, heard the message in an earpiece, then reported the story.

CBS News also depended on a relay: from Braver, who heard the sentence in the courtroom, to a producer in the corridor, who beamed the information by cellular phone to Chung, anchoring in New York, who passed the word to viewers. Braver, meanwhile, continued on to a camera position to discuss the sentence with Taira. CNN had planned well, but was almost undone by a technical failure. Two correspondents, Eugenia Halsey and Anthony Collings, were in the courtroom. Halsey was equipped with a cellular telephone to contact the Washington bureau—but the phone went dead. So Collings did the old-fashioned way—via shoe leather to a standup position outside the court.

NBC News also depended on fleetness of foot. As NBC News's law correspondent Carl Stern was awaiting the verdict in the courtroom, Jim Miklaszewski, who is normally a White House correspondent, was filling time at the camera position—until Stern showed up, somewhat breathless, to report the sentence.

Who was first on the air with news of the sentence? It appeared pretty much a dead heat at about 11:12. But CBS claimed a first, "by a matter of seconds."

"It was quite a few days," said O'Brien, when it was all over. The courtroom "fireworks" sandwiched around Independence Day, he said,"gives new meaning to the Fourth of July." —LZ

Source: *Broadcasting*, July 10, 1989. © 1989 by *Broadcasting*. Reproduced with permission.

public, but to a legal fraternity. The opinions are written in a style intended for a small group of attorneys, judges, and legal scholars. The Court does little to help reporters understand the opinions, which leaves much room for misunderstanding. Also, reporters say, the Court is to blame because it is unclear about its direction. Reporters say they cannot explain to the public the incomprehensible decisions of the Court. One reporter explained her dilemma in reporting a civil rights decision:

> It was literally impossible to decipher. All I could tell my readers is that the Court had done "x." I could not tell them why. One wire service hailed the decision as a great civil rights victory, while the other wire service called the decision a great civil rights defeat.[32]

A debate has ensued over whether the Court's work is so technical that only reporters with legal training should be assigned to cover the Court. In the early 1960s, Felix Frankfurter urged *New York Times* reporter Anthony Lewis to receive legal training to better report on the Court. Reporter-lawyers, such as Carl Stern of NBC News and Tim O'Brien of ABC News began to be assigned to this beat.[33]

The movement to reporter-lawyers has had its critics. One of the most prominent reporters assigned to the Court, Lyle Denniston of the *Baltimore Sun*, is not a lawyer and dissents vigorously from the view that lawyers make the best Court reporters. He contends lawyers who are reporters are too close to the judicial system. "If a reporter hangs around judges and lawyers too long he begins to smell like them. A journalist has his own smell and he should never trade that aroma for someone else's."[34] Diane Camper, a former correspondent for *Newsweek*, adds that such journalists don't relate well with the general readership: "There is a tendency to get bogged down in legal technicalities if you are a lawyer."[35]

Another problem with Court coverage originates with the way the press treats news. The time constraints of the news business, primarily the speed of transmission and rapid-fire delivery, do not lend themselves to thorough digestion of decisions and thoughtful analysis. Reporters are handed the decisions as they are announced by the justices. They must read, understand, and be able to summarize accurately the decision, including dissenting and concurring opinions, before the next deadline. For network television reporters and national newspapers, that deadline may be only hours away. For the wire service reporters, whose stories will circulate more than any other print stories, the deadline may be only minutes away. In their reporting of the Webster decision, network reporters began live broadcasting two minutes after the decision was released to the press.

The definition of news as what has occurred within the past 24 hours also prevents most of the press from returning to the decision the next day with longer, more reflective stories on the decision. Beyond the 24-hour period, the story of the latest Supreme Court decision is old news.

Where inaccuracy exists it is probably less the fault of reporters assigned to the Court, who have some familiarity with complex legal issues, than of editors and headline writers. Stephen Hess found that reporters assigned to the Court are more likely than their colleagues on other beats to disagree with editors over story language because of the technicality of legal terms.[36]

A more common and, indeed, a more subtle problem is reporter analysis of the decision. Most coverage of decisions consists only of a bare-bones description of the result, but when analysis is offered, the reporter determines its content. Reporters are free to frame the decision as they see fit, and the context a reporter sets for interpreting a given decision could be adherence to the Constitution, legal precedent, interest group pressure, or the personal values of the justices.

Reporters demand sources for stories, but since justices decline most requests for interviews, the press turns to non-Court sources. The choice of such sources is determined by reporters according to news values.

Reporters possess wide latitude in reporting decisions. A cross-media comparison of one decision on the constitutionality of sobriety tests for drunk drivers found wide variation in reporting.[37] One network evening news story focused primarily on the reliability of a breathalyzer, which was not a topic of the decision, and added conflict and skepticism to the story by highlighting problems with the breathalyzer. Two newspaper stories, however, seemed to reinforce the decision by including quotes from a supportive source, which in turn quoted generously from the majority opinion and minimized attention to any dissent.[38]

Why do reporters have such latitude? In part they do because the justices allow them to. Because of their own priorities—the need to maintain an apolitical and dignified image—the justices refuse to accommodate certain press priorities. Their reasoned arguments do not fit the media's needs for brevity and simplicity. If the justices explained their decisions in a format more suitable for the press, such as interviews or press conferences, reporters might gain a greater understanding of the decision. But, again, justices do not believe their decisions need to be explained more than they have already done in lengthy opinion, and they would run the risk of engaging in a post-decision fracas with legal scholars, interest group representatives and even with each other, which would only diminish the effect of the Court's decision. The Court's press officers might be capable of providing the analysis in a format desired by reporters. But press officers, probably in accordance with the wishes of the justices, have demurred at such requests. According to Supreme Court Public Information Officer Toni House:

> The justices spend anywhere up to nine months framing their opinions in the particular case. The idea that a press officer . . . would then come along behind and say, 'Well, in laymen's terms, this is what the Court really meant' is really mind boggling to me.[39]

Changes in the press have also affected the latitude that journalists who cover the Court claim. In the wake of the new journalism, reporters have tended to adopt a more interpretive role, one which treats Court decisions as parts of a larger context, interpreted by the reporter, rather than as stories unto themselves. Additionally, adversarial journalism has diminished reporters' deference toward the Court, as well as toward other national political institutions. The journalistic corps seems more inclined to regard the Court as a political institution than they once were.[40]

Covering a Political Institution

In 1979, a book by Bob Woodward and Scott Armstrong entitled *The Brethren* appeared in bookstores.[41] Unlike previous books about the Court, *The Brethren* explored the decision-making process and illuminated the role of personal relations, ideology, and other political actors. *The Brethren* also was unique in that it described recent cases and discussed activities of justices who were still on the Court. The reporting used for *The Brethren* demonstrated the potential of treating the Court as more of a human and a political body. Since the appearance of *The Brethren*, calls have been issued for changes in journalistic treatment of the Court. Some journalists and scholars have urged that the press cover the Court more and treat it more as a political institution.[42] They contend the Court too long has been handled by the press without the critical approach with which journalists view other institutions. According to scholar Lewis W. Wolfson, Supreme Court justices enjoy "an official's dream: reporters devote much of their time simply to reporting what they say."[43] *Baltimore Sun* reporter Lyle Denniston encourages journalists to treat the Court as an adversary rather than as a partner in newsgathering and reporting: "There is a mistaken notion that those who play the Court's game will get more information from the Court, but they actually get less."[44]

Greater coverage of the Court probably would change neither the relationship between the Court and the press nor even the Court itself, however. There is some evidence that the Court has been covered more since the 1970s without a concomitant decline in public support for the institution, which suggests that it is not the volume of coverage, but its tone that would impact on the Court.[45] But the calls for covering the Court more as a political institution are different; if heeded, the Court may be facing a more aggressive press corps less willing to abide by the traditional rules of deference.

One example is journalistic breach of Court secrecy. Several leaks of decisions in advance of their announcement have occurred in the 1970s and 1980s. In 1989, leaks about the decision writing in the Webster case on abortion emerged before the decision was announced.[46] In 1973, *Time* magazine reported the controversial *Roe v. Wade* decision legalizing abortion one day before it was announced. In 1986, an ABC News reporter broadcast the outcome of a decision on the constitutionality of the Gramm-Rudman-Hollings budget-balancing law two days before it was to be announced.[47]

Increased political coverage of the Court might well present greater difficulty for the Court as an arbiter of conflicts. The Court's position as a source of judgment aloof from political consideration would be undermined by coverage which emphasized political—even partisan—motivations or trends of the justices, and public deference for the Court, which is imperative to the maintenance of a significant role in national policy-making, might well decline.

Greater political coverage could in turn result in a more politicized body. The Court might be drawn into more political disputes with the president and the Congress, and perhaps urged to act in a more hasty manner with greatly reduced time for reflection.

The result eventually could be actual fragmentation of the Court mentioned earlier with each justice publicly pursuing independent individual objectives and seriously damaging the Court's ability to function as an institution.

Until recently, the Supreme Court has been the exception to the rule of increased dependency on the press by political institutions and processes. The Court has been relatively successful at keeping the press at arm's length in pursuit of the strategy of bolstering public deference.

However, that period may be closing if the trends continue. The Court may become more dependent on the press and the press will cover the Court from a more autonomous stance. Although the press will have a better story, it is not likely the nation would have a better Supreme Court.

NOTES

1. Quoted in David Shaw, *Press Watch*, New York: Macmillan, 1984, p. 120.
2. Federalist no. 78.
3. David M. O'Brien, *Storm Center*, Washington: CQ Press, 1986, pp. 295–297.
4. See Gallup Poll, July 1, 1968; Gallup Poll, May 27, 1969; and July 9, 1973.
5. Adam Clymer, "Opinion Narrows Over High Court," *New York Times*, July 13, 1986, p. 15; and Gallup Poll, July 13, 1987.
6. See Gregory Caldiera, "Neither the Purse nor the Sword: Dynamics of Public Confidence in the Supreme Court," *American Political Science Review* 80 (December 1986): 1209–1228.
7. See Gallup Poll, May 22, 1969, and July 9, 1973; and Roper Poll, October 1971.
8. NBC News/*Wall Street Journal* Poll, October 2, 1987; Gallup Poll, July 13, 1987.
9. Harris Poll, May 8, 1988.
10. O'Brien, *Storm Center*, pp. 295–297.
11. See William Rehnquist, *The Supreme Court: How It Was, How It Is*, New York: William Morrow, 1987, pp. 288–291; and O'Brien, *Storm Center*, pp. 122–124.
12. David L. Paletz and Robert M. Entman, *Media Power Politics*, New York: Free Press, 1981, p. 105.
13. Richard Davis, "Lifting the Shroud: News Media Portrayal of the U.S. Supreme Court," *Communications and the Law* 9 (October 1987): p. 46.
14. Davis, "News Media Portrayal of the U.S. Supreme Court," p. 46.
15. See David W. Rohde and Harold J. Spaeth, *Supreme Court Decisionmaking*, San Francisco: W.H. Freeman, 1976.
16. For samples, see Stuart Taylor, Jr., "Justice Stevens Is Sharply Critical of Supreme Court Conservatives," *New York Times*, August 5, 1984; "A Candid Talk with Justice Blackmun," *New York Times Magazine*, February 22, 1982; "Marshall Assails High Court Practice of Ruling Without Hearing Dissenters," *Philadelphia Inquirer*, April 28,

1987; Stuart A. Taylor, Jr., "Meese v. Brennan," *New Republic* (January 6 & 13, 1986): 17–21; "Marshall Faults the Justice Department," *New York Times*, December 13, 1987; Stuart A. Taylor, Jr., "Blackmun Provides a Peek at the People under Those Robes," *New York Times*, July 25, 1988, p. B6. For a more general discussion of these changes, see also Stuart A. Taylor, Jr., "Lifting of Secrecy Reveals Earthy Side of Justices," *New York Times*, February 22, 1988.

17. See Rehnquist, *The Supreme Court.*
18. See Mark W. Cannon and David M. O'Brien, *Views from the Bench*, Chatham, N.J.: Chatham House, 1985. See also Taylor, "Blackmun Provides a Peek at the People under Those Robes," p. B6.
19. *Chandler v. Florida*, 449 U.S. 560 (1981).
20. Eleanor Randolph and Al Kamen, "Chief Justice Considers Televising Supreme Court," *Washington Post*, April 12, 1986, p. 45.
21. "Light on the Supreme Court," *Washington Post*, April 22, 1986, p. A30.
22. Stuart A. Taylor, Jr., "Supreme Court Rejects Radio Coverage of Budget Argument," *New York Times*, April 20, 1986, p. 27.
23. "Supreme Court Press Officer Discusses Webster Case," *C-SPAN Update*, July 24, 1989, p. 8.
24. Elder Witt, "Shaping the Supreme Court for a Generation," *Congressional Quarterly Weekly Report*, October 6, 1984, p. 2452.
25. "Blackmun Has Sharp Opinions of Colleagues," *New York Times*, July 18, 1988.
26. Linda Greenhouse, "Rehnquist, in Rare Plea, Urges Raise for Judges, *New York Times*, March 15, 1989, p. A16.
27. See David Ericson, "Newspaper Coverage of the Supreme Court," *Journalism Quarterly* 54 (Autumn 1977): 605-607; and Michael Solomine, "Newsmagazine, Coverage of the Supreme Court," *Journalism Quarterly* 57 (Winter 1980): 661–663.
28. Richard Davis, "News Media Coverage of American National Political Institutions," unpublished doctoral dissertation, Syracuse University, 1986, p. 135.
29. See Davis, "News Media Coverage," pp. 127–136; and Ericson, "Newspaper Coverage," pp. 605–607.
30. For example, see Chester A. Newland, "Press Coverage of the U.S. Supreme Court," *Western Political Quarterly* 17 (March 1964): 15–36; and William Dahms, "Press Coverage of the Supreme Court: A Troubling Question," *Intellect* (February 1978): 299–301.
31. See David Grey, *The Supreme Court and the News Media*, Evanston, Ill.: Northwestern University Press, 1968; and Frank J. Sorauf, *Money in American Elections*, Glenview, Ill.: Scott, Foresman, 1988, pp. 223–225.
32. Mitchell J. Tropin, "What, Exactly, Is the Court Saying?" *The Barrister* (Winter 1984): 14.
33. William L. Rivers, *The Other Government: Power and the Washington Media*, New York: Universe, 1982, p. 95.
34. Tropin, "What Is the Court Saying?" p. 14.
35. Wolfson, *The Untapped Power of the Press*, New York: Praeger, 1985, p. 58.
36. Stephen Hess, *The Washington Reporters*, Washington: Brookings, 1981, p. 3n.
37. Davis, "News Media Coverage," pp. 50–52.
38. See Davis, "News Media Portrayal of the U.S. Supreme Court," pp. 50–51.
39. "Supreme Court Press Officer Discusses Webster Case," *C-SPAN Update*, July 24, 1989, p. 8.

40. For a discussion of Supreme Court reporters' views of their job, see Tropin, "What Is the Court Saying?"
41. Bob Woodward and Scott Armstrong, *The Brethren*, New York: Simon and Schuster, 1979.
42. For examples, see Shaw, *Press Watch*; and Paletz and Entman, *Media Power Politics*.
43. Wolfson, *Untapped Power of the Press*, p. 57.
44. Tropin, "What Is the Court Saying?," p. 70.
45. For a discussion of possible increased coverage of the Court, see Davis, "News Media Portrayal of the U.S. Supreme Court." For a discussion of recent increased public confidence in the Court, see Caldiera, "Dynamics of Public Confidence in the Supreme Court."
46. See Martha Sherill, "On Abortion, a Delayed Reaction," *Washington Post*, June 30, 1989, p. 1.
47. See Woodward and Armstrong, *The Brethren*, pp. 237–238; and Al Kamen and Helen Dewar, "A Court Ruling That Wasn't," *Washington Post*, June 17, 1986, p. A1.

SUGGESTED READINGS

Grey, David. *The Supreme Court and the News Media*. Evanston, Ill.: Northwestern University Press, 1968.
MacKenzie, John P. "The Warren Court and the Press." In *Mass Media and The Supreme Court*, 2d ed., edited by Kenneth Devol. New York: Hastings House, 1976.
O'Brien, David. *Storm Center: The Supreme Court in American Politics*. Washington: CQ Press, 1986.
Paletz, David, and Robert Entman. *Media Power Politics*. New York: Free Press, 1981.
Woodward, Bob, and Scott Armstrong. *The Brethren*. New York: Simon and Schuster, 1979.

PART IV

Media and Policy

The press is unique as a policymaking participant because it rarely has a stake in the policy outcome. Policymakers may lose their positions if voters assess their efforts negatively. Most interest groups have a concern due to economic consequences of government policy. Others seek to pursue social objectives. The general public is directly or indirectly affected by policy action.

The press as an institution possesses an interest in a small fraction of policy issues, specifically those regarding press freedom and regulation. Although such media giants as Time Inc., RCA, and CBS also are affected by economic consequences of policy, there is no evidence that such concern filters down to the newsroom and significantly alters news coverage of federal government.

This absence of a clear "stake" in policy-making suggests that the press is merely a neutral observer or mediator. This is not, however, entirely the case. Like all of us, members of the press approach their tasks in possession of certain norms and values. Also, the organization for which they work has certain imperatives which affect the way in which newsgathering is approached.

The question is whether these values and norms serve as a detraction from or even a distortion of the policymaking process. For example, the decision whether to cover live congressional hearings on the Vietnam War during the 1960s was fraught with economic considerations about the loss of advertising revenue for the networks. CBS eventually stopped live coverage and ran money-making reruns of "I Love Lucy."[1] The issue is not whether the networks misjudged, but whether policy decisions are actually affected by such considerations.

This section discusses the roles of the press in public policy-making generally and then examines that role specifically related to foreign affairs, and national security policy-making. In the first chapter, we begin by discussing various press roles in policy-making and then breaking the policy process into several successive stages and analyzing press involvement in policy-making at each stage. Then, we conclude that chapter with an overall analysis of the impact of the press on policy-making.

CHAPTER 11

Covering Public Policy

The press acts like "the beam of a searchlight that moves restlessly about, bringing one episode and then another out of darkness into vision."

Walter Lippmann[1]

PRESS ROLES

The press does serve as observer in society—recording events, statements, and policy decisions. But other roles in the policy process, more intrusive roles, also are performed.

In examining the press and foreign policy-making, Bernard Cohen has described three roles of the press—observer, participant, and catalyst.[2] But Cohen's categorization also can be fitted to public policy-making generally.

The press role as observer is the most obvious. The press observes and reports the events of the policymaking process. Theoretically, reporters stand at the elbows of policymakers and record what they observe. These recordings are disseminated to interested parties—other public officials, affected groups and individuals, and the general public.

As observer, the press serves as transmission belt conveying information from various participants, who do not communicate directly, in order to inform for future policy-making. Such a process is essential in a democracy where policy-making is a public enterprise and the participants include, at least at some level, the voters.

The press also acts as a participant in the policymaking process. According to Cohen, the press fulfills this role by serving as representative for the public, government watchdog or critic, advocate of certain policy positions, and actual policymaker. The press can be viewed by policymakers and the public as the voice of public opinion. As watchdog or critic, the press participates by watching over policymakers and offering criticism. Since this criticism is heard and responded to, the press moves from observer to actual participant in the process. This role, however, is fraught with potential danger for the press since it may transcend the public's expectations of press behavior vis-à-vis public officials and lead to public resentment of the press's intrusion.

The press also may act as participant through actual advocacy of policy options. Although such explicit advocacy, according to journalistic standards, is consigned to the editorial page, more subtle forms can occur in news reporting. For example, framing the issue in certain ways can be a form of position advocacy. The listing of available alternatives and the omission of others also can serve that function.

The press also participates by actually being a policymaker. A few, such as columnist George Will, actually have become unofficial advisors to policymakers. Journalists who are granted interviews with policymakers often reciprocate by delivering information and even advice solicited by the interviewee. Such information or counsel may relate to press policy or other policy areas.

The press also serves as catalyst because news content propels issues to the foreground and affects the public's issue agenda and, perhaps, the public's reaction to those issues. Issues which otherwise may have been ignored or minimized are emphasized in public debate.

THE POLICY CYCLE

Several stages in the policymaking process have been identified. These include problem identification, policy agenda setting, policy formulation, adoption, implementation, and evaluation. Although these stages in reality overlap and even fold back on each other, the sequential approach is a comprehensible system for identifying the role of the news media in the policy process.

Problem Identification

Only a handful of selected issues emerge from a universe of private conflicts to capture the attention of the public policy-makers. Two conditions typically serve to differentiate public policy issues from other problems: the public nature of the problem and the consensus that government has a legitimate role in resolving it.[3]

But many problems covered by the news media do not fit these two conditions—the search for an organ donor to serve an ill child, for example. This propensity to cover such problems reduces the media's impact, since when such content is portrayed primarily as human interest and not public policy, it is largely irrelevant to policymakers.

But when the story is recast as a public policy issue, television, because it is a nationwide medium, can transform localized conflicts into national public policy issues. For example, the story of toxic wastes dumped into upstate New York's Love Canal, which was broadcast by the news media in 1980, became a national policy story involving the White House as a policy decisionmaker.[4]

The problem identification stage is highly significant because it is the filter. From a wide range of potential issues only a relative few are identified as problems for governmental resolution. In its role as observer, the press chooses among events and issues. The selection process serves to illuminate some problems, while neglecting others.

In fact, this stage may be the point of most impact for the press in the policymaking process.[5] In accordance with the press's perceived role as voice of public opinion, members of Congress and White House officials look to the press to identify problems. They also know that even if the problem is not one of national public concern, in its role as catalyst, the press could help transform it into one.

For example, although presidents have power to shape the press agenda, they also are shaped by it. As two political scientists have noted about the Iran hostage crisis in 1979–1980: "It is awkward for the president to be shown ignoring a conflict that Cronkite, Chancellor and Reynolds [network news anchors at the time] all agreed was the most significant news of the day."[6]

The press does not identify problems alone, however. Interest groups, individual constituents, and policymakers themselves also play such a role. But they attempt to employ the news media in identifying problems for public policy resolution because the press reaches large numbers of people, including policymakers, and because the problems it identifies as significant are often perceived by political actors as significant. Policymakers react personally, but also in anticipation of a response by constituency groups as well as other policymakers—a response often precipitated by press attention.

Setting the Policy Agenda

Not all problems identified actually move on to the policy agenda where they receive serious attention by policymakers. The process of placing issues on the policy agenda is complex and unpredictable, and the very difficulty of the process mitigates against any single actor playing the consistently dominant role.

Presidents often shape the policy agenda. But even presidents have difficulty placing problems there consistently. Ronald Reagan's attempt to place federalism issues on the policy agenda failed when Congress and other political actors did not respond.

The press can be particularly effective in placing issues on the agenda in combination with other forces, and the agenda-setting efforts of a single politician, or a group such as a congressional committee or caucus or a special interest can be reinforced by press involvement on the issues.

At times, issues appear on the agenda without such direct effort. For example, the drug abuse problem became headline news in 1986 for several months following the sudden drug-related deaths of two star athletes. President and Mrs. Reagan and several members of Congress joined the debate, and the two political parties in an election year competed to serve as standard-bearer of the anti-drug abuse campaign.

More often, however, agenda placement clearly is intentional. The White House attempts to acquire press cooperation in coverage of the president's policy priorities, whatever they may be.

The press rarely pushes an issue onto the agenda all by itself. At times, sustained news coverage can rivet public attention on an issue over a period of time, as did the continuous coverage by NBC News of the Ethiopian famine relief in 1984. Private donations to relief agencies mushroomed. Members of Congress reacted and proposed larger amounts of U.S. aid.[7] But such sustained attention, absent external pressures, is unlikely. Thus, such singular success is rare.

Once an issue has been generated by the press, other players can take advantage of the boomlet in attention to push long-standing policy issues. In 1988, a major story of two gray whales trapped in Arctic ice prompted the Coast Guard to press the White House and the Congress for more icebreakers. News coverage of mass killings, for example, renews handgun control lobbying efforts.

Press interest in a policy or program can be a boon to a policymaker with a pet policy facing impossible odds in capturing the attention of other public officials as well as the general public. Like a starlet waiting to be discovered, many such programs hope for the lucky break of press notice to stimulate interest by other policymakers. Members of Congress fall primarily in this category. The power of the press to identify problems and place them on the agenda offers these policymakers a chance to push pet proposals and gain press and public recognition through identification with a "hot issue."[8]

Although policymakers may latch onto a media-generated issue or attempt to generate one of their own, the slippery nature of agenda setting makes the result difficult to predict. One study of policymakers found that most believed they could not control the policy agenda by initiating stories.[9] Timely events, actions by other players, and White House involvement all combine to shape the agenda. The press alone rarely possesses such power.

The placement of certain issues on the policy agenda also has a reverse side: the non-placement of issues. What doesn't get on the agenda and why can be just as enlightening as what does.

Policymakers occasionally try to lead the news media away from attention to certain policy issues. Carter Press Secretary Jody Powell explained White House strategy as "keeping the press focused on the issues [the president's staff] wanted it to deal with and away from questions and stories they didn't particularly want to tackle.[10]

Some policymakers intentionally avoid press coverage in order to resolve issues privately with a minimum of media fanfare. In other cases, the non-coverage is the product not of policymaker avoidance, but of press lack of interest. Neither the process nor the policy fits newsworthiness according to journalistic standards.

The press's own propensity for certain types of stories based on news values skews the agenda formation in a haphazard rather than a conspiratorial fashion. In fact, this predominance of news values constrains journalists who may well seek to advocate greater coverage of certain policy areas and options. Stories on policy objectives that individual journalists share may well languish in obscurity if lacking news value.[11]

Editorial constraints and the perceived interest of the audience also influence the press role in agenda setting. Time and space limitations keep many policy issues from finding their way into the news. News organizations can only concentrate their finite resources on a few continuing stories. Moreover, that selectiveness is heightened by the perception that the audience is interested in only a few major stories at a time. During the Reagan presidency, the Nicaraguan Contra aid story was followed from problem identification to evaluation, but other policy issues received scant coverage, or were only covered at certain stages.

As discussed in Chapter 8, the familiarity of the story raises the chances that some new, though minor, development will be reported. That measure—familiarity—ensures that many potential policy stories will never appear in the news at all and, as a result may not appear on the policy agenda either.

One key component the consequences of which reverberate throughout the process is how the context of the issue is framed. When the neutron bomb was announced in 1978, for example, it was described in initial press accounts as capable of killing people and leaving buildings intact. Many newspapers repeated the term in each new story.

Although the bomb was in fact designed to carry less permanent destructive capability in a European war, where large urban areas would be destroyed by existing nuclear weapons, the press description cast it in a sinister light. Congressional support remained elusive, and President Carter eventually opted not to deploy the weapon.[12] The press framed the issue as a Pentagon attempt to add a diabolical new weapon to the nuclear arsenal. Cast in that context, rather than as a deterrent to a Warsaw Pact invasion, the weapon faced a difficult—if not impossible—struggle for political survival.

The press role in framing issues is more likely when the press is the initiator in problem identification, as in the case of the neutron bomb coverage. The initial story was the product of extended research by a *Washington Post* reporter and was revealed by the reporter.

Policy Formulation and Adoption

The policy formulation stage is less influenced by the press than the two preceding stages due to several factors. Once the issue rests in the hands of policymakers, the press often will turn its attention back to another new problem. Also, the details of drawing up specific policy alternatives are more complex and less familiar to the general public and less interesting to reporters. Moreover, this stage is a less visible one. White House officials, members of Congress, executive branch officials, and interest group representatives often meet behind closed doors.

The policy adoption stage, where political support is garnered, also is a less visible stage than problem solving or agenda setting. When events during this stage are covered, the press concentrates on the final votes at each point—subcommittee votes, committee votes, etc. The process preceding that vote—hearings, negotiations, and committee mark-up of legislation—is largely ignored.

Seemingly, the earlier the event in this stage, the smaller the volume of news coverage. In a study of one week of congressional news coverage, Stephen Hess found that only three percent of newspaper stories concerned the introduction of legislation and only one of five focused on subcommittee work. Network television's bias for the latter phase—committee work and floor votes—was even more pronounced.[13] (See Table 11.1.) The work of gathering political support is largely an internal process not well suited for media coverage.

The press can have an impact at this stage, however, both indirectly by its impact at earlier stages (as in the case of the neutron bomb) and directly. Press stories about the issues can help crystalize or weaken political support. In the case of the waterway user-charge, the continual coverage of the bill throughout the formulation and adoption stages aided Domenici in acquiring support from key Republican senators who, in the words of one, wanted "the *Post* to show a Republican winning something for a change."[14] However, such impact is rare. If this stage is covered at all it is typically only the periodic votes on the issue, such as those in committee, and particularly the final votes in both houses of Congress.

Ironically, this stage and the preceding one constitute the best opportunity for the press to play a role since, as one scholar points out, this is "the time when decisionmakers are most impressionable."[15] Decisionmakers are sifting through various alternatives, and the press could affect the selection of options by open discussion of policy alternatives and consequences. Such discussion also would alert policymakers to likely press reaction if various options were chosen. But the lack of such discussion in the press at this stage minimizes the role of the press. According to a survey of senior federal officials, at this stage the press actually has the least impact on their decisions.[16]

Policy Implementation

Implementation is the stage following policy adoption when the relevant governmental agencies administer the policy. Other players such as the Congress and the courts can intervene, particularly by limiting administrative discretion.

TABLE 11.1. MEDIA COVERAGE OF LEGISLATIVE PROCESS

	Stories (percent)	
Legislative stage in story	**Newspapers**	**Television**
Introduction of legislation	3	0
Subcommittees	20	7
Committees	37	24
Floor action	35	58
Conference committees	5	11

Source: Stephen Hess, *The Washington Reporters,* Washington: The Brookings Institution, 1981, p. 104. Reprinted with permission.

At this stage of the process, media involvement is at its nadir. Coverage of federal agency activities is almost nonexistent in comparison with the attention devoted to the White House and Congress. For example, in 1988, only four reporters for the daily press covered the Environmental Protection Agency on a regular basis.[17] When the president is involved, news coverage increases. But absent that major player, bureaucratic administration is largely non-news.[18] Certain departments, such as State, Pentagon, Treasury, and Justice receive greater coverage, but other agencies are primarily ignored.[19]

Media critics bemoan the lack of coverage of the bureaucratic agencies. Ralph Nader has complained that the "biggest story in town is the escape of Cabinet secretaries from accountability.[20] Even journalists express concern with the lack of coverage.[21]

Why are agencies underreported by the media? A partial explanation lies with the agencies themselves. Some administrative agencies prefer anonymity. Following his study of government press offices, Stephen Hess concluded that "most executives would be satisfied with a press strategy of no surprises. All their press officers need do to be doing their job is provide a rudimentary early warning system [for crises] and issue routine announcements.[22] These agencies do not solicit the notice of the press and may even avoid it. One journalist covering the federal bureaucracy complained: "Congress makes itself easy to cover, the regulatory agencies don't."[23]

But the explanation rests largely with the press. This stage of the policy process is viewed as unnewsworthy. There are rarely news values in the stories of activities of agencies. The more familiar figures to press audiences—the president, congressional leaders, and even cabinet secretaries—have moved on to other issues. Few visuals or dramatic events occur in policy implementation. (Exceptions include the deployment of troops in combat to implement foreign and/or national security policy or inoculations for epidemics such as the swine flu in the mid-1970s.) Conflict also is usually absent.

Journalists claim that audiences simply aren't interested at this stage.[24] But journalists' own tastes intrude as well. Reporters generally say they do not like the bureaucratic beat because they view it as boring. Most journalists' interests lie elsewhere. One reporter explained that journalists are "bored with mechanics of government unless it produces a political issue or a scandal."[25] Another reporter laments the press work habits at the agencies:

Too often, reporters merely wandered from one press conference to another. . . . In succumbing to this comfortable routine they functioned essentially as mouthpieces for different viewpoints. . . .It takes energy and time—not to mention willingness to walk down blind alleys—to reach deep into the federal bureaucracy and extract stories that make news.[26]

Moreover, according to a former press officer for the EPA, technical, bureaucratic language can intimidate many reporters.[27]

As a result, the missing ingredient in news coverage of public policy tends to be the story of how that policy is implemented: How do federal agencies administer programs? How much flexibility do they possess? What administrative regulations have been adopted and how do they fulfill the intent of the law?

Policy Evaluation

Due to the involvement of more visible players, particularly members of Congress, the evaluation stage is not more visible than policy implementation. Members of Congress in their oversight role hold hearings, prepare reports, and issue statements on the effectiveness of policy. Interest groups and federal agency officials also participate.

These actors perceive policy evaluation as highly relevant because of its potential impact both on the continued existence of the policy and on the formation of the new policy. Moreover, policy evaluation coincides with press role as watchdog or critic.

The news media can have an impact on what policies are evaluated, since stories about policy effects can prompt evaluation. Following the Reagan administration domestic budget cuts in the early 1980s, a rash of new stories appeared featuring social welfare recipients losing government support. The stories, including a CBS documentary titled "People Like Us," provoked members of Congress to undertake an evaluation of the effects of the administration's policies.

When Congress initiates policy evaluation, press coverage of congressional hearings can both widen participation in policy evaluation and alter the evaluation process itself. Given the number of committee sessions underway in both houses of Congress (of which only a few are closed to the press), deciding which to cover bestows broad discretion on the press. Deciding which subjects to air and what amount of coverage to devote is a recurring dilemma. The consequences of such decisions may be significant. In 1966, two of the television networks decided to broadcast testimony before the Senate Foreign Relations Committee on U.S. military role in Vietnam. David Halberstam has argued that the hearings were significant in affecting policy-making on the war:

> [The hearings] were the beginning of a slow but massive educational process. . . .
> It was the ventilation of a serious opposition view. . . . From that time on, dissent
> was steadily more respectable and centrist.[28]

Most public policy evaluation occurs beyond the network news programs and the print media, however. Most does not concern highly visible policy such as the Vietnam War or Reagan administration social welfare cuts, and the evaluation is accomplished primarily by the bureaucracy and congressional committees. As we have already noted, coverage of the bureaucracies is slim, and the vast majority of congressional committee hearings where policy is evaluated publicly go unreported by the press.[29]

Press and the Congress share the blame for this neglect. The proliferation of congressional committees has simply overwhelmed the press; if Congress offered a centralized priority list, coverage of evaluation might improve. But policy evaluation coverage, or the lack thereof, is a responsibility of the press. The press follows journalistic standards. Lacking news values, as the evaluation stage usually does, this aspect of the process is largely ignored. Hence, the role of the press in affecting the outcome of the policy evaluation stage is minimal.

IMPACT ON THE POLICY PROCESS

As noted at the beginning of this chapter, the press acts like "the beam of a searchlight that moves restlessly about, bringing one episode and then another out of darkness into vision."[30] The media's coverage of the policy process is much like that searchlight approach described by Lippmann. Much of the policymaking process remains in the dark, but the glare of press attention may suddenly—and often unpredictably—descend on policymakers in the midst of policy formulation, adoption, or evaluation. The attention may be unexpected and, for many players, unwanted. The focusing of that searchlight on a policy at any stage of the process is due to the combination of forces which include the efforts of political actors who seek to illuminate the process for their own purposes, as well as the particular news values of the media.

Policymakers constantly anticipate media attention; sometimes they court it, and often they attempt to avoid it. They wonder: What if this policy action or decision received widespread notice? What kind of reaction would it engender? The odds of media attention for any given issue are slim, but the uncertainty remains and affects decision making.

Then, often without warning, the searchlight passes. Another problem is illuminated. A scandal occurs or a crisis ensues; some other event with higher news value intrudes. The once-illuminated area becomes dim, and policymakers return to their routine.

Some policymakers—publicity-hungry members of Congress or administration officials—chase after the light in an attempt to remain in the public glare. Many try to move the light to their policy area to achieve political objectives through press assistance, while others in the same policy area may be tugging in the opposite direction, attempting to dampen media interest.

In terms of policy coverage, one could argue that there is also a second light, a spotlight, which is permanently set on the president. The president is the subject of constant press attention and is expected to respond to the events exposed by the searchlight.

As the searchlight sweeps, the whole policy process is rarely exposed. More commonly the searchlight identifies a problem, places it on the agenda, and then moves on, ignoring the more complicated stages. As a result, as policymakers begin to resolve problems, the public's attention shifts to other problems. Although certain events such as final congressional votes will merit some level of press attention, other action will be ignored—and congressional inaction on such issues, since it does not fit the discrete event-oriented nature of news, also passes unnoticed.

This failure to follow through limits the press's impact on policy. Framing of the issue is the press's primary means to affect how the problem will be resolved. Once the issue is dropped by the press, then the impact is diminished. Other players with greater persistence, such as interest groups, become more significant in the latter stages.

The lack of follow-through is beneficial to policy output. Better policy emerges when policymakers are not legislating in an environment where every movement is scrutinized. The process of compromise is more difficult when negotiators' initial positions are made and locked in publicly, guaranteeing eventual dissonance over the final product and predictable criticism of politicians' hypocrisy. Senator Pete Domenici of New Mexico, frustrated by such media attention, once remarked: "You can't negotiate in a fishbowl."[31]

One consequence of the media's searchlight approach is policymakers' realization that media attention will soon pass. If those who seek to shun the exposure wait out the public attention by appearing to satisfy the demands of outsiders—the press, the public, and/or interest groups—through gestures such as appointed commissions or studies of the problem, policy-making can return to its state before press illumination. These policymakers can get on with their own agenda which may have been temporarily interrupted by the media's priorities.

On the other hand, the pressure to act in a more substantive way while under the glare of the news media may be so great that policymakers reach for a quick solution to a complicated problem. In order to appear responsive to public will, policymakers are tempted to resolve an issue hastily. For example, in 1985, responding to news coverage of huge budget deficits, the Congress passed the Gramm-Rudman bill quickly that fall. A major component of the bill was later declared unconstitutional. Both the Congress and the president later distanced themselves from responsibility for passing the law.

Congress is less likely than the White House to act quickly due to the many time-consuming obstacles to rapid action inherent in the legislative branch. But members of Congress are often guilty of joining the chorus for immediate presidential action to resolve a newly identified problem quickly or at least to offer an initiative to the Congress.[32]

Television in particular has had a major role in accelerating the process of decision making. Former presidential advisor Lloyd Cutler has written of television's doomsday clock as it relates to foreign policy, but application can be extended to other policy areas:

> If an ominous foreign event is featured on TV news, the president and his advisers feel bound to make a response in time for the next evening news broadcast. . . . If he does not have a response ready by the late afternoon deadline, the evening news

may report that the president's advisers are divided, that the president cannot make up his mind, or that while the president hesitates, his political opponents know exactly what to do.[33]

The doomsday clock can lead to policy miscalculations. In the case of foreign policy, those errors can cause serious damage to U.S. relations with other nations.[34]

The press also may have shortened the trial period for a policy proposal. Two decisions by the Reagan administration—one involving tax exemptions for racially discriminatory schools and the other on restrictions on Social Security benefits—both had a short life due to quick and overwhelmingly negative press reaction. Explanation and justification of the policies were discarded in favor of hasty reversal.[35] Negative press coverage is a potent tool for forcing policymakers to reassess policy quickly, if not reverse it.

SUMMARY

The massive impact of the press on public policy feared by many is a myth. The press does, however, affect policy-making. The press does have a substantial role in setting the issue agenda of policymakers. The press attention is powerful at affecting what issues policymakers talk about, but it is substantially less important in affecting what they actually do. Substantive impact is likely to occur when the press generates an issue and/or frames it—but most issues are neither media-generated nor media-framed.

Most issues are not illuminated more than briefly by the media's searchlight unless a major political figure, almost always the president, becomes involved, or a newsworthy event such as a crisis or a scandal occurs.

When an issue does receive media attention, the coverage can affect substance by impelling policymakers to respond rapidly, perhaps with ill-considered solutions. But other factors such as the press's spotty coverage of the process, particularly the critical middle and latter stages, mitigate against substantive impact by the press. In a study of six cases of the media's role in policy-making, researchers found significant media impact on policy in only three; moreover, each case was an issue widely publicized at the time and therefore more likely to be affected by press coverage.[36]

In fact, policymakers involved in these policy areas said they were unaffected by the press coverage of their decision-making. They indicated that press coverage affected only the process, and not the actual content of policy.[37]

NOTES

1. Walter Lippmann, *Public Opinion*, New York: Macmillan, 1938, p. 364.
2. Bernard Cohen, *The Press and Foreign Policy*, Princeton, N.J.: Princeton University Press, 1963.

3. James E. Anderson, David W. Brady, and Charles Bullock, III, *Public Policy and Politics in America*, North Scituate, Mass.: Duxbury Press, 1978, p. 7.
4. Martin Linsky, *How the Press Affects Federal Policymaking: Six Case Studies*, New York: Norton, 1986.
5. Martin Linsky, *Impact: How the Press Affects Federal Policymaking*, New York: Norton, 1986, pp. 135–136.
6. William C. Adams and Philip Heyl, "From Cairo to Kabul with the Networks 1972–1980," *Television Coverage of the Middle East*, Norwood, N.J.: Ablex, 1981, p. 31.
7. Christopher J. Bosso, "Setting the Agenda: Mass Media and the Discovery of Famine in Ethiopia," in Michael Margolis and Gary A. Mauser, *Manipulating Public Opinion*, Pacific Grove, Calif.: Brooks/Cole, 1989, pp. 153–174.
8. Linsky, *Impact*, pp. 139–140.
9. Linsky, *Impact*, p. 92.
10. Quoted in Stephen Hess, *The Government/Press Connection*, Washington: Brookings, 1984, p. 105.
11. For a sample, see A. Clay Schoenfeld, "The Press and the NEPA: The Case of the Missing Agenda," in Doris A. Graber, *Media Power in Politics*, Washington: CQ Press, 1984, pp. 260–266.
12. See Martin Linsky, *How the Press Affects Federal Policymaking*, pp. 145–217.
13. Stephen Hess, *The Washington Reporters*, Washington: Brookings, 1981, p. 104.
14. T. R. Reid, *Congressional Odyssey*, New York: W. H. Freeman, 1980, p. 57.
15. Lewis Wolfson, *The Untapped Power of the Press*, New York: Preager, 1985, p. 79.
16. Linsky, *Impact*, p. 130.
17. Jim Sibbison, "Dead Fish and Red Herrings: How the EPA Pollutes the News," *Columbia Journalism Review* (November/December 1984), p. 26.
18. Hess, *Washington Reporters*, pp. 107–108.
19. Hess, *The Government/Press Connection*, pp. 102–106.
20. Dick Kirschten, "The White House Press: Public Watchdog or Megaphone for President's Messages," *National Journal*, November 16, 1985, p. 2583.
21. Hess, *Washington Reporters*, p. 64.
22. Hess, *Government/Press Connection*, p. 106.
23. Hess, *Washington Reporters*, p. 64n.
24. Hess, *Washington Reporters*, p. 64n.
25. Quoted in Sibbison, "How the EPA Pollutes the News," p. 28.
26. R. Jeffrey Smith, "Covering the EPA, Wake Me Up If Anything Happens," *Columbia Journalism Review* (September/October 1983): 29–34.
27. Sibbison, "How the EPA Pollutes the News," p. 28.
28. Halberstam, *Powers That Be*, p. 507.
29. Hess, *Washington Reporters*, p. 106.
30. Lippmann, *Public Opinion*, p. 364.
31. Reid, *Congressional Odyssey*, p. 36.
32. See, for example, Pat Towell, "Failed Coup against Noriega Stirs Hill Frustrations," *Congressional Quarterly* (October 7, 1989): 2660.
33. Lloyd Cutler, "Foreign Policy on Deadline," *Foreign Policy* (1984): 114.
34. See Cutler, "Foreign Policy on Deadline," pp. 114–121.
35. See Linsky, *How the Press Affects Federal Policy Making*, pp. 254–305.
36. Linsky, *Impact*, pp. 112–118.
37. Linsky, *Impact*, p. 114.

SUGGESTED READINGS

Graber, Doris, *Media Power in Politics*. Washington: CQ Press, 1984.

Hess, Stephen. *The Washington Reporters*. Washington: Brookings, 1981.

Hess, Stephen. *The Government/Press Connection*. Washington: Brookings, 1984.

Linsky, Martin. *Impact: How the Press Affects Federal Policymaking*. New York: W.W. Norton, 1986.

Linsky, Martin. *How the Press Affects Federal Policymaking: Six Case Studies*. New York: W.W. Norton, 1986.

Wolfson, Lewis W. *The Untapped Power of the Press*. New York: Praeger, 1985.

CHAPTER 12

Covering Foreign Affairs

You're interested in the drama of the news. What we are working for is the repose of solutions. . . . Our business is, in a sense, to get foreign policy off the front page back to page 8.

Former Secretary of State Dean Rusk to CBS News Reporter
Walter Cronkite, 1966[1]

THE NATURE OF FOREIGN AFFAIRS NEWS

Foreign affairs news constitutes a significant proportion of news coverage of American national politics. According to one study, over 40 percent of network television news is devoted to foreign affairs.[2]

However, although elite newspapers stress foreign relations and economics, much of foreign affairs reporting on television emphasizes crises such as civil wars, political violence, and natural disasters;[3] peaceful relations between countries or even less dramatic activities within nations are largely ignored. One scholar has concluded:

> Too often the Asian or African story becomes a pictorial guide to the natural wonders of the area rather than a discourse on the ideas of nation-building, emerging nationalism, socialism, and modernization that are the forces actually affecting these continents.[4]

Many media critics argue that the U.S. news media offer a distorted view of the Third World.[5] Although ABC's evening news program is titled ''World News Tonight'' and the other television networks claim worldwide coverage, one study found that two-thirds of TV's foreign affairs news concerns Western Europe and the Middle East, while only 20 percent covers Eastern Europe, the Soviet Union, Latin America, Canada, and Africa combined.[6] (See Table 12.1.)

One foreign reporter suggests a double standard in international reporting: "The problem is that when people die, if they are Western people, white people, there is a greater sense of newsworthiness in the West than if blacks or if Third World people die."[7] William C. Adams, in his study of news coverage of natural disasters, found that location made a substantial difference in the amount of coverage accorded. Adams concluded that "the globe is prioritized so that the death of one Western European equaled three Eastern Europeans equaled nine Latin Americans equaled 11 Middle Easterners equaled 12 Asians."[8]

Theoretically, U.S. news organizations cover the world. The capability to cover any event anywhere is a theme of all news organization marketing, especially the television networks. One network claims it is "uniquely qualified to bring you the world."

In reality, however, where news originates is closely correlated with the location of major news organization bureaus.[9] The proximity of a news reporter clearly contributes to the newsworthiness of events, and the proximity of a camera for television news is even more important. Events outside camera range must possess other news values in high degree to receive time on the nightly news. This process is to some extent circular, however, since news organizations decide where to place journalists and bureaus according to their expectations of where news will originate.

Only rarely does a story command such significance to the American press that the absence of a bureau is overridden. One example is the Iraqi invasion of Kuwait in August, 1990, a nation where few news organizations had stationed reporters.

In an era of news organizations budgetary cutbacks, which has particularly affected the television networks, the cost of foreign newsgathering has become crucial. According to one ABC News executive, even small overseas bureaus cost

TABLE 12.1. PERCENTAGE OF REFERENCES TO EACH MAJOR WORLD REGION AND CANADA, ALL NETWORKS

Region	1972–1981
Western Europe	30.7
The Middle East	29.3
Asia	28.1
Eastern Europe	20.2
Latin America	11.1
Africa	7.2
Canada	2.3

Source: James F. Larson, *Television's Window on the World: International Affairs Coverage on the U.S. Networks*, Norwood, N.J.: Ablex, 1984, p. 68.

the network over one million per year.[10] Due to the importance of the "bottom line," the result is more reliance on news gathered by major bureaus and increasing neglect of other parts of the world.

CBS Evening News anchor Dan Rather, in a newsmagazine commentary, expressed his concerns and attributed the cause to business decisions when he wrote: "Make no mistake, the trend line in American journalism, print and broadcast, is toward decreasing foreign coverage." Rather assigned the blame for cuts in foreign coverage to a network business decision that foreign news is too expensive.[11]

Another factor in determining foreign news is the ease of journalistic access to various nations. Non-democratic nations have learned this lesson, and they use media access as a tool to encourage or stifle coverage to satisfy their own political purposes. After the Iraqi invasion of Kuwait, Saddam Hussein initially restricted access to Western media, but then decided that he could improve coverage of his side of the conflict by cooperation. One indication of this effort was the Iraqi government's choice of "Nightline" as the first forum to present its side since, as ABC news executive Roone Arledge admitted, the Iraqis "have always felt that "Nightline" was a fair program to the Arab point of view."[12]

Probably the most successful example of avoiding Western press coverage occurred in Cambodia in the mid-1970s when an estimated one to three million citizens were exterminated by their government. Because the government closed the country to the Western press, American news media virtually ignored the story.[13]

It appears that the American media are merely "following the flag." In other words, they report on foreign affairs in accordance with the priorities of the U.S. government. Political factors certainly help explain the American news media's emphasis on Western European affairs, which are treated as news because of the close political and economic ties between the United States and these countries. Western European countries also share similar social customs and political institutions, which are more familiar to American audiences. Moreover, the ethnic background of most Americans is rooted in Western Europe.

Middle East stories, which also comprise a substantial part of U.S. foreign news, are primarily about Israel and its relations with other Middle Eastern nations. Many Americans, including journalists, feel a close affinity with Israel due to the historical relationship between the United States and Israel.[14]

In addition to regional bias, foreign affairs coverage is slanted towards selected "continuing sagas."[15] Television news in particular tends to return to episodes of long-running stories such as Israel and Middle East affairs, the U.S. role in El Salvador, and the U.S. hostages in Lebanon. Some dramatic events produce saturation coverage; specific recent examples include the U.S. military deployment into Saudi Arabia and the collapse of the Berlin Wall. More generally, saturation coverage is devoted to events such as a critical election in a foreign nation or a hostage release.

Saturation coverage means the story receives large amounts of coverage for extended periods of time. For example, the June 1985 hijacking of a TWA airliner en route from Cairo to Rome was the subject of nearly two-thirds of evening news time on all three major networks for a 16-day period.[16]

Occasionally stories burst upon the scene and cannot be ignored because of their potential to disrupt U.S. or international affairs or due to their high dramatic quality. The fall of Communist governments in Eastern Europe in the autumn of 1989 is one example.

Foreign affairs reporting is primarily and predictably coverage of U.S. relations with other nations, and secondarily coverage of countries close to the United States such as the Western European nations, Israel, and Canada. A third and distinctly subordinate category is coverage of events which do not specifically affect the United States and which occur in countries other than those listed.

USING THE PRESS TO CONDUCT FOREIGN POLICY

The news media's capabilities for dissemination of information have expanded to worldwide reach, and the content of American news is followed by foreign political leaders. Consequently, the American press has become a conduit for information between nations.

In states where news media, particularly broadcast media, are owned and/or operated by the government, the media serve directly as state organs. Even in some Western democracies, certain newspapers affiliated with the government or ruling political party are similarly viewed. In the United States, no such explicit relationship exists at the national level. Journalists for the networks and elite publications attempt to discover and convey accurately the thinking of senior administration officials in order to boost the organization's credibility as a source of accurate news.

Those who make foreign policy often use the press's highly credible status and access to wide audience, as well as its willingness to report administration views, to communicate messages to foreign governments. This tool is especially useful when no other form of communication exists. For example, during the Iran hostage crisis in 1979–1981, the communication between the U.S. government and the Iranian students holding the hostages in the U.S. embassy was occasionally conducted exclusively through the press.[17] But even in non-crisis situations, the press can become a vehicle for communicating with foreign governments.

Using the press in this manner raises serious questions about the conduct of foreign policy. Does this role reduce the press's independence? Is the press failing to fulfill its role in American politics when concentrating on communicating U.S. government policy? Journalists who follow the lead of the U.S. government may be poorly serving the U.S. public since this practice may lead them away from stories of administration embarrassments, which policymakers are not likely to tout, and from challenging the objectives of policymakers.[18]

Stories are sometimes simply too dramatic to be ignored. Media coverage of the fall of the Berlin Wall in November 1989 is an example. *Source:* © UPI/Bettmann Newsphotos.

Is it an effective conduit? Even if the conduit role is accepted as legitimate, another question is whether the press can serve as an effective conduit for intergovernmental messages? Both policymakers and journalists defend the press as conduit. Policymakers do so because of the high level of credibility of the American press, which suggests that messages transmitted through such a channel will be taken seriously. Policymakers also appreciate that messages so transmitted do not carry the imprimatur of the U.S. government. Thus, foreign governments can be given suggestions or warned of U.S. actions without formal involvement by the U.S. government.

Journalists do not view such usage as inimical to their independent status, since no coercion is involved. Journalists are free to air their views of governmental actions along with their descriptive reporting of them. In fact such usage enhances their reputation for accurate information, and their role as participants in the process.

However, is the press a competent conduit? In a study of television news coverage of the Iran hostage crisis, David Altheide found contradictory media messages within two days of each other; one message hinted at likely U.S. military response, while the second ruled out such force.[19] Iran or another foreign country using the news media to discern U.S. intent might be forgiven for misunderstanding U.S. policy. Even on a more subtle level, will all the nuances be preserved? Also, given the frequency of unofficial leaks, will the unofficial message be mistaken for authoritative?

Still another issue is: If the press is a legitimate channel for sending foreign policy messages, is the government justified in sending "disinformation" through the same channel in support of U.S. policy?

In August and September of 1986, the Reagan administration launched a disinformation campaign through the U.S. media intended to convince Libyan leader Colonel Muammar Qaddafi that the United States would attack Libya or that he would be overthrown.

Although it denied it had lied outright, the administration admitted the campaign and justified it as in the best interest of U.S. foreign policy. President Reagan remarked that he would "just as soon have Mr. Qaddafi go to bed every night wondering what we might do," and Secretary of State George Shultz remarked:

Frankly, I don't have any problems with a little psychological warfare against Qaddafi. . . . If I were a private citizen reading about it, and I read that my Government was trying to confuse somebody who was conducting terrorist acts and murdering Americans, I would say, 'Gee, I hope it is true.'[20]

Press reaction to the campaign was immediate and predictably negative.[21] Although most journalists supported the use of the press as a communication channel, they overwhelmingly rejected employment of disinformation as a corruption of the process. Acceptance of the first, however, almost inevitably guarantees that such attempts will occur.

The role of the press has not been limited to communication of U.S. policy. The press has played a feedback role as well. Particularly through editorials, the press provides a government outsider reaction to foreign policy-making.

EFFECT ON PUBLIC OPINION

Does news coverage of foreign affairs affect the public's opinions about foreign policy? Doris Graber concluded that because most Americans lack knowledge of foreign affairs (and are not interested in gaining more), they are easily swayed by television coverage.[22] Some evidence does suggest a correlation between opinion change and news content.[23]

William C. Adams suggests that three factors influence how much news media coverage of foreign affairs will impact on public opinion: the magnitude of visibility of the story (How much press time/space is devoted to it?); the level of congruence with established public values toward foreign affairs (Is the story in accordance with the ideals and beliefs of its audience?); and the degree of consistency with existing public information about international affairs and international figures (Does this information agree with what Americans already know about foreign affairs?).[24]

It is almost a given that stories not given saturation coverage are not likely to affect public opinion, and most foreign affairs issues and events do not receive this level of news attention. In fact, the vast majority of U.S. foreign policy decisions are made without much general media or public notice, which mitigates against much effect.

The other two factors explain why foreign affairs events such as Reagan's visit to the Bitburg cemetery in Germany in 1985 do not alter public opinion. In the case of the Bitburg visit, although the story was highly visible, the message that the president was paying homage to Nazi soldiers was incongruent with public values of Ronald Reagan and U.S. foreign policy in Germany. Hence, it was rejected by the public.[25]

The filter of public values and information aids in understanding why media coverage of foreign affairs-related issues or events does not change public attitudes in predicted directions. For example, it was expected that viewers surveyed after watching "The Day After," an ABC network docu-drama on the aftereffects of a nuclear strike, would become more antimilitary or anti-Ronald Reagan. This did not happen.[26] Thus saturation coverage of an event does not guarantee altered public views.

Public opinion can be impacted by news coverage of foreign affairs. But certain factors affect that process, and saturation news coverage alone is not sufficient.

Effect on Foreign Policy-Making

At the conclusion of a half-hour CBS News special on the status of U.S. involvement in Vietnam in March 1968, Walter Cronkite concluded that the war was not winnable and the U.S. government should negotiate its way out of Vietnam. As the story goes, President Johnson turned to his aides and declared that if Walter Cronkite thought the war was over, so would the rest of the country.[27]

This anecdote suggests the power of the news media on U.S. policy-making. However, the anecdotal evidence has not been reinforced with systematic research. In fact, it has been contradicted. For example, in a study of news coverage of the Vietnam War, Daniel C. Hallin concluded that press content became oppositional only after the policymakers involved split over U.S. involvement.[28] The bulk of scholarly attention has been on media role in foreign policy crises such as the Iran hostage crisis rather than on the effect on the conduct of non-crisis foreign policy— and, like the domestic public policy process, the vast majority of foreign policy-making is conducted in a non-crisis atmosphere. Certainly, foreign policy in general receives more press attention than other types of policy.[29] And the president is more likely to become involved in foreign policy than in domestic policy. Nevertheless, most foreign policy is developed outside the glare of the lights and cameras.

How much of this type of foreign policy is affected by the press is unknown, but it is unlikely the press plays a direct role in such policy decisions. It is also unlikely the press has an indirect role via public opinion since minimal coverage is given, and the mass public is unlikely to respond.

But coverage of foreign policy, like other policy areas, is affected by the searchlight nature of the press. When a hostage-taking, a dramatic coup, or a revolution occurs, foreign policy in that area is quickly illuminated. The discrete event focuses attention on the policy; the policy itself is not newsworthy. The press has failed to explain the social forces producing these crises because they are not considered news.

As a result, when foreign events become news, the audience lacks understanding of the context for the event.[30] Lack of context may be salient when the public demands certain policy options, such as military action, that are incongruent with the imperatives of the situation.

James Larson argues that television coverage affects foreign policy by conveying emotion and a sense of intimacy in reporting on the human effects of foreign policy. For example, President Reagan was said to be touched by coverage of the plight of the families of the hostages held in Lebanon, which spurred the Iran arms-for-hostages deal. Also, Reagan reportedly acted to limit Israeli bombing in Lebanon after viewing highly emotional film clips of civilian casualties from the bombing.[31]

The portrayals may affect the public first and pressure from the public may be placed on government policymakers to respond.[32] However, it is more likely that foreign policy elites and a small, attentive audience for foreign policy issues will affect foreign policy-making. The news media provide a vehicle for participation in the dialogue and acquisition of information for meaningful participation.

Due to the news media's role as information source, the press portrayal of foreign affairs can affect policy by shaping the views of policymakers. Although those who are directly involved in foreign policy-making have access to other sources, the press serves as a valuable source given its surveillance capability and speed of delivery.

In fact, information from the press may precede that from other sources, especially in a crisis situation. In the case of a fast-breaking event, a journalist on the scene merely reaches for a telephone to report the event. If properly equipped, a broadcast crew can send pictures instantaneously via satellite. A government employee, on the other hand, is concerned with obtaining a secure telephone line or communications link. Even then, the information will pass through several layers of bureaucracy before reaching chief policymakers. Moreover, the government employees are not usually assigned such tasks. One government official explained: "The embassies do not attempt to cover the news; they assume that people in the State Department read newspapers."[33] The press can impact policy through the portrayal of the world it provides policymakers.

SUMMARY

Press coverage of foreign affairs is a substantial portion of the total news pie. Coverage is skewed towards certain regions and has a sporadic quality concentrating on "continuing sagas."

The press and foreign policy leaders cooperate to communicate foreign policy. However, the press may not be well suited as a conduit, particularly when used exclusively. The media's effect on foreign policy-making seems to hinge on the extent of media coverage, public reaction, and policymakers' direct reaction to the media's coverage or to the public's reaction. It is a convergence of all three elements.

NOTES

1. Quoted in Stephen Hess, *The Government/Press Connection,* Washington: Brookings, 1984, p. 104.
2. See James F. Larson, *Television's Window on the World: International Affairs Coverage on the U.S. Networks,* Norwood, N.J.: Ablex, 1984.
3. See Carolyn Garrett Cline, "The Myth of the Monolity," *Newspaper Research Journal* 5 (Winter 1983): 17–28; Larson, *Television's Window on the World;* William C. Adams and Philip Heyl, "From Cairo to Kabul with the Networks," in William C. Adams, ed., *Television Coverage of the Middle East,* Norwood, N.J.: Ablex, 1981, pp. 1–39; and Waltraud Queiser Morales, "Revolutions, Earthquakes, and Latin America: The Networks Look at Allende's Chile and Somoza's Nicaragua," in William C. Adams, ed., *Television Coverage of International Affairs,* Norwood, N.J.: Ablex, 1982.
4. Robert M. Batscha, *Foreign Affairs News and the Broadcast Journalist,* New York: Praeger, 1975, p. 216.
5. See for example, Mort Rosenblum, *Coups and Earthquakes,* New York: Harper & Row, 1970; and Michael X. Delli Carpini, "Television and Terrorism: Patterns of Presentation and Occurrence, 1969 to 1980," *Western Political Quarterly* 40 (March 1987): 45–64.

6. Larson, *Television's Window on the World;* and David H. Weaver and G. Cleveland Wilhoit, "Foreign News Coverage in Two U.S. Wire Services," *Journal of Communication* 31 (Spring 1981): 55–63.

7. Landrum R. Bolling, ed., *Reporters under Fire,* Boulder, Colo.: Westview Press, 1985, p. 31.

8. William C. Adams, "Whose Lives Count? TV Coverage of Natural Disasters," *Journal of Communication* 36 (Spring 1986): 113–122. For an opposing view, however, see Gary D. Gaddy and Enoh Tanjung, "Earthquake Coverage by the Western Press," *Journal of Communication* 36 (Spring 1986): 105–112.

9. Larson, *Television's Window on the World;* and Edward J. Epstein, *News from Nowhere,* New York: Vintage, 1974, pp. 100–102.

10. James F. Larson, *Global Television and Foreign Policy,* New York: Foreign Policy Association, 1988, p. 39.

11. Dan Rather, "The Threat to Foreign News," *Newsweek,* July 17, 1989, p. 9.

12. Tom Shales, "Baghdad Breakthrough," *Washington Post,* August 16, 1990, p. D1.

13. William C. Adams and Michael Joblove, "Unnewsworthy Holocaust," in Adams, ed., *Television Coverage of International Affairs,* pp. 217–226.

14. See Adams and Heyl, "From Cairo to Kabul with the Networks," pp. 1–39; and S. Robert Lichter, "Media Support for Israel: A Survey of Leading Journalists," in Adams, ed., *Television Coverage of the Middle East,* pp. 40–52.

15. William C. Adams, "Mass Media and Public Opinion about Foreign Affairs: A Typology of News Dynamics," *Political Communication and Persuasion* (1987), p. 264.

16. Larson, *Global Television,* p. 25.

17. David Altheide, "Iran vs. U.S. TV News: The Hostage Story out of Context," in Adams, ed., *Television Coverage of the Middle East,* pp. 138–158.; and James F. Larson, "Television and U.S. Foreign Policy: The Case of the Iran Hostage Crisis," *Journal of Communication* 36 (Autumn 1986): 108–130.

18. See William A. Dorman and Mansour Farhang, *The U.S. Press and Iran: Foreign Policy and the Journalism of Deference,* Berkeley, Calif.: University of California Press, 1987. For an argument that the press used to engage in such behavior, but does no more, see I. M. Destler, Leslie H. Gelb, and Anthony Lake, *Our Own Worst Enemy: The Unmaking of American Foreign Policy,* New York: Simon and Schuster, 1984.

19. David Altheide, "Iran vs. U.S. TV News: The Hostage Story out of Context," in Adams, ed., *Television Coverage of the Middle East,* pp. 153–154.

20. Quoted in Bernard Gwertzman, "Schultz Calls Use of Press to Scare Libyan Justified," *New York Times,* October 3, 1986, p. A1.

21. For samples, see Robert D. McFadden, "News Executives Express Outrage," *New York Times,* October 3, 1986, p. A7.

22. Doris Graber, *Mass Media and American Politics,* Washington: CQ Press, 1988, p. 353.

23. Adams and Heyl, "From Cairo to Kabul with the Networks," pp. 15–23.

24. Adams, "Mass Media and Public Opinion about Foreign Affairs," pp. 263–278.

25. Adams, "Mass Media and Public Opinion about Foreign Affairs," pp. 263–278.

26. See William C. Adams et al., "Before and after 'The Day After': The Unexpected Results of a Televised Drama," *Political Communication and Persuasion 3* (1986): 191–213. For another example of unexpected public reaction to a televised issue presentation, see Michael J. Robinson, "Public Affairs Television: The Case of the

'Selling of the Pentagon,' " *American Political Science Review* 70 (June 1976): 409–432.

27. David Halberstam, *The Powers That Be,* New York: Knopf, 1979, p. 514.

28. Daniel C. Hallin, *The Uncensored War,* New York: Oxford University Press, 1986.

29. Stephen Hess, *The Ultimate Insiders: U.S. Senators in the National Media,* Washington: Brookings, 1986, p. 35; Stephen Hess, *The Washington Reporters,* Washington: Brookings, 1981, pp. 107–110; Michael B. Grossman and Martha Joynt Kumar, *Portraying the President,* Baltimore Md.: Johns Hopkins University Press, 1981, pp. 270–272; and Richard Davis, "News Media Coverage of American National Political Institutions," unpublished doctoral dissertation, Syracuse University, 1986, pp. 162–164.

30. See, for example, Larson, "Television and U.S. Foreign Policy," pp. 108–130.

31. Michael A. Ledeen, *Grave New World,* New York: Oxford University Press, 1985, p. 104.

32. Ledeen, *Grave New World,* p. 104.

33. Bernard C. Cohen, *The Press and the Foreign Policy,* Princeton: Princeton University Press, 1963, p. 209.

SUGGESTED READINGS

Adams, William C., ed. *Television Coverage of the Middle East.* Norwood, N.J.: Ablex, 1981.

Adams, William C., ed. *Television Coverage of International Affairs.* Norwood, N.J.: Ablex, 1982.

Batscha, Robert M. *Foreign Affairs News and the Broadcast Journalist.* New York: Praeger, 1975.

Cohen, Bernard C. *The Press and the Foreign Policy.* Princeton, N.J.: Princeton University Press, 1963.

Dorman, William A., and Mansour Farhang. *The U.S. Press and Iran: Foreign Policy and the Journalism of Deference.* Berkeley, Calif.: University of California Press, 1987.

Larson, James F. *Television's Window on the World: International Affairs Coverage on the U.S. Networks.* Norwood, N.J.: Ablex, 1984.

Larson, James F. *Global Television and Foreign Policy.* New York: Foreign Policy Association, 1988.

CHAPTER 13

National Security Policy

"You people in the news business enjoy not allowing the U.S. to do anything in secret, if you can help it. The higher the classification the quicker you will report it. So you are predictable in that sense."

Secretary of State George Shultz[1]

COVERING AN INVASION

On January 16, 1991, U.S. bombers began a massive aerial bombardment of Iraq and Kuwait in preparation for a ground assault against Iraqi forces barricaded in Kuwait. President Bush, Secretary of Defense Richard Cheney, and General Colin Powell, chairman of the Joint Chiefs of Staff, were gathered in the White House for the crisis eagerly awaiting word from the military commanders relaying information on the status of the operation. But the first news on the success of the bombing came not from secret transmissions through the military chain of command, but from the television set as three CNN reporters huddled in a hotel room in Baghdad reported live by telephone. The first information about the mission's success given to the president was the same information simultaneously relayed to millions of households in the United States and all over the world, including the presidential palace of Saddam Hussein in Iraq.

This mass technological achievement aptly demonstrates the capability of the news media for news reporting in wartime and the potential difficulties for policymakers attempting to control information about military operations. As over 700 news organizations sent reporters to the Middle East to cover the early days of the war, U.S. policymakers were faced with the loss of power to determine the nature and extent of news reporting.

In response, the U.S. military instituted the most stringent restrictions on the press since World War II, including limitations on access to combat zones, sketchy information delivered at press briefings, and prior censorship of press reports sent back to the United States. Journalists criticized the military for using the restrictions not only to prevent military information from reaching the Iraqis, but also to portray the war in the most positive terms.[2]

Some news organizations included warnings with their stories about the war such as the following from the *New York Times*:

Censors Screen Pooled Reports
The American-led military command in Saudi Arabia has put into effect press restrictions under which journalists are assembled in groups and given access to military sources.

The pool reporters obtain information while under military escort, and their accounts are subject to scrutiny by military censors before being distributed. Some of the information appearing today on American military operations was obtained under such circumstances.

However, the public did not seem to mind. Polls taken immediately after the start of the war indicated strong public support for military censorship.[3]

Ironically, press coverage of U.S. involvement following Iraq's invasion of

Source: Cartoon of February 14, 1991 by Don Wright. *Washington Post National Weekly Edition.* Reproduced by permission of Don Wright.

Kuwait was highly supportive. One study of press coverage found 62 percent of the people quoted as sources in the United States were supportive of U.S. policy. Many of the stories focused on human interest. Stories about soldiers packing their bags and being loaded on military air transports, tales of a soldier's life in the desert including boredom and frustration, and accounts of the varied efforts of Americans back home to support the troops through cards, letters, and free copies of newspapers dominated national news.

Early in the operation, journalists quickly identified the "good guys" and the "bad guys" in the conflict and expressed indirect support for the expeditionary force. In a *Christian Science Monitor* article of August 21, 1990, on a visit of General Colin Powell to troops departing for the Middle East, reporter Scott Pendleton wrote: "Rarely in recent memory has a general offering such dockside sentiments spoken for so much of the United States as Powell did last Friday—and the Marines there knew it."[3] The president was praised specifically as seen in *Time* magazine's cover story of August 20, which opined that "only the U.S., most everyone acknowledges, has the capacity to muster the international effort required to stop the power-grab of a vain, amoral crusader like Saddam Hussein. It appears that George Bush has the will and skill to do so." *Newsweek*'s lead story on August 20 was similarly patriotic:

> From the Middle West to the Middle East, American fighting men were on the move last week—and as the Pentagon began what was clearly the biggest U.S. mobilization since the Vietnam War, the nation watched with mingled pride and apprehension. Ahead, in the oil kingdoms of Arabia, American boys faced all the horrors of modern war: tanks, missiles, even poison gas. They shouldered their gear and boarded the transports, kissing their sweethearts goodbye. The cold war was over but there were new threats to peace from a hard-eyed adventurer in Iraq. And if the mission was uncertain and the conflict far away, it was time, as George Bush said last week, to stand up for what's right.

This latest U.S. military incursion once again raised the issue of the proper role of the press in covering U.S. troop movement in hostile or potentially hostile conditions. Does the press hamper the operations of the military in such conditions or undermine public support at home? Should the press be able to cover military operations in the same way other events—domestic or foreign—are covered or should restrictions be placed on their reporting in conjunction with national security interests? If restrictions are favored, what kind of restrictions are appropriate?

These questions are not new. Since the Vietnam War, during each new U.S. military incursion, administrations have sought to exercise control over the press's activities and news organizations have bridled at perceived unnecessary restrictions. Each time, the debate over the press's role has been reengaged.

On December 20, 1989, 10,000 American troops invaded Panama and took over the country. Over several days of battles, the existing government was defeated and a new government, backed by the United States, was installed. The de facto leader of Panama, General Manuel Noriega, was captured and flown to the

United States for trial. The Bush administration defended the invasion as necessary to save American lives, although its displeasure with the whole Noriega regime was long-standing.

Unlike military strikes during World War II, Korea, and Vietnam, journalists were not invited to accompany the troops. Reporters who were assigned to a Pentagon military operation press pool were purposely delayed in leaving Washington and were shunted away from the fighting when they did arrive in Panama. The only still photos and videotape of the battles available to the public were those provided by the Pentagon itself. Rather than being allowed to see the fighting, reporters were taken to view Noriega's homes. When reporters arrived at battles, the action was already over.

Journalists covering the invasion were prohibited from filming damaged helicopters or caskets of dead servicemen, interviewing wounded soldiers, or visiting Panamanians taken prisoner by the U.S. troops.[4]

Journalists' experiences in Panama were similar to those of journalists covering the Grenada invasion in 1983. In Grenada, only after the initial fighting had subsided were reporters allowed to visit the island. The commanding officer later related that he had "other priorities to be dealt with" besides press access, and that the press "would have to make the best of the situation."[5]

In the case of Grenada the press reacted strongly to the denial of access. *Time* labelled the action "a bad mistake, an outrage to press freedom, and an ominous symptom of a tendency in the Reagan administration to try to control the flow of information."[6] The *Washington Post* called the act of denial of access "inexcusable" and opined "the government set aside tried-and-true rules for ensuring that the media and through them the people would see, know, and understand in the most timely and credible way how it was exercising military power in their name."[7]

However, public opinion apparently varied sharply from the views of the press. *Time* found its letters on the issue running eight to one in favor of the restrictions on access, and the vast majority of calls to ABC and NBC also sided with the government.[8]

U.S. military actions in the Middle East, Panama and Grenada each, coupled with the press and public reactions, have raised the question of the role of the press in covering national security policy. No other policy area has provoked as much tension between political leaders and the press as has this one.

The tension has resulted from the press's greater surveillance capability in such situations, as well as the political system's dependence on the press. The general public rely on the press to comprehend national security policy and the administration depends on the press to explain policy and rally public support.

THE PROBLEM OF ACCESS

One of the thorniest issues has been the problem of press access. The issue still remains: Should the government limit the presence of the press in potential or actual combat situations?

Proponents of such limitations argue they are needed to preserve national security. If the press accompanies the troops, military secrecy will be violated. The enemy will be aided by negative coverage of military efforts. These arguments all assume that the press will not maintain confidentiality and will relay largely critical coverage of U.S. military involvement.

Opponents counter that the access provided during earlier conflicts should be maintained. Denial of access from the early 1980s on was a departure from accepted practice. They also contend that in a democracy the public must be kept informed about military operations. Hence, restrictions on the presence of the press in combat situations weakens our democratic system of government, for which we are supposed to be fighting.

News coverage of combat has occurred since the Revolutionary War. More recently, in World War II, Korea, and Vietnam, journalists did accompany U.S. troops into combat. Due to the cooperation of the military, in Vietnam reporters were provided easy access to the battlefront, usually riding in empty medical evacuation helicopters. One reporter even termed the Vietnam conflict "a notably convenient war to cover."[9]

Yet the Middle East conflict and the Panama and Grenada invasions' controversies suggest a dramatic shift. What has changed? Have journalists changed? Were journalists in the past more patriotic, more accepting of military authority, more committed to the war effort than those today?

George Shultz voiced such sentiments:

> These days in the advocacy journalism that's been adopted, it seems as though reporters are always against us and so they're always trying to screw things up. And when you're trying to conduct a military operation, you don't need that.[10]

Advocates of this view point to the press's reporting in Vietnam as evidence of a journalistic shift. The reporting of atrocities, gory battle scenes, and body bags hampered the war effort and led to the the U.S. pullout.[11] Lack of access in Panama and Grenada denied the press such battle scenes and forced coverage to focus on policymakers in Washington and the outcome of the policy following the conflict.

Opponents respond that the Vietnam War was different. The war coverage at that time reflected public indecisiveness and confused U.S. administration objectives.

Magnifying the question of access is the introduction of television and the rapid relay of information. Television provides visuals for stories. Combat situations feature scenes of injured soldiers and mangled bodies. Television can transmit pictures of those scenes from battleground to living room.

Vietnam was the first conflict where television was available to portray war so vividly. The indictment of the press stems largely from this capability. The fear is that such coverage will turn the electorate from support of a war, that emphasis on bloody scenes and body bags will deter U.S. citizens from supporting the objectives of a war.

One factor in determining access has been the greater presence of the press in

combat situations. An estimated 400 members of the press sought to cover the
Grenada invasion on its first day. That number equalled approximately one-fourth
of the early U.S. military force. About 750 journalists were on the island within
several days.[12] Reporters are accompanied by an army of technicians and producers,
whose number exceeded the size of the press corps in Vietnam at the height of the
Vietnam War.[13]

One outgrowth of the Grenada invasion was formation of a National Media
Pool to cover the early stages of a military action.[14] A 16-member pool was assigned
to the Panama invasion, but, as discussed above, the pool was prevented from
covering the invasion. The theory was that news organizations would not attempt to
use their greater independent capability which offers more autonomy today in
covering overseas military operations than ever before. During Grenada, for example, the press chartered their own boats and planes, which was unheard of during
World War II or Vietnam.

Following media criticism of its handling of the press in Grenada, the Joint
Chiefs of Staff of the Armed Forces commissioned a panel including military
officers and journalists to advise the Pentagon on future press access policy. Known
as the Sidle Panel after its chairman, retired General Winant Sidle, the group
recommended the military allow news coverage wherever possible. Concurrently,
the report urged greater responsibility by the press in following voluntary censorship rules set by the military. However, the application of such guidelines is yet
untested. The guidelines assume an attitude of trust and cooperation between press
and the military, and that attitude may have unraveled in recent years.

The whole issue of access may even become moot in the 1990s if news
organizations can use highly advanced satellites for newsgathering. With finely
detailed pictures from their own satellites, media organizations may be able to
follow and report on military operations without direct access to the field of combat.
This technology was used by the broadcast networks to follow events in Iraq and
Saudi Arabia in 1990.

The U.S. government has licensed commercial satellites, from which news
organizations have bought imagery. But some news media organizations have
discussed construction and launching of a joint media satellite which would assure
news organization access to satellite pictures and speed the newsgathering process.
The need for such direct access became more apparent to the networks when the
French government refused to sell imagery from its SPOT satellite to media
organizations covering the Kuwaiti invasion. With a resolution of just 33 feet
across, SPOT can see structures such as individual houses. The news organizations
were able to buy imagery from the American-owned Landsat satellite.[15] In the
future, they plan to contract with the Soviet Union, which launched, in the fall of
1990, a satellite with resolution sharper than SPOT's.[16]

Clearly, with news media organizations eavesdropping on secret military
operations with their own satellites, such activities would be far more difficult to
undertake. In response to these concerns, the U.S. Commerce Department in 1986
established a rule that operations of such satellites could be suspended on national
security or foreign policy grounds. As an alternative, former CIA Director Stans-

field Turner suggested creation of a new government agency designed to release all remote sensing imagery, private- or government-owned, not jeopardizing national interests.[17] The issue of how to deal with this new form of media surveillance has yet to be determined, but it has the potential of reshaping the role of news media in covering combat operations.

COMBAT NEWS COVERAGE

In 1965, a CBS Evening News report by correspondent Morley Safer showed American marines setting fire to thatched-roof huts with cigarette lighters in the Vietnamese hamlet of Cam Ne. President Johnson immediately called the network executives and complained that they were trying to sabotage U.S. policy by this kind of reporting.[18]

The press has regularly been accused of bias in covering combat situations. Peter C. Rollins describes a distorted picture of the Battle of Khe Sanh conveyed by reporters during the Vietnam War. According to Rollins, accounts of death and defeat were emphasized while victories were ignored.[19] Similar charges of negativism have been made about subsequent U.S. military encounters, particularly the 1983 Grenada invasion.

The issue involves the role of the news media in wartime situations. What should the press cover? For television, what pictures constitute the reality of the conflict?

Some military officers claim that the presence of reporters affects military strategy. Fighting wars becomes more difficult not simply politically but also tactically. As one naval officer commented: "There is no 'nice way' to conduct house-to-house searches for a TV camera."[20]

Reporters' preexisting assumptions can lead to inaccurate or biased reporting. According to Peter C. Rollins, many reporters approached the U.S. involvement in Vietnam assuming it would repeat the French conflict in Vietnam in the early 1950s with the same anticipated result—eventual defeat.[21] Certainly there have been press suggestions of similar links between U.S. involvement in Central America and Vietnam—complete with predictions about an eventual U.S. military role, political morass, and final defeat.

We know little about the impact of the press in a combat situation, however. The United States has not waged a conventional war involving large numbers of troops since Vietnam, and the press's technical capability—satellite uplinks, minicams, live transmission—to cover such a conflict has greatly increased.

Moreover, the size of the press contingent has mushroomed with the proliferation of news outlets covering national affairs. Add to that number the growth in the size of the foreign press covering U.S. affairs, and we must acknowledge that the press presents enormous tactical problems for U.S. forces.

Politically, the administration pursuing a war policy faces a press that is more capable than ever before of undertaking independent surveillance. Short of direct censorship, which is constitutionally suspect according to the Supreme Court and problematic in enforcement, policymakers face a press with the capability of damaging the administration's best efforts at gaining public support.

SECRECY AND CENSORSHIP

Winston Churchill was said to have remarked during the height of World War II: "In wartime, truth is so precious that she should be attended by a bodyguard of lies."[22] The issue of government's right to lie is the end product of the confluence of governmental secrecy requirements and press capability for surveillance and transmission.

Journalists stumbling onto information about a foreign policy decision at the time of Thomas Jefferson probably would not have been able to affect the outcome, even if they had found a use for the information. But such information today is more likely, first, to be learned and, second, to be transmitted to a mass audience within minutes of its revelation to a reporter. This vast increase in the press's capabilities and potential power to influence means greater dependence by policymakers on the cooperation of the press.

In World War II, the growing power of the press was still new to journalists. They were willing to cooperate with government officials. Moreover, in World War I, the press had suffered under the provisions of various legislation—the Espionage Act, the Trading-with-the-Enemy Act, the Sedition Act, all passed in 1917–1918 and all restrictive of press content. The Sedition Act made criminal the writing or publication of "any disloyal, profane, scurrilous, or abusive language about the form of government of the United States or the Constitution, military or naval forces . . ." or any language intended to bring the above "into contempt, scorn, contumely, or disrepute." More than 75 newspapers lost their mailing privileges under this law or agreed not to print certain material.[23]

The memory of such prohibitions was still fresh at the onset of World War II. When no similar legislation was enacted for that conflict and a voluntary self-censorship was sought, reporters and editors responded with gratitude and circumspection. The overwhelming public support for the war effort also contributed to press cooperation.

The Second World War cooperation is hailed as a model for government-press relations. But much has occurred in the intervening years to change relations between the government and the press. By the time of Vietnam, press capability and independence had increased. The opportunity for a break from governmental cooperation was ripe. But the fissures had occurred even prior to that point. Journalists were upset with the government's prevarication in the case of the U-2 shot down over the Soviet Union in 1960. For its part, the administration also began to criticize press coverage of the early U.S. role in Vietnam.[24]

During Vietnam, many reporters perceived a gap between administration assessments of the war and reality. As discussed in Chapter 5, many journalists were affected by developments in journalism and the larger society. By 1967 and

1968, journalists were sending back more critical stories of the war, particularly after the Tet Offensive in January and February 1968.[25]

The break did not close following the beginning of U.S. withdrawal from the Vietnam War. The Pentagon Papers revelation, the Nixon administration's claim of national security for protecting Watergate-related activities and other events confirmed the fears of the press that the government used secrecy as a cloak for illegal or unethical activities or at the least to save political embarrassment. State Department spokesman Hodding Carter's admission that "at least 90 percent of all classified matter that crossed my desk could have been declassified and made public with no effects on national security" reflected many journalists' views of governmental secrecy.[26]

Government officials faced a press increasingly capable of acquiring information independently of government due to its enhanced surveillance capacity. Since journalists' independent efforts could uncover national security policy decisions and actions, the press no longer needed to rely as much on government for initial information. The only potential barrier to publication was confirmation. Confirmation from a reliable source frees the press from using itself as authority for information.

Politicians believed the press was able to affect negatively their programs. Moreover, through reliance on television and publicity efforts, they could bypass the press in communicating with the public and mobilizing public support. Journalists began to be treated as outsiders, even potential enemies.

When faced with press knowledge of national security information, government officials face a dilemma. If they do not lie, but remain candid with reporters about national security actions, what are the possible consequences? Reporters, then, would determine whether to use national security information or contain it. The journalist becomes the decisionmaker about potential threats to national security in the release of information.

But a journalist's decision whether or not to publish is complicated by the kinds of factors that we have discussed earlier: news values, competition with other reporters, or even skepticism or naiveté about any real danger to national security. The problem of relying on journalists to make such decisions is illustrated by the response of a CBS News reporter when asked what he would have done had he known about the Grenada invasion plans beforehand. He replied: "I don't know. We would have tried to find some way to use what we knew without endangering the operation."[27]

If, on the other hand, government officials lie, what may result? Their own credibility may be damaged. And what about the need for an informed public in decision-making: Doesn't lying negate that role?

Some public officials have defended the right to lie to the press to contain knowledge of a national security decision and lead reporters away from a story prior to an action. In order to straddle the issue, some presidents have also chosen to exclude press secretaries from knowledge of military incursions such as the Grenada invasion so they need not lie. However, their omission robs the president of an advisor with knowledge of press relations at a crucial time. Moreover, the press secretary quickly gains a reputation as an outsider in policy-making and is thereafter regarded by the press as an unreliable source.

But the issue of government lying is highly complex; it is not necessarily a straightforward government-versus-press issue. Some press secretaries have opposed any government right to lie, while many journalists have recognized a qualified need for deception. Philip Geyelin of the *Washington Post* admitted that "the president has an inherent right—perhaps even an obligation in particular situations—to deceive," and other journalists have expressed agreement.[28]

Wartime censorship has been practiced in the past by the United States government. However, the question of censorship during an undeclared or "cold" war is still debated. Moreover, the United States has declared other "wars"—on terrorism and illegal drug importation, for instance. Which rules apply to coverage of these wars? The press argues that, absent a declaration of war, peacetime rules of broad access should apply. Many policymakers contend that conditions have changed since World War II. Full-scale conventional wars are unlikely today, given the threat of nuclear war. The press must be willing to adapt to changing circumstances and not demand a declared war before censorship is imposed.

News coverage of terrorists' acts, for example, has engendered criticism of the press as an unwitting promoter of terrorist activity and propaganda. According to one survey, a majority of the general public believe the press gives too much attention to terrorists and that coverage acts as a stimulus for future terrorist actions.[29]

Moreover, the press has been accused of distorting the public's image of terrorism by emphasizing terrorist activity in the Middle East while downplaying such activity in Latin America.[30] In 1986, NBC News was strongly criticized for airing a lengthy interview with Abdul Abbas, accused mastermind of the 1985 Achille Lauro hijacking. A State Department spokesman commented that "terrorism thrives on this kind of publicity," and *Time* magazine chided the network by suggesting that "greater care should be exercised to ensure that a terrorist does not use the interview simply for his own means."[31]

Pre-publication censorship has never been seriously considered, but the Supreme Court left open the possibility that in some circumstances such as a "grave and irreparable danger" such censorship would be constitutional. But the justices did not provide more specifics.[32] The Reagan administration prosecuted or fined employees who leaked intelligence information and threatened to prosecute news organizations who published national security secrets.[33]

Many journalists respond that secrecy is inconsistent with a democratic society and censorship of any kind is a violation of the First Amendment. How can Americans make decisions about national security policy when they are denied relevant information? Can a veil of secrecy foster government actions incongruous with democracy and the will of the public, and even produce decisions harmful to the national interest? They also contend that they can be trusted to withhold sensitive information when the government makes a convincing case.

No satisfactory permanent resolution has appeared. However, government and press officials have sought accommodation on a case-by-case basis. In fact, the Reagan administration's confrontation over possible prosecution is an exception rather than the rule. The more common practice in cases of possible sensitive national security information has been consultation with news organizations. According to Howard Simons, former managing editor of the *Washington Post,* representatives of his newspaper and government officials consult before publishing such material:

> It was all done very quietly. They would call you over to the CIA or the White House. They wouldn't ask you not to publish. They would outline what damage would be caused by a story. Then, you went back and made your own decision.[34]

In 1961, President John F. Kennedy persuaded the *New York Times* not to publish detailed information it possessed on the upcoming Bay of Pigs invasion, and in 1986 President Reagan urged Katherine Graham, publisher of the *Washington Post* not to publish details of U.S. eavesdropping technology acquired by the Soviet Union.[35]

The mixture of hostility and attempts to understand the perspective of the other side illustrates both the level of dependence on the press by government and the high level of independence by the press. Although not in an autonomous state, the press is treated by government as an equal player to be approached warily due to its perceived power. The press also seeks to enhance its independent role by avoiding actions resulting in future legal restrictions.

EFFECT ON PUBLIC SUPPORT
FOR U.S. MILITARY ROLE

Does news coverage of national security policy affect public opinion? Many critics of the media have argued that news coverage diminished public support for U.S. involvement in Vietnam and continues to affect public support for U.S. military role abroad, although journalists deny the charges.[36] Some foresee the press hampering any future military intervention, with the result that the U.S. will decline to play a military role abroad.[37]

Conversely, the press has been charged with legitimizing U.S. involvement in the Vietnam conflict. Philip Knightly argues journalists failed to report atrocities committed by U.S. troops for several years until the My Lai incident became public and made such stories newsworthy.[38] Daniel C. Hallin concluded that television coverage of the war actually tended to support the administration's view prior to the Tet Offensive. Even editorial statements by journalists during this period were biased towards the U.S. and South Vietnamese forces.[39] Robert M. Entman and David L. Paletz also demonstrated the absence of any serious press challenge to U.S. involvement prior to the 1968 Tet offensive.[40] In a *Newsweek* poll taken in

1967, a majority of respondents said watching television did not make them more opposed to the war, while less than a third said it did.[41]

Whether or not the press would play a role in affecting public opinion would certainly depend both on political factors such as the clarity of objectives and the visible pursuit of those objectives, and on journalistic factors, such as access to the battlefield and the degree of trust between government and press. Nothing inherent in media values necessarily leads to coverage either for or against war.

SUMMARY

No other issue has created such tension between press and policymakers as press freedom versus national security. The role of the press in combat situations remains a thorny issue; although the military and the press have attempted to reach agreement for future cooperation, the absence of trust is still apparent. Increased technical capabilities enhance the press's capacity to survey military actions and decrease the military's ability to control press access.

The absence of trust has led government officials to turn to secrecy, censorship, and occasionally to lying to accomplish political and military objectives. However, the role of the press and the public in determining national security policy may be endangered by such behavior.

Whether public support for future wars will be affected by the press coverage is unknown. The press has been accused in the past, particularly in Vietnam, both of hampering military policy and of legitimizing it.

Absent the existence of trust between the military and the press, it is unlikely these two salient players in national security policy will come to a workable agreement on the role of the press in combat. Yet the administration's failure to involve the press in a workable process has heightened tensions, rather than reduced them.

There is no evidence the news media are united in opposition to U.S. military involvement nor that any future war coverage automatically would be negative. Nor is there evidence that a majority of Americans turn against a military action because of news reports.

In fact, it is likely that the administration would be highly successful in affecting what the news content is. But the key to that success is not in muzzling the press, but assuring that military action taken in the name of the United States is, in fact, supported by a broad majority of the citizens of the United States.

NOTES

4. Fred S. Hoffman, Review of Panama Pool Deployment December 1989, internal report prepared for the Assistant Secretary of Defense for Public Affairs, March 1990.
5. Joseph Metcalf, III, "Decision Making and the Grenada Rescue Operation," in James G. March and Roger Weissinger-Babylon, eds., *Ambiguity and Command: Organiza-*

tional Perspectives on Military Decision Making, Marshfield, Mass.: Pitman Publishing, 1986, p. 290.

6. *Time*, November 7, 1983, p. 102.
7. *Washington Post*, October 28, 1983, p. A22.
8. Landrum R. Bolling, *Reporters under Fire: U.S. Media Coverage of Conflicts in Lebanon and Central America*, Boulder, Colo.: Westview Press, 1985, p. 2.
9. Charles Mohr, "The Media," in George K. Osborn et al., eds., *Democracy, Strategy, and Vietnam*, Lexington, Mass.: Lexington Books, 1987, p. 180.
10. Quoted in Anthony Marro, "When the Government Tells Lies," *Columbia Journalism Review* (March/April 1985): 38.
11. See, for example, Colonel Richard C. Upchurch, USMC, "Wanted: A Fair Press," *Naval Institute Proceedings* (July 1984): 70.
12. "Conference Report on U.S. Military Operations and the Press," *Political Communications and Persuasion* 3 (1985): 75.
13. Peter Braestrup, *Big Story*, Boulder, Colo.: Westview Press, 1977, pp. 11–12.
14. "Strict Media Rules Opposed for Future Military Actions," *Washington Post*, February 9, 1984, p. A4.
15. Telephone interview with Mark E. Brender, ABC News defense producer, September 21, 1990.
16. Mark Brender and Peter Zimmerman, "The Day the Open Skies Closed," *Space News*, August 13–19, 1990, p. 15.
17. See Peter E. Glaser and Mark E. Brender, "The First Amendment in Space: News Coverage from Satellites," *Issues in Science and Technology* (Fall 1986): 60–67.
18. David Halberstam, *The Powers That Be*, New York: Knopf, 1979, p. 490.
19. Peter C. Rollins, "TV's Battle of Khe Sanh: Selective Images of Defeat," in William C. Adams, ed., *Television Coverage of International Affairs*, Norwood, N.J.: Ablex, 1982, pp. 203–215.
20. Quoted in David K. Hall and Captain Richard M. Butler, USN, "The Grenada Invasion," unpublished manuscript, National Security Decisionmaking Department, U.S. Naval War College.
21. Rollins, "TV's Battle of Khe Sanh," pp. 203–215.
22. Kay Halle, ed., *Irrepressible Churchill*, Cleveland, Ohio: World Publishing, 1966, p. 230.
23. Frank Luther Mott, *American Journalism, A History: 1690–1960*, 3d ed., New York: Macmillan, 1962, pp. 623–624.
24. Braestrup, *Big Story*, pp. 2–3.
25. See Braestrup, *Big Story*, pp. 2–3.
26. Lewis W. Wolfson, *The Untapped Power of the Press*, New York: Praeger, 1985, p. 129. See also David Wise, *The Politics of Lying*, New York: Random House, 1973.
27. Jody Powell, *The Other Side of the Story*, New York: William Morrow, 1984, p. 233.
28. Anthony Marro, "When the Government Tells Lies," *Columbia Journalism Review* (March/April 1985): 35.
29. Times-Mirror, *The People and the Press*, January 1986, pp. 11–12.
30. Michael X. Delli Carpini, "Television and Terrorism: Patterns of Presentation and Occurrence, 1969 to 1980," *Western Political Quarterly* 40 (March 1987): 45–64.
31. James Kelly, "Caught by the Camera," *Time*, May 19, 1986.
32. *New York Times v. U.S.*, 403 U.S. 713 (1971).
33. Stephen Engelberg, "CIA Director Requests Inquiry on NBC Report," *New York Times*, May 20, 1986.

34. Quoted in Stephen Engelberg, "U.S. Aides Said to Have Discussed Prosecuting News Organizations," *New York Times,* May 20, 1986, p. A18.
35. Engelberg, "U.S. Aides Said to Have Discussed Prosecuting News Organizations," p. A18.
36. For a sample of the debate, see Daniel C. Hallin, *The Uncensored War,* New York: Oxford University Press, 1986; Upchurch, "Wanted: A Fair Press," pp. 68–74; Lloyd Cutler, "Foreign Policy on Deadline," *Foreign Policy* (1984): 114; and Charles Mohr, "Once Again—Did the Press Lose Vietnam?" *Columbia Journalism Review* (November/December 1983): 51–59.
37. See for example, William A. Rusher, "The Media and Our Next Intervention: Scenario," *Parameters* (September 1988): 3–12.
38. Philip Knightly, *The First Casualty,* New York: Harcourt Brace Jovanovich, 1975, pp. 373–401.
39. See Hallin, Table 2.
40. See Hallin, *The Uncensored War;* and Robert M. Entman and David L. Paletz, "The War in Southeast Asia: Tunnel Vision on Vietnam," in William C. Adams, ed., *Television Coverage of International Affairs,* Norwood, N.J.: Ablex, 1982.
41. "The Press: Room for Improvement," *Newsweek,* July 10, 1967, p. 76.

SUGGESTED READINGS

Bolling, Landrum R. *Reporters under Fire: U.S. Media Coverage of Conflicts in Lebanon and Central America.* Boulder, Colo.: Westview Press, 1985.

Braestrup, Peter. *Big Story.* Boulder, Colo.: Westview Press, 1977.

Hallin, Daniel. *The Uncensored War.* New York: Oxford University Press, 1986.

Heise, Juergen Arthur. *Minimum Disclosure: How The Pentagon Manipulates the News.* New York: W.W. Norton, 1979.

Rollins, Peter C. "TV's Battle of Khe Sanh: Selective Images of Defeat." In *Television Coverage of International Affairs,* edited by William C. Adams. Norwood, N.J.: Ablex, 1982.

PART V

The Mass Public and the Electoral Process

One question that has intrigued scholars, politicians, and news professionals and has been the subject of numerous essays by media critics and apologists is whether the mass media affect political behavior, especially in relation to the electoral process. Do news stories, editorials, commentaries, documentaries, public affairs programs and other forms of media coverage of American national politics actually affect the mass public, particularly as voters?

The answer has been widely viewed as crucial because of the implication of the growing role of an external, unelected, and unaccountable political force—the mass media—in American politics, particularly in influencing elections. The involvement of the mass public is a cardinal principle of a democratic system. Could the media's effects shape the way people are socialized politically, their feelings about the utility of participating in the process, the issues they think are important, and even the way they vote in elections?

The electoral process, as the mechanism for the selection of political leadership in a democracy, has been accorded particular interest by those concerned about the maintenance of that function. If the mass media affect that process, is the alteration somehow detrimental to its continuance? Can media role affect the very nature of electoral campaigns, particularly the only national race—the race for the presidency? Is the choice of our president a media-driven process?

This section addresses those questions and offers really a mixed assessment of media power over mass political attitudes and presidential campaigns.

CHAPTER 14

The Media and the Mass Public

The press "may not be successful much of the time in telling people what to think, but it is stunningly successful in telling its [audience] what to think about."

Bernard Cohen[1]

In the 1930s Germans were spellbound by the radio oratory of Adolf Hitler. Hitler's usage of radio to stir Germans to support Nazi ideas caused great concern among scholars and others that media could be highly successful in altering people's political attitudes and behavior.

It was widely believed that the mass media acted like a hypodermic needle on the public—directly shaping public opinion with great impact. The consequences for political behavior were serious, particularly if these new communication technologies could be used by ideological extremists to gain political power.

The earliest modern studies of mass media and political behavior were conducted by scholars at Columbia University in the 1940s.[2] Paul Lazarsfeld and Bernard Berelson conducted research on mass political behavior and electoral campaigns in Erie County, Pennsylvania, and in Elmira, New York. Waves of interviews with local residents were conducted in 1940 and in 1948. They found the mass media influence's was minimal.

They concluded the mass media had little impact on political attitudes and behavior. The media, they found, primarily reinforced partisan tendencies rather than altered them. Lazarsfeld, Berelson, and others suggested the presence of a two-step flow in communication: messages flowed from the mass media to opinion leaders and from opinion leaders to voters. This process mediated the direct effects of the mass media on voters. Opinion leaders were more attuned to media messages than others and were more influential in affecting vote decisions. Interpersonal influence played a mediating role in the mass media's effect on political attitudes and behavior.

Moreover, the study identified large-scale barriers blocking media effects, including the social networks of the individual, selectivity in media exposure, attention and retention, and partisanship.

The dearth of hard evidence of media impact on political behavior spawned the minimal effects theory, which suggested that media have little impact on voting.[3] This theory prevailed for several decades. Consequently, succeeding large-scale studies of mass political behavior ignored the mass media.[4] Leading political scientists also minimized media effects.[5]

But the study of media effects over three decades has moved far beyond the conclusions of the two-step flow and the minimal effects theory. The study of media effects now includes media role in political socialization, agenda-setting, vote choice, and political efficacy and participation. However, understanding media effects requires an appreciation of the factors limiting the media's role, most of which do not inhere from the nature of the media. The audience and the social and psychological environment surrounding an individual's use of the media also impinge on media effects.

MITIGATING FACTORS

The News Audience

The audience for news initially was thought of by scholars as passive, meaning that people absorbed news content willingly and unquestioningly. But audience studies have suggested that activity, not passivity, is actually the rule for audiences. To begin with, the very decision to be a part of a news audience—to watch or read the news—is an active one. For example, most people choose not to be in the audience for television network news each day. Fewer than one-third of adults in the United States watch television news—local or national—on a given day. Only one percent of households with television sets watch CBS News as often as four or five nights a week.[6]

Another indication of the less than expected size of television network news is the result of a 1985 survey that less than half of the general public could recognize a photograph of CBS News anchor Dan Rather. Only one-third knew NBC News anchor Tom Brokaw. Many more do include themselves in the audience for print news; more than two-thirds of adults read at least part of a newspaper each day.[7]

One aspect of activity is the decision to be part of the news audience. The decision to attend to news and public affairs separates the news audience from others.

Uses and Gratifications. One theory suggests that individuals use the media to fulfill certain needs and gratifications.[8] The uses and gratifications theory implies that the audience helps determine media effects by drawing on media to fulfill social and psychological needs, which may include information and entertainment, as well as specific personal needs.

Since not all individuals possess the same needs nor do they seek uniform ways to meet these needs, this approach to media effects perceives the audience as more diverse than originally imagined. We know that mitigating factors such as interest in and prior knowledge of public affairs affect the audience for news. People who possess a greater interest in politics are more likely to be exposed to news, which in turn reinforces interest.[9]

Selectivity. One thing we do know about news audiences is that they are selective, but not in the way we might think. We might suspect that people would avoid exposure to discordant viewpoints by selecting media that reinforce their own views.[10] Research suggests the contrary, however; dissonant information not only is seen or read, but also is recalled.[11] One barrier to selective exposure is the television news format, which reduces choice of information selection.

The real barrier is selective perception—people receiving the same message but perceiving it differently. Cognitive learning of dissonant views does not necessarily produce attitudinal and behavioral change because selective perception remains a barrier. One example is the viewers' varying responses to political advertisements. In the 1988 presidential campaign one of Dukakis's ads showed actors portraying political consultants discussing how to "package" George Bush for the campaign. Dukakis supporters reacted favorably to the subtle criticism of Bush. But Bush supporters liked it too because positive aspects about Bush were discussed in the ad.

Nature of News and Audience Recall. The nature of news content itself mitigates against attitudinal changes. For example, Thomas E. Patterson discovered in his study of news coverage of the 1976 presidential campaign that most news stories did not mention candidates' abilities or stances.[12] In turn, voters in his study responded to questions about the candidates more often with evaluations of the candidates' winning abilities than with an assessment of candidate qualifications, record, or issue stances.[13]

News content does not emphasize the latter aspects, which makes it unlikely the press will alter the voter's views on candidates on these points. What attitudinal changes do occur are the result of the assessments of a candidate's ability to win.

The capabilities of the audience and the medium as well combine to limit media effects. The messages of TV news in particular are not presented in a strongly persuasive mode. Most stories are assembled daily, their visual and audio components developed hastily and with little time for organization. The audio and visual components may even conflict. Moreover, the rapid delivery of television news may well contribute to information overload.

Audiences have low recall of TV news stories.[14] Even when individuals remember TV news stories, that memory does not necessarily translate into understanding.[15] Moreover, recall is short-term, and there is an extremely high level of forgetting.[16]

One reason for low recall and understanding is the nature of television news. It is not designed primarily for knowledge, but, as Dan Nimmo and James E. Combs label it, as an "acquaintance medium" which offers familiarity with disparate bits of information:

> Television news provides single pieces of information on a daily basis. It unites
> that fragmentary communication, not by building a body of understanding based
> on a testable theory that explains events, but by weaving bits and pieces into an
> appealing story.[17]

News messages delivered in the print media lend themselves to greater recall and comprehension.[18] People learn more from newspapers, but they say they rely more on television for news and information.[19]

The audience for news and public affairs, then, is active rather than passive, but several factors mitigate against the potentially massive media effects often conjectured. The way the audience uses and reacts to media messages must be considered in any discussion of media effects.

POLITICAL SOCIALIZATION

The process by which people from childhood on develop cognitions, attitudes, and behavioral patterns about politics has been termed political socialization. The political socialization process and the role of various agents such as the family, schools, and peer groups have been the subject of a significant body of research.[20]

Scholars in the 1950s and 1960s initially ignored the role of the mass media as a socializing agent because they generally accepted the "minimal effects" theory of media's role, in which the media were perceived simply as information carriers and reinforcers of existing political orientations.[21] They had only minimal effects on people's attitudes. Moreover, effects were minimal because they were mitigated by interpersonal communication with people whose opinions were respected and who vocalized them.

The News Media as Agent of Political Socialization

More recent research in the 1970s and 1980s has suggested a larger role for the news media, however, particularly as the roles of other socializing agents, such as parents, have diminished.[22]

Simultaneously, evidence suggested a higher than expected level of news content exposure, especially for teenagers. Exposure is significant because it is a necessary precondition for media impact; we must watch or read before we can be affected. Exposure patterns set in pre-adult years predict later media usage in adult years, and exposure is an indicator of involvement in politics at this period in life.[23]

Most children and teenagers do not watch television news, but about one-half of all high school students read newspapers most days, and most elementary school children watch "In the News" segments on Saturday mornings. There is also evidence of at least moderate exposure to campaign news and commercials during presidential election years, and one study of youths between 18 and 25 found an increased reliance on television for public affairs by age 25, though the level of newspaper reading remained constant.[24]

Not only news and public affairs, but also entertainment media may affect the political socialization process.[25] Television entertainment programming is more frequently watched by children and teenagers than is news, and many entertainment programs contain overt political themes. Others may carry subliminal or even unintended messages about such themes as authority, conflict, and group relations.

The mass media in both their news and entertainment functions clearly have the potential for acting as a salient agent in the political socialization process. But is that potential realized?

Effect on Political Learning

There is a growing body of evidence that mass media exposure does affect cognitions—awareness and knowledge—of politics.[26] Children pick up their political vocabulary from the media.[27] Heavy political media exposure does predict a greater knowledge of politics. Learning from media is higher for older age groups than for younger ones.[28] The motivation to acquire information is significant, however. A strong correlation exists between interest in politics and exposure to news media use, but correlation does not prove exposure causes interest or vice versa.[29]

Children and teenagers reported television as their primary source of information about news.[30] But television actually may have less impact on political knowledge than newspapers.[31]

Have the media replaced parents and schools as primary sources of political learning for children and teenagers? According to the children and teenagers, the answer is yes.[32] There is some evidence in addition to self-reporting.[33] But, youth, like adults, may well overestimate their own usage of television. Given the higher than expected exposure to political media and the declining role of family as agent, however, the role of the media as a primary cognitive source is plausible.

Effects on Children's Values, Attitudes, and Opinions

With the dissemination of television, the opinions about media's role in political socialization began to change. One scholar in the early 1970s termed television "the new parent."[34] However, though cognitive effects have become clear, that does not mean the media necessarily impact on a child's attitudes, opinions, and even basic values. Rather than displacing parents, there is evidence political television broadcasts stimulate interpersonal discussion of politics.[35]

Children are likely to perceive the mass media as influential in the formation of their opinions, but little independent confirmation exists beyond self-reporting.[36] Some studies have found correlations between news exposure and attitudes toward governmental figures, presidential candidates, party affiliation, and political efficacy.[37] But such correlations do not demonstrate conclusively that an attitude change was caused by media exposure, since children who attend to the media may do so because they are more politically interested or have favorable views of governmental leaders. Some evidence suggests that interpersonal communication is more influential than mass media in political socialization.[38]

Adults who use news media for information do so, at least in part, because they anticipate participating in politics ranging from a political discussion to the act of voting. However, children and adolescents are not able to participate in voting, and we cannot study voter decisions to determine behavioral effects of media on children. Other forms of political behavior have been studied, however, and positive correlations between news media exposure and partisan political activity (such as wearing buttons, attending rallies, and working in campaigns) have been found.[39] Positive correlations between exposure to news media and political discussions with others, including parents and friends have also been discovered.[40]

As we suggested earlier, however, correlation does not indicate cause and effect. Political discussions and activity may prompt heightened exposure or political interest may stimulate both news exposure and political activity.

The final judgment on how the media affect children's and teenagers' political attitudes and behavior is still out. Moreover, some researchers have questioned the theory that children's cognitions and attitudes actually affect later attitudes. They suggest that children's attitudes are unstable and that early learning is transformed by later learning. They argue the adolescent stage offers a more accurate explanation of adult attitudes and behavior.[41] Hence, studies of news and public affairs media use by children to explain adult political attitudes and behavior would be of questionable value.

Unfortunately many of the studies of the news media's effect on the political socialization process are now dated, and little more is extant. It will be some time before we can answer that question conclusively.

We do know that the media play a major—perhaps even the primary role—in cognitive learning about politics, and this fact alone suggests the potential effect that media may have an attitude and behavior.

In what areas might that potential be realized? We will look at three: agenda-setting; vote choices; and political participation and efficacy.

AGENDA-SETTING

Setting the Agenda

It has been said the press affects the way we prioritize public issues through its power to channel public debate. This power is sometimes wielded as the agenda-setting efforts of various political actors such as presidents or members of Congress, but it may also be an independent tool in the hands of a highly autonomous press. Two early researchers of the media's agenda-setting role argued that:

> The press is far more than a conduit for the concerns and issues of others. In the process of transmitting others' concerns and issues, it re-works and re-translates them. In the process of deciding each day which items to report and which to ignore, the editors of the news media guide our attention and elements in the larger political arena.[42]

Factors of Agenda-Setting

Agenda-setting in fact comprises not one function, but at least three. Minimally, media content heightens awareness of issues. But the media's agenda-setting capability also concerns salience—which issues are generally viewed as important. Finally, agenda-setting also involves setting priorities or the exact ordering of issues. It is on this last issue—media's role in determining priorities—that most agenda-setting study centers.[43]

Research on the agenda-setting function of the media has consistently found that the public share the press's agenda on major issues, and has also found some evidence of a causal relationship under certain conditions.[44]

But agenda-setting research does not support the conclusion that the media's role in agenda-setting is uniformly pervasive. The media's ability to set the agenda is affected by the audience and the nature of the issue.

Those most susceptible to media agenda-setting are those with less education, political independents, and those who demonstrate less political interest and activity.[45] Moreover, those who are in a personal predicament related to the media's agenda are more likely to copy that agenda, and others may respond similarly if the issue persists on the media agenda. For example, even those who are untouched personally by unemployment will begin to treat it as a priority issue if the media cover it as an important issue over a long period of time.[46]

The type of issue also influences the media's agenda-setting role. The media agenda is more likely to be adopted for issues where the media are the primary source of information on the topic. These "unobtrusive issues" include such areas as foreign affairs. For other issues, such as inflation or unemployment, where individuals have alternative sources of information—personal experience, interpersonal sources—the media's priorities can be balanced and may not be accepted as readily by the individual.[47] The volume of issues also intervenes. The individual can follow a short list of media issue priorities, but not a lengthy one.[48]

Political Effects

Agenda-setting by the media can have political consequences. Shanto Iyengar and Donald R. Kinder argue that television news affects American viewers' political choices by priming the pump—emphasizing certain aspects of national politics and ignoring others.[49] Agenda-setting necessarily implies focusing on certain issues and not on others, and since perceptions are based on available information, information can affect choices.

Audience members are likely to assign greater weight to certain problems as a result of the attention paid to them in the media and use such weighting to assess the performance of national government, particularly the president. Hence, agenda-setting can clearly influence public approval and perhaps even vote decisions.

The way in which media "frame" an issue may also influence how it affects the public. If the media-identified problem is framed primarily as specific to an individual rather than as systemic, then the individual and not the institution bears the blame. Such framing can serve to place the responsibility on the doorstep of political leaders or elsewhere.[50] The propensity of the press to personalize issues—for reasons we discussed in talking about news values—mitigates against audience attribution of the problem to the national government.

VOTE CHOICES

Minimal Effects Theory

As mentioned at the beginning of this chapter, it was noted that originally scholars believed mass media had little impact on vote choice. These early scholars had examined supposed persuasive effects of the news media rather than cognitive effects. By the 1960s and 1970s, a shift in emphasis occurred.[51] Only when research methods began to concentrate on cognitive effects such as agenda-setting, voter awareness and images, rather than exclusively on vote change, was the minimal effects theory challenged. Several more recent studies of media and voting have determined that various aspects of the vote decision—awareness of candidates, image of candidates, and issue information—are in fact affected by the media.

Awareness of Candidates

Name recognition is crucial to electoral success. The press play a significant role in increasing name recognition for presidential candidates. In a study of the 1976 presidential campaign, Thomas E. Patterson found a strong correlation between news media coverage of presidential candidates and the public's awareness of the candidate. Surprisingly, newspaper coverage was a more effective tool for building public recognition than television. Newspaper readers were more likely than television viewers to increase their awareness of candidates during the course of the campaign.[52]

Patterson also found a strong correlation between voter awareness and vote choice. Few voters choose presidential candidates about whom they know nothing; they prefer candidates about whom they possess some information. Much of that information, particularly for new candidates, comes from press coverage.

Patterson estimated that in the primary elections of 1976, Jimmy Carter, who had received a far greater amount of news coverage than his opponents, gained 12 percent more votes than he would have had candidate awareness been equal.[53]

IMAGES OF CANDIDATES

The press has been accused of determining the images of candidates. Empirical studies support the conventional wisdom that the mass media do affect voters' perceptions of candidates, particularly at earlier stages of a campaign.[54]

Television has been accused of shaping the images of presidential candidates, but newspapers may, in fact, play a greater role. According to Patterson, television plays a significant role in defining image early in the primary season and affects judgments about a candidate's character. But newspaper coverage is important in filling out the candidate's image in voters' minds throughout the campaign.

> The newspaper, then, is more instrumental in the formation of images. Underlying this is the fact that impressions are created mainly by words rather than pictures. . . . [Voters'] thoughts about a candidate's primary victories or his political record, for example, depend mostly on verbal communication, and in this the newspaper excels.[55]

There is some evidence that voters' images of candidates are formed after they watch or read news about the candidates, particularly candidates initially unfamiliar to voters.[56] Moreover, initial image formation—the first impression of the candidate—sticks in the minds of voters and reduces the impact of later coverage. This enhances the value of early news coverage in candidate image formation.[57] New candidates, then, are most susceptible to media image-making. They have no previous image, and the media can affect voters' perceptions of them.

Issue Information

Voters acquire information about issues, as well as candidates, from news media content. Newspapers contribute more to issue awareness than television; television news viewing has little effect on issue learning.[58] Surprisingly, more learning comes from exposure to paid political advertisements than from network television news content. This stems from television news programs' lack of issue content, as will be discussed in the next chapter.[59]

Studies suggest that issue learning is related to voter interest. Those voters with high interest in politics gain the most from newspaper content. But even those with low and moderate interest acquire some issue information.[60] The less interested voter acquires the highest gain of information from campaign commercials; but there may be a threshold beyond which commercials no longer transmit new information.

Issue learning, particularly for low- and moderate-interest voters, is dependent on the emphasis given to the issue in media coverage. As we will discuss in the next chapter, issues do not constitute a major part of campaign news coverage. As a result, all but high interest voters find it difficult to learn about candidate issue positions when they are largely ignored in news content.

The major vehicles for issue transmission by television are those events where candidates and supporters are given time to state the candidate's positions. The debates and the conventions are instructive, then, particularly for low-and moderate-interest voters, because they allow candidates time to outline their views.

POLITICAL EFFICACY AND PARTICIPATION

Finding Media Effects

While the preponderance of media effects studies have been directed at the voter and the electoral process, one question has largely been ignored: What role do the media play in the formation of attitudes about the political system and the individual's role in it? In other words, do media messages affect people's trust in government and their views of their own efficacy in the political system?

The role of the media in shaping attitudes of trust and feelings of efficacy was largely ignored as long as the minimal effects theory was accepted. As we suggested earlier, however, more recent studies contradict the minimal effects theory. A 1969 study of a British election campaign concluded that due to news and public affairs content, media usage had produced a mild form of alienation on the part of some voters.[61]

In the United States, a landmark study on the influence of public affairs media on political efficacy was conducted by Michael J. Robinson. Robinson analyzed the effects of a CBS television documentary entitled "The Selling of the Pentagon" and found that viewers' feelings of political efficacy declined after exposure to the program. He also analyzed historical election data and found a trend of feelings of diminishing political efficacy among people who relied on television for news. Those reliant on other media also experienced decline, but not at the same level. Robinson concluded that television produced a destabilizing effect on viewers, especially on those who were less interested in politics and were an inadvertent audience to news through television's entertainment.[62]

But Robinson's conclusions were not wholly supported. In another study, where a correlation between highly critical newspaper content about national government and distrust in government by readers was found, feelings of political efficacy were not affected.[63]

Media as Cause

The issue of media effect on political efficacy and participation arose after public opinion pollsters noticed a marked increase in Americans' cynical attitudes towards government during the 1960s and 1970s, as opposed to the 1950s. A majority or a plurality in the 1960s and 1970s were agreeing with statements such as "I don't think public officials care much what people like me think," "People like me don't have any say about what the government does," and "There are quite a few crooks in government."[64] Although the cynical attitudes began to dissipate somewhat in the 1980s, trust and efficacy levels remained below those measured in the 1950s.

Scholars began to look for causes.[65] Some sociologists pointed to the socially wrenching events of those decades—political assassinations, the civil rights movement, the Vietnam War, and Watergate—as causes. Blame was also placed on the failure of systems of government. But television, due to its emergence as a new pervasive phenomena during this period, also was identified as a possible cause of the new "malaise" in the populace.[66] Television received attention because of its role in disseminating political information. Public opinion polls indicated people were relying on television more than newspapers for news and information.

Bad News and Cynicism

People were watching television; sales and audience use of television sets soared during the 1950s and 1960s. But during this period were they receiving negative portrayals of American government which fed cynicism? Were newspapers during these years providing the same?

One study of television network news found bad news was placed higher in the broadcast, giving it added weight and was more often accompanied by an audio-visual aid.[67]

Some content analysis has suggested media content is negative toward government institutions and leaders,[68] while other studies suggest that the press actually conveys support for governmental institutions.[69] The middle ground is that press content is largely neither favorable nor unfavorable, but neutral.[70]

One important caveat is the institution involved. As we have seen earlier, the Court usually receives highly supportive institutional coverage, and the president much the same. But the Congress does not.

However, when media content is negative, is there an effect? Critical newspaper content has been found to be correlated with reader distrust of government, but efficacy has not.[71] Correlations between heavy exposure to news and public affairs information and high levels of feelings of political efficacy have been found.[72] However, this does not mean that exposure to political media content necessarily causes an increase in feelings of efficacy. It may say more about the audience for political media. Those who feel politically inefficacious are less likely to be interested in politics and, if they use media, use it not for informational purposes, but for vicarious gratification. They choose to attend to those aspects of politics that excite or distract them.[73] Attention, and not simply exposure, is a significant factor in studying media effect on trust and efficacy.[74]

The Media and Political Participation

Does the media's content affect political participation? According to Elisabeth Noelle-Neumann, a scholar of public opinion, the media do affect political involvement. She suggests people are reluctant to participate if they perceive their opinions are not shared by the majority. She has observed a "spiral of silence" where people are cowed into nonparticipation in politics—ranging from active campaigning to merely discussing politics with others.[75] The key factor, according to Noelle-Neumann, is the individual's perception of the climate of public opinion. The media help shape those perceptions. They contribute to the creation of, in the words of Walter Lippman, the "pictures in our heads" by which we perceive the rest of the world.

If Noelle-Neumann's theory is accurate, this behavior would not likely change vote choices, since such decisions are made privately, but it would impact on the discourse on public issues, both at an interpersonal level, where people would be unwilling to express themselves in political discussions, and at the mass level, since individuals on one side of an issue would be passive. Moreover, the very decision to vote could be affected when individuals perceive themselves as part of a decided minority. However, the empirical support for such an effort in the United States is still lacking.

SUMMARY

Do the news media affect mass political attitudes and behavior? The answer is both yes and no. It is clearly negative if one means massive effects in persuasion on political matters. The mitigating factors of motives for use of the news media, selectivity in media use, and the nature of the news itself reduce the influence of the news media on political behavior.

Those who have accused the press of causing large-scale tremors in the body politics have not been supported by the empirical evidence. We need not worry that the news media are manipulating our minds on matters political.

However, those who suggest there is little or no effect cannot rest easy either. The answer is affirmative when you examine more subtle effects. The news media apparently do have some impact on socializing people to politics, setting the agenda for public debate, determining voter learning and attitudes towards candidates and issues in electoral campaigns, and shaping people's perceptions concerning their political efficacy and the value of political participation.

To what extent these subtle effects can cumulatively result in major changes in the political system is unknown. However, news media effects have not led the mass public in any specific direction—partisan or ideological—that Americans were not already inclined to go. Nor are they likely to do so in the future. The barriers the mass public raise against news media effects and the lack of a press mission to alter radically the audience's political views combine to rule out any large scale media-directed conversion in the body politic.

NOTES

1. Bernard Cohen, *The Press and Foreign Policy,* Princeton, N.J.: Princeton University Press, 1963, p. 13.

2. Paul Lazarsfeld et al., *The People's Choice,* New York: Columbia University Press, 1948; and Bernard Berelson et al. *Voting,* Chicago: University of Chicago Press, 1954.
3. For a summary of the literature supporting this theory, see Joseph T. Klapper, *The Effects of Mass Communication,* New York: The Free Press, 1960.
4. See Angus Campbell, Gerald Gurin, and Warren C. Miller, *The Voter Decides,* Evanston, Ill.: Row, Peterson, and Co., 1954; Angus Campbell et al., *The American Voter,* New York: Wiley, 1964; Gerald Pomper, *Voters' Choice,* New York: Dodd, Mead, 1975.
5. See, for example, V. O. Key, Jr., *Public Opinion and American Democracy,* New York: Knopf, 1965, pp. 344–369.
6. Lawrence W. Lichty, "Video Versus Print," *Wilson Quarterly* (Special Issue 1982): 49–57.
7. Lichty, "Video Versus Print," pp. 49–57.
8. For a discussion of the uses and gratifications theory, see Jack M. McLeod and Lee B. Becker, "The Uses and Gratifications Approach," in Dan D. Nimmo and Keith R. Sanders, *Handbook of Political Communication,* Beverly Hills, Calif.: Sage, 1981, pp. 67–100; Jay G. Blumer and Elihu Katz, eds., *The Uses of Mass Communications: Current Perspectives on Gratifications Research,* Beverly Hills, Calif.: Sage, 1974; and Elihu Katz, Jay G. Blumler, and Michael Gurevitch, "Uses and Gratifications Research," *Public Opinion Quarterly* 37 (Winter 1973–1974): 509–523.
9. See for example, Thomas E. Patterson, *The Mass Media Election,* New York: Praeger, 1980, p. 71; and Doris Graber, *Processing the News,* 2d ed., New York: Longman, 1988, pp. 107–113.
10. See Lazarsfeld et al., *The People's Choice;* Jay G. Blumer and Denis G. McQuail, *Television in Politics,* Chicago: University of Chicago Press, 1969; Thomas E. Patterson and Robert D. McClure, *The Unseeing Eye: The Myth of Television Power in National Elections,* New York: Putnam, 1976; and Patterson, *Mass Media Election.*
11. Patterson, *Mass Media Election,* pp. 79–84. For a critical assessment of selectivity, see David Sears and Jonathan Freedman, "Selective Exposure to Information: A Critical Review," *Public Opinion Quarterly* 31 (Summer 1967): 194–213.
12. Patterson, *Mass Media Election,* pp. 87–89.
13. Patterson, *Mass Media Election,* pp. 89–90.
14. W. Russell Neumann, "Patterns of Recall among Television News Viewers," *Public Opinion Quarterly* 40 (Spring 1976): 115–123; Graber, *Processing the News,* pp. 107–113; Patterson, *Mass Media Election,* pp. 63–64.
15. John K. Robinson and Dennis K. Davis, "Comprehension of a Single Evening's News," in John K. Robinson and Mark R. Levy, eds., *The Main Source: Learning from Television News,* Beverly Hills, Calif.: Sage, 1986, pp. 107–132.
16. Graber, *Processing the News,* pp. 107–116.
17. Dan Nimmo and James E. Combs, *Mediated Political Realities,* 2d ed., New York: Longman, 1990, p. 49.
18. Robinson and Levy, *Main Source,* p. 87–105; Patterson, *Mass Media Election,* pp. 63–64.
19. See, for example, Leo Bogart, *Press and Public,* Hillsdale, N.J.: Lawrence Erlbaum, 1981, pp. 182–183. For evidence of more reliance on newspapers, see Patterson, *Mass Media Election,* p. 57.
20. See, for example Stanley W. Moore, James Lare, and Kenneth A. Wagner, *The Child's Political World,* New York: Praeger, 1985; Robert W. Connell, *The Child's Construction of Politics,* Victoria, Austral.: Melbourne University Press, 1971; Robert M.

Liebert et al., *The Early Window: Effects of Television on Children and Youth*, 2d ed., New York: Pergamon, 1982, Richard Niemi, *The Politics of Future Citizens*, San Francisco: Jossey-Bass, 1974; Richard G. Niemi and M. Kent Jennings, *Generations and Politics*, Princeton, N.J.: Princeton University Press, 1981; and Robert Hess and Judith Torney, *The Development of Political Attitudes in Children*, Chicago: Aldine, 1967.

21. See Steven Chaffee, Scott Ward, and Leonard Tipton, "Mass Communication and Political Socialization," *Journalism Quarterly* 47 (1970): 647–659. For another discussion of avoidance of use of media as an independent variable, see Sidney Kraus and Dennis Davis, *The Effects of Mass Communication on Political Behavior*, University Park, Pa.: Pennsylvania State University Press, 1976, pp. 21–25.; and Richard E. Dawson et al., *Political Socialization*, 2d ed., Boston: Little, Brown, 1977, pp. 195–198.

22. See R. W. Connell, "Political Socialization and the American Family: The Evidence Re-Examined," *Public Opinion Quarterly* 36 (Fall 1972): 323–333; Hess and Torney, *Development of Political Attitudes in Children;* M. Kent Jennings and Richard G. Niemi, *The Political Character of Adolescence*, Princeton, N.J.: Princeton University Press, 1974.; Richard G. Niemi et al., "The Similarity of Political Values of Parents and College-Age Youths," *Public Opinion Quarterly* 42 (1978): 503–520; and Niemi and Jennings, *Generations and Politics*.

23. Charles K. Atkin, "Communication and Political Socialization," in Dan D. Nimmo and Keith R. Sanders, eds., *Handbook of Political Communication*, Beverly Hills, Calif.: Sage, 1981, pp. 301–307.

24. See Jennings and Niemi, *Political Character of Adolescence*, p. 259; Niemi and Jennings, *Generations and Politics*, pp. 129–132; Charles K. Atkin and Walter Gantz, "Television News and the Child Audience," *Public Opinion Quarterly* 42 (1978); 183–198; Chaffee, Ward, and Tipton, "Mass Communication and Political Socialization," 647–659.; and Charles K. Atkin, "Effect of Campaign Advertising and Newscasts on Children," *Journalism Quarterly* 54 (1977): 503–508.

25. For example, see Thomas R. Marshall, "The Benevolent Bureaucrat: Political Authority in Children's Literature and Television," *Western Political Quarterly* 34 (September 1981): 389–398.

26. For a review of the literature before 1980, see Atkin, "Communication and Political Socialization," pp. 301–307.

27. See Olive Stevens, *Children Talking Politics*, Oxford: Martin Robertson, 1982; and Connell, *Child's Construction of Politics*.

28. Atkin and Gantz, "Television News and the Child Audience," pp. 183–198; Atkin, "Effects of Campaign Advertising and Newscasts on Children," 503–508; and Moore, Lare, and Wagner, *Child's Political World*, pp. 132–133.

29. For example, see Dan Drew and Byron Reeves, "Children and Television News," *Journalism Quarterly* 57 (1980): 45–54.; and Marilyn Jackson-Beeck, "Interpersonal and Mass Communication in Children's Political Socialization," *Journalism Quarterly* 56 (1979): 48–53.

30. Chaffee, Ward, and Tipton, "Mass Communication and Political Socialization," pp. 647–659; and Joseph R. Dominick, "Television and Political Socialization," *Educational Broadcasting Review* 6 (February 1972): 48–57.

31. Steven Chaffee et al., "Mass Communication in Political Socialization," in Stanley A. Renshon, *Handbook of Political Socialization*, New York: Free Press, 1977, pp. 231–233.

32. See Chaffee, Ward, and Tipton, "Mass Communication and Political Socialization," 647–659; Dominick, "Television and Political Socialization," pp. 48–57; and Connell, *Child's Construction of Politics.*

33. Chaffee, Ward, and Tipton, "Mass Communication and Political Socialization," pp. 647–659.

34. Neil Hollander, "Adolescents and the War: The Sources of Socialization," *Journal Quarterly* 48 (Autumn 1971): 472–479.

35. Stevens, *Children Talking Politics,* p. 166.

36. Chaffee, Ward, and Tipton, "Mass Communication and Political Socialization," pp. 647–659; Kraus and Davis, *Effects of Mass Communication on Political Behavior,* pp. 25–26.

37. See for example, Gary C. Byrne, "Mass Media and Political Socialization of Children and Pre-Adults," *Journalism Quarterly* 46 (Spring 1969): 140–144; and Atkin, "Effects of Campaign Advertising and Newscast on Children," pp. 503–508.

38. For example, see Jack Dennis, "Preadult Learning of Political Independence: Media and Family Communications Effects," *Communication Research* 13 (July 1986): 401–433.

39. Chaffee et al., "Mass Communication in Political Socialization," pp. 231–233; and Chaffee, Ward, and Tipton, "Mass Communication and Political Socialization," 647–659.

40. For example, see Atkin and Gantz, "Television News and the Child Audience," pp. 183–198.

41. See Connell, *Child's Construction of Politics;* and S. A. Peterson and A. Somit, "Cognitive Development and Childhood Political Socialization," *American Behavioral Scientist* 25 (1982): 313–334.

42. Donald L. Shaw and Maxwell E. McCombs, *The Emergence of American Political Issues,* St. Paul: Minn.: West Publishing, 1977, p. 15.

43. Shaw and McCombs, *Emergence of American Political Issues,* pp. 99–100.

44. See Maxwell E. McCombs and Donald L. Shaw, "The Agenda-Setting Function of the Mass Media," *Public Opinion Quarterly* 36 (1972): 176–187; Shaw and McCombs, *Emergence of American Political Issues;* George R. Funkhouser, "The Issues of the Sixties: An Exploratory Study in the Dynamics of Public Opinion," *Public Opinion Quarterly* 37 (1973): 62–75; Shanto Iyengar and Donald R. Kinder, *News That Matters,* Chicago: University of Chicago Press, 1987; and Shanto Iyengar et al., "Experimental Demonstrations of the 'Not so Minimal' Consequences of Television News Programs," *American Political Science Review* 81 (1982): 848–858.

45. Iyengar and Kinder, *News That Matters,* pp. 54–62.

46. Iyengar and Kinder, *News That Matters,* pp. 47–53.

47. Maxwell E. McCombs and Sheldon Gilbert, "News Influence on Our Pictures of the World," in Jennings Bryant and Dolf Zillman, *Perspectives on Media Effects,* Hillside, N.J.: Lawrence Erlbaum, 1986, p. 11.

48. Shaw and McCombs, *Emergence of American Political Issues,* p. 99.

49. Iyengar and Kinder, *News That Matters.*

50. See Shanto Iyengar, "Television News and Citizen's Explanations of National Affairs," *American Political Science Review* 81 (September 1987): 815–832; and Iyengar and Kinder, *News That Matters,* pp. 82–89.

51. For a cogent analysis of this trend, see Lee B. Becker, Maxwell E. McCombs, and Jack M. McLeod, "The Development of Political Cognitions," in Steven H. Chaffee, ed., *Political Communication,* Beverly Hills, Calif.: Sage, 1975, pp. 21–63.

52. Patterson, *Mass Media Election,* pp. 107–114.
53. Patterson, *Mass Media Election,* pp. 115–117.
54. See Donald H. Weaver et al., *Media Agenda-Setting in a Presidential Election,* New York: Praeger, 1981; and Patterson, *Mass Media Election.*
55. Patterson, *Mass Media Election,* pp. 142–143.
56. Patterson, *Mass Media Election,* pp. 134–135.
57. Patterson, *Mass Media Election,* pp. 134–136.
58. Patterson, *Mass Media Election,* pp. 134–136.
59. See Thomas E. Patterson and Robert McClure, *The Unseeing Eye: The Myth of Television Power in National Elections,* New York: Putnam, 1976; and Harold Mendelsohn and Garret J. O'Keefe, *The People Choose A President: Influences on Voter Decision-Making,* New York: Praeger, 1976.
60. Patterson, *Mass Media Election,* pp. 159–165.
61. See Jay G. Blumer and Denis McQuail, *Television in Politics,* Chicago: University of Chicago Press, 1969.
62. Michael J. Robinson, "Public Affairs Television and the Growth of Public Malaise: The Case of the Selling of the Pentagon," *American Political Science Review* 70 (June 1976): 409–432.
63. Arthur H. Miller, Edie N. Goldenberg, and Lutz Erbring, "Type-Set Politics: Impact of Newspapers on Public Confidence," *American Political Science Review* 73 (March 1979): 67–84.
64. See, for example, Angus Campbell, *The Sense of Well-Being in America: Recent Patterns and Trends,* New York: McGraw-Hill, 1981; Arthur H. Miller, "Political Issues and Trust in Government: 1964–1970," *American Political Science Review* 68 (September 1974): 951–972; Jack Citrin, "Comment: The Political Relevance of Trust in Government," *American Political Science Review* 68 (September 1974): 973–988; Philip E. Converse, "Change in the American Electorate," in Angus Campbell and Philip Converse, eds., *The Human Meaning of Social Change,* New York: Russell Sage Foundation, 1972; and Seymour Martin Lipset and William Schneider, "The Decline of Confidence in American Institutions," *Political Science Quarterly* 98 (Fall 1983): 379–402.
65. See Arthur H. Miller, "Political Issues and Trust in Government: 1964–1970," pp. 951–972; and Joel O. Aberbach and Jack L. Walker, "Political Trust and Racial Ideology," *American Political Science Review* 64 (1970): 199–219.
66. Robert Dahl, "The City in the Future of Democracy," *American Political Science Review* 61 (December 1967): 967.
67. Dennis T. Lowry, "Gresham's Law and Network TV News Selection," *Journal of Broadcasting* 15 (Fall 1971): 399–408.
68. Edith Efron, *The News Twisters,* Los Angeles: Nash, 1971; and Michael J. Robinson et al., "With Friends Like These . . .," *Public Opinion* (June/July 1983): 2–3.
69. David L. Paletz, Peggy Reichert, and Barbara McIntyre, "How the Media Support Local Government Authority," *Public Opinion Quarterly* 35 (1971): 80–92.
70. Miller, Goldenberg, and Erbring, "Impact of Newspapers on Public Confidence," pp. 67–84.
71. Miller, Goldenberg, and Erbring, "Impact of Newspapers on Public Confidence," pp. 67–84.
72. See Jerome D. Becker and Ivan L. Preston, "Media Usage and Political Activity," *Journalism Quarterly* 57 (Spring 1970): 122–129; and Heinz Eulau and Peter Schnei-

der, "Dimensions of Political Involvement," *Public Opinion Quarterly* 20 (Spring 1956): 128–142.

73. See Jack McLeod, Scott Ward, and Karen Tancill, "Alienation and Use of the Mass Media," *Public Opinion Quarterly* 29 (Winter 1965): 584–594.

74. Garret J. O'Keefe and Harold Mendelsohn, "Nonvoting and the Role of the Media," in Charles Winick, ed., *Mass Media and Deviance,* Beverly Hills, Calif.: Sage, 1978.

75. Elisabeth Noelle-Neumann. *The Spiral of Silence,* Chicago: University of Chicago Press, 1984.

SUGGESTED READINGS

Blumler, Jay G., and Elihu Katz eds. *The Uses of Mass Communications: Current Perspectives on Gratifications Research.* Beverly Hills, Calif.: Sage, 1974.

Chaffee, Steven H., ed. *Political Communication: Issues and Strategies for Research.* Beverly Hills, Calif.: Sage, 1975.

Chaffee, Steven H., et al. "Mass Communication in Political Socialization." In *Handbook of Political Socialization,* edited by Stanley A. Renshon. New York: Free Press, 1977.

Graber, Doris. *Processing the News.* 2d ed. White Plains, N.Y.: Longman, 1988.

Iyengar, Shanto, and Donald R. Kinder. *News That Matters.* Chicago: University of Chicago Press, 1987.

Kraus, Sidney, and Dennis Davis. *The Effects of Mass Communication on Political Behavior.* University Park, Pa.: Pennsylvania State University Press, 1976.

Lang, Gladys Engel, and Kurt Lang. *Politics and Television Re-Viewed.* Beverly Hills, Calif.: Sage, 1984.

Nimmo, Dan D., and Keith R. Sanders. *Handbook of Political Communication.* Beverly Hills, Calif.: Sage, 1981.

Noelle-Neumann, Elisabeth. *The Spiral of Silence.* Chicago: University of Chicago Press, 1984.

Patterson, Thomas E. *The Mass Media Election.* New York: Praeger, 1980.

Robinson, John P., and Mark R. Levy, eds. *The Main Source: Learning from Television News.* Beverly Hills, Calif.: Sage, 1986.

Weaver, Donald H., et al. *Media Agenda-Setting in a Presidential Election.* New York: Praeger, 1981.

CHAPTER 15

Effects on Presidential Campaigns

*"For the large majority of voters, the campaign [for president] has little reality
apart from its media version."*

Thomas E. Patterson[1]

ELECTORAL INTERMEDIARY

With political party reform and campaign finance reform, our system for choosing
the president has experienced significant restructuring in the past thirty years. As we
suggested in earlier chapters, major unintended by-products of reform have been an
increased dependency on the mass media as electoral intermediary and the emergence of the press as an independent force in the electoral process. The various
participants in the electoral process—voters, candidates, political parties—have
become increasingly dependent on the mass media.

Today, voters' perceptions of candidates and the campaign are affected by the
media's portrayal. When the voter seeks information about the campaign, the media
is the major, if not the sole, source of that information.

Aware of the media's role in shaping voters' perceptions and lacking any other
vehicle with the same reach, candidates have come to rely on the media (primarily
the news media and not paid advertising) in crafting an image of themselves.
Although paid political advertising is widely viewed as the main vehicle for image
making (and does play a larger role in the general election campaign than in the
primaries), candidates view news coverage as the most important factor in communicating with voters.

In the primaries, paid media have little effect on the voters' decisions. One study of advertising in presidential primaries found the candidate who spent the most in the campaign lost 12 of 18 primaries in large states. Michael J. Robinson argues paid media work only when the advertisements reinforce impressions from elsewhere—debates, news coverage, and known facts.[2]

Democratic political consultant Robert Squier commented:

> In a presidential race, most of the campaign has run its course before they get into paid media. In a sense, presidential candidates are their own spot-makers as they get their messages across on the stump before the cameras.[3]

The major political parties also have become increasingly reliant on the media. The grassroots network used by the parties in the past to disseminate information has deteriorated. In the 1970s, the two major political parties used telethons to raise money and strengthen partisan loyalties.

In the 1980s, both parties developed and aired political advertisements instead. In 1980 through 1984, they aired party, or sometimes called institutional, advertisements, as opposed to ads for specific candidates. The Republican ads used in 1980, for example, urged voters to ''Vote Republican for a Change'' using a Tip O'Neill look-alike to disparage Democratic-controlled government.

By 1982, however, the parties flip-flopped with the Republicans cautioning voters to ''Stay the Course'' with scenes of joggers panting and sweating through a difficult and painful exercise, while the Democratic party ads urged change by criticizing the Republicans for their lack of compassion and fairness. One 1982 Democratic party ad showed an elephant in a china shop destroying plates labelled Social Security and other social programs. Usage of the ads demonstrated that the political parties in their national campaigning were adapting to the media age.

As a result of this increasing reliance on mass media, the role of the press as the gatekeepers for news coverage in campaigns has grown. More news organizations—including metropolitan newspapers and local broadcast stations—cover presidential campaigns. More reporters seek interviews with the candidates. More debates are scheduled by news organizations. More journalists serve as moderators or panelists for these debates. More journalists follow the candidates. During the pre-primary stage in 1988, about 35 news organizations regularly followed George Bush alone.[4] By contrast, in 1976, almost all news organizations used zone coverage—sending a reporter to cover all the candidates in a state's primary. In 1976, during the pre-primary period, Jimmy Carter had a media entourage of two journalists.[5]

Changes in the media business have also increased the role of the press in campaigns. The rise of alternatives, such as CNN and Independent Network News, to the three national television networks has increased the journalistic presence on the campaign trail and the demands on the candidates' and the campaign staffs' time. Moreover, local television stations offer larger doses of national news through network stories and through their own staff and resources.

This chapter will discuss how the electoral system's growing dependency on the media has facilitated the media's role in the conduct of political campaigns today. That discussion will begin with an analysis of press roles and the effects of the media's intervention on several aspects of the presidential campaign.

PRESS ROLES

The press has acquired various roles in the process of presidential campaigns. Some were previously performed by others, particularly the political party and its leadership. Also, some roles, such as mentioner, are far more important in the primary season than in the general election campaign. The roles the press now plays are mentioner, categorizer, expectation-setter, agenda-setter, winnower, and chief critic.

Mentioner

Prior to the 1988 presidential campaign, veteran newspaper columnist James Reston wrote of the then-current crop of presidential candidates: "What they need is a chance to be heard honestly and fairly in the coming three years without being diminished even before the campaign starts."[6]

But the press does affect how the candidates will be heard. In fact, the press has become a major assessor of candidates' performance and possibilities, particularly before any votes are cast.

Candidates are enhanced or diminished by the press simply as a result of the amount of coverage devoted to their campaigns. Since there is only one national election in this country and since presidential candidates often enter the race with little national name recognition and low voter awareness, the press plays a significant role in introducing the current crop of presidential contenders to the electorate.

The press now functions as the "Great Mentioner." Journalists cover some candidacies more extensively than others. This role is especially critical in the pre-primary stages of the campaign, when no primary or caucus results exist. This is a period when "polls, punditry, and seat of the pants assessment" dominate news coverage of the campaign,[7] and the effect can be substantial coverage for certain candidates and near obscurity for others.

For example, before the first primary in 1984, former Vice President Walter Mondale received more than twice the coverage given another contender, Gary Hart, and more than four times the coverage accorded a second opponent, Alan Cranston.[8] This situation shifted after Hart earned a surprising upset over Mondale in the New Hampshire primary. In the post-primary coverage, the front-page stories of the *New York Times* accorded Hart more than 60 percent of the news content, while all other Democratic presidential candidates combined received the rest.[9]

In 1988, before the Iowa caucus, George Bush and Senator Bob Dole together received well over half of the coverage of the Republican race. This occurred even though they constituted only one-third of the Republican field.[10]

The criteria for mentions is vague. Reporters say they use discussions with party officials and political consultants, straw poll results, polling data, the extent of the campaign organization, the size of the campaign treasury, and the amount of perceived support in the party. However, reporters probably rely heavily on intuition and the behavior of other journalists with more experience or expertise.

Clearly, priority in coverage is given to those candidates who are widely known and are considered as potential winners. Nationally recognized candidates with existing widespread support within the party (former Vice President Walter Mondale in 1984, for example) automatically receive more early coverage than less well-known candidates (Alan Cranston, for example)—a situation that serves to compound the already existing inequity.

In the 1988 presidential campaign, Democratic candidate Bruce Babbitt and Republican candidates Jack Kemp, Alexander Haig, and Pete Dupont, all of whom lacked the prerequisites for mention, were never able to acquire the level of coverage given those candidates perceived as having a chance of winning the nomination such as George Bush, Michael Dukakis, and Robert Dole.

The press serves as mentioner even before the candidates enter the race. By referring to some public figures as potential presidential candidates, the press may affect later candidate decisions to run. In 1986, two years before the next presidential election year, *New York Times* columnist James Reston wrote a highly favorable nationally-syndicated column about the record of Governor Michael Dukakis and suggested Dukakis as a possible presidential candidate.[11] This kind of reference likely helped position Dukakis as a strong contender when others such as Senator Edward Kennedy and New York Governor Mario Cuomo declined to run.

Does this mentioner role really affect the campaign? The value of these mentions lies in perceptions. The perception of momentum on the part of certain candidates can translate into greater awareness of and support by activists, financial donors, and voters. *New York Times* reporter R. W. (Johnny) Apple noted this phenomenon after assessing the candidates for the 1976 campaign:

> But early calculations have a life of their own, because they are the backdrop against which politicians and the media tend to measure the performance of the various candidates. . . .[12]

After winning a surprise second place in the 1984 Iowa caucus, Gary Hart's news coverage increased dramatically. According to one study, Hart received ten times more coverage on one network than he had the previous week.[13] He also gained votes for a string of primary and caucus victories during the following three weeks. Hart had achieved enough name recognition and familiarity among voters to be viewed as the major alternative to Mondale.

A New Star for the Democrats' Firmament

Nebraska's Bob Kerrey makes his media debut

By Paul Taylor
Washington Post Staff Writer

When Democratic Sen. Bob Kerrey of Nebraska returned from the jungles of Southeast Asia last week, he completed one rite of passage and began another.

Kerrey, 46, has made his first trip back to the region since 1969, when his right foot was blown off by a grenade after he led a seven-man Navy SEAL team up a 350-foot cliff during a night raid on a Viet Cong command post on an island in Nha Trang Bay.

Now midway through a nine-day, Senate-sponsored fact-finding mission, Kerrey, a critic of both the Vietnam War and the Bush administration's policy in Southeast Asia, has visited the killing fields in Cambodia and had a testy exchange with a Khmer Rouge leader at a refugee camp in Thailand.

His appearances after his return included NBC's "Today" show, ABC's "Good Morning America" and CNN's "Newsmakers," and a live segment on a Peter Jennings-hosted retrospective on the Vietnam War.

In short, Kerrey is making his first foray into the national media spotlight, and this is who America is meeting: A boyishly handsome Medal of Honor winner, the boyfriend of a movie star, a self-made millionaire entrepreneur, a former governor, a freshman senator and a man who a growing number of Democrats consider the fastest-rising star in their party.

"I know of a lot of bright young issue activists and political types who are ready to draft him to run for president," says one Democratic official who asked not to be identified. "What sets him apart is he has this lively, aggressive, straightforward candor. His whole demeanor says: 'I'm here to do some good, so get out of my face.' He's an anti-politician politician, and a lot of people find that very attractive."

Kerrey's first 15 months in the Senate have been relatively uneventful. He stood out by casting one of only nine votes against the 1989 savings and loan bailout, which he calls "money down a rat hole." He won praise in some quarters for an impassioned floor speech last summer against the flag-desecration constitutional amendment. He's gotten into the thick of farm policy as a freshman member of the Agriculture Committee.

But most of all, he has been quietly boning up on a subject on which he's yet to make a mark, but about which he says he has "an intense interest."

"It is time for us to declare war on poverty again," Kerrey declared in a speech to the Mississippi Jefferson-Jackson Day Dinner April 7 on the eve of his departure to Southeast Asia.

In a similar speech last fall in Boston, Kerrey extolled the successes and acknowledged the failures of the original War on Poverty. "In fighting poverty there is really no such thing as victory," he said, "It is not like landing a man on the Moon. There is no finish line. The effort does not end with the passage of legislation. In fact, we learned the effort simply never ends. . . ."

"In America today," he continued, "another baby is born into poverty every 40 seconds. Every 40 seconds. For example, *now*."

Kerry punctuated the remainder of the speech with the refrain: "And we must do it quickly, because yet another child is born into poverty, *now*."

Do what? For all of his urgency, he is the first to admit he is not sure. His fervent belief in the obligation of the federal government to do something is matched only by his fervent skepticism about the ability of the federal government to do anything.

"I've got substantial mixed feelings about . . . government," he told the Mississippi Democrats. ". . . Government almost killed me in Vietnam. But after that it saved my life. Government also helped me get started in business in 1973 and then it seems it spent the next 17 years trying to put me out of business." (Kerrey and his brother-in-law own a chain of restaurants and exercise salons in Nebraska.)

Kerrey got the star treatment in Mississippi. He made a brief, evocative speech to a veterans' group about the honor of "going in harm's way" for one's fellow soldiers and the moral obligation to give of oneself "not just to our loved ones, but to the strangers among us." The crowd gave him a rousing reception.

"He certainly knows how to use the English language," says Frank Barber, secretary of the Mississippi Senate.

At a briefing on the problems of the Mississippi Delta, Jackson State University Graduate School Dean Leslie McLemore offers an unsolicited pledge to support Kerrey if he runs for president. "He is a genuine hero and we don't have enough men in public life who meet Kennedy's standards in 'Profiles in Courage,' " the educator explains.

When Democratic Rep. Mike Espy of Mississippi introduced Kerrey later that night to the Jefferson-Jackson Day Dinner, the congressman closed with what he called a personal request: "All I want is an autographed picture of Debra Winger." The audience cheered.

Kerrey and Winger started their relationship in the early 1980s, when he was governor of Nebraska and the actress was in the state to film "Terms of Endearment." They broke up, she married actor Timothy Hutton, had a child and got divorced. Now they are seeing each other again.

"There is a word that describes Bob and it's overused but it applies—he has charisma," says his pollster, Harrison Hickman. "He is genuine and direct with people; he doesn't try to finesse things. People pick up on it instantly."

"I have heard him compared to Gary Hart," says Harrison Golden, a Democratic national committeeman from Mississippi and a former Hart statewide coordinator, "but there is one area of incredible contrast. Hart had real problems showing his emotions, Kerrey isn't afraid to wear them on his sleeve. He has the rare ability to touch people when he speaks."

Kerrey became active in the anti-war movement after he returned from Vietnam, and has retained an interest in the region. Last fall, he testified before the State Foreign Relations Committee against the administration's policy of providing covert aid to two guerrilla groups in Cambodia, arguing that the money indirectly helped the Khmer Rouge.

In a meeting at a refugee camp in Thailand earlier this month, Kerrey heard a Khmer Rouge leader say the guerrillas had changed since the mid-1970s, when they were responsible for the killing of more than a million Cambodians. "I don't trust the Khmer Rouge," Kerrey replied, according to an account in Wednesday's Omaha World Herald.

Kerrey has taken two reporters with him to Southeast Asia, one from the Omaha paper, another from the Wall Street Journal. Three dozen other news organizations asked to tag along; all were turned down. "He wants this to be a fact-finding trip about policy options," said his press secretary, Steve Jarding. "If he had wanted to make a big splash in the media, he would have taken the camera crews along. The place to get footage is when you're in Southeast Asia, not when you come back."

But when Kerrey came back, the cameras were waiting. ■

The classic case of effects from the mentioner role is the candidacy of Jimmy Carter in 1976. Carter began his presidential campaign as a little-known former governor of Georgia. He was widely viewed as a long shot. However, after the Carter campaign packed a state party gathering with supporters and won a straw poll in Iowa, the *New York Times* published a front page story on Carter's victory and began a flood of stories on Carter's candidacy. The extensive coverage helped Carter break out of a pack of largely unknown candidates and gain further press notice and public support.[14]

The mentioner role can also be significant in the general election campaign. Although both major party candidates are generally unaffected, since both receive massive coverage, third and minor party candidates receive little or no attention from the national press. One of the most successful recent minor party candidates for president, Libertarian Ed Clark, received less than one-third of one percent of CBS News campaign coverage during his 1980 presidential campaign.[15]

Third party candidates fare better if they are familiar to voters as political figures, but their campaigns remain seriously unreported compared to the two major party candidates. They are excluded from candidate debates and denied media interviews and coverage of news conferences, which would provide greater legitimacy for their campaigns. The media role of "great mentioner" in the general election campaign provides clear advantages to the two major party candidates and damages other parties' attempts to reach voters and achieve credibility as a viable alternative.[16]

Categorizer

Candidates work diligently at crafting an image of themselves for presentation to voters during the campaign. The image is designed to highlight their strengths as well their opponents' weaknesses.

The press also present images of candidates—images that fit press needs for simple, handy identification of candidates. The press attaches labels to candidates in order to simplify the process of describing them to readers or viewers, and to remove "image-making" from the hands of the candidates' media consultants.

These press labels may be derived from the candidate's personal or professional background, issue positions, coalitions of support, or personal style. Labeling is especially frequent when candidates are new to the national arena. Candidates who already possess a national record with voters, such as incumbent presidents, are less easily stereotyped.

During the 1984 and 1988 presidential campaigns, there were several examples of media labeling: Jesse Jackson, the black candidate; John Glenn, the astronaut; Pat Robertson, the preacher; and George Bush, the preppie. Gary Hart's label changed between the two campaigns from the "new ideas" candidate to the "playboy."

In fact, in the 1988 campaign, the press often labeled the whole Democratic presidential field as "Snow White and the Seven Dwarfs," referring to Colorado

Representative Patricia Schroeder, who ultimately did not run, and the seven male candidates. The implication was that all of the candidates were of less than presidential stature.

The labels are confirmed through constant linking of the candidate to the origin of the label. For example, John Glenn's status as a former astronaut was almost always noted in stories about his candidacy.

In some cases, the labels coincide with the candidates' own desired image. In 1984, Gary Hart sought recognition as a candidate with new ideas, appealing to younger voters as a fresh alternative. That same year, Alan Cranston appealed to nuclear freeze advocates and became known as the "freeze" candidate.

Other candidates try to shake images perceived as highly negative, inaccurate, or restrictive, but they often find such images, once established, hard to lose. In 1988, Gary Hart wanted to be treated as a candidate with substantive ideas about the future of the nation, but he could never remove the categorization as an adulterer. In 1984, John Glenn finally gave up trying to fight the astronaut image and attempted to turn it to his advantage.

Labels can be damaging to campaigns, since voters are often attempting to sort out candidates in the early stages of the campaign, precisely when the press is beginning to attach labels. Such labels can determine or interfere with voter perceptions of candidates at a particularly vulnerable time in the election process. For example, California Governor Jerry Brown found it difficult to be taken as a serious presidential contender after reporters began to call him "Governor Moonbeam" because of some of his futuristic policy proposals. As discussed in the preceding chapter, the voters' perceptions of candidates are affected by the media during the early stages when voters are seeking information and the press are simultaneously attaching the candidate labels.

Expectation-Setter

In assessing presidential candidates, the press tends to rely on a game analogy: There are winners and losers. The press coverage tends to look like coverage of a horse race, providing "handicapping" information and establishing who's ahead and who's behind at various points in the process. As in a horse race, expectations are established in advance for the performance of the participants. Candidate A is expected to run well and win, while candidate B is a decided long shot.

The expectations game not only heightens interest in a long and often unexciting campaign, but also structures the reporting of the candidates. The numbers produced by primaries and caucuses take on greater meaning when weighed against expectations of performance.

For example, if a candidate who was supposed to win by a large margin in a state actually garners only a bare majority, the press can challenge the candidate's claim of victory. This occurred in the classic case of the 1968 New Hampshire primary when President Lyndon Johnson narrowly beat Senator Eugene McCarthy, but reporters called the Johnson win a "defeat" because of the narrow margin of victory.

Although reporters often become their own sources for political analysis, they do not set expectations in a vacuum. Reporters base their predictions on polls and interviews with candidates, political leaders, and campaign staff, as well as on observations of crowd response, organizational efforts, and the candidate's campaign skills. Candidates and their campaign staffs attempt to shape the press's role in expectation-setting by dampening expectations of their own performance and raising those for their opponents.

A major contributor to the expectation-setting role of the press has been the extensive use of polls, particularly polls commissioned by the news media organizations themselves. Today, several major news organizations, including CBS News, the *New York Times*, ABC, the *Washington Post, USA Today*, and the *Los Angeles Times* conduct independent or shared polls, especially during presidential campaigns. Increasingly, poll results have been the theme of stories about the campaign. In 1988, polls were the subject of one-fourth of the stories about the horse race.[17]

Does the press's expectation-setting role make any difference in the course of the campaign? The expectation game can have consequences. In 1972, Edmund Muskie won the New Hampshire primary with 46 percent of the vote. But Muskie's failure to achieve a majority of the vote in a state next door to his own was interpreted by the press as a defeat and severely damaged Muskie's ultimately unsuccessful candidacy.

" I'M STILL UNDECIDED—I LIKE DUKAKIS' MAKE-UP AND CAMERA ANGLES, BUT I'M IMPRESSED WITH BUSH'S BACKDROPS AND TWENTY SECOND SOUND BITES!"

Cartoon of September 26, 1988. *Washington Post National Weekly Edition.* Reprinted by permission of Doug Marlette and Creators Syndicate.

Criticism of the press for minimizing Muskie's victory provoked a decision on the part of the some of the press corps in the 1976 campaign to focus on the victor of a primary no matter how narrow the victory. The prime beneficiary of this new policy was Jimmy Carter, who was the center of press attention after winning a plurality of 28 percent of the vote in the New Hampshire primary. And in 1988, the victory of Michael Dukakis in the New Hampshire primary was viewed as a sweeping win even though he garnered only 35 percent of the vote in a state next door to his own.

Since setting expectations is a subjective endeavor, the effects may not be as random as they appear. Determining whether the glass is half-full or half-empty suggests the subjectiveness of the expectation-setter role. Whether Richard Gephardt's 33 percent plurality in the Iowa caucus in 1988 was a victory or a defeat depends on what factors are considered.

Reporters' consideration of some factors and not others in the expectation game may cause them to make errors in their assessments—errors that may lead to serious consequences. In the 1984 presidential debates, the press expected Ronald Reagan, the Great Communicator, to triumph over Walter Mondale, who was faring badly in the polls. These high expectations were fallacious. Reagan's reputation had been built largely on controlled encounters with the press, not more spontaneously structured debates; and Mondale, unlike Reagan, had had years of debate experience in the Senate and had debated frequently during the primaries earlier that year.

Rather than admit the inaccuracy of their previous expectations, reporters attributed Reagan's poor performance to mental or physical problems. *Washington Post* columnist Richard Cohen wrote a classic journalistic explanation of Reagan's problems in the debate:

> If Reagan is slowing down, if at 73 he's slipping off to senility, is occasionally befuddled, unable to come up with the precise word and verbally treads water by repeating himself, it's indeed a cause for concern and should be discussed. He is, after all, the president, and the job calls for mental acuity. . . . [But] we all have our off nights. Maybe Reagan did not sleep well. Maybe he ate something that disagreed with him. Maybe, for some unexplainable reason, he simply was not himself.[18]

The expectation game continued with the second debate. By that point, the press expectations of Reagan had dropped so low that the president needed only to put in a fair performance in order to exceed them.

Similarly in 1988 the expectations the press placed on George Bush during the two presidential debates with Michael Dukakis were lower than those of Dukakis. Bush only needed to avoid any major gaffes while Dukakis had to excel in order to be considered a "winner."

The expectations game can lead the press to assess candidates according to their own standards of success and not those of the candidate. When candidates do not perform according to media expectations, the reporting is affected.

For example, after the second presidential debate between Bush and Dukakis in 1988, NBC anchorman Tom Brokaw revealed his own expectations: "I really thought that Michael Dukakis would have something in his hip pocket, some kind of dramatic new position."[19] Dukakis's own objective was to define himself to voters, including his policy goals as president. His strategy was not to create a new and dramatic stance.

It is difficult to believe these expectations do not color reporters' post-performance assessments of candidates. Brokaw and other journalists may have been quick to claim a Bush victory in the debate precisely because of the expectations for dramatic flair which they themselves placed on Dukakis's performance, but which were completely out of keeping with the personality or campaign strategy of the candidate.

The expectations game magnifies the candidate's gain or loss: the highs are higher and the lows are lower. Gary Hart's nine-point lead (equalling 12,000 votes) over Walter Mondale in New Hampshire was a stunning upset. For a candidate, a lackluster debate performance is the end of the road.

Some candidates with strong internal party support prove the journalistic assessments wrong. The presidential campaigns of both Ronald Reagan and George Bush were nearly written off by many journalists following their Iowa caucus defeats in 1980 and 1988 respectively. Both went on to win the nomination and the presidency those years. However, the snowball effect of expectations can be a serious detriment for most candidates.

Agenda-Setter

> He who determines what politics is about runs the country, because the definition
> of the alternatives is the choice of conflicts, and the choice of conflicts allocates
> power.[20]

Candidates and the press are often at cross-purposes during electoral campaigns. Candidates seek to transmit messages to voters which identify the candidate's record, personal characteristics, and stances on policy.

Journalists, on the other hand, possess a contrasting agenda. They seek news, which is not the candidate's stump speech or electoral appeals. Candidate positions are assumed to be constant and, by definition, not news. Rather, it is conflict between the candidates, a revelation of an indiscretion, some indication of candidate disingenuousness, or candidate responses to journalists' queries about issues high on press agendas.

The campaign becomes a struggle for control of the agenda. Candidates complain that their messages are not transmitted to the voters and they cannot address voters' concerns. Journalists argue that candidates ignore the real issues and attempt to create false images for their own campaigns. Reporters accuse the candidates of manipulating campaign news coverage. For instance, in 1988, former CBS News reporter Marvin Kalb called George Bush's media director, Roger Ailes, a "de facto producer of the evening news."[21] The outcome of the struggle determines the shape of the campaign.

There is evidence that the press wins most of the time. Several studies of news media coverage of presidential campaigns have concluded that press coverage is preoccupied with aspects of "hoopla" and "horse race," such as "winners and losers," campaign strategy, poll results, and campaign appearances.[22] In 1988, one study of network news coverage during the primaries concluded 40 percent of the election stories were about the horse race.[23] Another study found news of the horse race far exceeding news of other topics such as policy issues or the candidates' orientation. (See Table 15.1.) Another study, this of news coverage of three candidates during the 1984 campaign preprimary period, discovered that the candidates' own issue priorities, as measured by their campaign speeches, were included in less than one-tenth of the articles specifically about those candidates.[24]

Such coverage displaces reporting of policy issues. Even when issues are discussed in the news content, they are more likely to be campaign than policy issues. Campaign issues are those issues developed from campaign incidents,[25] as, for instance, from the 1988 campaign: Michael Dukakis's mental health record, Gary Hart's extramarital affairs, Joe Biden's plagiarism, and Dan Quayle's military record. According to Michael J. Robinson, campaign issues in 1984 accounted for nearly 40 percent of all election news.[26]

A fraction of content is devoted to policy issues. In the 1988 primary season, news media discussion of campaign issues far outweighed discussion of policy issues, and the fall general election campaign was not substantially more policy-oriented than the primary season.[27] Thomas E. Patterson found newsmagazines covering the 1988 presidential campaign had a similar emphasis, with less than 20 percent of news about the campaign devoted to policy issue coverage.[28]

However, even when policy is discussed, they may not be the policy issues stressed by the candidates. The press favors certain types of policy issues, particularly those which are clear-cut and neatly divide the candidates.[29] These are issues that can be expressed simply and involve high emotion and conflict. Examples in 1988 included abortion, a tax increase, and aid to the Nicaraguan Contras.

TABLE 15.1. THEMES OF 1988 ELECTION NEWS

	Proportion of news
Horse race (e.g., winning and losing, strategy and tactics, fund raising)	32%
"Campaign" issues (e.g., facts and rumors of scandals, allegations, of dirty or low-level campaigning)	13
"Campaign" images (e.g., candidates' styles of campaigning, posturing, likability)	15
"Governing" images (e.g., leadership ability, trustworthiness)	7
Policy issues (e.g., foreign policy, domestic economy)	17
Candidates' orientation (e.g., personal and political backgrounds, ideology, group support)	16
	100%

Source: Thomas E. Patterson, "The Press and Its Missed Assignment," in Michael Nelson, ed., *The Elections of 1988,* Washington: CQ Press, 1989, p. 98.

Cartoon by Mike Luckovitch. *Newsweek*, September 19, 1988. © 1988 by Mike Luckovitch. Reprinted with permission of Mike Luckovitch and Creators Syndicate.

Journalists gravitate to campaign issues rather than policy issues because they more neatly fit news values. Policy issues are not dramatic nor unexpected, and they presuppose some familiarity with the issue. They are rarely new. Campaign issues, on the other hand, are new, unpredictable, and generally less complex. For example, in 1988 Republican vice-presidential candidate Dan Quayle's military record in the National Guard rather than in Vietnam, in light of his conservative defense policy views, was a surprising and dramatic story. During that campaign, due to this ongoing story, press coverage of Quayle far exceeded that of Democratic vice-presidential candidate Lloyd Bentsen.[30]

According to F. Christopher Arterton, journalists also favor these issues because they provide the press with more control over the campaign agenda. Candidates are thrown off their carefully managed speeches and themes when press queries focus on a single unexpected issue.[31] Candidates are forced to fit their own campaign priorities to those of the press.

Candidates, on the other hand, prefer policy issues which are diffuse in nature, help build electoral coalitions, and provide flexibility for governing. Issues such as economic prosperity, national defense, and welfare reform generally do not alienate voters and appeal to key groups within the electorate.[32]

This divergence in the types of policy issues given priority by the press and the candidates has consequences for the candidates. The press agenda dominates news coverage of the campaign, and the messages that candidates wish to send to voters, especially those concerning general policy direction and specific policy issues, are rarely included in campaign news coverage.[33]

The press's role as agenda-setter also has consequences for voters. Interpersonal discussions are more likely now than in the past to include references to the hoopla and horse race aspects of a campaign. Voters are more likely to view the "game" as a campaign's most significant aspect.[34] Voters' perceptions of which candidates are likely winners or losers appear to follow closely those images presented by the press.[35]

Does the agenda-setting role of the press affect voters' ability to learn about the policy issue positions of candidates, especially given the press's heavy emphasis on "game"? Evidence indicates that voters do learn about candidate positions on issues, but that they learn much more quickly about a candidate's viability than about the candidate's issue stances.[36] Also, they learn most about candidate policy positions not during the primary season when new candidates are introduced and the winnowing process is under way, but during the convention and general election periods when the contest has already been narrowed usually to only two major party presidential contenders.[37]

Winnower

Through the performance of these roles, the press has acquired a broad role as winnower in relation to presidential candidates. Through mentioning, categorizing, and expectation-setting, the press play a significant role in winnowing the presidential candidate field down to two major party nominees.

Although voters actually pull levers in voting booths and cast votes in caucus meetings, voter perceptions of the candidates and the campaign are shaped largely by the press portrayal. This is especially true in the primary contests where partisan affiliation is useless, since competing candidates are all of the same party.

The meaningfulness of that participation also is interpreted by the press. Press coverage is tilted towards the first two contests—the Iowa caucus and the New Hampshire primary. (See Figure 15.1.) Although these two states possess only three percent of the total population of the United States, one-third of the 1988 network news coverage of presidential primaries centered on their electoral contests.[38]

Extensive media coverage of the Iowa caucus and the New Hampshire primary adds weight to their results; candidates who win there are given major boosts in name recognition and positive voter familiarity, both of which translate into more volunteers and financial donations. States which vote later in the process, although larger and more representative of a national electorate, are often under-reported.

Party leaders and public officials have tried to affect that weighted interpretation by altering primary schedules. The agreement by a large number of Southern states to hold their 1988 primaries simultaneously early in the season was an attempt to boost the Southern role in the selection process—and perhaps to give a Southern

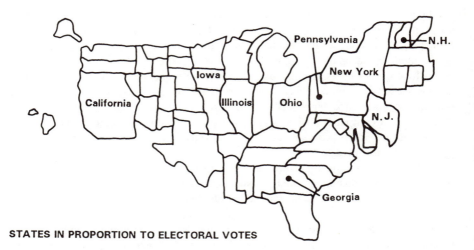

STATES IN PROPORTION TO ELECTORAL VOTES

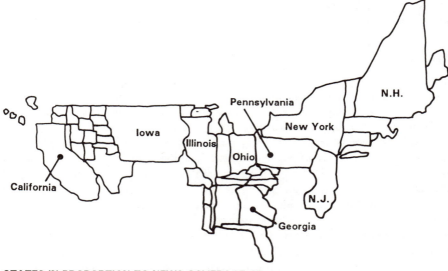

**STATES IN PROPORTION TO NEWS COVERAGE OF
CONTESTS FOR THE 1984 PRESIDENTIAL NOMINATION**

Figure 15.1. Over the course of the presidential nomination campaign, two states, Iowa and New Hampshire, are given media attention far out of proportion to their significance in the general election. William C. Adams, "As New Hampshire Goes . . ." In Gary R. Orren and Nelson W. Polsby, eds. *Media and Momentum: The New Hampshire Primary and Nomination Politics*, Chatham, N.J.: Chatham House, 1987, p. 43–44.

candidate a boost in national media coverage as well as delegates early in the race. The hope was that scheduling a number of the state primaries each with its own separate result would minimize the media's role as winnower since more people would be voting at one time rather than in a succession of one or two primaries every few days followed by extensive media coverage.

Although one candidate in 1988, Tennessee Senator Albert Gore, did bypass the two early contests without being ignored by the press, the role of New Hampshire that year was not diminished. Michael Dukakis was able to parlay his large New Hampshire victory into the needed momentum for the rest of the primary campaign. The change in scheduling may have affected the salience of the Iowa caucus. Both winners in 1988—Missouri Representative Richard Gephardt (Democrat) and Kansas Senator Bob Dole (Republican)—failed to translate their early wins into any lasting success.

Chief Critic

In addition to the above roles, the press also has become chief critic of candidates during the campaign. While voters participate only as passive observers, except when voting, the journalists can repeatedly vocalize their reaction to the candidates. During the course of the campaign, journalists express their assessments of candidates or include evaluations by others who serve as news sources of the candidates' personality, campaign style, ideology or issue positions, electoral strategy and tactics, and base of electoral support.

These assessments, particularly for television news stories, are largely negative. During 1988, negative judgments on television news outweighed positive by two to one for both George Bush and Michael Dukakis.[39] Bush was criticized for his trip to Boston Harbor, the pledge of allegiance issue, negative campaign ads, and his choice for a running mate. Dukakis was panned for dullness, failure to respond to Bush's attacks, organizational ineptitude, and attention to his gubernatorial duties.

The 1988 campaign was not unusual in that regard. In 1980, for example, Jimmy Carter received on the CBS Evening News nearly three times as many negative evaluations as positive. Carter was an incumbent president running on a mixed record of success. But then challenger Ronald Reagan's reviews in press stories were almost as bad.[40]

In television news coverage of presidential nominees, the negative is accentuated. In fact, in 1980, for all the candidates running for president, both Democrats and Republicans, negative assessments outweighed positive in news stories by two to one.[41] (The print media may be different. Michael J. Robinson and Margaret A. Sheehan's study of UPI wire copy found most candidate evaluations in that medium were positive.)[42] The 1984 campaign was similar. Both Reagan and Walter Mondale earned more negative than positive assessments. And George Bush, who was running for reelection as vice-president, was not mentioned positively even once.[43]

Negative treatment is usually reserved for front-runners or at least for candidates viewed as serious contenders. George Bush, who was considered the front-runner for the Republican nomination throughout 1988, received less positive assessments than rivals Dole or Kemp. Ironically, the only exception was after his third-place finish in Iowa when his underdog status earned him a significant boost in positive press assessments.[44]

Bush's "good press" actually conforms to press treatment of underdogs, candidates who face major uphill battles to win the nomination. They are accorded either favorable press attention or neglect. For example, in 1988, Democratic presidential candidate Jesse Jackson was given highly positive coverage until he began to be treated as a serious contender for the nomination midway through the campaign. Even then, Jackson still fared slightly better in press assessments than the other Democratic presidential candidates.[45]

Why is press coverage so critical of presidential candidates? One reason may be the press's perceived role as watchdog. The press takes seriously its responsibilities to uncover anything that the public might not otherwise know about candidates. Another reason is the fear that failure to criticize will make it harder to resist candidate attempts to use the press for image-making purposes.

As for the watchdog role, the press clearly perceives such a role. Speaking of the press, *New York Times* publisher Arthur Ochs Sulzberger once remarked, "Our function is to serve as the eyes and ears of the public."[46] Others outside the press concur. Sociologist Herbert Gans calls the news media "stand-ins for the national constituency."[47] With this role perception, journalists feel they must do more than just cover the news of the campaign; they must uncover the candidate's attempts to waffle on the issues, create a false image, glorify a record of public service, or manipulate the press to achieve any of the above.

Generally both presidential candidates are the subject of negative press coverage during the fall campaign. Recent negative assessment of candidates has been summarized by Dan D. Nimmo and James Combs with a distinct ring of familiarity for those familiar with these campaigns:

1976: Two nice, well-meaning, largely unknown and faceless men, average in achievement and vision, seek the presidency [Carter and Ford]. What difference does it make? Ho-hum, how dull.

1980: Carter lacks the strength and vision to make a difference; Reagan's proposals, although tenable, will never clear Congress. What difference does it make? Ho-hum, how dull.

1984: Reagan's not vulnerable; Mondale doesn't play on TV; nice guys finish last. What difference does it make? Ho-hum, how dull.

1988: NBC Nightly News' John Chancellor five months before the election: "Two of the dullest presidential candidates in memory . . . decent, honorable, and quite boring men." Ho, hum. Need we add, what difference does it make?

Source: Nimmo and Combs, *Mediated Political Realities,* 2d Ed., White Plains, N.Y.: Longman, 1990, p. 65.

Journalists also may become critical in order to display independence from the candidates. Since candidates are directing their campaigns to a large extent at the media, including journalists, reporters may respond by accentuating the negative as a balancing mechanism.

Finally, the press's role as chief critic may be the product of journalistic disdain for politicians. Journalists reveal this bias when, early in a campaign, they speak positively of nontraditional politicians such as John Anderson in 1980, Gary Hart in 1984, and Bruce Babbitt in 1988. Journalists see these candidates as more like them. Tom Wicker wrote of John F. Kennedy that he received positive coverage from the press because of "a feeling among reporters that he probably liked us more than he liked politicians, and that he may have been more nearly one of us than one of them.[48]

These candidates appear to eschew traditional electoral coalitions of their party; they take unpopular stances and often even inveigh against the party leadership. Journalists are soon disappointed, however, when these candidates, sensing the possibility of winning, begin to pursue the traditional path necessary for victory.

Perhaps some combination of all of the above reasons best explains the media's criticism of presidential candidates. If so, the critic role is based, at least partially, on false expectations on the part of the press. The campaign for president is rarely dramatic. Through the journalistic prism, the campaign has become a melodrama in an attempt to liven up the event for reporting purposes.[49] The result is eventual disappointment. Competitors for the presidency are not heroes, but traditional politicians who, rather than ride a white horse to victory, forge compromises and construct tenuous electoral coalitions in typical political style.

MEDIA-BASED CAMPAIGNS

The Candidates

The increased role of the media in the campaign for president, particularly the nomination process, has affected those who run and those who do not.

Television has been accused of changing the nature of candidates—of producing candidates who are all image and no substance, who perform well on television, but may not be capable of governing. As the argument goes, neither Thomas Jefferson nor Abraham Lincoln nor Franklin Roosevelt would win an election today because television would spotlight physical flaws.

Television seems to have altered the preferred image for political candidates. There are several traits which are viewed by politicians, media consultants, and journalists as important for successful campaigning in the age of television: an attractive, youthful (but not too young) physical appearance; a mellifluous voice; and no obvious physical impairments.

To judge candidates on such traits may seem unfair, but every medium possesses its own biases. In the day of literal stump speeches, a strong pair of lungs divided the successful campaigner from the others. In the time of George Washington, John Adams, and Thomas Jefferson, writing skill was an advantage for candidates in an era of campaigning by correspondence and essay.

The effect of television's emphasis on candidate physical appearance has been overemphasized, however. Long before television, Warren G. Harding was widely viewed as successful because of his handsome personal appearance. Thomas E. Dewey, the Republican presidential candidate in 1944 and 1948, was described as looking like the man on the wedding cake.

Conversely, even in the television age, candidates have been serious contenders for and have even won their party's presidential nomination without possessing all the "essential" traits. George McGovern, the 1972 Democratic presidential nominee, has a nasal voice. Robert Dole is disabled from a war injury; and George Bush's voice often becomes high-pitched. But all three were taken seriously by fellow politicians, the press, and the public.

With the rise of television, fears have arisen that the successful candidates would be those with media backgrounds or those highly skilled in media use, as witness the electoral triumph of former actor, sports broadcaster, and radio commentator Ronald Reagan in 1980 and 1984 over less telegenic candidates. One scholar has argued that Reagan provided the blueprint for future presidential candidates, and the winners of future presidential elections will be those who perform best on television.[50] Indeed, Walter Mondale felt television contributed to his 1984 electoral defeat. "I think that, more than I was able to do, modern politics today requires a mastery of television," Mondale told reporters. "I think you know I've never really warmed up to television. And . . . it's never really warmed up to me."[51]

But a background in the communications field has not been uncommon for candidates for office in the past. Well-known politicians who possessed press backgrounds include Theodore Roosevelt, Warren G. Harding, and William Randolph Hearst.

However, Ronald Reagan clearly is the exception rather than the rule. Most presidential candidates, including the winners, have not possessed media backgrounds or extensive media skills. Moreover, those with such backgrounds or skills cannot necessarily attribute their victories to that; Ronald Reagan ran for president three times before winning. In fact, neither George Bush nor Michael Dukakis, the major party nominees in 1988, were highly regarded for their media skills. In the race for their respective party nominations, they bested opponents such as televangelist Pat Robertson and former journalists Albert Gore and Paul Simon.

Candidates do sometimes hesitate to undergo the increased media scrutiny that characterizes the modern media-based campaign. In 1988, Governor Mario Cuomo of New York, widely regarded as the likely front-runner for the Democratic presidential nomination, based his decision not to run at least partially on his desire to shield his family from intense media attention.[52]

The rules of scrutiny have changed. Practically all aspects of a candidate's personal and professional life may become matters for public exposure. In 1987 and 1988, stories about candidates' personal backgrounds flourished, ranging from tales of extramarital affairs to military, health, and academic records.

This change has sparked a controversy over the responsibility to investigate and report on candidates' personal lives. Proponents of the new scrutiny contend that press coverage of personal matters is part of the public scrutiny candidates must endure when they run for public office. For its part, they argue, the press is merely performing a necessary function as watchdog in the process. Opponents respond that the press goes too far in publicizing aspects of candidates' personal life which are irrelevant to governance.

Such scrutiny is not entirely new. For example, stories of Grover Cleveland's siring a child out of wedlock were widely circulated by the press during his presidential campaigns over one hundred years ago.[53]

But such charges were used for partisan purposes since the press of that day still largely reflected partisan views. With the rise of an independent press, the repetition of such charges came to be viewed as unworthy of the press's newly emerging professionalism and a signal that journalists no longer were the handmaidens of politicians.

However, the reemergence of investigation of personal and family issues is under a different pretext. The press scrutinizes and uncovers personal activities of candidates today to serve not political ends, but journalistic and commercial ones. Journalistically, such reporting reinforces the press's role as public trustee and watchdog. Journalists ferreting out scoundrels and hypocrites in government are viewed as performing a valued function—one that clearly establishes the press's independence by distinguishing in the public's mind the journalists from the politicians they cover. It also serves notice on politicians that journalists will not be servants of the politicians' interests. Moreover, commercially, scandal is big news. In the wake of Watergate, Koreagate, and Abscam, news of political corruption again is highly salable because it is more readily believed in this climate.

The journalistic view towards such reporting is not monolithic, however. Several newspapers criticized the *Miami Herald* for its stakeout of Gary Hart in May 1987 which led to his withdrawal from the presidential race. But abstention from this type of scrutiny becomes difficult given competitive instincts and commercial pressures.

According to one study, stories about Dan Quayle, especially those emphasizing his use of family connections both to avoid Vietnam service and to gain entrance to law school, constituted more than 25 percent of evening news broadcasts for two weeks following his nomination for vice president. The print media reacted similarly. On one day alone, the *Washington Post's* coverage of Quayle included three national news stories, two columns, two "style" features, and two op-ed commentaries.[54]

Is this trend dangerous? Should the press engage in such scrutiny? Does this scrutiny discourage candidates from running? Does it force out of public life candidates for reasons irrelevant to their governing capabilities? Does it divert the presidential campaign from a discussion of policy issues and qualifications for governance to a prurient exercise?

On the other hand, isn't such scrutiny really germane to government? Don't candidates' personal lives indicate their character? Isn't character an overriding

Gary Hart on Why Our Media Miss the Message

By Gary Hart

I s it any wonder that in an age of television "sound bites" produces bite-sized policies? Or that a culture that treats politics like a sport—and lumps political figures with soap-opera characters—is producing more celebrities than statesmen?

We are, in a word, trivializing our own leadership—together with the offices to which they aspire, including the presidency.

I'll put my argument directly, because it's a central dilemma of our age. Solutions to our problems cannot pass through a media filter which demands simplicity, rewards tactics and is transfixed by personality—particularly when those solutions are complex and require serious debate by an informed public.

What forces have contributed to the creation of this media filter? Competition is clearly a factor. News producers seek to be faster, and often more sensational, at lower cost. Local news programs in Denver offer cash giveaways to attract viewers. Two full minutes of news time have been re-allocated to advertisers by CBS Evening News. So-called innovations such as CNN and USA Today represent sophisticated news packaging, not news collection. More diversity has not increased competition in serious news gathering. As in other industries, competition in news media has occurred in the style and form of presentation, not in improved substantive quality.

Finally, journalistic standards are eroding, as they did earlier in Great Britain, because of a blurring of the distinction between the seri-

Former senator Gary Hart re-entered the Democratic presidential race last week. This article presenting Hart's critique of the news media is adapted from an address he delivered at Yale University on Nov. 11.

ous and the sensationalist press. To keep or capture a worried or confused reader or viewer, sex is ofter more expedient than seriousness.

I know this moment a headline is being composed by someone whose attention span has just been exhausted which reads: "Hart Bashes Press." Wrong. First, we are all the press. The distinction between producer and consumer, where news is concerned, is practically non-existent. Second, we all want our news simple and our politics spicy. How else to account for USA Today and the ABC News-Break? And someone out there is buying the National Enquirer.

As a candidate, I have been driven nearly mad by questions from concerned citizens that began, "Why isn't anyone saying . . . ?" Because more often than not some of us were saying close to what the questioner was listening for but hadn't heard. Why the confusion? Because the questioner assumed practically anything a presidential candidate said was newsworthy and would be printed or screened. Therefore, if it wasn't seen in the papers or on television, quite obviously it wasn't being said. And, for all practical purposes, the questioner was right.

Recently, I proposed a national course of strategic investments of public and private resources to ensure opportunity and a stable living standard for our children. But few have heard of these ideas because of greater fascination with stories that dominated the evening news—such things as, for example, the ephemeral charisma of Col. North.

Who wants, after all, to hear about tedious subjects like investments in our future when all television eyes focus on a fascinating or sensational personality. "Television," recently said the eminent historian Barbara Tuchman, "has become our monarch. It has been a great boon to the ill and lonely, but the degree to which it has impaired the brain cells of the general population has not been measured."

While we sat transfixed by such personalities as the charismatic Col. North, the termites of debt continued to undermine the long-neglected foundations of our national economy. In a single day $500 billion worth of corporate America evaporated on the floor of the New York Stock Exchange like raindrops in the sub-Sahara.

And, as Kurt Vonnegut says, so it goes.

We have created—all of us—a media filter that gives us reality short and sweet—as sweet as possible. The filter lets through simplicity, tactics and personality. It resists complexity, strategic thought and genuine character.

Ideas, new policies, are electronically squeezed like lemons. A recent survey measured the average "sound bite" on CBS News at 12 seconds. Military reform, a proposal for a new foreign policy framework, a plan for strategic investment for national restructuring—such new departures must find a home on the too-frequently-unread "op-ed" page, where they can be explicated at the great length of 800 words.

Campaigns, the vehicles by which we select our magistrates, are interpreted as if they were sports events. Political endorsements, fund-raising techniques, clever staffs, media strategies, manipulative consultants, sly tactical ploys, all dwarf in media attention the lowly "issues" effort, traditionally relegated to the mustiest, smelliest cranny in the national headquarters.

At the first Democratic candidate debate in 1983, a well-respected, senior political journalist fled the hall within minutes of the opening statements—complaining vigorously that "issues" bored him. And so it goes.

"Personality" has ever been with us in American politics. And, in proper perspective, that's as it should be. But this year's buzz word is "character," and character is defined in a totally negative sense as everything a candidate lacks or every mistake a candidate has made. Now clearly, one must be of sound character to seek to guide our nation. Soundness being judged by a lifetime of performance, the caliber and quality of public service, the demonstration of independence, courage, and conviction in voting, imagination and initiative in governance, utmost respect for the public trust, scrupulous integrity and honesty in campaign finance and handling the public's tax dollars. And cause should not given to doubt the candidate's ability to conduct the people's business.

But are we seeing a new departure—a departure disturbing, if not dangerous? How far are we prepared to go as a society to peek into areas hitherto precluded? Should candidates be surreptitiously surveilled by reporters or private individuals? Should hidden cameras be used? How far should anonymous tips be pursued? Should rumors and gossip be widely printed? Should reporters tell untruths to obtain sensational responses? What are the limits?

In the occasionally exciting prying into a candidate's minutes and hours, are we not obscuring the years of a lifetime and undramatic acts of courage, fortitude, and determination that reveal true character?

That we are even asking such questions seems a far cry from the America of Jefferson and Madison, from John Winthrop's City on a Hill. More like what might occur in police-state capitals such as Managua, Sofia or Santiago. Little wonder we are the objects of wonder or ridicule around the world from people who simply cannot understand how a news organization can afford to fly six reporters a thousand miles to hide in a candidate's bushes and peek in his windows and cannot send one reporter to the White House to ask the president why he let 250 young marines lose their lives in a barracks in Beirut.

Who's questioning the character of a State Department official who lies to Congress? Or a White House staffer who shreds papers while Justice Department officials wait next door? What about the character of an administration riddled with people who blithely abuse the public trust and get away with it?

Could the very simple human response be that we all find sex more interesting than sound government? Could it be we have confused what's interesting and pruriently exciting with what's important? Could it be we've come to the new point in our history where we entrance ourselves with our leaders' personal lives because we either cannot or will not explore their ideas, their policies, or their vision?

I quote again Ms. Tuchman:

"The passionate interest the Gary Hart episode aroused in the public, contrasted with the flaccid reaction to lost lives and broken laws, illustrates the shallowness and frivolity of public opinion. If the American people do not grow angry when their son's lives are sacrificed to official negligence, or when statutes are casually violated by the caretakers of the nation's security, one cannot expect any change to a steadier government that commands more respect. Anger when anger is due is necessary for self-respect and for the respect of our nation by others."

Serious people now believe we have put image over substance in our choice of government officers. By our demand for simple answers, we have trivialized ideas, policies and serious debate. By our elevation of political techniques, we have trivialized the process for selecting our leaders. By our acceptance of a cult of personality, we have trivialized the true meaning of character.

A process may be judged by its system of rewards. Our process today rewards simple solutions, media manipulators, political consultants, mal[l]eable personalities, and candidates who are neither controversial nor complex. You must decide for yourself whether such a process and system of rewards is designed to produce superior leaders—the Roosevelts, Churchills and DeGaulles of the future.

My fear is that things are going to get worse, not better. There is no privacy—for anyone. And the new rule is that all information—however obtained—is relevant. And, given modern technology, all can be learned.

But, you will naturally ask, if someone has nothing to hide, why should they mind? Part of the answer is self-evident. No one enjoys being spied upon, particularly as a condition for holding public office. But consider the rest of the answer. Rumor and gossip have become the coins of the political realm. When rumor is treated as legitimate news, it not only leads to suspicion but also can be rationalized as authority for surveillance—or spying. Spying, done well or poorly, can produce bits of information, innocent or otherwise. Information thus produced can lead to the threat of publication—an unsubtle form of blackmail— or actual publication and the destruction of a candidacy.

The issue isn't whether a candidate has something to hide. The issue is one of self-respect and the self-evident value of privacy. Take that away and we'll have not only bite-sized policies, we'll have pint-sized leaders.   ■

aspect of choosing a president? Don't candidates invite discussion of character when they emphasize character traits—honesty, compassion, steadiness—in their campaigns?

The trend toward personal scrutiny of candidates is another product of the political system's dependency on an increasingly autonomous mass media. It would be erroneous to argue that the media dominate the process, but the strength of the media's role does mean that journalistic imperatives will affect the course of the campaign—and that political imperatives will have to co-exist with the journalistic. As long as journalists define the scrutiny of candidates' personal background as one of their tasks, it will continue to be an element of the process.

The standards for assessing candidates have become, at least partly, press standards. The weakening of the political institutions which have traditionally organized the election process has created a new process influenced by rules and standards which may or may not be relevant to political decision making.

George Reedy, a journalism professor and former White House press secretary under Lyndon Johnson, argues that "the media should not have to make judgments about what to disclose or withhold. They should not have to say, 'This is unworthy for the public to know; I have good judgment and good taste and will decide what [the voters] should know or not know'."[55]

That kind of wholesale abdication of responsibility in favor of the press is unsatisfactory to both candidates and the public. The resurrection of political standards by mediating political institutions would minimize the importance of journalistic standards in the electoral process.

Campaign Scheduling and Media Events

Much of the modern presidential campaign is designed for media purposes. The public campaign is particularly visual-oriented; candidates schedule pseudo-events to attract television attention and shape those events for optimal coverage, as well as transmission of messages to voters. Thus we see activities like a walk through an Italian market, a drive on a tractor, or a visit to a factory gate, planned largely for the benefit of cameras.

In 1988, for example, George Bush held a rally at a flag factory complete with a mammoth American flag in the background. The event was designed to reinforce Bush's verbal message that he favored having schoolchildren say the Pledge of Allegiance and that Michael Dukakis, who as governor vetoed a Massachusetts state law requiring such recitation, did not. Other similar events included Bush's boat ride around the Boston Harbor to demonstrate his opponent's failure to clean it and Dukakis's ride on a tank designed to symbolize his support for a strong national defense.

The events are not merely photogenic. They communicate messages about the candidate without reliance on speeches, and not coincidentally, they fit news values more appropriately than candidate speeches.

As we pointed out earlier, news media coverage is not a given for all candidates during the early days of a campaign. Candidates must vie for the attention of news organizations, who must choose from among a dozen or more active, serious presidential contenders.

One campaign staff director suggested the desperation of candidates attempting to attract the media: "Everywhere we go, we're on a media trip; I mean we're attempting to generate as much free television and print, as much free radio, as we can get."[56]

Later in the campaign, however, and for front-runners early in the campaign, that desperation is replaced with a concern for controlling rather than seeking press coverage. Candidates continue to stage the photogenic pseudo-events, but events may be limited to one per day so a candidate's event doesn't end up competing with another event and allow the press to chose the theme for the day.

The public campaign is an exercise in media market hopping. Candidates travel from one media market to another in an attempt to pick up local media coverage, and at each stop, candidates are interviewed by local print and broadcast journalists.

Satellite links, mobile studios, and portable cameras have altered campaign coverage just since the early 1980s. Both candidates and journalists have utilized the new technology in their struggle over the agenda. Candidates now hold satellite news conferences in a studio in one location and answer questions from reporters in different locations, or link up with the whole nation from a remote, but visually appealing site.

As Donald Foley, former press secretary to 1988 presidential candidate Richard Gephardt explained:

> You can rent a satellite truck, a dish, and crew for about $5,000 a day, hold 10 or 12 one-on-one interviews, call the local studios and have them pull it down and air it live or tape it for their newscasts. The difference is you can do it in the middle of a cornfield rather than in a studio.[57]

Such technology can ease the candidate's job of reaching media markets in several states in a short period of time.

The hand-held lightweight portable video camera has also affected campaign coverage. Every appearance, practically every public word of a candidate can be recorded. Candidate gaffes are more accessible. For example, Democratic presidential candidate Joe Biden's offhand claim of academic excellence in law school, offered before a small audience early in the 1988 campaign, was recorded by such a camera, aired nationally on C-SPAN, and, when his actual record was made public, contributed to his campaign's demise.

The National Nominating Conventions. The major political parties' nominating conventions used to be a gathering of local and state party leaders and activists for the primary purpose of selecting presidential and vice presidential nominees and patching together a platform stating the party's most important issue concerns. Today the convention is a media event, a live prime-time television program, and the first media event of the general election campaign.

Conventions have been altered to fit television needs. In 1952, delegates were informed they should remember they were on television, and should avoid behavior such as dozing off during speeches that would cast the convention and the party in a bad light. Since then parties have discontinued other practices such as prolonged sessions, spontaneous candidate demonstrations, and numerous and lengthy seconding speeches—all unfit for the scripted television image. In fact, in 1972, journalists discovered that the Republican National Convention actually ran according to a script which even specified when the convention chair would ask the delegates to clear the aisles.

Scheduling of dates, convention hall logistics, arrangement of business and speeches are negotiated not only with the television networks in mind, but actually with the networks themselves. The parties want to make sure the press, especially television, can cover the event with a minimum of difficulty.

The conventions today are a showcase for the parties. The party's nominee, previously selected through the state primaries, is introduced to a nationwide prime-time audience. Valuable prime-time television is used to praise the nominee as well as the party. At the podium, speaker after speaker glorifies the party's nominee and the party and rails against the opposing party. The convention also serves as a means for establishing the party's themes for the fall campaign and, through positive coverage, acquiring a well of public favor at the outset of the campaign.

Television coverage may actually meet all these expectations by the party. Although studies of television coverage of conventions in the 1970s suggested press emphasis on disunity and conflict, according to a study of 1988 network convention coverage, positive evaluations of the party's candidates and other party leaders far outweighed negative assessments. Conversely, in coverage of each party's convention, little in the way of positive statements was aired about the opposing party.[58] More importantly for a presidential candidate, the conventions, via televised coverage, tend to give the party's candidate a temporary lift in the polls. In 1988, both Bush and Dukakis emerged from their respective party conventions with a stronger poll standing. Such a lift has been common in recent presidential election years.

But one major worry for the parties and the networks is the diminishing interest in the conventions. Convention watching has declined since its inception in 1952 and the novelty of televised conventions has worn off.[59] Audiences have become bored with the anticlimactic gatherings which the conventions have become. Moreover, the growing availability of alternative programming via cable, satellite, and independent television stations has attracted many viewers who previously lacked such a choice.

In order to regain audience interest, the two major political parties have incorporated movie stars, entertainment routines, and professionally produced documentaries in their convention proceedings.

If the conventions now are primarily public relations tools for the parties, why do the news media, particularly the television networks, continue to cover them? Actually, they do not cover them as they used to. Since 1984, the networks have abandoned the gavel-to-gavel coverage which was the hallmark of convention coverage. News coverage now is limited to two to three hours in prime-time each of the four nights of the convention.

In 1988, the three networks—ABC, CBS, and NBC—combined devoted 60 hours of air time to the two conventions.[60] By contrast, in 1952 gavel-to-gavel coverage ran for 47 hours for the Democratic convention alone on each network.[61]

Also, other networks have filled that role. Today, CNN provides gavel-to-gavel coverage, and C-SPAN offers viewers complete coverage of podium activity—roll call votes, speeches, films, and other business.

Even when the networks are airing the conventions, they do not cover every event on the convention agenda. Only one-half of the television coverage features podium activity.[62] Battles have raged between network and party representatives over network resistance to coverage of party-produced films, which the parties promote to meet the network's entertainment imperatives and which the networks label as ''propaganda'' for the party. Much of the television coverage of the conventions is generated by the network, such as correspondent reports, interviews, panel discussions, and anchor analysis.

The networks do continue to cover the conventions, primarily because they demonstrate the networks' commitment to public service. Lack of coverage would lead to criticism that the networks were sacrificing public interest for commercial gain. Another reason is the possibility a convention will produce ''hard'' news. The 1988 Republican convention featured the selection of a controversial vice presidential candidate. Finally, each network is there because their competitors are. Though one or another network has attempted to significantly deemphasize convention coverage, all have not joined in simultaneously.

Shaping the Image

The 1988 presidential campaign was reported as the most image-oriented of any in recent American history. One newsmagazine described the campaign this way:

> [George Bush] owed [his election] in important part to his paid handlers, the cosmeticians who had made a mild man look hard and the armorers who had made a genteel man look like a schoolyard bully; no recent president had been . . . so completely an artifact of packaging and promotion.[63]

Candidates and their supporters have long attempted to establish or manipulate images. In 1840, William Henry Harrison was portrayed by his supporters as a man who drank hard cider and lived in a log cabin. Harrison's macho image, particularly appealing in the frontier-oriented midwestern states, contrasted favorably with Van Buren's image, fostered by the Harrison supporters, as effeminate and aristocratic. A glance at the nicknames of famous politicians suggests the emphasis on image-making: Honest Abe (Abraham Lincoln), Silent Cal (Calvin Coolidge), Dwight ''Ike'' (who was liked) Eisenhower. Moreover, the press was used to promote such images. Creating a negative image of the opponent has been equally important— witness ''To Err is Truman'' (Harry Truman), ''egghead'' (Adlai Stevenson), and Tricky Dick (Richard Nixon).

However, the enlarged role of an independent press has changed the process of image-making. First, the rise of primaries and the media's increased significance during the nomination process has extended image-making beyond the general election period backwards into the nomination stage. Also, the personalized nature of the modern presidency and the rise of television have contributed to the expansion of image considerations in voters' minds and in the candidates' campaigns.

Candidates today probably are judged as people by voters more than in the past, perhaps because television allows voters to observe candidates at close range. The danger of this kind of "person-to-person" assessment lies less in the characteristics of television in the process, but in the unrealistic expectations placed by viewers on the medium.

There is greater emphasis placed on presidential character than in the past. The greater demands of the office both domestically and internationally, as evidenced by the campaign issues of recent presidential campaigns, coupled with the removal of the psychological distance between president and public, have contributed to this expectation.

With the exception of candidate debates, the vast majority of voters see candidates only in situations which are filtered either by journalists (news and documentaries) or by campaign consultants (paid political advertisements). Image-making has become more demanding with reliance on brief news clips and 30- or 60-second paid commercials which do not allow much room for explanation of ideas.[64] Though voters may be exposed to many seconds of a candidate's commercial message through repetition, the candidate's total message through several different spots still totals less than five minutes. The desired image of the candidate must be conveyed in that brief time. Voters' images of candidates are acquired through the prism of the media, particularly television. Candidates know this and concentrate on creating a desired image.

The media-based campaign, in tandem with the other developments discussed above, has produced the aura of proximity while retaining the reality of distance that allows image construction.

Voters will never be able to assess candidates with as much realism as may be expected in an age of television. The facade of honest assessment lures voters into thinking they can make almost interpersonal-based judgments about the candidates through the mass media.

The packaging of candidates has become a predominant theme of the press since the publication of Joe McGinniss's *The Selling of the President 1968* about Richard Nixon's campaign.[65] In fact, packaging itself has become the theme of presidential campaigns. In 1988, political advertisements for Michael Dukakis criticized the Bush "handlers," and Dukakis and Paul Simon included as part of their campaigns that they refused to be packaged. Such anti-packaging themes have also become part of the image-making process.

Candidates and their campaign consultants attempt to craft images which encompass various, both substantive and stylistic, features. Television particularly emphasizes style—personal background, personal characteristic traits, and campaign style—rather than substance because of television's preference for drama and visuals.[66] However, the facets significant for governance include capability for governing, public service background, and issue positions.

Candidates have adjusted to this shift in emphasis by concentrating on stylistic images encompassing family life, compassion, personal warmth, candor, and spirituality. They celebrate their roots—middle class, small town, perhaps immigrant ancestors.

Symbols of personal characteristics are highlighted: Dukakis's old snowblower to indicate frugality, George Bush's extended family to demonstrate kindness and gentleness, and Jimmy Carter's hometown of Plains to suggest small town purity and wholesomeness.

Political consultants have been credited with an extraordinary ability to sell candidates, but the truth is well short of the supernatural. Consultants have clearly become a major part of presidential campaigns. Media consultants such as David Garth, Roger Ailes, and Jerry Rafshoon have become famous in their own right; candidates even compete for their services. Other consultants—particularly pollsters such as Republicans Richard Wirthlin and Robert Teeter and Democrats Peter Hart and Patrick Caddell—have also become major figures in presidential campaigns. But any candidate for the presidency already possesses a public record. The public has preconceived notions about some of these candidates. As one political consultant put it: "You can't put a candidate completely in a new package.[67]

Consultants do have greater possibilities of affecting images with lesser known candidates, where the public's conception is yet unformed. But since advertisements compete with free media—news—the message can be highly diluted. The most successful message is the one that conforms to a candidate's free media image. For example, in 1984 Walter Mondale's advertisements stressing Gary Hart's immaturity conformed with what the free media was already saying about Hart.[68]

Political consulting is not new. The task used to be performed by the party leadership, but with the decline of party involvement in both the nomination process and the general election campaign at the presidential level, the new political gurus for presidential candidates are not party leaders but political consultants.

The major difference between the two is the latter's disconnected status from the political party organizations. Today's political consultants, much like the candidates they serve, do not hold responsibility for the party's welfare. However, political consultants are not political "hired guns" willing to accept any client. They divide along partisan and ideological lines. One could even argue that the media consultants are more principled than party leaders since the leadership necessarily supports the party's candidate, while media consultants accept candidates with whom they share ideological views.

Research suggests that the effects of consultants' work, particularly in the paid media, are minimal in importance. According to Michael J. Robinson, paid media in 1984 served only to counter the effects of other candidates' paid media and as a measure of viability to the press.[69] In other words, such messages were not the primary means for selling the candidate to the voters.

The Message

The messages of candidates are not covered automatically by the press. Candidates must compete vigorously even for press attention, and even front-runners do not always see their messages transmitted through the media.

As a result, candidates have learned to revise their messages to improve the chances of attracting news attention. Candidate statements are more often than not presented in a format appropriate for sound bites—15-second snippets of video— and the more interesting or entertaining the statements, the more likely it is that they will be used.

Jesse Jackson, former Democratic presidential candidate and a widely acknowledged master of the sound-bite genre, explained:

> If there is anything I have developed over a period of time, it is to speak in epigrams. . . . So we say, 'we're going to have demonstrations without hesitation and jail without bail.'. . . I know if I take a minute and a half to say, 'we're going to demonstrate this afternoon, and we're not going to think about it any longer, and we're willing to go to jail and will not pay the price of the bail and bond, there is no telling whether that would get picked out.[70]

Candidates quickly learn the message must be transformed to fit news values in order to attract press coverage and be communicated to voters, and it sometimes

Source: © UPI/Bettmann Newsphotos.

appears that they reduce their messages to oversimplified solutions. The issues used by George Bush in the 1988 presidential campaign such as the pledge of allegiance and prison furloughs were viewed as trivial but media-attractive. They also rely on negative personalized slogans, as did Walter Mondale's use of ''where's the beef'' in attributing more style than substance to Gary Hart during the 1984 presidential campaign.

Presidential campaigns have always included simplified issues and ad hominem attacks. Television has not changed that. But the increased dependence on the news media for candidate and campaign information and the organization of the campaign ensures that these facets of campaigning acquire an importance they did not have in the past.

Candidates rely on the press for communication with voters to a greater extent than they did in past campaigns. In the past, the messages were transmitted more directly through political parties or a less autonomous press. Only when candidates are no longer required to conform to news values to reach voters will their messages be more in accordance in substance and style with their own political imperatives.

SUMMARY

The electoral system has become dependent on the press for the conduct of campaigns and elections. The press today performs roles which affect the nature of the campaign, particularly at the primary stages. Campaigns have become oriented toward media coverage. Candidates gear their presentation of themselves to the media, with the presumption that the media will transmit that presentation to the voters. The media's role in campaigns has not radically altered the image-making process which has always been a part of American presidential campaigns, but candidates have learned to adjust to a new environment which places emphasis on different skills than in the past. Television, particularly, creates the dangerous illusion that voters can personally know the candidates. Candidates also have learned to adapt their message. This reliance on the press has enhanced the status of negative aspects of the message.

NOTES

1. Thomas E. Patterson, *The Mass Media Election*, New York, Praeger, 1980, p. 3.
2. Michael J. Robinson, ''Where's the Beef? Media and Media Elites in 1984,'' in Austin Ranney, ed., *The American Elections of 1984*, Durham, N.C.: Duke University Press/ AEI, 1985, pp. 172–177.
3. Quoted in Dom Bonafede, ''Hey, Look Me Over,'' *National Journal*, November 21, 1987, p. 2967.
4. Bonafede, ''Hey, Look Me Over, p. 2968.
5. F. Christopher Arterton, ''The Media Politics of Campaigns,'' in James David Barber, ed., *Race for the Presidency*, Englewood Cliffs, N.J.: Prentice-Hall, 1978, pp. 32–33.

6. James Reston, "Mean Politics Starting Early for '88 Race," *New York Times*, January 24, 1986.
7. Michael J. Robinson and Margaret Sheehan, *Over the Wire and on TV*, New York: Russell Sage, 1983, p. 85.
8. Thomas E. Patterson and Richard Davis, "The Media Campaign: Struggle for the Agenda," in Michael Nelson, ed., *The Elections of 1984*, Washington, D.C.: CQ Press, 1985, p. 114. See also Henry E. Brady and Richard Johnston, "What's the Primary Message: Horse Race or Issue Journalism," in Gary Orren and Nelson Polsby, *Media and Momentum: The New Hampshire Primary and Nomination Politics*, Chatham, N.J.: Chatham House, 1987, pp. 141–150.
9. Patterson and Davis, "Media Campaign," p. 115.
10. S. Robert Lichter, Daniel Amundson, and Richard Noyes, *The Video Campaign: Network Coverage of the 1988 Primaries*, Washington: AEI, 1989, p. 53.
11. James Reston, "The View From Beacon Hill," *New York Times*, October 1, 1986.
12. Quoted in Arterton, "Media Politics of Campaigns," p. 21.
13. Brady and Johnston, "What's the Primary Message," pp. 142–143. See also William C. Adams, "Media Coverage of Campaign '84: A Preliminary Report," *Public Opinion* (April/May 1984): 10–11.
14. See Patterson, *Mass Media Election*.
15. Michael J. Robinson, "Just How Liberal is the News?" *Public Opinion* (February/March 1983): 55–60.
16. For a discussion of media coverage of other parties, see Frank Smallwood, *The Other Candidates: Third Parties in Presidential Elections*, Hanover, N.H.: University Press of New England, 1983, pp. 266–273. For a candid analysis of the role of media coverage from the perspective of a third-party presidential campaign staffer, see Mark Bisnow, *Diary of a Dark Horse: The 1980 Presidential Campaign*, Carbondale, Ill.: Southern Illinois Press, 1983.
17. Lichter et al., *Video Campaign*, p. 36.
18. Richard Cohen, "How to Handle the Age Issue," *Washington Post*, October 12, 1984, p. A23.
19. Quoted in Andrew Rosenthal, "After Third TV Debate, Networks' Policy Shifts," *New York Times*, October 15, 1988.
20. E. E. Schattschneider, *The Semi-Sovereign People*, New York : Holt, Rinehart, Winston, 1960, p. 68.
21. Quoted in S. Robert Lichter, Daniel Amundson, and Richard E. Noyes, "Election '88 Media Coverage," *Public Opinion* (January/February 1989): 18–19.
22. See Patterson, *Mass Media Election*, pp. 21–30; Arterton, *Media Politics*, pp. 44–48, 143; and Robinson and Sheehan, *Over the Wire and on TV*, pp. 144–166. For a somewhat dissenting view, see Brady and Johnston, "What's the Primary Message," pp. 142–143.
23. Lichter et al., *Video Campaign*, pp. 14–15.
24. Patterson and Davis, "Media Campaign," pp. 116–117.
25. Patterson, *Mass Media Election*, pp. 34–38.
26. Michael J. Robinson, "The Media in Campaign '84, Part I," in Michael J. Robinson and Austin Ranney, eds., *The Mass Media in Campaign '84*, Washington: AEI, 1985.
27. Lichter et al., *Video Campaign*, p. 15; and Marjorie Randon Hershey, "The Campaign and the Media," in Gerald M. Pomper et al., *The Election of 1988*, Chatham, N. J.: Chatham House, 1989, pp. 97–98.

28. Thomas E. Patterson, "The Press and Its Missed Assignment," in Michael Nelson, ed., *The Elections of 1988*, Washington: CQ Press, 1989, pp. 96–98.
29. Colin Seymour-ure, *The Political Impact of the Mass Media*, Beverly Hills, Calif.: Sage, 1974, p. 223.
30. Patterson, "Press and Its Missed Assignment," p. 103.
31. Arterton, "Media Politics of Presidential Campaigns," p. 48–54.
32. See Benjamin I. Page, *Choices and Echoes in Presidential Elections*, Chicago: University of Chicago Press, 1978.
33. Patterson and Davis, "Media Campaign."
34. Patterson, *Mass Media Election*, chap. 9.
35. Patterson, *Mass Media Election*, chap. 11.
36. Brady and Johnston, "What's the Primary Message," pp. 175–177.
37. Patterson, *Mass Media Election*, chap. 13.
38. Lichter et al., *Video Campaign*, p. 12.
39. Lichter, Amundson, and Noyes, "Election '88," pp. 18–19.
40. Robinson and Sheehan, *Over the Wire and on TV*, pp. 111–112.
41. Robinson and Sheehan, *Over the Wire and on TV*, pp. 111–112.
42. Robinson and Sheehan, *Over the Wire and on TV*, pp. 111–112.
43. See Martha Clancey and Michael J. Robinson, "General Election Coverage Part I," *Public Opinion* (December/January 1985): 49–54.
44. Lichter et al., *Video Campaign*, pp. 89–91.
45. Lichter et al., *Video Campaign*, p. 79.
46. Quoted in Tom Goldstein, *News At Any Cost*, New York: Simon and Schuster, 1985, p. 101.
47. Herbert Gans, *Deciding What's News*, New York: Pantheon Books, 1979, p. 292.
48. Tom Wicker, *On Press*, New York: Viking Press, 1978, p. 113.
49. Dan Nimmo and James E. Combs, *Mediated Political Realities*, 2d ed., New York: Longman, 1990, pp. 64–65.
50. See Robert Denton, Jr., *The Primetime Presidency of Ronald Reagan*, New York: Praeger, 1988.
51. Quoted in Elizabeth Drew, *A Campaign Journal*, New York: Macmillan, 1985, p. 763.
52. "Letting the Cup Pass," *Time*, March 2, 1987, p. 18.
53. Richard E. Welch, Jr., *The Presidencies of Grover Cleveland*, Lawrence, Kans.: University Press of Kansas, 1988, pp. 36–39.
54. Dom Bonafede, "Snoop or Scoop," *National Journal*, November 5, 1988, p. 2794.
55. Bonafede, "Snoop or Scoop," p. 2793.
56. Quoted in F. Christopher Arterton, "Campaign Organizations Confront the Media Environment," in Barber, ed., *Race for the Presidency*, p. 5.
57. Quoted in Bonafede, "Hey, Look Me Over," p. 2465.
58. S. Robert Lichter and Linda S. Lichter, "Covering the Convention Coverage," *Public Opinion* (September/October 1988): pp. 41–44. For a study of earlier convention coverage, see David L. Paletz and Martha Elson, "Television Coverage of Presidential Conventions: Now You See It, Now You Don't," *Political Science Quarterly* 91 (Spring 1976): 109–131.
59. Christopher Sterling, *Electronic Media*, New York: Praeger, 1984, p. 169.
60. Lichter and Lichter, "Covering the Convention Coverage," p. 41.
61. Judith H. Parris, *The Convention Problem*, Washington: Brookings, 1972, p. 150.

62. Lichter and Lichter, "Covering the Convention Coverage," p. 41; Joe Foote and Tony Rimmer, "The Ritual of Convention Coverage in 1980," in William C. Adams, ed., *Television Coverage of the 1980 Presidential Campaign*, Norwood, N.J.: Ablex, 1983, pp. 69–88; and Paletz and Elson, "Television Coverage of Presidential Conventions," pp. 109–131.
63. *Newsweek*, November 21, 1988, p. 146.
64. Larry Sabato, *The Rise of Political Consultants*, New York: Basic Books, 1981, p. 146.
65. Joe McGinniss, *The Selling of the President 1968*, New York: Pocket Books, 1969.
66. Patterson, *Mass Media Election*, pp. 21–30.
67. Sabato, *Rise of Political Consultants*, p. 144.
68. Robinson, "Where's the Beef?" pp. 172–177.
69. Robinson, "Where's the Beef?" pp. 172–177.
70. Quoted in John D. Callaway et al., eds., *Campaigning on Cue*, Chicago: The William Benton Fellowships Program in Broadcast Journalism, The University of Chicago, 1988, p. 165.

SUGGESTED READINGS

Arterton, F. Christopher. *Media Politics*. Lexington, Mass.: D.C. Heath, 1984.

Barber, James David, ed. *Race for the Presidency*. Englewood Cliffs, N.J.: Prentice-Hall, 1978.

Davis, James W. *National Conventions in the Age of Reform*. London: Greenwood Press, 1983.

Hershey, Marjorie Randon. "The Campaign and the Media." In Gerald M. Pomper et al. *The Election of 1988*. Chatham, N.J.: Chatham House, 1989.

Lichter, S. Robert, Daniel Amundson, and Richard E. Noyes. *The Video Campaign: Network Coverage of the 1988 Primaries*. Washington: AEI, 1989.

Orren, Gary, and Nelson Polsby, eds. *Media and Momentum: The New Hampshire Primary and Nomination Politics*. Chatham, N.J.: Chatham House, 1987.

Patterson, Thomas E., and Robert D. McClure. *The Unseeing Eye: The Myth of Television Power in National Elections*. New York: Putnam, 1976.

Patterson, Thomas E. *The Mass Media Election*. New York: Praeger, 1980.

Patterson, Thomas E. "The Press and Its Missed Assignment." In *The Elections of 1988*, edited by Michael Nelson. Washington: CQ Press, 1989.

Robinson, Michael J., and Margaret Sheehan. *Over the Wire and On TV*. New York: Russell Sage, 1983.

Robinson, Michael J., and Austin Ranney, eds. *The Mass Media in Campaign '84*. Washington: AEI, 1985.

CONCLUSION

The Media's Role in American Democracy

Early U.S. political leaders envisioned a press that would play a significant role in the functioning of American democracy. Certainly their vision has become a reality—but in ways that the nation's founders probably did not anticipate. In areas that include government performance evaluation, elections, the formulation of public opinion, and policy-making, the press is a major player—not simply a vehicle for communication, but a force which to a greater or lesser extent influences the democratic process.

As we have seen, a political system which is dependent on an autonomous press to fulfill certain requisite functions of government produces inevitable tensions. Political leaders frequently criticize the press for accumulating and wielding too much power, and even for usurping roles traditionally undertaken by other actors, such as the major political parties. In return, the news media often criticize government leaders and agencies for attempting to manipulate the gathering and reporting of news.

What *is* the proper role of the press in a democratic society? What solutions exist that allow the press to assist in the effective functioning of our democratic process while maintaining its independence? Three possible areas of change suggest themselves: press reform; political reform; and a return to more traditional intermediaries for the functions the press is now called upon to perform.

PRESS REFORM

Does the press in this country now perform in ways that basically reflect the public interest? Do the news media help sustain a viable democratic political system, or are they driven by economic imperatives that sustain only their own self-interest?

The news media have come in for their share of criticism in recent years. Liberals suggest that the press is too easily manipulated by establishment interests, that it is insensitive to those who are without political power, and that profit for the few—those at the top of the handful of media conglomerates who own the majority of media outlets—now outweighs any sense of social or political responsibility. From the right, on the other hand, come charges that the press is overly critical of corporate and professional interests, and that it romanticizes the plight of the poor. From all sides come attacks on current trends toward sensationalism and super- ficiality, which have given rise to what the public sees as invasions of privacy and undermining of the judicial system.

The press has even taken to engaging in frequent bouts of introspection and self-criticism, particularly since 1972 in the months immediately following presi- dential elections. Without fail, journalists who analyze press coverage of presiden- tial campaigns have faulted themselves for not forcing the candidates to discuss issues, and for permitting personality and "sound bites" to dominate their report- ing. Press "gadflies" like columnist Les Brown and "Nightline" host Ted Koppel join academics like Tom Goldstein and Norman Isaacs and special interest groups like the national Parent-Teacher Association in finding fault with the way the news media define, gather, and report the news.[1]

Journalists frequently conclude that more aggressive reporting would counter attempts at manipulation by White House, congressional, and even Supreme Court public relations experts. But such increased zeal would probably, in the end, only heighten the tension. A more aggressive stance only leads newsmakers to try to become more adept at manipulating the news in order to avoid the bad publicity which they anticipate will result from such reporting.

Political leaders suggest, on the other hand, that what is called for is more cooperation between press and government. Those who govern would provide the news, as well as more supportive "care and feeding" for the press (opportunities to follow the troops into Grenada or Panama, for example), in return for journalists' agreement to focus on stories that are, by the politicians' standards, not negative or unfair. Although the news media in practice already accept substantial help from the sources they cover, they are unanimous in their rhetorical rejection of this kind of explicit agreement. Any increase in cooperation between newsmakers and news- gatherers would inevitably lead ultimately to an increase in tension, since journalists would feel less and less in control of their own stories.

What would constitute effective press reform? Only a basic restructuring of the newsgathering process would allow any real reduction in tension. Our definition of what constitutes *news* would have to change, so that substantive policy replaced conflict, novelty, and personality as a primary value. The "beat system," which accepts the primacy of certain sources like the White House (and therefore of certain kinds of news) in the reporting process, would have to be abandoned in favor of more issue-oriented and expert-based journalism.

The fact is that, given the psychological and economic bases for traditional values and habits in reporting, no such changes are likely to occur. The various factors supporting the roles of the news organization and news professionals in the newsgathering process run counter to any major changes in the operation of the press.

POLITICAL REFORM

If real reform in the news media is unlikely, are there other arenas where change might reduce the potential for tension? The political process where the press is perceived to wield the greatest power is the electoral process, and particularly the presidential election process. As we have seen, the enhanced press role has significantly altered the way presidential campaigns are run today.

Are there possible electoral reforms that would diminish the impact of the news media on campaigning? Most attention has been directed to the nominating stage of national campaigns, where the press clearly plays a significant role.

One proposal aimed at reducing media's influence is the establishment of four regional primaries to select convention delegates, with rotating primary dates so that no one region would always go first. Candidates would not then be able to parlay victory in one early, small primary or caucus state—Iowa or New Hampshire—into extensive media attention. Although such a change might diminish the power of one or two small states to initiate a media extravaganza, media coverage of early primary results would continue to impact on succeeding ones, whether the first primary were state-wide or regional.

Others have called for a single, national primary, which would eliminate the power of media coverage to "snowball" a small victory into a succession of larger ones. Such a move, however, would destroy the last vestige of "retail" politics left in presidential campaigns. Only in states like Iowa, with its small-town caucuses, and New Hampshire, with its early primary, are candidates still forced to run "person-to-person" as they might for a local or state office, with media supplementing and not supplanting their interaction with voters.

In a single primary, candidates would be forced to rely even more heavily than they do now on media resources—broadcast advertising, staged events, satellite news conferences, and televised debates. News stories would provide the only channel for those candidates without massive advertising budgets to reach the citizenry, and consequently candidates' efforts to shape news coverage would grow even more intense.

Neither regional nor national primaries address the very real question of the role the press plays before any balloting takes place. In fact, in both instances, candidates for national office would find themselves more dependent on early press coverage, rather than less. The greater dependence on the media that would result from such changes would serve only to heighten the already-existing tensions between press and politician.

A RETURN TO TRADITIONAL INTERMEDIARIES

The tensions produced by the increasing dependency of the political system on the press, and the press's increasing autonomy, might be reduced by retarding one or both of these trends.

As we have suggested, however, any reduction in press independence is unlikely. The trend toward greater press autonomy, as well as the traditional support for a free press, have deep roots in American political culture. The general public (not to mention the press itself) would not tolerate increased governmental control without a clearly defined justification. Even then, the Supreme Court might well stand in the way of enforcement.

Any attempt to reduce press autonomy would be potentially dangerous; if any group of individuals is capable of punishing the press for news content, or of preventing publication or broadcast of a story, the potential for abuse looms large. The effect on American politics would also be deleterious. A vigorous, free press is essential as a check on the exercise of power in a democratic system.

The second alternative, then, is to reduce the system's dependency on the news media. At first glance, the idea sounds impractical. As we have suggested, proposals for campaign reforms would not address the problem. In addition, technology cannot be uninvented. Nor can political leaders simply be advised to stop using the media for political purposes. The public could turn off their televisions and cancel their newspaper subscriptions, but that cure—a loss of information altogether—is worse than the disease.

The primary cause for the system's dependency on the press rests with fundamental changes in the system itself. A vacuum within the political system has facilitated the rise of press influence in recent years, and that vacuum is a result of the absence or diminishment of traditional, strong political mediating institutions.

As I suggested at the outset of this book, the major political parties traditionally played the linking role between political system and public. But beginning in the 1960s, political parties have been shunted aside in the electoral and policymaking processes. Party leaders, in response to calls for more open selection of candidates, have allowed the nominating process for national candidates to slip from their control. By assisting in the creation of a wide-ranging system of primaries and caucuses, parties gradually turned the nominating process over to the general public—and to the press. Today, the role parties play in the organization of presidential campaigns is minimal. Journalists identify the candidates, establish the issues, and provide the public with the information on which they base their decisions.

During the 1980s, the parties attempted to return some power to the party leadership. Ex-officio national delegate slots to nominating conventions were reserved for party leaders, as a first step toward providing leaders with more influence and returning some semblance of real power to the conventions themselves. Even with these changes, however, the party's power at the convention stage is still miniscule in contrast to its former status.

Political parties have the ability to regain the role they once played in the nomination process. Restructuring the nominee selection process is within their power. Party leaders have been unwilling to act in this direction, fearing the specter of cronyism and undemocratic control, but only the return to party control can reduce the present dependency on the news media.

If nomination for national office once again becomes the internal business of the major political parties, the press would not be a necessary intermediary in organizing the campaign for voters. Candidates would no longer need to appeal to masses of voters (not, at least, until they were nominated and faced a national campaign for office), and voters would not need to rely on the media to make decisions about candidates with whom they are largely unfamiliar. We would return to a *representative* system, in which elected delegates are responsible for choosing a nominee who best reflects the party's values and can appeal to voters.

Would such a change bring widespread outcries from both press and public? Not necessarily. NBC news commentator John Chancellor has called for abolishing primaries in favor of 50 state conventions for each party, and a proviso that convention delegates not be bound to specific candidates in primaries.[2] Chancellor contends that such a system would "lead us away from expensive advertising and the crazed 340 days of campaigning in Iowa, to an emphasis on ideas rather than stamina."[3] Hal Bruno, Director of Political Coverage at ABC News expresses a similar sentiment: "I'd like to see party leaders coming back in and taking charge of their parties at the state and local level and having a lot more to say about who goes to conventions."[4]

Comments like these suggest a growing realization that the media-oriented nominating process is lengthy, expensive, and draining for both the candidate and the public. Moreover, it is clearly no more—and by all signs less—issue-oriented than the previous system.

Reinvigorating the party's role at the nominating stage for national candidates also reintroduces the party into the general election campaign, since candidates will be more indebted to parties than they have been in recent elections, and parties themselves will have a greater stake in electing the candidates they nominate. Repercussions also exist for governance. Candidates who rely on their parties for nomination and on support from their parties for election are more likely to act in harmony with the party's goals in policy-making. Presidents may find their parties more effective as tools for mobilizing public opinion, since they constitute potential cores of public support. This kind of interaction between president and party would reduce the current isolation of the presidency.

Reinvigoration of the parties would not mean a return to the "good old days" of corrupt political machines. In fact, the nearly instantaneous transmission of information by the news media, the increased size and visibility of the political press corps, and the autonomy of the press would guarantee that. Political party leaders act now within a technological context that virtually demands open negotiations, and they would face constant scrutiny during electoral periods.

What I'm suggesting, then, is that political parties must *use* the news media rather than be replaced by them. Political scientist Robert Entman has suggested creating partisan media subsidized by the government. Broadcast and print media owned and operated by the political parties might present not a replacement for but an alternative to independent media, and might aid in restoring partisan allegiance and political participation.[5] Such a system would allow partisan messages to be transmitted directly to voters without the filter of a medium understandably more attuned to journalistic and commercial imperatives than to political ones.

SUMMARY

The weakening of other mediating bodies such as the political parties places expectations on the press which are inherently inimical to the role a free press should play in a democratic society. The press must play a significant role in American politics, but it does not have the capability to perform roles traditionally filled by other bodies in a way that serves the interest of the political system. Reforming the media's role cannot be accomplished by initiating reforms in how the press gathers or reports news, nor by tinkering with the political or electoral processes, nor by reducing the independence of the press. The reform that would most significantly lessen the impact that the news media have on how our political process operates is the revitalization of political parties. The parties need to reclaim their responsibility and capacity to act as linking mechanisms between governed and governors. They need to retrieve the political function which has fallen, by default, to the press—an institution ill-equipped to perform that role.

NOTES

1. Tom Goldstein, *The News at Any Cost: How Journalists Compromise Their Ethics to Shape the News*, New York: Simon and Schuster, 1985; Norman Isaacs, *Untended Gates: The Mismanaged Press*, New York: Columbia University Press, 1986.
2. John Chancellor, "Putting Zip, Juice—Interest—into Campaigns," *New York Times*, November 29, 1988, p. A25.
3. As quoted in John D. Callaway et al., eds., *Campaigning on Cue*, Chicago: William Benton Fellowship Program, 1988, p. 54.
4. Callaway et al., *Campaigning on Cue*, p. 54.
5. Robert Entman, *Democracy without Citizens*, New York: Oxford University Press, 1989, pp. 136–139.

Index